Structure, Agency and the Ir

The central problem of social theory is 'structure and agency'. How do the objective features of society influence human agents? Determinism is not the answer, nor is conditioning – as currently conceptualised. In general, 'conditioning' only accentuates the way structure and culture shape the social context confronting the individual. What it completely neglects is our personal capacity to define what we care about most and to design courses of action to realise our concerns in society. Instead, the author maintains that through their 'internal conversations', individuals reflect upon their social situations in the light of their personal concerns – asking themselves 'what should I do?' and answering their own question.

On the basis of a series of unique, in-depth interviews, Margaret Archer identifies three distinctive forms of internal conversation. These govern agents' responses to social conditioning, their individual patterns of social mobility and whether or not they contribute to social stability or change. Thus the internal conversation is seen as being the missing link between society and the individual, structure and agency.

MARGARET S. ARCHER is Professor of Sociology at the University of Warwick. An internationally respected social theorist, she was the first woman to become President of the International Sociological Association and is a former editor of *Current Sociology*. Previous publications include *Culture and Agency* (1998), *Realist Social Theory* (1995) and *Being Human: The Problem of Agency* (2000).

Structure, Agency and the Internal Conversation

Margaret S. Archer

University of Warwick

CAMBRIDGE UNIVERSITY PRESS

PUBLISHED BY THE PRESS SYNDICATE OF THE UNIVERSITY OF CAMBRIDGE
The Pitt Building, Trumpington Street, Cambridge CB2 1RP, United Kingdom

CAMBRIDGE UNIVERSITY PRESS
The Edinburgh Building, Cambridge, CB2 2RU, UK
40 West 20th Street, New York, NY 10011–4211, USA
477 Williamstown Road, Port Melbourne, VIC 3207, Australia
Ruiz de Alarcón 13, 28014 Madrid, Spain
Dock House, The Waterfront, Cape Town 8001, South Africa

http://www.cambridge.org

First published 2003

Printed in the United Kingdom at the University Press, Cambridge

Typeface Plantin 10/12 pt.   *System* LATEX 2$_\varepsilon$ [TB]

A catalogue record for this book is available from the British Library

Library of Congress cataloguing in publication data
Archer, Margaret Scotford.
Structure, agency and the internal conversation / Margaret S. Archer.
    p.   cm.
Includes index.
ISBN 0 521 82906 2 (hardback) – ISBN 0 521 53597 2 (paperback)
1. Social structure.   2. Agent (Philosophy).   3. Self-knowledge, Theory of.
4. Social perception.   5. Interviews – Great Britain.   I. Title.
HM708A73 2003   301 – dc21   2003043804

ISBN 0 521 82906 2 hardback
ISBN 0 521 53597 2 paperback

To the memory of
Ninian McNamara S. J.
For our years of good companionship

'To be human is to exist in the tension *between* solitude and society'
Vincent M. Colapietro

Contents

Figures

E·S·R·C

ECONOMIC & SOCIAL RESEARCH COUNCIL

Produced under the aegis of an ESRC
Research Fellowship

Acknowledgements

I am a lone writer who gets on best without distraction. Therefore, my first thanks are to the ESRC, for a Research Fellowship that allowed me to retreat to my study at home for three years of semi-eremitic research.

Shortly after beginning what was to be 'another theory book', I knew it was going to be necessary to interview real people and, with trepidation, set out to locate these interlocutors. My gratitude to the generosity of the twenty men and women who collaborated is boundless, because their personal disclosures form the most exciting and original part of the book. May they all succeed in developing or maintaining a way of life that enables them to realise their ultimate concerns!

Although a lone writer, I would not thrive as a lonely person. Three friends, in particular, must be thanked for their constant support. First is the late and much missed Ninian McNamara, who convinced me that I should investigate the internal conversation and became as excited as I did when its different modes began to emerge. Second is my husband, Andrew Jones, to whom an on-going thank you for reading every word of the original text – on behalf of the society for the defence of the English language. Residual barbarities are my responsibility alone. Third is Doug Porpora, whose encouragement has been rock-like and whose gift of friendship is as rare as the depth with which it is appreciated.

Lastly, my thanks go to my son, Kingsley Jones, for producing the diagrams and designing the cover, to Mandy Eaton for patiently transcribing the interview tapes, and to Frances Jones, whose competence covered up my computing deficiencies.

Introduction: how does structure influence agency?

How does structure influence agents? To ask the question invites social theorists to advance a process, that is a causal mechanism linking the two. On the whole, they have reached a negative consensus about what this process is *not*. It is not social determinism. Structural and cultural influences cannot be modelled on hydraulic pressures. If they cannot, then something else is involved in the process. That something could be the properties and powers of agents themselves, which is the thesis of this book.

How structures are variously held to influence agents is dependent upon what 'structure' and 'agency' are held to be. There is no ontological consensus whatsoever about what they are within social theory. The sole and slim agreement is that in *some* sense 'structure' is objective, whilst in *some* sense 'agency' entails subjectivity. Both logically and traditionally, this minimal accord was compatible with accounts of the process by which one influenced the other that are diametrically opposed. Either structure or agency could be held to be dominant, and the other element to be correspondingly weak, so weak that it was deprived of causal powers – such that structure melted into 'constructs' or agents faded into *träger*.

More recently, it has become popular to suggest that we abandon the quest for a causal mechanism linking structure and agency, in favour of 'transcending' the divide between objectivity and subjectivity alto-gether. Basically, this enterprise rests upon conceptualising 'structures' and 'agents' as ontologically inseparable because each enters into the other's constitution.[1] Arguments 'against transcendence'[2] protest that the *interplay* between the objective and the subjective can only be occluded by the attempt to transcend the difference between the two. Those who are 'for transcendence' are denying that objectivity and subjectivity re-fer to two causal powers that are irreducibly different in kind and make

---

[1] For a critique of such 'central conflation', see Margaret S. Archer, *Realist Social Theory: The Morphogenetic Approach*, Cambridge University Press, 1995, ch. 4.
[2] Nicos Mouzelis, 'The Subjectivist–Objectivist Divide: Against Transcendence', *Sociology*, 34: 4, 2000.

relatively autonomous contributions to social outcomes. Moreover, the 'duality' of structure and agency (or arguments about the homology between the positional and the dispositional), which conceptualise them as inextricably intertwined, are both hostile to *the very differentiation of subject and object* that is indispensable to agential reflexivity towards society. Consequently, the potential of such reflexivity for mediating the influence of structure upon agency is lost in advance.

Realist social theory is obviously 'against transcendence' because it is 'for emergence'. Ontologically, 'structure' and 'agency' are seen as distinct strata of reality, as the bearers of quite different properties and powers. Their irreducibility to one another *entails examining the interplay between them*. Hence the question has to be re-presented in this context – how do structures influence agents? In other words, how does objectivity affect subjectivity, and vice versa? Social realists have not given a fully satisfactory answer. We have advanced a rather vague process of 'conditioning'[3] – one that is far too imprecise to do service as a causal mechanism.

Central to realist social theory is the statement that 'the causal power of social forms is mediated through social agency'.[4] That is surely correct, because unless we accept that structural and cultural factors ultimately emerge from people and are efficacious only through people, then social forms are reified. However, what explanatory work does this statement do and what does it fail to accomplish?

Basically, it is little more than a condensed statement about realist social ontology. It refers to structural and cultural emergent properties, which are held to have temporal priority, relative autonomy and causal efficacy *vis à vis* members of society. Only because social forms do possess these three characteristics can they be held to exert an irreducible influence upon something different in kind and pertaining to a different level of stratified reality, namely people. Agents possess properties and powers distinct from those pertaining to social forms. Among them feature all those predicates, such as thinking, deliberating, believing, intending, loving and so forth, which are applicable to people, but never to social structures or cultural systems. Beyond that, the statement specifies only that the causal power of social forms 'is mediated through agency', but it does not tell us anything about the mediatory process involved. Obviously, the word 'through' requires unpacking before the process of mediation has begun to be conceptualised.

---

[3] See Roy Bhaskar's most developed diagram of his 'Transformational Model of Social Action', *Reclaiming Reality*, Verso, London, 1989, p. 94. Equally, see my own basic diagram of the 'Morphogenetic Approach', *Realist Social Theory*, p. 157. See figures 1.1 and 1.2.

[4] Roy Bhaskar, *The Possibility of Naturalism*, Harvester Wheatsheaf, Hemel Hempstead, 1989, p. 26.

outcome

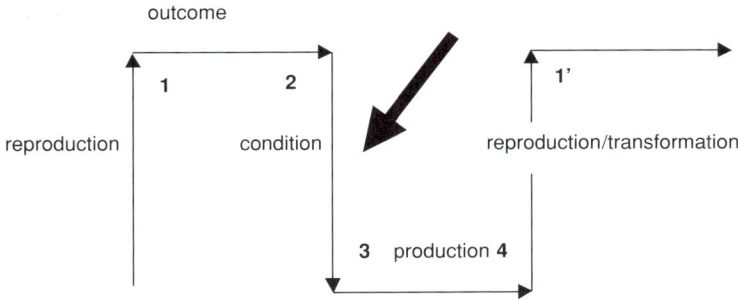

reproduction   1   2   condition   1'   reproduction/transformation

3   production 4

Source. Roy Bhaskar, *Reclaiming Reality*, Verso, London, 1989, p. 94

Figure 1.1 The place of conditioning in Bhaskar's transformational model of social action.

structural conditioning

T^1

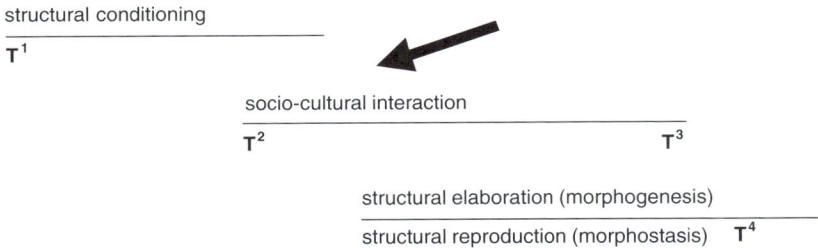

socio-cultural interaction

T^2 T^3

structural elaboration (morphogenesis)

structural reproduction (morphostasis) T^4

Source. Margaret S. Archer, *Realist Social Theory*, Cambridge University Press, 1995, p. 157

Figure 1.2 The place of social conditioning in Archer's morphogenetic approach.

However, the unpacking has been far from complete. Generically, it has consisted in replacing the word 'through' by the process of 'social conditioning'. Since to condition entails the existence of something that is conditioned, and because conditioning is not determinism, then this process necessarily involves the interplay between two different kinds of causal powers – those pertaining to structures and those belonging to agents. Therefore, an adequate conceptualisation of conditioning must deal with the interplay between these two powers. Firstly, this involves a specification of *how* structural and cultural powers impinge upon agents, and secondly of *how* agents use their own personal powers to act 'so rather than otherwise', in such situations.

Realist social theorising, like much other social theory, has been almost exclusively preoccupied with the first problem, which is why it is considered to be incomplete as yet. It has concentrated upon the question of transmission, or how it is that structural properties can impinge upon agents so as potentially to be able to condition their actions. Frequently, this has been answered by construing these influences as 'constraints' and 'enablements'. They are transmitted to us by shaping the situations (structural or cultural) in which we find ourselves, such that some courses of action would be impeded and others would be facilitated.

However, it should be noted that these two very useful concepts *themselves* imply the exercise of agential powers. Constraints require something to constrain, and enablements something to enable. If, *per impossibile*, no agent ever entertained any course of action, they could neither be constrained nor enabled. Only because people envisage particular courses of action can one speak of their constraint or enablement, and only because they may pursue the same course of action from different social contexts can one talk of their being differentially constrained and enabled.

In other words, this preliminary unpacking of the word 'through' acknowledges that the two different causal powers of structural objectivity and agential subjectivity are *both* entailed by the concepts of 'constraints' and 'enablements'. This is also the case for all other ways in which structures can be held to influence us as agents. Here, it could be objected that we sometimes talk of structural factors working upon us, without our awareness – as in the 'unacknowledged conditions of action'. It might seem that if these are influential, but unacknowledged, then their effects must be independent of their subjective reception. Equally, references are also made to the influences of objective structural and cultural factors in creating vested interests and motivating us to defend them, or in reducing our aspirations by limiting our social horizons. In such cases, it might be thought that if objectivity shapes subjectivity in these ways, then the latter makes no independent contribution to outcomes. However, it would be erroneous, in all three instances, to believe that subjectivity has been banished from these processes of conditioning.

For example, where the unacknowledged conditions of action are concerned, a native English speaker may advance her academic career, thanks to the predominance of the English language, without any acknowledgement on her part that the conditions of her action are the heritage of British colonialism. That is perfectly correct, but what she is responding to, in pursuing her academic projects, is the ease and rewardingness of her situation. This is all she needs to know, and she will only know that under her own descriptions, for example, 'I won't have to wait long for that book to be translated', or her presumption that English will always be an official language at conferences. Her subjective response, namely exerting her personal powers to write further articles and papers, does not depend upon her understanding the generative mechanisms that structured the situations she encounters; it is enough that she is aware of her situation.

Similarly, a vested interest is an interest vested in a position, and for it to move an agent then it has to be found good by that person, under her own descriptions. Human subjectivity has not been eliminated, as is demonstrated when some people use their personal powers to renounce or repudiate their vested interests. Then again, the differential life-chances allocated to those differently situated in society are influential because they assign different opportunity costs to the same course of action (such as buying one's own house). Yet, it is agential deliberations that determine whether or not the price is deemed worth paying, even if its costs to them, in terms of saving, overtime and foregoing other things, are higher than to those who are better placed. Therefore, we can never explain who becomes a homeowner without consulting agents' subjectivity. Otherwise we would be confined to making empirical generalisations of the kind, 'the greater the costs of a project, the less likely are people to entertain it'. Yet, even there, subjectivity has not entirely made its exit.

Of course, if we did all respond to social forms in identical fashion, reference to 'personal powers' would not be redundant, but it would lose much of its interest. Instead, explaining what people do, in all of the above cases, involves reference to agents' subjective and reflexive formulation of personal projects – in the light of their objective circumstances. This being the case, then the influence of constraints and enablements will be taken as paradigmatic of how structure conditions agents – such conditioning being a process that involves both objective impingement and subjective reception.

Structural constraints or enablements and human projects

There are no constraints and enablements *per se*, that is as entities. These are the potential *causal powers* of structural emergent properties, such as distributions, roles, organisations, or institutions, and of cultural emergent properties, such as propositions, theories or doctrines. Yet, to constrain and to enable are transitive verbs; they have to impede or to facilitate something. As with all potential causal powers, they can remain unexercised because it is a wholly contingent matter whether they are activated. In other words, constraints and enablements do not possess an intrinsic capacity for constraining or enabling in abstraction. For anything to exert the power of a constraint or an enablement, it has to stand in a *relationship* such that it obstructs or aids the achievement of some specific agential enterprise. The generic name given to such enterprises is 'projects'. Obviously a project is a human device, be it individual or collective, because only people possess the intentionality to define and design courses of action in order to achieve their own ends. Animals, of course, have a limited intentionality when stalking prey, for example. But only the higher primates, who can use sticks to reach what is beyond their grasp, can be credited with primitive projects; tigers do not dig traps or lay snares for gazelles. In other words, a project involves an end that is desired, however tentatively or nebulously, and also some notion, however imprecise, of the course of action through which to accomplish it.

This is the reason why constraints and enablements are terms in social science, which refer to causal powers that can be exercised in society, but are not terms employed in natural science. Where chemical reactions are concerned, a different terminology would be used, for instance that of 'inhibitors', 'catalysts' and 'retarding agents'. Importantly, this recognises that simply by virtue of their composition, two substances will, *ceteris paribus*, necessarily interact in determinate ways. There is no entity involved which possesses the reflexivity to deliberate about how to respond to the causal power(s) which have been activated (apart, of course, from the experimenter). Consequently, terms are adopted which straightforwardly tell us how the reaction is necessarily blocked, speeded-up or slowed-down when other substances or processes (such as heating) intervene.[5]

The language of social constraints and enablements is entirely other because they work quite differently in relation to human projects. The first difference is that they can operate through anticipation. Reflexive agents can sometimes foresee the impediments that certain projects would encounter and thus be deterred from pursuing them. Equally, they may anticipate the ease with which other projects could be advanced, and the benefits that would accrue, and thus be encouraged to adopt them. This *sui generis* difference from inert matter does not depend upon human agents being correct in their forecasts and expectations; indeed they are not, but inert matter cannot anticipate at all.

The second difference is that when a project is constrained or enabled during its execution, agents can act strategically to try to discover ways around it or to define a second-best outcome (where constraints are concerned). Equally strategically, they can deliberate about how to get the most out of propitious circumstances, which may mean adopting a more ambitious goal, so that a good outcome is turned into a better one (where enablements are concerned). Thus, by their nature, humans have

---

[5] The *ceteris paribus* clause has to be invoked again, but only to refer to further contingent intrusions in laboratory experiments, which are rarely perfectly closed.

degrees of freedom in determining their own courses of action. These certainly vary with the stringency of constraints and the strength of enablements, but agents enjoy their own powers of reflexive deliberation, in contrast with inert matter, which merely manifests indeterminacy or inertia if causal powers are weak (for example, if insufficient amounts of a substance are present).

In short, constraints and enablements derive from structural and cultural emergent properties. They have the generative power to impede or facilitate projects of different kinds from groups of agents who are differentially placed. However, the activation of their causal powers is contingent upon agents who conceive of and pursue projects upon which they would impinge. Otherwise, constraints and enablements remain unexercised. Because they are relatively enduring, structural and cultural emergent properties retain their generative potential to exert constraints and enablements *were* anyone or a group to adopt a project upon which they would impinge.

In other words, *it is essential to distinguish between the existence of structural properties and the exercise of their causal powers.* Properties pertain *to* structures and cultures; for example, science will always now contain the potential for the construction of nuclear bombs, regardless of a global prohibition upon their manufacture. Conversely, whether constraints and enablements are exercised as causal powers is contingent upon agency embracing the kinds of projects upon which they can impact. Moreover, the influences of constraints and enablements will only be tendential because of human reflexive abilities to withstand them and strategically to circumvent them. The effect of these structural and cultural causal powers is at the mercy of two open systems; the world and its contingencies and human agency's reflexive acuity, creativity and capacity for commitment.

In sum, the activation of the causal powers associated with constraints and enablements depends upon the use made of personal emergent properties to formulate agential projects. Thus, a top-heavy demographic structure simply cannot constrain a generous pension policy unless and until some group, which is in a position to introduce it, does in fact advocate such a policy. Similarly, the necessary contradiction[6] between two sets of beliefs or theories remains a purely logical matter, which is without social consequence, unless there are people whose project it is to uphold one of these sets of ideas.

As these examples show, it is not the mere *co-existence* of structural and cultural properties with any kind of project held by agents that realises the

---

[6] See Margaret S. Archer, *Culture and Agency*, Cambridge University Press, 1988, p. 145f.

powers of constraints and enablements. Instead, the projects have to be of such a nature that they activate particular causal powers. There is no necessity that this should always be the case. Certain intentional human activities, like private prayer, can never be the objects of structural or cultural constraints, though they may be socio-culturally discouraged. Conversely, private drinking may or may not be constrained according to variations in taxation, availability or legality.

The answer to the question, 'what is required for structural and cultural factors to exercise their powers of constraint and enablement?' can be summarised as follows. *Firstly*, such powers are dependent upon the existence of human projects; no projects mean no constraints and enablements. *Secondly*, to operate as either an enabling or a constraining influence, there has to be a relationship of congruence or incongruence respectively with particular agential projects. *Thirdly*, agents have to respond to these influences; which being conditional rather than deterministic, are subject to reflexive deliberation over the nature of the response. In sum, no structural or cultural emergent property is constraining or enabling *tout court*. To become constraints or enablements involves a relationship with the use made of personal emergent properties. *Whether or not* their causal power is to constrain or to enable is realised, and for *whom* they constitute constraints or enablements, depends upon the nature of the relationship between them and agential projects.

Until we understand this relationship, any account of 'conditioning' remains unilateral, since it concentrates exclusively upon how the situations and circumstances that we confront are structurally and culturally moulded for us. Conversely, specifying *how* structures and agents combine entails two stages. Firstly, it involves theorising about how structural and cultural forms can *impinge upon people*. This, realism is held to have conceptualised adequately when dealing with social forms as constraints and enablements, although it has underplayed the *indispensability of agential projects* to the activation of these social powers. Secondly, the specification of how social forms are influential *also* entails the *reception of these objective influences*, with their potential power to condition what people may do, by reflexive agents whose subjective powers ultimately determine what they do in fact do. Here, Hollis and Smith criticise social realism because 'it does not make sense of how we *integrate* structures and agents in a *single* story'.[7] In short, we realists have failed to 'specify how structures and agency are to be combined'. If this criticism means that we have not theorised how 'transmission' and 'reception' come together

---

[7] Martin Hollis and Steve Smith, 'Two Stories about Structure and Agency', *Review of International Studies*, 20, 1994, p. 250.

as two elements of a single mediatory process, then the point is well taken and this book is dedicated to producing the necessary account – which I believe is possible and they do not.

In brief, this book aims to replace the 'inevitability of two stories' (the 'external' and the 'internal') with the 'tale of two powers' – with a single account of the necessary interplay between objectivity and subjectivity. Without this, the realist proposition that the 'causal power of social forms is mediated through social agency' rightly repudiates reification, but it remains far too indefinite to give due recognition to the personal powers of human agents. That will be the case while ever we realists fail fully to theorise the mediatory process denoted by that word 'through'.

Therefore, we need to be a good deal more precise about the agential process involved. After all, 'constraints and enablements' only indicate the difficulty or ease with which certain projects could be accomplished, *ceteris paribus*, by groups of people standing in given relations to (part of) society. They tell us absolutely nothing about which projects *are* entertained, even though they can inform us about who has an objective material or ideational interest in adopting a maintenance project rather than a transformatory one. Much more is involved; agents have to diagnose their situations, they have to identify their own interests and they must design projects they deem appropriate to attaining their ends. At all three points they are fallible: they can mis-diagnose their situations, mis-identify their interests, and mis-judge appropriate courses of action. However, the fundamental question is not whether they do all of this well, but how they do it at all. The answer to this is held to be 'via the internal conversation'. This is the modality through which reflexivity towards self, society and the relationship between them is exercised. In itself it entails just such things as articulating to ourselves where we are placed, ascertaining where our interests lie and adumbrating schemes of future action.

Personal reflexivity: the missing link in mediation

The account of how structures influence agents, which will be developed throughout this book, is entirely dependent upon the proposition that our human powers of reflexivity have causal efficacy – towards ourselves, our society and relations between them. However, reflexivity, which is held to be one of the most important of personal emergent properties, is often denied to exert causal powers – in which case it becomes considerably less interesting or of no importance at all in accounting for any outcome. To revindicate the influential nature of reflexivity is thus essential to the present enterprise.

The opposition to be overcome can be summarised by considering Graham's statement below and what he says about himself in relation to his actions, compared with how others would interpret his words.

I'm very cautious in what we spend – I like to be right if I'm going to do something out there. And the caution is don't jump straight in. Just stand back . . . and make plans. Stand back, don't stand forward. (Graham, 62-year-old construction site foreman)

The lay person's reaction would probably be that he is thinking about himself, his finances and his spending, and it is the fact that he dwells upon these relationships which makes Graham a cautious spender. If lay people are invited to be imaginative, they might also picture what he does when shopping. He 'stands back', meticulously aware of his income and expenditure; he knows what is within his means and what is beyond them; he is not an impulse buyer, but is alert to good value; he will be attentive to quality and so will shop around; and what he eventually purchases will be the closest approximation to what he set out to buy, at the best price available. In short, what Graham does in the marketplace cannot be explained without reference to Graham himself. Specifically, his *doings* are a product of how he thinks about himself and how he monitors his activities, 'out there' in the market.

A formal description of his statement would be that Graham is exercising his personal capacity for reflexivity to deliberate about himself in relation to his circumstances in order to plan his future actions. However, there would not be consensus upon that description, which is very close to the lay understanding. Instead, theorists would disagree amongst themselves about what part Graham's deliberations play in accounting for his actions. Their disagreement is firmly rooted in how Graham, the agent, is conceptualised. The disputants can be placed on a continuum, which ranges from those who maintain that 'Graham' is the proper name given to a particular neural network, to those who hold that he is a 'cultural artefact'.[8] At the one extreme, his *thinking* explains nothing about his *doing*, because his thoughts have no independent power to affect his actions; at the opposite extreme, his *thoughts* may account for his deeds, but these are not *his* thoughts, since they have been internalised from society. In between these two poles are various concepts of the agent, which accord his thoughts different amounts of responsibility for his actions. Let us briefly characterise three theoretical positions whose protagonists would dispute what Graham says of himself.

(A) At one pole, neurological reductionists would not deny that Graham *felt* as if he were planning his budget carefully, but this feeling

---

[8] Rom Harré, *Personal Being*, Basil Blackwell, Oxford, 1983, p. 20.

would only be a phenomenological accompaniment to the workings of his hard-wiring. Since the latter alone is causally responsible for his spending, then his feelings do not account for his doings. When he talks of 'standing back and making plans', he rightly characterises how it feels to him when about to make a purchase, but he wrongly concludes that his sensation of deliberating about his purchases is causally responsible for what goes into his shopping basket. His sense of planning is only phenomenological 'froth' – an epiphenomenon. Thus his notion that he can monitor himself to act cautiously rather than rashly is also pure delusion. Graham lacks the personal powers to make a difference, for 'Graham', the neural network, will do just what his brain-events make him do in the shopping mall. Graham's characterisation of himself as a 'cautious man' is not necessarily uninteresting, but only as a further candidate for reducing to 'Graham's'[9] neural-firings. Thus Graham is the embodiment of the shopper, who performs all the actions entailed in shopping, but what is going through his head as he does so is a subjective irrelevance; his deliberations have no causal efficacy, and he is wrong in believing that they do. How does structure influence agency? It does so in exactly the same way that the natural environment influences non-human organisms – that is without any mediation by subjectivity.

(B) In the middle of the continuum are those who would countenance what Graham says of himself, but would also draw attention to what he is not saying and what he may lack the 'discursive penetration' to say. Both of the latter are needed in order to provide a complete account of his actions. Attention might be drawn to his careful budgeting as a disposition, acquired semi-consciously and quasi-automatically from his working-class position,[10] because money has been tight throughout his life. Here, his subjectivity is not disregarded. He might indeed mentally debate between buying a barbecue or re-laying the patio, and he may plan in which order to obtain the two, but he will be largely unaware that his horizons have been socially reduced, such that he does not even consider acquiring an outdoor jacuzzi.

In similar vein, it might be pointed out that Graham's subjective conception of his spending plans necessarily means that he tacitly draws upon many objective factors,[11] precisely in order to be able to plan. His deliberations presuppose various things about his social context, yet he

---

[9] Daniel C. Dennett, *Consciousness Explained*, Penguin, London, 1993. Theorists can agree 'about just what a subject's heterophenomenological world is, while offering entirely different accounts of how heterophenomenological worlds map onto events in the brain', p. 81.

[10] Pierre Bourdieu, *Outline of a Theory of Practice*, Cambridge University Press, 1977 and *The Logic of Practice*, Polity Press, Oxford, 1990.

[11] Anthony Giddens, *Central Problems in Social Theory*, Macmillan, London, 1979 and *The Constitution of Society*, Polity Press, Oxford, 1990.

may not be fully aware of making these presumptions. For example, he is drawing on the fact that the construction industry furnishes him with a steady income, that those on steady incomes can readily buy a barbecue on credit, and that someone with his contacts can re-do the patio at less than the commercial cost. The outcome could be that Graham ends up with a new barbecue standing on a new patio this summer. If he does, he probably *also* remains unaware that objectively he has helped to keep the garden suppliers in business and that subjectively his neighbour is now considering his own garden improvements.

This sounds quite plausible, but it has one drawback, namely it is now not clear where Graham starts and finishes in relation to his context. If, in making his plans, *he has to draw upon* these social factors, then how much of what he says is about himself and how much is about his circumstances? To appreciate the difficulty that this creates, suppose one tries to allow that Graham is indeed a 'cautious man', as he says of himself. If 'caution' is characteristic of him as a person, he will not even entertain a plan until he has 'stood back', examined the ins and outs, and finally reassured himself that it is a modestly non-risky enterprise. The problem is encountered immediately. For Graham to deem a course of action to be a low-risk one entails him drawing upon further presuppositions about his social context – that his suppliers are reputable, that he will not be made re-dundant, that home improvements increase re-sale value etc. Thus, there never comes a point at which it is possible to disentangle Graham's personal caution (a subjective property of a person) from the characteristics of his context (objective properties of society). In any case, as was seen above, his very disposition towards careful budgeting is not entirely his own, but a refraction of his social origins. 'Graham' has now become so inextricably intertwined with his social background and foreground that it is no longer clear *who* is 'standing back'. All that is certain is that he does not have the last word about himself, his intentions or actions. Therefore, it becomes impossible that Graham can deliberate upon his circumstances as subject to object, because these are now inseparable for 'Graham'.

(C) At the opposite extreme, Graham's utterance can stand, but only as part of the ongoing 'conversation of society'. Interpersonally, his community will have developed a set of meanings about the appropriate spatial uses of house and garden. That these are negotiated constructs, which are therefore subject to re-negotiation, is witnessed by the fact that Graham's parents would not have invited friends and family to eat spare ribs on their (non-existent) patio. Here, however, we are in still bigger trouble with Graham's statement about his 'plans' and his belief that his subjective deliberations are his own. This is because the direct implication of holding that we are 'cultural artefacts' is to void our 'inner lives' in order to vaunt our discursive production. Indeed, the very 'I' that Graham employs to speak about his 'own' deliberations is not self-referential. Its use merely demonstrates his mastery of the first-person pronoun, which indexes the spatial location of his body. 'Graham' has appropriated the very notion of being Graham, a self, as a theory which he has learned from society, just as all his internal dialogue is secondary and derivative from 'society's conversation'. Since there can be 'nothing in the mind that was not first in the conversation',[12] then 'Graham' cannot privately deliberate upon his personal plans.

Therefore, in characterising himself as 'cautious', 'Graham' is stressing his accountability to society's moral order and demonstrating that he has internalised its prudential discourse. For instance, he appropriates the term 'cautious' because he does not gamble (dubious practice), although he takes his 'credit worthiness' for granted (standard practice). The problem now is that his society has also been re-conceptualised. Objectively, our economy is one that encourages people to extend their use of credit to the limit. Since 'Graham' will be as susceptible to this encouragement as others in his community, then he may talk as if he is planning cautiously, whilst objectively he is living quite dangerously. How matters are can never be substituted for how any community (of discourse) takes matters to be. People who found themselves in negative equity or having their homes re-possessed confronted real structural powers and not a social meaning. Once again, it is impossible for 'Graham' to deliberate on his circumstances as subject to object; his 'subjectivity' has dissolved into 'society's conversation' and his objective context has melted away into social constructs.

In none of these theories is Graham taken at his word, that is as a person who subjectively reflects upon himself in relation to his objective circumstances. This is because both the subjective and the objective have been re-defined. On the one hand, Graham is not whom he considers himself to be. Instead, he becomes one of three different versions of 'Graham'. No 'Graham' has the subjective reflexivity that Graham himself claims to possess. In place of this personal property, which allowed him to 'stand back' and privately make sure that he was 'right' about what he intended to do, each 'Graham' has a quite different property. For 'Graham' A, his subjectivity has become an epiphenomenon of his brain-events, for 'Graham' B it has become inseparable from his social context, and for 'Graham' C it is a derivative from the collective discourse of his community. On the other hand, Graham was deliberating in order

---

[12] Rom Harré, *Personal Being*, p. 116.

to 'be right' when doing things 'out there' in the real social world. Instead, 'Graham' A, cannot be a knowing subject in relation to objective reality, for 'Graham' B, 'out there' has become blurred with 'in here', and for 'Graham' C, the objective reality of society has been transformed into how his community takes it to be, not how it is. All three theories have completely re-defined 'subjectivity' and 'objectivity', such that they cannot stand in the relationships supposed by Graham when making his original statement.

In other words, none of these approaches allows that Graham is doing what he thinks he is doing, that is reflecting upon himself in relation to his circumstances – as two distinct parts of reality with different properties and powers. In saying what he does, he endorses a belief in his own subjectivity and that his reflexive deliberations affect his actions within the objective social situations that he finds himself.

In this book, I want to maintain that Graham is correct. Firstly, he is right about his subjectivity, that it is his own internal property, that it is real and that it is influential. In other words, it is a *personal interior property*, with a *first-person subjective ontology*, and with powers that can be *causally efficacious* in relation to himself and to his society. Secondly, he is also right that he lives in a social world that has different properties and powers from his own – ones which constrain (and enable) his actions. These are *temporally prior* to his conceiving of a course of action, *relatively autonomous* from how he takes them to be, but can *causally influence* the achievement of his plans by frustrating them or advancing them. Thirdly, he is again correct that since he is capable of reflexively monitoring himself in relation to his circumstances, whilst they are incapable of doing the same towards him, then he is able to adopt a 'stance' towards his social context, in his case that of a 'cautious man'. In other words, Graham believes that he had best be aware (and beware) of his society, as best he can, and then carefully 'plan' before acting. In defending these three elements of his outlook, this does not imply, and does not need to imply, that either his 'self-knowledge' or his 'societal-knowledge' are correct, or that the 'stance' he adopts in order to accomplish what he seeks is appropriate, let alone optimal, to his ends.

Conclusion

To defend these three elements is to endorse the notions that 'structure' and 'agency' constitute two distinctive and irreducible properties and powers, and that human reflexive deliberations play a crucial role in mediating between them. Many will object to both propositions. On the one hand, only if the ontological difference between 'structure' and 'agency' is accepted (acceptance precluding their conflation) does the question arise as to how the influence of the one is *mediated* to the other. More exactly, it is only if the subjectivity of 'agents' and the objectivity of 'structures' are credited not only with being different kinds of properties, but also with the capacity for exerting different kinds of *causal powers* that the process of mediation becomes problematic. Only then do we have to ask questions about how 'structure' impinges upon 'agency' and how the powers of 'agents' affect its reception. Simply to recognise that there is a difference between subjectivity and objectivity does not entail the problem of mediation. This has been seen for the neurological reductionists, who do not deny that we are subjective beings but view our phenomenology as epiphenomenal, and thus deprived of causal powers. On that premise the question of mediation is redundant.

On the other hand, among those who do endorse the distinctively different and irreducible properties and powers of 'structures' and 'agents', there should logically be an acceptance of the need for identifying a mediatory process that links them. Nevertheless, there may well be resistance to the particular mediatory mechanism that I am advancing in this book, namely the reflexive deliberations of social agents. Since these obviously entail epistemology, then to hold them responsible for mediation might also appear to involve committing the 'epistemic fallacy';[13] that is, wrongly substituting how agents take things to be for how they really are. In fact it does not. Certainly, agents can only know themselves and their circumstances under their own descriptions, which are ever fallible, as is all our knowledge. If they get either of these seriously wrong, then they will pay the objective price, which may give them occasion to correct their views.[14] Not to acknowledge this would spell a collapse into idealism, whose irrealism withholds objective properties and powers from 'structure'. However, to insist that we pay an objective price for getting reality wrong is irrelevant to the proposition being advanced. This merely asserts that unless agents did subjectively conceive of courses of action in society, then nothing would activate the causal powers of structural and cultural properties to constrain or to enable them. Therefore, how people reflexively deliberate upon what to do in the light of their personal concerns has to form *a* part of a mediatory account. My aim will be to convince fellow realists, as well as other social theorists, that human reflexivity is *central* to the process of mediation.

---

[13] See Andrew Collier, *Critical Realism*, Verso, London, 1994, pp. 76–85 on the 'epistemic fallacy'.

[14] How matters are plays a regulatory role towards how we take matters to be; one which stops very far short of determinism and is better seen as associating 'bonuses' with getting reality right and 'penalties' with getting it wrong.

Yet, to advance the 'internal conversation' as the process of mediation 'through' which agents respond to social forms – fallibly and corrigibly, but, above all, intentionally and differently – is to attribute three properties to their reflexive deliberations. The 'internal conversation is held to be (a) genuinely interior, (b) ontologically subjective, and (c) causally efficacious. However, as has been seen in relation to Graham, there are strenuous forces at work that are concerned to withhold these three predicates from human reflexivity. The next chapter is an attempt to rebut such arguments, at their *fons et origo* – within the philosophy of mind.

Only if the 'internal conversation' can be upheld as an irreducible *personal* property, which is real and causally influential, can the exercise of its powers be considered as the missing mediatory mechanism that is needed to complete an adequate account of social conditioning. In fact, the defence of the 'internal conversation' and the task of conceptualising it defensibly will occupy the next three chapters. Only if it can be established that two sets of emergent, and thus irreducible, properties and powers are involved can we return to the central problem about the *interplay* between objectivity and subjectivity. Then it would indeed be necessary to resist the 'transcendence' of subjectivism and objectivism, on the grounds that this would be to conflate two different ontological levels and their distinctive properties and powers. Only at that point can we properly examine how all agents attempt subjectively, because reflexively, to establish their own personal *modus vivendi* in objective social circumstances which were not of their making or choosing.

Part 1

Solitude and society

1 The private life of the social subject

Were we humans not reflexive beings there could be no such thing as society. This is because any form of social interaction, from the dyad to the global system, requires that subjects know themselves to be themselves. Otherwise they could not acknowledge that their words were their own nor that their intentions, undertakings and reactions belonged to themselves. Without this, no two-person interaction could begin, let alone become a stable relationship. Similarly, not one social obligation, expectation or norm could be owned by a single 'member' of society. This would then make the very term 'social agent' meaningless.

This basic statement scarcely figures in introductory textbooks and many elaborate social theories have been presented without any reference to human reflexivity. Why? Reflexivity tends so to be taken for granted that its implications are rarely reflected upon themselves. The ability to know ourselves to be ourselves is simply presumed whenever reference is made to social agents, just as it is pre-supposed that these agents are also embodied, intelligent and open to social influences. It is as if these predicates were background assumptions, devoid of any further interest. However, we know from disputes at the beginning of the twentieth century that the issue of human intelligence was highly controversial and we know from those at the end of the century that human embodiment became problematic. In both cases, our understanding increased once we ceased taking them for granted. Perhaps the time has come for reflexivity to be moved under the spot-light.

Moreover, the moment that these four background assumptions[1] are considered together, then they become very interesting indeed. Someone who knows herself to be herself also knows that she inhabits her own body and, in so doing, she knows a good deal about it, some of which will be known to her alone. Already we seem to have arrived at 'private knowledge'. Next, a reflexive being, who is also an intelligent being, has

---

[1] There are probably far more than four. These four are highlighted because of the significance of their interrelationships.

the capacity to ask herself, how do other things, including people, affect me? The combination of reflexivity and intelligence has produced someone who can reflect upon the world. Already, reflexivity is no longer a discrete attribute, but a generative ability for internal deliberation upon external reality, which cannot be assumed to be inconsequential. The 'mean' interpretation of reflexivity, as a taken for granted human faculty, seems necessarily to have become much more generous and correspondingly much more interesting.

Finally, this being, who now appears to have private knowledge and to engage in internal deliberations, is also held to be open to social influences. There is every reason to agree that the latter is the case, just as there are compelling reasons to accept the other background assumptions. Yet, something even more interesting now emerges, namely why should it be assumed that these external social influences are immune from internal reflexivity? We have no good reason to do so at all, unless we are committed to a much more dubious proposition, which is that *all* social influences work behind our backs and therefore *cannot* be matters for internal deliberation. In that case, what we think we are doing when we marry, vote or apply for a job becomes truly mysterious if it is totally irrelevant. It could still remain the case that *some* social influences are immune from internal deliberations, but the onus would then be on the theorist to delineate these and to justify what accords them this immunity. Furthermore, a social influence can *itself* be immune to what people think about it, and yet what they make of it reflexively can profoundly influence what they do about it.

If there is no good reason for deeming these reflexive activities to be irrelevant to social outcomes, then the nature of their relevance requires examination. However, before one can get to such an examination of the role of reflexive deliberations in mediating between structure and agency, a detour has to be taken through the philosophy of mind. This is because the critical onslaught upon Cartesian notions of how we obtain knowledge of our own mental doings, what authority our subjective reports possess and whether our internal deliberations are causally efficacious has gone well beyond disposing of 'Descartes Myth'. 'Private knowledge', 'first-person authority' and 'subjective causation' have been jettisoned as indefensible notions on *any* interpretation. Such, at least, was the intended effect of exorcising the mental ghost from the human machine.[2] Without any inclination to defend Cartesian dualism, I have every intention of defending a generous version of reflexivity, as one of the properties and powers which are particular to people. Sociologists

---

[2] Gilbert Ryle, *The Concept of Mind*, Hutchinson, London, 1949, pp. 13–14.

of a nervous disposition might well prefer to press 'fast forward' at this stage. They are probably believers in 'folk philosophy' anyway, and I do not propose to do much more than to defend it in the present chapter. This is prior to exploring the role of reflexivity in relation to the properties and powers particular to social forms.

Taking the 'inner eye' out of introspection

Most lay folk would probably subscribe to the notion that what goes on in our own minds is something private to us, which we alone can know better than anyone else. This is because each person has the ability to know his or her mind in a manner that is quite different from the ways in which they can know other people's minds, or non-mental objects in general. In folk parlance, this special capacity is often referred to as 'seeing with the mind's eye'. These ideas of 'looking inwards', and thus obtaining transparent self-knowledge from a privileged standpoint, are the folk versions of what Descartes called 'introspection' and Locke 'reflection'. To Locke this signified 'that notice which the mind takes of its own operations'. It is the 'perception of the operations of our own mind within us', which is accomplished through an 'internal sense'.[3] This metaphor of 'looking inwards' implies that we have a special sense, or even a sense organ, enabling us to inspect our inner conscious states, in a way which is modelled upon visual observation. This analogy between perception and introspection is what has borne the brunt of criticism. Etymologically it derived from the Latin *spicere* ('to look') and *intra* ('within'). Those who insisted upon the *dis*-analogy between perceiving and introspecting were surely correct. In perception, there is a clear distinction between the object we see and our visual experiences of it, whereas with introspection there can be no such differentiation between the object and the spectator, since I am supposedly looking inward at myself. Over the last half century, the critical response to this misplaced perceptual metaphor has been overkill. It generically consists in turning our heads inside out, so that our inner doings are learned from our external behaviour, rather than *vice versa*, where behaviour traditionally betokened the workings of the mind.

In this way, behaviourists and their successors scuppered the 'internal sense' by substituting a third-person account for the first-person one. We thus learn about our own intentions, motives, feelings, commitments and so forth by watching what we do or listening to what we ourselves say out loud, which is identical with how we come to know other people. Now,

---

[3] John Locke, *An Essay Concerning Human Understanding*, Book II, ch.2.

this manoeuvre has undoubtedly eliminated any need to posit an 'inner sense', since it works by exteriorising our interiority, because everything 'inner' can be read from its public behavioural manifestations. Secondly, and rather ironically, the one continuity (which the revised behaviourist version(s) maintain), is that self-knowledge is still about *observation*. In fact, by substituting the third-person stance for the first-person perspective, it has brought 'introspection' directly into line with perception by effectively re-conceptualising it as 'extrospection'; I now observe what 'she' is doing, even though 'she' is myself, in just the same way that I observe a tree.

What I want to maintain is that the villain of the story to date is the notion that self-knowledge has anything to do with perception and its cognates, such as the 'internal sense' or the 'mind's eye', but also *including* behavioural observation and its latter-day cognates like 'self-scanning'.[4] The force of this critique consists in pointing out that many aspects of the life of the mind cannot be known by 'extrospection', or from the third-person stance, because they are fundamentally different from visual perception. This hinges on what has properly been called the 'problem of privacy'.[5] It consists in the fact that although certain mental states, like being excited, can be externally attributed to me by observing my shining eyes and general agitation, this is hardly possible for mental states which have no necessary external behavioural manifestations, that is, those which roughly fall under the heading of 'deliberating'. Therefore, what will be defended is that we do indeed have *inner* lives, hermetically sealed against 'extrospection' and knowable only by our first-person selves. That this form of knowing can be construed on the model of internal perception will be rejected, and I offer no resistance to *The Disappearance of Introspection* as the term used to capture such knowing. What I do defend is that there is something very important to be known, which is indeed inner and private, but that is much better captured by conceptualising it as the 'inner conversation' whose reporting has nothing in common with observational reports.

For present purposes, Ryle's influential, behaviourist critique can stand for that radical revisionism which sought to expel introspection whilst retaining, by other means, that which introspection was supposed to have provided, that is, various forms of self-knowledge. His argument was that there is no need to posit the mind as constituting or embracing

---

[4] See David M. Armstrong, *A Materialist Theory of the Mind*, Routledge and Kegan Paul, London, 1968.
[5] William Lyons, *The Disappearance of Introspection*, MIT Press, Cambridge, Mass., 1986, p. 52.

another organ of sensing by which we *spect intra*, for we do not need this piece of apparatus to deliver the self-knowledge that we possess. It can be attained without invoking any 'mind's eye' because I learn about myself in exactly the same way as I learn about you, that is by external observation of our doings, sayings and actions. Thus if I doubt whether you have understood something, I can test your understanding by asking you for a paraphrase, translation or application, but these are exactly the same means I would have to use on myself to satisfy myself about my own mastery of the same material. To behaviourists, whether concerned with the self or others, ascertaining their mental states, 'capacities and propensities is an inductive process, an induction to law-like propositions from observed actions and reactions'.[6] So, there is no difference in kind between a person's knowledge about herself and her knowledge about other people; behaviourism had lifted the Iron Curtain between self and other. It had done so by turning the mind inside out so that there was no inner cavern requiring inspection; if you like, we all now wear our minds on our sleeves. Hence, '(s)elf-consciousness, if the word is to be used at all, must not be described on the hallowed paraoptical model, as a torch that illuminates itself by beams of its own light reflected from a mirror in its own insides. On the contrary, it is simply a special case of an ordinary more-or-less efficient handling of a less-or-more honest and intelligent witness.'[7]

The basic problem with behaviourism's method of banishing introspection, by smashing the un-needed metaphysical looking glass, was its failure to cope with the 'problem of privacy'. In other words, behaviourism was impotent to deal with covert mental acts, which have no behavioural manifestations. There remained important mental states and activities, inaccessible to 'extrospection', about which a person could normally claim knowledge (for example, about her thinking, imagining, believing and feeling), that were unavailable to others and for which introspection could still be invoked. Interestingly, defenders of the Cartesian view that each person has special access to (at least some) of her mental states, renamed this process with other terms like 'self-acquaintance'[8] or 'self-knowledge',[9] in order to escape the perceptual connotations of 'introspection'.

---

[6] Gilbert Ryle, *The Concept of Mind*, p. 172.   [7] Ibid., pp. 194–5.

[8] Sydney Shoemaker, in his later work tends to use the term 'self-acquaintance'. See *The First-Person Perspective and Other Essays*, Cambridge University Press, 1996. Earlier work showed a preference for the term 'self-knowledge'. See *Self-Knowledge and Self-Identity*, Cornell University Press, Ithaca, New York, 1963.

[9] Quassim Cassam, 'Introduction', to his (ed.), *Self-Knowledge*, Oxford University Press, 1994.

Self-knowledge without introspection?

To sustain a successful defence against behaviourism entails upholding three arguments coherently: (a) that there is a domain of mental privacy within consciousness, (b) which is inaccessible to 'extrospection' and, (c) of which the person has awareness through means other than introspective observation. The same three propositions also need to be upheld against more recent and more radical assaults upon the possibility of authentic 'self-knowledge'.

Lately, there are two more summary ways of banishing introspection, 'internalism' and 'externalism', both of which work in the same manner as behaviourism by voiding the consciousness of any 'inner' contents. After Ryle had exorcised the ghost from the machine, those who considered he had done a workmanlike job were left with only the machine inside the head. 'Strong internalists', who believe that all that goes on there are brain states, have eliminated the problematic notion of introspection, because they have reduced consciousness itself to an epiphenomenon. And the one thing epiphenomena cannot do is to exert a causal power like reflexivity. This is true even were the feat of introspecting one's own neural firings to be capable of revealing anything meaningful at all. Thus the 'strong internalist' presents us with nothing more than brain states inside the body and behaviour outside it; what used to be held to exist between them is filled in with 'mere' phenomenology. Thus, to Dennett, what may be in the head, is a soft-core of phenomenological 'seemings', which it is interesting to excavate, but only with a view to their downward reduction to sub-personal and non-intentional brain mechanisms.[10] 'Strong Externalists'[11] simply do the reverse. The ghost is similarly exorcised from the machine, but meanings too are called out of the head and take up their abode in the local environment. We are left with the brain as a contentless processing device, which broadly garners meanings from where they are distributed around its local habitat. Hence the slogan, deriving from Putnam, meanings 'just ain't in the head'.[12] Either way,

---

[10] Dennett's posited relationship between phenomenology and brain states is avowedly reductionist. The subject's phenomenological world is 'determined by fiat', as a fictional text is by its author. 'This permits theorists to agree in detail about just what a subject's heterophenomenological world is, while offering entirely different accounts of how heterophenomenological worlds map onto events in the brain', D. C. Dennett, *Consciousness Explained*, Penguin, London, 1993, p. 81.

[11] See Colin McGinn, *Mental Content*, Basil Blackwell, Oxford, 1989, pp. 31f.

[12] Hilary Putnam, 'The Meaning of "Meaning"', repr. in *Philosophical Papers, ii. Mind, Language and Reality*, Cambridge, 1975, pp. 227. For a critique of this view see Donald Davidson, 'Knowing One's Own Mind', *The Proceedings and Addresses of the American Philosophical Association*, 60, 1987, pp. 441–58.

introspection is not the gateway to reality; this lies somewhere 'beneath it' in the neurons, or 'outside it', in the environs.

Since this is not the place for an overview of general theories from the philosophy of mind (and in any case it will become clear that I reject the claims of eliminative materialism), let me now change tactics. Instead of reviewing attempts to rescue or to demolish introspection, let us instead examine what arguments can be marshalled to satisfy the three desiderata, listed above, of an account that allows for 'self-acquaintance'.

Defending a domain of mental privacy   The defence of what I have termed a domain of mental privacy is intended to refer to *activities* of mind of which the subject is consciously aware. By emphasising activities, I am not seeking to defend the existence of supposed entities like *qualia* or 'raw feels', which is a different issue. In stressing that our inner thoughts are matters of conscious awareness, I do not exclude matters of which we can become aware through self-examination, but obviously do not include those of which we remain unconscious.[13] These delimitations are made in the light of why such (putative) internal deliberations are interesting. It is their potential role in shaping agential activity, towards ourselves or towards our society, which is important, and, consequently, for how structure is actively mediated by agency. On the one hand, the 'entities' discussed as *qualia* are irrelevant to these concerns. On the other hand, non-conscious features may play a part in the depiction of the passive agent, to whom things happen, but by definition can play no part in the conscious, *reflexive deliberations* of the active agent.[14]

What are the proper candidates for making up the domain of private mental activity? First-order desires, beliefs, thoughts and so forth are inappropriate because they may fall into either the private or public domains, or straddle the two, and this is a matter of contingency. For example, holding 'secret beliefs' was a way of life in Eastern Europe, until a few years ago; now those identical beliefs may be the basis of electoral campaigns. The same goes for much thoughtful activity; we can do sums in our heads or on the blackboard. What I am looking for is a kind of mental activity which of its nature *has* to originate in the private domain; that is one where it is a matter of pure contingency whether it is given public articulation or any determinate behavioural manifestation.

---

[13] Here it will be seen that I am in full agreement with Searle's argument about the relationship between the unconscious and consciousness. See John R. Searle, *The Rediscovery of the Mind*, MIT Press, Cambridge, Mass., 1995, ch. 7.

[14] Although a repressed thought could potentially divert a reflection or possibly even censor it, the fact remains that unconscious items cannot *enter into* our reflections.

The only candidate, which necessarily fits this bill, is *reflexivity itself*, as a second-order activity in which the subject deliberates upon how some item, such as a belief, desire, idea or state of affairs pertains or relates to itself. By definition, reflexivity's first port of call has to be the first-person and the deliberation, however short, must be private before it can have the possibility of going public. We do not solve questions of 'how do I feel about this?' or 'what do I believe about that?' by appeal to third parties, except as rhetorical devices. On the contrary, we may well tell third persons that we will have to think about it, thus signalling our need for inner deliberation. Apparent counter-instances where a subject immediately reacts to some proposition by saying that, 'No, I couldn't possibly φ', merely indicate that private deliberation has been completed on that issue and thus the public response requires no further thought. For example, adults have normally defined their personal stance towards drug use, and thus would have ready responses to recreational offers. Hence 'reflexive deliberation' is the mental activity which, in private, leads to self-knowledge: about what to do, what to think and what to say.

Of course, this presumes that 'reflexive deliberation' is an activity and one of which the agent is aware and involved in *qua* agent. It is thus opposed, for example, to theories like Rational Choice,[15] where various desires and beliefs are pitted against one another and their relative strength determines the individual's preference schedule. As Shoemaker comments, if 'this were right, it would seem unnecessary that the deliberator should have knowledge of the contending beliefs and desires; he would merely be the subject of them, and the battleground on which the struggle between them takes place. But this model seems hopelessly unrealistic, in part because it entirely leaves out the role of the person as an *agent* in deliberation, it represents deliberation as something that happens in a person, rather than as an intentional activity on the part of the person.'[16] Instead, deliberation is self-reflexive because it is a self-critical exercise. In it, one must not only have the desires, beliefs and so on which are under review, but also be aware of having them to be able to review them, and then to be capable of revising them in the light of one's deliberations.

This line of argument is the one that I followed in *Being Human*. Often it is the case that our desires and especially our emotional commentaries

---

[15] See Margaret S. Archer, 'Homo Economics, Homo Sociologicus and Homo Sentiens', in Margaret S. Archer and Jonathan Q. Tritter (eds.), *Rational Choice Theory: Resisting Colonization*, Routledge, London, 2000.

[16] Sydney Shoemaker, 'On Knowing One's Own Mind', in his *The First-Person Perspective and Other Essays*, p. 28.

upon them are in conflict, but the mere fact of their conflicting will not by itself prompt activity that automatically brings about conflict resolution. On the contrary, the desire to flee, prompted by some fear in the natural order, may well be prejudicial to our desire for subsistence through our performative achievements in the practical order (like the fleeing hunter who leaves his spears behind), or our desire for self-worth in the social order, where flight may mean cowardice and a court martial. We are aware of all three desires, because our emotional commentaries make us so, but the dilemma of competing desires is not something that re-solves itself. Simply to maintain that the strongest urge will prevail, at any given time, is a recipe for disaster, because of the above knock-on effects.

Instead, it was argued at length[17] that we have to prioritise our con-cerns and find a means of accommodating those that cannot be repudi-ated, but must be subordinated. Here it was maintained, following Harry Frankfurt,[18] that we all have to deliberate upon and define our 'second-order concerns'. These prioritise which of our first-order concerns will be most influential in defining our lives' activities and which will be least important. This individual *modus vivendi* defines our identities. Our per-sonal identities derive from the pattern of our concerns together with how we believe that we can live it out. Although each *modus vivendi* is both fallible and subject to revision, it implies a conscious awareness of our concerns and an active agent who deliberates over their ranking, patterning and pursuit. Here, the very elaboration of a second-order de-sire presupposes a prior self-acquaintance with our various concerns and a subsequent growth in self-knowledge about the importance to us of 'what we care about' most. As agents, our private mental awareness is predicated throughout this account, for how else could we perform such operations?

Ever ingeniously, it might be suggested that *we* don't: it is our hard-wiring that does it for us, without any awareness of our part. Thus, in the first place, it could be maintained that it is the *existence* of our con-cerns, rather than *self-knowledge* of their existence, which generates the behaviour they rationalise. But note that by insisting upon the connection between concerns and behaviour, such an objection violates my require-ment (b). If concerns always give rise to behaviour, then they are open to 'extrospection'; they have to be because there is no other way that we could know them, without presuming huge leaps forward in the existing

---

[17] Margaret S. Archer, *Being Human: The Problem of Agency*, Cambridge University Press, 2000, ch.7.

[18] Harry G. Frankfurt, *The Importance of What We Care About*, Cambridge University Press, 1988, ch. 7.

brain sciences.[19] By futuristic fiat, the privacy of reflexive deliberations, which do not result in overt behaviour, have been ruled out. This would simply mean that I am wrong about all persons having a private domain of mental reflexivity. So we must now consider that someone is hardwired for their set of beliefs and desires, *without* self-awareness and *without* any second-order deliberative process. This means making the acquaintance of a character whom Shoemaker calls George. He is 'self-blind', meaning that although George can have a comprehension of mental states in a third-person way, he can never be aware that they pertain to him. Thus, let us say, he knows what belief in God means, but can never avow whether he himself does or does not so believe, even though he does have a belief to which he is blind. George lacks reflexivity and, if so, he necessarily also lacks any private mental activity. Thus to defend my fundamental argument that we all do have a private domain of consciousness, I must show that we cannot be George-like, self-blind to our own beliefs, desires and so forth, which I have just been claiming we have the capacity to reflect upon internally and to prioritise.

Self-knowledge as publicly indispensable but publicly inaccessible   If George can exist, then his self-blindness means that we can only examine him through behaviourism, which makes him the precise opposite of the reflexive agent whom I have in mind and whose private deliberations I am defending. The question is, can George 'pass' as a human agent, that is someone who gets through life in the third-person, and is thus indistinguishable from someone acting in a first-person manner? If so, he therefore makes the very notion of first-personhood into something whose existence is extremely doubtful and fundamentally unnecessary. The argument would be that George can know that 'p' is true, but his self-blindness leaves him unaware if *he* believes that 'p' is true or not. However, if he is cognitively intact, then he can well simply learn to say 'p', and later to utter the words 'I believe in "p"', as the result of practical reasoning, namely, that is what people who accept 'p' do say when questioned. Now George is beginning to look like a normal person, because he can learn to speak like one.

Nevertheless, if his belief-statements can 'pass' in the present tense, it does not seem that they can do so in the future or past tenses without self-awareness. How can his publicly stated beliefs about what is *now* the case give him any indication about how he will behave in the future? He has

---

[19] This abolition of 'psychological states', seen as vestigial 'folk psychology', must be replaced by a 'cognitive science', whose invention lies in the future, is the response given by Steven Stich, *From Folk Psychology to Cognitive Science*, MIT Press, Cambridge, Mass., 1983.

no reason to suppose that matters will remain constant, but in that case how can he learn what other people will say in the future under changed circumstances? He cannot, because he cannot predict this, but neither can he do what they do, by virtue of their self-awareness, namely formulate their intentions – which they may not voice – and from which George thus cannot learn. In the absence of self-awareness, he cannot formulate intentional actions or necessarily acquire the information upon which to pretend intentionality. This seems to make him different from normal people. Yet, it might be objected that practically George could just learn to say 'I'm not sure'; he will have plenty of role models for this and would thus appear indecisive rather than abnormal.

However, can people be indecisive about their *pasts*? Certainly, one often does know of one's past beliefs on the basis of third-person evidence, when other people remind one of them. However, here we come up against the problem of privacy again because 'there is an additional way normal people can know about past beliefs. Sometimes a belief does not manifest itself in any behaviour, verbal or otherwise. Additionally, in some such cases, information about what evidence was available concerning a certain matter may be insufficient to indicate what the person believed about it.'[20] If George is self-blind, and thus has no self-acquaintance, then he cannot have this kind of knowledge about his past beliefs. Can he pass as normal under these circumstances? Well, it still seems that he can again pretend, and given enough role models he could hide behind third-person formulations like 'It seems we all believed φ in those days.' George will appear stiffly aloof and personally non-committal, but maybe that's just the way George is, so he can still pass.

However, Shoemaker rightly suggests that he will be in hotter water with his desires than his beliefs. Among propositional attitudes, 'desire' is different from belief because belief is unique in that it entails having available as a premise the proposition that is the 'object' of the attitude, and this lies in the public domain. Here, George has a premise 'p', well supported by public arguments, from which he can reason that it is to his practical advantage to learn to say that he believes in 'p'. Desire is different, because among its premises feature statements about the agent's *own* wants or goals. Can it merely be sufficient that he *has* a desire, without being aware of it, for it to lead to action? Perhaps, in parallel to beliefs, he might learn to say 'I want dinner' when the herd generally declare it to be dinnertime; but if he does so, his conventional behaviour may be at variance with his desire, the hunger of which he is unaware. A state of desiring has no independent 'object', in the way that the truth of 'it

---

[20] Shoemaker, 'On Knowing One's Own Mind', p. 43.

is raining' gives public reasons why it is practically sensible to proclaim a belief in it and to carry an umbrella. Desiring is *self-referential*, and hence Shoemaker claims that 'we get to the conclusion that it requires self-knowledge with respect to desire, and hence that self-blindness is impossible'.[21]

Nevertheless, he gives some weight to the objection that the premises involved in practical reasoning need not be about the agent's own desires but could be based instead upon premises about what is desirable. Thus, instead of saying, which he cannot, 'I want x', George could still reason from the premise that 'it is desirable that I should have x, because x of itself is desirable'. It does seem possible that he could do so, but then what he learns to say he wants may still be at variance with his desires which remain unknown to him. George has now become a repressed conventionalist, which may not be too good for his long-term mental well-being, but it does not stop him from passing.

Frankly, George is becoming rather a bore and the long literature about him does not lessen the impression. However, society has its quota of bores, so this is hardly relevant. What is highly relevant is a sociological point, which to my knowledge has escaped attention. Let us remember that George started off life as an exemplar. If he could pass in society with his lack of self-awareness, then why should we not assume that the whole human race was not in the same position? Well, there is a very good reason, because all of George's passing successfully depended upon his learning appropriate expressions, 'I believe . . .' 'I want . . .', from what I have deliberately called role models. Now, these are normal people, who, because of their own self-knowledge, naturally generate statements that abnormal George learns to imitate for practical purposes. Yet, if everyone were like George, there could be no such fund of role models, and the argument breaks down because nobody can learn from anybody else. There would be no public conventions to follow and, if all were indeed self-blind, not a single private prompt to follow either. A society that tried to run in entirely the third-person is a non-starter. As I argued elsewhere,[22] a 'sense of self' on the part of its members is a transcendental necessity for society existing. Unless people accepted that obligations were incumbent upon them themselves, unless they accepted role requirements as their own, or unless they owned their preferences and consistently pursued a preference schedule, then nothing would get done in society.

George was invented to test whether someone could get by in a state lacking in self-awareness, that is as a prototype of agents who lacked a private inner life. The argument has gone backwards and forwards, but

---

[21] Ibid., p. 47.   [22] Margaret S. Archer, *Being Human*, ch. 4.

this is simply not a case where what might conceivably be true for each individual could possibly be true for all. Whatever conceptual credibility George himself may have collected, his 'passing' remains utterly dependent upon the rest of society's members being fundamentally unlike him in this crucial respect. If they are, then the claim that everything about him is publicly observable falls too. George's living exclusively in the public domain has been shown to be parasitic on other members of society having private lives involving self-knowledge of their beliefs, desires, intentions and memories. Nothing whatsoever has shown that all of these have to be manifest in the public domain; some will remain matters of private deliberation and prioritisation. To uphold the reality of a private domain of mental deliberation which may not be publicly manifest is, it has been argued, necessary to society's existence and to the existence of each of its normal members.

Replacing introspection by the 'internal conversation'   The philosophical debate about self-blindness has revolved around whether this is a contradiction in terms, or if someone like George could get by in everyday life. I have taken a different tack and argued that a society of the self-blind is a non-starter. This leaves the argument agnostic about George as an individual, but justifies the assertion that were it possible to demonstrate the existence of such individuals, we can legitimately deem them to be abnormal. Here, the sociological thought-experiment trumps the psychological one. That being the case, we are still left asking what it is that normal people do when they obtain self-knowledge about their beliefs, desires, intentions and so forth. If I have indeed shown that the possession of self-awareness on the part of the vast majority of its members is a transcendentally necessary condition for the working of any society, then an account is needed of how the vast majority obtain this by means other than introspective observation. The suggestion here is that we should break with the perceptual analogy entirely though without jettisoning the core of what is misleadingly known as 'introspection'.

Let us begin by noting that people have many different experiences within the course of a single day, of which they are aware to some degree, or we would not be warranted in saying that these were *their* experiences. If they sleep through a particular sunrise, then that dawn is something that has happened, but which is no part of their experience. If they were up and about, with curtains open and so on, then that dawn was part of their experience. Yet, they may have been busy and paid it scant attention. If we press them to tell us something about that dawn, we are asking for attentive retrospection. This is not like taking a second *look* at a filed photograph; it is much more like police procedure where witnesses are asked to recall 'any detail, however trivial'. In this case a response might be given such as, 'it must have been a pretty miserable morning because it was raining when I got the milk in'. Note, this does not necessarily entail consulting a visual image; the subject may not be able to picture getting the milk in, but only recall that it was wet, perhaps via the thought, which the rainy dawn had occasioned, that 'I must wear my mackintosh today.'

Attention is the key to the accuracy of retrospection and so it is to 'introspection', but neither entails something that could be called having 'another look'. When we have a pain or a feeling of guilt we can and often do give it our undistracted attention, in an attempt to diagnose precisely what it is, how important, how familiar and what we should do about it. These are all activities which, in the first instance, can only be conducted in the first-person. They are our own attempts to diagnose our own condition. This mulling over is cognitive rather than perceptual, a matter of self-probing rather than self-observation. If the conclusion is that the condition requires professional help, then the self-same process of attempting to articulate one's pain or feelings to oneself continues in interlocution with the doctor or therapist. The first stage of paying attention in so-called 'introspection' is a process of discursive diagnosis. Through the inner conversation self-knowledge is (fallibly) attained and articulated, which may or may not later be extended into discourse with third-parties, such as doctors.

Occurrent pains and feelings are only the tip of the iceberg; internal questioning and answering are the real modalities by which we develop our self-acquaintance. Generically, we 'introspect' when we interrogate ourselves: be this practically, as in planning what to do next; or meditatively, as in pondering what our responses were to some event or information; or speculatively, as in considering our reactions to a problem or how we think we would react to a change of circumstance. Most important of all, our 'internal conversations' are evaluative. As I argued in *Being Human*,[23] through inner dialogue, we prioritise our 'ultimate concerns', with which we identify ourselves. Simultaneously, we accommodate other, ineluctable concerns to a subordinate status within an overall *modus vivendi*, which we deem worthy of living out and also one with which we think we can live. This is the stuff of our inner lives; a reflexive defining of ourselves, based upon self-knowledge clarified through the internal conversation. Dialogical reflexivity thus integrates ourselves around what we care about most. Simultaneously it monitors our participation in

---

[23] See Ibid., ch. 7.

society, since our voluntaristic social activities are sieved through our internal commitments and our involuntary ones are scrutinised in the same manner.

Thus I am in full agreement with Gerald Myers, for both of us are advocating replacing a concept of introspection, which is based upon perceptual observation, by one which refers instead to the 'inner conversation'. As he puts it, '(w)e can think of introspection . . . as a self-dialogue, and its role in the acquisition of self-knowledge, I believe, can hardly be exaggerated. That it plays such a role is a consequence of a human characteristic that deserves to be judged remarkable. This is the susceptibility of our mind/body complexes to respond to the questions that we put to ourselves, to create special states of consciousness through merely raising a question. It is only slightly less remarkable that these states provoked into existence by our questions about ourselves quite often supply the materials for accurate answers to those same questions.'[24] What we are both doing here is replacing internal observation with internal conversation. The replacement of the observer/observed by the speaker/respondent will have far-reaching consequences in the next two chapters for the conceptualisation of our reflexivity.

Conclusion

In this section, three propositions have been advanced and defended. First, it was maintained that there is a domain of mental privacy within every conscious human being. This was presented as a busy place where the private life of the social agent was lived out. The main activity, which went on within this privacy, was reflexive deliberation. Through it, people exercised their powers as 'strong evaluators'[25] to define where they stood in relation to external reality. In this way, our reflexivity, which is part and parcel of our human consciousness, defined our personal identities by reference to what is of ultimate concern to us in the world. Secondly, this life of the mind was held to be inaccessible to outside inspection, because our internal deliberations have no necessary behavioural manifestations. We thus have to take the agent very seriously indeed because he or she is a crucial source of self-knowledge. Far from such knowledge being a dispensable personal commentary, going on in the privacy of each head, it was maintained that the very existence of society depended upon the self-acquaintance of its individual members. Unless people knew themselves,

[24] Gerald E. Myers, 'Introspection and Self-Knowledge', *American Philosophical Quarterly*, 23:2, April 1986, p. 206.
[25] Charles Taylor, 'Self-Interpreting Animals', in his *Human Agency and Language*, Cambridge University Press, 1985, pp. 65f.

their own beliefs, desires, feelings, evaluations and intentions, they were incapable of accepting any social expectations as applying to them or of actively personifying any social role. A society of the self-blind is a contradiction in terms, because each would be waiting upon the rest to give a lead, which none would be capable of doing, since they did not know what they desired of (or believed about) any state of affairs. Finally, this private life of the mind was not a passive matter of 'looking inward' to see what we found there, but an active process in which we continuously *converse* with ourselves, precisely in order to define what we do believe, do desire and do intend to do. In other words, it is the personal power that enables us to be the authors of our own projects in society.

The existence, ineradicability and causal efficacy of the internal conversation

Now, each of these three propositions raises an important philosophical issue, which has to be clarified before we can proceed. Thus, (i), to assert the existence of a 'domain of mental privacy' immediately raises the question about its ontological status. In other words, are these subjective mental activities real? Already, it has been seen that many would deny them this status, by maintaining that they are epiphenomenal, reducible and therefore, eliminable. As a realist I reject these designations, but have to demonstrate their fallacy by showing the causal effects of these mental activities, that is their capacity to modify persons themselves and, through them, to modify their environments.

Next, (ii), to stress the non-observability of this life of the mind raises the important question of how we gain access to it. Can this be done in any third-person manner? It has already been seen that behaviourism, as the most radical attempt to cast all knowledge of ourselves and of others in the third-person mode, came to grief on the basic 'problem of privacy' itself. To rebut any other third-person manoeuvres, it will be necessary to uphold the fundamental ineradicability of the first-person perspective.

Lastly, (iii), to view the 'internal conversation' as (irreducibly) causally efficacious raises all the problems surrounding the existence of first-person authority. In what sense, if any, does this imply that our self-knowledge is incorrigible, or carries some special kind of epistemic privilege? Conversely, if such knowledge is corrigible because fallible, in what way, if any, can we be said to know ourselves better than others can know us? Here, I will be defending the causal efficacy of our internal conversations *vis-à-vis* ourselves and the world, without seeking to uphold its incorrigibility. It is indeed corrigible because, like anything else, we can know ourselves only under particular descriptions, which can always be erroneous. Also, as with every other form of knowledge, there can be growth of self-knowledge, through the application of judgemental rationality to ourselves. It should be noted, however, that the growth in self-knowledge, which obviously entails corrigibility, also takes place *through* the internal conversation, which thus cannot be side-stepped.

The strange reality of reflexivity

The previous section introduced a matter with which all normal people are fully familiar. In fact, ironically, they are most likely to be more familiar with it and agreed upon its existence than about any other aspect of reality. This is the fact that they all enjoy a lively inner life of the mind. The irony is that so much philosophical energy should have been spent on trying to convince us that we are all deluded. Just because our reflexive deliberations had become caught up in a technical debate about 'introspection', and just because its mis-conception as an 'inner eye' had an unfashionable Cartesian pedigree, we are variously encouraged to regard the private life of the mind as a vestige of 'folk psychology'. As citizens of late-modernity, the basic message to us was to ignore these inner mental doings. Even if behaviourism had come a cropper on this very 'problem of privacy', we are now asked to make a blind act of faith in future neuroscience. One day this will reveal our active imaginings, intimate feelings and self-probing thoughts to be mere epiphenomena, which can be reduced to brain processes. Alternatively, we could reconcile ourselves to being some kind of throughput, which simply registered external meanings. In that (Putmanian) case, our inner clamourings were confined to a few 'narrow' personalised issues arising within the bodily envelope.

Instead, my purpose here is to defend the reality of the life of the mind. Of course it is not the case that when we mull things over, make evaluations, clarify our beliefs and desires, formulate our intentions or dedicate ourselves to some commitment, that these internal deliberations are in any way like tables and chairs or trees and mountains. That has nothing to do with whether they are real or not. Reality itself is not homogeneous; rather it is made up of entities whose own constituents are radically different from one another. Believing otherwise is very much the after-effect of Enlightenment positivism, which conceived of all reality as 'matter in motion'. In this tradition, any non-observable 'entity' was denied ontological status. At its extreme, logical positivists not only declared non-observables to be unreal, but to be metaphysical postulates at best and nonsense at worst. Yet, progress in modern science has depended upon the basic rejection of the 'perceptual criterion' for assigning reality-status to entia, and has taken a fundamentally realist turn. For something to be entertained as having reality status, we no longer ask for visual evidence of it, but utilise the 'causal criterion'; ontology is ascertained according to something's effects. Reality is therefore assigned indirectly, fallibly and thus provisionally. It may seem strange to talk about the provisional nature of known reality, but, after all, science has been more often wrong than right about the entities it has considered to furnish the world. Yet, as physical reality is conceived of today, it is constituted as much by quarks and black holes as it is by gravity and magnetism or by rocks and plants. The point of raising this is to emphasise that the physical world itself is not homogeneous, which prepares us for the acceptance of plural ontologies.

It is now more than thirty years since Popper advanced his statement about the 'three worlds'.[26] These are ontologically distinct sub-worlds: the first being the physical world or world of physical states, the second being the mental world or world of mental states, and the third being the world of intelligibles or world of objective ideas. The three share objective reality; they are 'equally' real, but utterly different and variously related. All I want to underline here is Popper's support for the 'thesis that a subjective mental world of personal experiences exists'.[27] I do so, not just because I also defend it, but because Popper has formulated the genuine oddity about World Two: it is both objectively real and also subjective in nature. This is indeed its peculiarity: namely, it has a subjective ontology.

Conscious states, such as the reflexive deliberations under discussion, exist only from the point of view of some agent who has them. As John Searle puts it, they have a 'first-person ontology'.[28] A pluralistic ontology refers to the different modes of existence of different types of entities in the world. Thus, mountains, plants and chairs have an objective mode of existence, whereas desires, thoughts and feelings have a subjective mode. In other words, it is only as experienced by some subject that a pain or a thought exists; there are no such things as disembodied pains or thoughts. (I reserve the term 'idea' for World Three, or what I have called the Cultural System,[29] that is theories or beliefs which are part of the public domain and whose mode of existence is that of being lodged in the Universal Library of Humankind.) Thus my current thoughts about the internal conversation have a first-person mode of existence; just as does my thought that it's time I took the dog out or decided what to have for dinner. No one has the latter couple of thoughts but me, although they can have their own thoughts about their own dogs and their own dinners. Conversely, I am busy sharing my ideas about inner dialogue

---

[26] Karl R. Popper, 'On the Theory of the Objective Mind', in his *Objective Knowledge*, Clarendon Press, Oxford, 1972. Lecture first delivered in 1968.

[27] Ibid., p. 136.   [28] John Searle, *Mind, Language and Society*, p. 42.

[29] See Margaret S. Archer, *Culture and Agency*, Cambridge University Press, 1988, ch. 5.

with you. Since this is done by publishing them, they will then take on a life of their own and take up their abode as a theory in the Universal Library. The inner conversation never does so. It remains ineluctably tied to the subject who conducts it. Of course any agent can choose to make public a stylised version of their inner dialogue; all they need for this is a diary or a publisher. Popper himself has given us a good example of this migration from World Two to World Three with his intellectual autobiography, *Unended Quest*.[30] The point, however, is that all ideas begin life as thoughts, because someone has to have them and unless and until they are publicly shared, they retain their subjective ontology.

Our thoughts are as first-person dependent as are our pains, and the vast majority of our thinking retains its subjective status. Perhaps it may be objected that there is a difference, namely that I cannot share my toothache with you, whilst you may think that I am busy sharing my thoughts. I do not agree. This is because I do not and cannot literally share my thoughts with you. I cannot share what it qualitatively felt like to have them, nor how, above all, I deliberated internally about exactly what I meant. In fact, I can only share my *ideas* with you, in much the same way that a patient tells the dentist where it hurts and how it hurts. Properly, neither pains nor thoughts can be shared. However, the question of sharing is beside the point, as is the question of epistemic access. There may indeed be some of my mental states which others are in a better position to recognise and identify than I am myself; I may protest humility, but you might well detect its falsity and proclaim my arrogance. Instead, as Searle maintains, 'the sense in which I have an access to my states that is different from that of others is not primarily epistemic... rather each of my conscious states exists only as the state it is because it is experienced by me, the subject'.[31]

This is what makes the ontology of mental states distinctive. Most other parts of reality have a third-person mode of existence.[32] The reality of objects in the physical world does not depend upon their being experienced by subjects; a mountain exists whether anyone has come across it or not. The existence of ideas in the world of intelligibles is not reliant upon their being known by any living agent; a theory or a recipe is real knowledge, which is independent of a current knowing subject. In other words, they both have an objective ontology.[33] The peculiarity of the 'mental world'

---

[30] Karl Popper, *Unended Quest: An Intellectual Autobiography*, Routledge, London, 1992.
[31] John Searle, *Mind, Language and Society*, p. 43.
[32] Obviously, transcendental reality would also be first-person in kind.
[33] See Margaret S. Archer, *Culture and Agency*, Cambridge University Press, 1988, ch. 5, for the argument that ideas, as opposed to thoughts, have an objective ontology in the public domain as part of the 'Cultural System'.

is that it has a subjective ontology; objectively it exists, but subjectivity is its mode of existence.

The main consequence of this oddity is well known to everyone. Their own mental states are accessible to them in a way in which they are not accessible to others. Yet many would challenge this epistemic consequence of the first-person ontology of our conscious mental deliberations. I admitted above that *sometimes* another could provide a more accurate diagnosis of one of my attitudes than I did myself (arrogance rather than false humility). However, that is very different from asserting that such can *always* be the case and for the entirety of our mental deliberations. Anyone who maintains the latter is denying that agents have privileged access to their own mental states, and thus that their distinctively subjective ontology has this distinctive epistemological implication. Consequently, they are also denying that our reflexive deliberations constitute a domain of privacy for each one of us, because if you can know my thoughts better than I can know them myself, then there is no sense in which my thinking is private to me.

Yet such assertions are gaining in momentum. The Freudian strand in psychology places the therapist in this more knowledgeable position, discourse theory in sociology has the same effect for the academic analyst, and both strong 'internalists' and 'externalists' represent the same trend in philosophy. In their different ways, what all of these are seeking to do is to replace a first-person account of our mental states by a third-person one. Effectively they are trying to succeed in the same enterprise where behaviourism failed. Were they to be successful, then there would be no such thing as a private life of the social agent, together with its personal properties and powers. Instead, the life of the mind would have become transparent to the investigator. Our 'folk' feeling of having privileged access to our own thoughts would be shown up as a deceptive bit of phenomenology.

Instead, I want to argue that these third-person manoeuvres cannot succeed. The counter-arguments that I will present are fundamental links in the chain of propositions, which present the internal conversation as essential to solving the problem of how agency and structure are linked. Our reflexive deliberations are held to be the processes through which we agents selectively mediate structural and cultural properties and also creatively contribute to their transformation. Therefore to rob agency of its first-person powers, by accrediting them to third parties, is to cut back on the causal powers which make each and every agent an active contributor to social reproduction or transformation. Agency needs to be granted autonomous properties in order to play this role. To eliminate

their first-person perspective on themselves deprives them of this autonomy by discrediting its powers and explaining them away as the results
of childhood influences, society's discourse or brain states.

The ineradicability of the first-person perspective

Let us begin by stating something rather obvious but very important. A
self-conscious being *is* someone who has a first-person perspective on
reality, such that they think of themselves as a subject who is distinct
from all else in the world. In *Being Human* I supplied an account[34] of
how this continuous sense of self, as someone distinct from other objects
and other subjects, emerged from our practical, relational encounters
with the world. The work of Merleau-Ponty and of Piaget was used to
show how our practical referential detachment from objective reality was
achieved through our active doings. By virtue of our practices we acquired
the 'object concept', the first form of conservation, which distinguished
each of us from all other things in our environment, including other
people. From further active practice, we also learned the limits to and
distinctiveness of our own properties and powers, compared with the
properties and powers of other things and people.

Inextricably linked to this development of self-hood, namely that each
individual knows herself to be one and the same being over time, is reflexivity. As Frankfurt maintains, 'being conscious in the every day sense
does (unlike unconsciousness) entail reflexivity: It necessarily involves a
secondary awareness of a primary response. An instance of exclusively
primary and unreflexive consciousness would not be an instance of what
we ordinarily think of as consciousness at all. For what would it be like to
be conscious of something without being aware of this consciousness? It
would mean having an experience with no awareness whatever of its occurrence. This would be, precisely, a case of unconscious experience. It
appears, then, that being conscious is identical with being self-conscious.
Consciousness *is* self-consciousness.'[35] This, of course, is only the case
for human beings. A computer can be programmed to monitor its own
responses, as in error-correction, but lacks consciousness as a machine.
Since the continuous sense of self is something that develops with practice, then very young children will not display reflexivity. It remains a
matter of speculation how far down the animal kingdom we go before

[34] Margaret S. Archer, *Being Human*, ch. 4.
[35] Harry G. Frankfurt, 'Identification and Wholeheartedness', in his *The Importance of What We Care About*, pp. 161–2.

consciousness attenuates to a point where it excludes reflexivity, although Gallup's experiments with chimpanzees[36] strongly indicate its presence and thus serve to confirm its language-independence.

Now there is already something special about possession of this reflexive first-person perspective, which leads directly to an affirmation of privileged access by each (normal) person to one of her most important mental activities. To possess it means that one can conceive of oneself as oneself, and that one has the ability to conceive of oneself as having a subjective point of view, beliefs, desires, attitudes and so forth. This means that I can conceive of myself quite independently of a name, a description or any other third-person referential device; reflexivity is quintessentially a first-person phenomenon. Significantly, it is the case that I can be mistaken about third-person references like names. Having a common first name, I may respond to a call like, 'Margaret, over here', only to discover my mistake, that it was another Margaret who had been called. By contrast, and this is where privileged access makes its *entrée*, I can never be mistaken over who is referred to when I think or speak of 'I myself'. I do not have to identify the person in question any further, nor am I capable of the mistaken belief that I refer to someone else. This is the only claim that will be made for the infallibility of the first-person perspective.

The causal powers of reflexivity: individual and social   However, this infallible ability of all normal people to think of themselves as themselves has far reaching consequences for each individual and for society. As Lynne Baker rightly puts it, '(i)f one can think of oneself as the bearer of first-person thoughts, then one has a concept of a subject of thought and can think of others as subjects of thought'.[37] Note that this is precisely the reverse of social constructionists, like Rom Harré, who view us as cultural artefacts. He treats the use of 'I' as a *theory* that we appropriate from society, which makes the first-person perspective derivative from the third-person plural.[38] That view would simultaneously deny any privileged access, and it is very dubious whether it can ever properly account for or accommodate reflexivity, since that could only feature as another learned theory. However, I have criticised Harré's views at length elsewhere,[39] and how Baker continues is more germane to the present concern. Using the asterisk to indicate reflexivity, she maintains

---

[36] Gordon Gallup Jr, 'Self-Recognition in Primates', *American Psychologist*, 1977, 32, pp. 329–38.

[37] Lynne Rudder Baker, 'The First-Person Perspective: A Test for Naturalism', *American Philosophical Quarterly*, 35: 4, 1998, p. 331.

[38] See Rom Harré, *Personal Being*, Basil Blackwell, Oxford, 1983, p. 26.

[39] Margaret S. Archer, *Being Human*, ch. 3.

that 'if one can think of oneself as oneself*, then, in addition to having desires (say), one can reflect on one's desires *as one's own*. Conversely, without the ability to think of oneself as oneself*, one could not have the attitudes toward one's own desires ("second-order volitions") that some take to be definitive of being a person.'[40]

In *Being Human* (ch.7) I maintained that it was by monitoring and then prioritising our concerns that we acquired our personal identities. This process was seen as being firmly embedded in the internal conversation and entailed the three stages of 'discernment', 'deliberation', and 'dedication'. 'Dedication' signalled the emergence of our personal pattern of commitments. This pattern was a result of our 'second-order volitions', to use Frankfurt's term.[41] In turn, it led on to a transvaluation[42] of the imports which different features of the world then had for a person who, through inner dialogue, had determined where their 'ultimate concerns' lay and had committed themselves internally to them. This is the first causal power, which stems from our reflexive first-person perspective; namely, that we can modify ourselves by reflecting upon what we most care about and how we must accommodate all our other concerns to it. Thus, the private life of the mind was held to be crucial to the singular identity which the person lived out in public.

There is a second major causal power, which our reflexive first-person perspective exerts, and this concerns our ability to function as social actors. As the incumbents of roles, actors need their reflexivity to know that the associated duties and expectations apply to them, themselves, rather than just being diffuse obligations, which are binding upon no one in particular. Only if I acknowledge that it is I, myself, who am responsible for taking the 10 o'clock class, which is down to MSA, does anyone turn up to discharge the responsibility. Equally, when expectations clash, there is no dilemma or attempted resolution unless the actor reflexively accepts that both pertain to her, herself. Consider Antigone, whose dilemma cannot be understood unless she is credited with a reflexive first-person perspective. If Antigone did not know that she herself were both Polynices' sister and also King Kreon's niece and subject, then she could have no dilemma about whether to comply with the family duty to bury her brother or to obey the royal prohibition on the burial of traitors. She has to know that she herself is one and the same person, who is both sister and subject, before she can have a dilemma. Without reflexivity, she might still lose her life through a fleeting act of compassion, but could not die a thousand deaths in anticipation, since Antigone could not have

[40] Lynne Rudder Baker, 'The First-Person Perspective', p. 331.
[41] Harry G. Frankfurt, *The Importance of What We Care About*, essay of same title.
[42] Charles Taylor, 'Self-Interpreting Animals'.

determined that she herself would carry out the burial. Without reflex-ivity, she might save her life, but then she could not keep it either as a loyal subject or as a disloyal sister, because both roles imply that she accepts them as her own. Certainly, she could grasp the dilemma in the third-person, that is, 'sisters should bury dead brothers: subjects must not bury traitors', but deprived of reflexivity, it could have no personal application.

It is not social realism, alone, which requires a reflexive first-person perspective of its actors; every social theory does, because society itself cannot exist without them. Thus, *homo economicus* (of rational choice the-ory) requires reflexivity if he is consistently to pursue his own preference schedule, for he has to know both that they are his own preferences and also how he himself is doing in maximising them over time. At the other extreme, *homo sociologicus* (of functionalism) needs reflexivity not only to know that social obligations pertain to him himself, but also that when expectations do not cover some eventuality, then he himself must meet the occasion with an unscripted performance.

Why our reflexivity cannot be eliminated   If, as argued above, re-flexivity exercises causal powers, then this is an argument for its inelim-inability. Logically, those causal effects for which it is responsible will remain unexplained without the inclusion of reflexivity in explanatory statements. There is another way of demonstrating its indispensability. This is to confront those who maintain that the reflexive first-person per-spective can always be re-formulated in third-person terms, and to show that this manoeuvre fails to work. Such attempted re-formulations prob-ably appear to all of us as strained academic exercises, because we do not live life in the third-person; no day begins with some detached thinking that 'after MSA has got up, she must go shopping before a considera-tion of Russell's ideas takes place'. Nevertheless, the internal moans and groans about getting up, the deliberation about whether or not the food cupboard will hold out for another day, and the thoughts that come and go about Russell over the breakfast cereal, are, supposedly, phenomenologi-cal froth which can be eliminated without loss. However, the third-person argument is not merely about how things seem, but whether or not we can do without the grammatical first-person, whilst still conveying the same meaning in simple sentences.

A classic example is Bertrand Russell's attack upon the Cartesian *cogito*. Here, he maintains that the 'I', in 'I think', could be eliminated in favour of 'There is thinking'. In that case, the latter sentence would not lead to the conclusion that 'I exist', but would only serve to call attention to the speaker. This is the same line taken by Rom Harré and Peter

Geach: 'I' refers to a location, it is a site, like '39N 77W', the geographical coordinates of Washington. As such, it retains the speaker's *perspective*, which is essential, but subtracts the first-person from it. This is supposedly without loss, because 'I' only indicates a point of view, it does not refer to a substantive self or to an emergent sense of self. Hence Geach, with his cross-hairs still on Descartes, claims that had the latter said, 'I am getting into an awful muddle', he could have substituted the sentence 'This is an awful muddle', thus eliminating the 'I' without detriment. But, 'this', in the alternative sentence, is an indexical expression, meaning it is tied to '*my* thoughts', and thus cannot be identified without the reintroduction of the 'I'. Harré would presumably spring to the defence by offering the alternative reformulation, 'there is an awful muddle at site X', the physical location of the bodily Descartes. Sometimes, the 'I' can indeed be taken as a literal point of view in direct speech (for instance, 'I can see trees from my window'), but reflexive uses of the 'I myself' cannot be rendered in the third-person.

Such reflexive uses are intrinsic to the internal conversation, but Geach also maintains that even in soliloquy, the 'I' is 'idle, superfluous'[43] and thus eliminable. Baker comes back to the defence of reflexivity with the argument that 'there is no third-person way to express the Cartesian thought, "I am certain that I* exist." The certainty that Descartes claimed was certainty that *he** existed, not certainty that *Descartes* existed. And these states of certainty are not equivalent.'[44] They are not. My thought that 'I myself undertake x' is not equivalent to my thought 'MSA undertakes X.' I can be sure of what I commit myself to (whether I faithfully carry it out or not), but MSA is a proper name which may or may not properly belong to me. I myself can always make undertakings, and it makes no difference to this were it to transpire that MSA's legal name was something other.

Furthermore, although Geach might sometimes be able to sustain his point about the superfluity of the 'I' in *monologue*, this cannot be the case in *soliloquy*. Hamlet's best-known monologue could possibly be rendered as, 'At a precise location to the extreme east of Denmark, the pros and cons of suicide were rehearsed.' Interestingly, the speech itself never uses the first-person and since, in the play, the speaker is present on stage, his third-person identity is not in doubt. Yet, even here there is a glitch. Hamlet points out to the audience that suicide is necessarily a reflexive act. The line, 'When he himself might his quietus make with a bare bodkin', is not one from which the reflexive can be eliminated. To commit suicide,

[43] Peter Geach, *Mental Acts*, Humanities Press, New York, 1957, p. 118.
[44] Lynne Rudder Baker, 'The First-Person Perspective', p. 336. The previous two pages owe much to her arguments.

though not accidental death, one has to know that one is killing one's own self and that the quietus will pertain to the self-same person. Thus, 'he fell upon his sword' may serve as a third-person account of another's action, but it cannot capture the act of suicide, where the reflexive 'I' is far from being superfluous.

In soliloquy 'I' can only be 'idle' if reflexivity is taken for granted. The only alternative is to abolish the concept of soliloquy itself, by turning all soliloquising into internal monologues, which address an imagined audience. Occasionally, this is the case, as, for example, when we rehearse a speech, imagine just what we will say to an offensive neighbour, or how we will put our case for a pay-rise. It is not, however, possible as a generic characterisation of the internal *conversation*. In internal dialogue, the question, 'With whom am I deliberating', remains intriguing. Now, I consider this to be a genuine inner dialogue, which requires real interlocutors, rather than depending upon an imagined audience, and will defend the idea in chapter 3 that we can and do indeed speak to ourselves. When entertaining plans, the present 'I' considers its future self, the 'You', and we often say things to ourselves like 'You couldn't do it.' The past 'I', which has now become the memory bank, the 'Me', may also supply material for the thought, 'You couldn't go through that again.' The present 'I', which alone is capable of action, basically has to weigh future aspirations against past self-knowledge. Whether a course of action is forthcoming or not, the 'I' could not have been busier and there is nothing more reflexive than the internal conversation.

So far, the elimination of the reflexive first-person perspective has been considered in relation to its reformulation in third-person terms. In concluding this section, the indispensability of the first-person perspective in connection with psychological explanation also repays consideration. Many explanations of individual actions work by attributing attitudes, which are only available to agents who exercise their reflexive first-person perspective. How, for example, could we explain Oedipus blinding himself once he discovered that he himself was the killer of Laius? None of the story makes sense without reference to reflexivity. At the start, only the assumption that he himself was *not* the killer accounts for Oedipus' search for the killer of Laius. Later, when he comes to the realisation that he himself killed Laius, he demonstrated his ability to think of himself as himself, which is a thought impossible to anyone lacking the reflexive first-person perspective. Finally, his subsequent self-blinding cannot be explained by adverting to a third-person syllogism: 'Whoever killed Laius should be blinded; I killed Laius; therefore, I should be blinded.' 'Rather, Oedipus blinded himself because of the horror of the realisation that *he himself* had killed Laius. Nothing less than a first-person perspective would do justice to Oedipus' motivation. If this is right, then . . . a psychology that aims to be a complete theory of behaviour cannot afford to ignore the first-person perspective.'[45] In other words, if elements like our attitudes and feelings, such as our horror, necessarily figure in full explanations, they cannot be dispensed with as 'phenomenological froth'.

The lesson from Antigone was that many complete sociological explanations are dependent upon explicit inclusion of the reflexive first-person perspective, whilst Oedipus showed the same for psychology. This still leaves us a long way short of the stated goal, namely to show that our reflexive deliberations are what articulate structure and agency together. Before we can even start towards it, there is a final philosophical tangle to clear. All that has been shown so far is that the fact that our agents, Antigone and Oedipus, do know themselves to be themselves, is essential to explanations of their actions. Of this, I have maintained that their self-knowledge is infallible, but what of the rest that they might reveal to us about the lives of their minds? We cannot, it has been maintained, exclude the first-person perspective, but the aim is to go much further and to *explore* it. Does this mean that another step is taken and that 'first-person' authority is accepted? In other words, are Oedipus and Antigone the best authorities on their own reflexive *deliberations* and do we therefore have to take them at their word on the lives of their minds?

First-person authority: how great is it?

The previous section dealt with the most fundamental power of agents, namely their reflexive ability to know themselves to be themselves over time. For all (normal) agents, this personal emergent property or PEP emerges in childhood from the relationship between our human embodiment and our necessary relations with the environment – natural, practical and social. It is a matter of natural necessity, for I cannot know myself to be myself without the simultaneous differentiation of myself from other things and people. This emergent property was deemed fundamental because it was equally crucial to the survival of the individual and to the workings of society. However, if we possess this *continuous* sense of self, it follows that we must also have memories, both of our singular biographies and of the environmental contexts, including the social settings, which we have encountered. The two together give rise to the further emergent power, namely that we can reflect upon ourselves in relation to our circumstances.

The reflexive first-person perspective was seen as *indispensable* to explaining the problems faced by Antigone and Oedipus (whether to bury a traitor, who happened to be one's brother, and how to punish a killer, who happens to be oneself). It was also clear that matters did not end there. Their continuous sense of self had to be invoked in order for either Antigone or Oedipus to have a dilemma at all. This was the lesson which the last section was concerned to draw. However, it was impossible even to sketch their problems without indicating that the second personal emergent property (PEP) came into play. Confronted with their dilemmas, both Antigone and Oedipus made decisions and acted. Now, it seems necessary that both of their actions entailed *personal deliberation*, precisely because their dilemmas arose from the absence of normative guidelines to action, since the relevant social norms were themselves in conflict, that is, those of sister/subject and avenger/assassin. Their subsequent actions were socially unscripted, but rather than remaining paralysed, both Antigone and Oedipus acted. This constitutes strong *prima facie* grounds for considering that they both deliberated how they might act, since each had alternatives, and the one they chose did major damage to each of them. Their 'cases' do not clinch an argument about the power of reflexive deliberation, because we have only a playwright's *interpretation* on which to go, which is, of course, a third-person perspective.

However, there is a general 'folk' assumption that people do not sacrifice their lives or blind themselves on the throw of a dice; they agonise over such actions precisely because they are reflexively aware of the severity of their consequences. Jesus' agony in the garden was a paradigmatic human response. I want to maintain that we are correct in this 'folk thinking'. Yet in order to assert that our 'reflexive deliberations' have causal powers, that is intrinsic ones which enable us to monitor and modify ourselves, and extrinsic ones which allow us to mediate and modify our societies, something more has to be demonstrated. I hope already to have shown that the fundamental 'sense of self' cannot be eliminated as phenomenological froth, but now the same indispensability has to be established for the 'internal conversation' in relation to human action.

To begin with, if our reflexive deliberations are held to be crucial to our actions, I have to show that they are neither epiphenomenal nor eradicable. Now, our inner dialogue could not even be a candidate for indispensability in explaining action without showing that there is 'first-person *authority*' in addition to a 'first-person perspective'. Unless internal conversations can be credited with (some) authority in relation to our actions, then they are dispensable. By authority, I mean that our reflexive deliberations have causal efficacy *because* they derive from us, that is from certain of our mental states. If that is the case, then logically we have to include them in proper explanations of action. This remains the case even when we allow, as we must, that structural and cultural conditioning also and necessarily have to be incorporated into complete explanations. It is only believers in structural or cultural determinism who can write-off mental deliberations as epiphenomenal, but such 'downward conflationists' have sacrificed any conception of the active agent in advance and have settled for agential passivity. Obviously, social realists dissociate themselves from this view, as do many other schools of thought, or there would not be a problem of structure and agency.

Yet to maintain that the causal efficacy of our reflexive deliberations derives from *us*, in an inalienable and authoritative manner, involves much more than rebutting determinism. If first-person deliberations are to earn an ineradicable place in sociological explanations, then it follows that agents do have privileged access to their deliberative mental states. Otherwise, the agent's point of view, outlook or intentionality can be dropped in favour of statements about the agent on the part of the investigator. Unlike determinism, this would not entail the passive agent, but it would involve commitment to the 'transparent' agent; one whose sense of mental privacy is illusory. Then the explanatory framework would only involve indirect reference to agents, for methodologically, the investigator would enjoy greater authority *about* the subject than would the subject herself.

To block this manoeuvre, it is necessary to maintain that the causal powers stemming from reflexive deliberation not only belong to the agent, but also that subjects have a special knowledge of them, which cannot be matched by that of an investigator. In other words, what has to be defended is some version of the common view that the kind of knowledge that an agent has of her own mental deliberations is both fundamentally different from, but also superior to, the knowledge of her mental activities that is available to anyone else. Often however, this is reduced to nothing more than common sense phenomenology (no one can know what it feels like to be me or to have my experiences better than I myself do). What is commonly denied is that subjects enjoy any privileged epistemic access to their own minds. Agassi provides a forceful statement of this denial: 'the doctrine of privileged access is that I am the authority on all my own experiences . . . The thesis was refuted by Freud (I know your dreams better than you do), Dühem (I know your methods of scientific discovery better than you), Malinowski (I know your customs and habits better than you), and perception theorists (I can make you see things which are not there and describe your perceptions better than you can).[46] Shorn of epistemic privilege, the agent's 'internal conversations' would have no claim to be

---

[46] Joseph Agassi, *Science in Flux: Boston Studies in the Philosophy of Science*, 27 (R. S. Cohen and M. Wartofsky eds.), 1975, p. 120. It is only the claim about Freud which is of concern here.

the generative mechanism which, tendentially, directs their own lives and also the many differences that they make to their societies. Someone else always knows that something else really drives the subject. Reflexive deliberations are deceptive and incomplete knowledge; therefore the investigator substitutes an alternative generative mechanism. Reflexivity thus loses any ontological claim to be the basis of agential causal powers because it is other factors and forces that move us.

The authority of our 'reflexive deliberations'   It is crucial to the present argument that this is not taken as an either/or situation, in which supreme authority is accorded, either to agent or investigator. The claim made here is that it is perfectly possible to uphold a defensible version of first-person authority whilst accepting much of what Agassi says, short of his conclusion that we know the mental states of other minds better than we know our own. The first point to concede is that historically there have been various excessive claims made about the epistemic authority of the first-person. Alston[47] has usefully produced a typology of four such claims, none of which is defended here:

(i) *Infallibility* This imputes to agents the impossibility of their making mistakes in their judgements on beliefs about their own mental states (held by Descartes).

(ii) *Omniscience* Not only must every belief formed about any element of consciousness be correct (infallibility), but also every feature of those mental states must be represented in those beliefs (ignorance is excluded as well) (held by Hume).

(iii) *Indubitability* A weaker version than infallibility, which does not hold agents never to be in error about their mental states, but only makes the weaker claim that they could never have grounds for doubting their beliefs (held by Hamilton).

(iv) *Incorrigibility* A weaker version than indubitability, since incorrigibility only rules out someone else having grounds that are sufficiently strong to show that the agent was mistaken (held by Ayer).

Now, all of these claims are about our 'dispositional states', specifically our beliefs, rather than our phenomenal states, such as feelings and sensations. Since the internal conversation involves both, this means it is impossible to rest the case for first-person authority upon our phenomenology, as Shoemaker does in concentrating upon our pain and visual sensations,[48] or as Nagel did in accentuating the singularity of 'what

---

[47] William Alston, 'Varieties of Privileged Access', *American Philosophical Quarterly*, 8:3, 1971, pp. 225f.

[48] Sydney Shoemaker, 'How is Self-Knowledge Possible?', in his *Self-Knowledge and Self-Identity*, Cornell University Press, Ithaca, New York, 1963.

it feels like'.[49] Both, I believe, are correct, but the internal conversation is more extensive, and, as maintained earlier, is very much concerned with clarifying our 'dispositional states': what we do believe and desire and what our attitudes are. Indeed, this clarificatory *process* was precisely what was deemed to make the 'observational' model of introspection inappropriate (see this volume pages 31–33).

If there is anything in the basic psychoanalytical claim (that we conceal various beliefs and desires from ourselves and attribute other desires and beliefs to ourselves, which we do not have), then this represents a strong reason for denying that the agent enjoys omniscience, infallibility, indubitability or incorrigibility in relation to her 'dispositional states'. In that case, the same goes for making such claims, on behalf of agents, in relation to the internal conversation. However, it does not dispose of personal authority; indeed Davidson has argued that psychoanalysis itself depends upon such authority. This is because 'in psychoanalytic practice, recovery of authority over an attitude is often considered the only solid evidence that the attitude was there before being non-inferentially appreciated by its holder . . . So I do not think that the existence of unconscious attitudes threatens the importance of first-person authority.'[50]

What we now need is a definition of first-person privileged knowledge about their own mental states which defends the authority of the first-person, relative to third-persons, without making any of the four excessive claims listed above. Alston proffers the following formulation of privileged access, which he terms 'self-warranted' belief. 'Each person is so related to propositions ascribing current mental states to himself that it is logically impossible both for him to believe that such a proposition is true and not to be justified in holding this belief; while no one else is so related to such propositions.'[51] It is a weaker and conciliatory formulation because it admits of cases in which a person is mistaken about her mental states and allows for any degree of ignorance about them; it can even accommodate instances in which someone else can show an agent that she is mistaken. All of this follows from not insisting that what the agent holds to be the case about their beliefs and so forth is in fact truly the case. However, 'at the same time it specifies a very definite respect in which a person is in a superior epistemic position *vis-à-vis* his own mental states'.[52]

In other words, I enjoy self-warrant whenever I truly believe that I am thinking (or feeling) X at the moment; *ipso facto*, I am justified in

[49] Thomas Nagel, 'What Is it Like to be a Bat?', reprinted in David M. Rosenthal, *The Nature of Mind*, Oxford University Press, 1991.
[50] Donald Davidson, 'First-Person Authority', *Dialectica*, 38: 2–3, 1984, p. 105.
[51] William Alston, 'Varieties of Privileged Access', p. 235.
[52] Ibid., p. 236.

claiming to know my own state of belief, even if that belief itself turns out to be untrue. Self-warrant is methodologically more useful too, since it is usually much easier to determine whether an agent believes that she has a certain thought, than it is to establish whether in fact she does have that thought. Sociologically, it also fits the internal conversation nicely, because they are the thoughts that an agent is justified in believing that she has which will occupy her inner deliberations. (As I insisted earlier, we cannot be reflexive about matters unconscious or unknown.) Simultaneously self-warrant accords first-person cognitive superiority to the agent over third-person accounts of their beliefs; self-attributions thus retain a special epistemic status.

Davidson introduces some helpful fine-tuning here. Specifically, he wants to get away from talking about first and third-person relations to *propositions*, as in Alston's formulation, because this assumes that the two parties are entertaining the same proposition. If I report that 'I believe I am happily married', it is of course very questionable that your recording, 'MSA believes she is happily married' addresses the same proposition, since we can mean very different things by being happily married. Thus Davidson replaces *propositions* by *utterances*, and then proceeds to explain why there must be an asymmetry between first and third-person knowledge about an agent's beliefs. This 'difference follows, of course from the fact that the assumption that I know what I mean necessarily gives me, but not you, knowledge of what belief I expressed by my utterance'.[53] Thus the asymmetry derives from the necessary presumption that the utterer is not wrong about what her words mean, whereas the hearer can never be in the same position because she is an interpreter. 'To put the matter in its simplest form: there can be no general guarantee that a hearer is correctly interpreting a speaker; however easily, automatically, unreflectively and successfully a hearer understands a speaker, he is liable to general and serious error. The speaker cannot, in the same way interpret his own words ... cannot wonder whether he generally means what he says.'[54] It is important to note here that reference has now switched from talking about the (introspective) observer to discussing the internal *speaker*.

Davidson concludes therefore that there is an unavoidable presumption built into the equally unavoidable act of interpretation, namely that the speaker generally knows what he means. Hence, there is also the presumption that if a speaker knows that he holds what he says to be true, he also knows what he believes. Two things follow from this. Firstly, such a modified view of first-person epistemic privilege is quite sufficient to leave the agent with authority in her own mental life. Within the internal

---

[53] Donald Davidson, 'First-Person Authority', p. 110.   [54] Ibid.

conversation the question of interpretation does not arise; in speaking to herself, her deliberations are made up of internal sayings that she holds to be true of herself. It is freely admitted that she may be wrong *in* her beliefs, but not *about* holding them. What she does with self-warrant is to question and answer herself about her mental states and the relations between them, knowing what she means as she deliberates to herself about them. In so doing, she does what no one else can. In basing her private and public conduct upon her reflexive deliberations, she draws *directly* on meanings known to her, which can only be known *indirectly* by others, through fallible interpretation.

Conclusion

The above is sufficient to leave the subject with privileged authority in her own life. What it serves to reinforce is the fundamental nature of the 'problem of agency'. It would cease to be either fundamental or problematic if third parties could 'read their minds' as well as agents do themselves. Facts about agents' mental doings would then become just further psychological data to be integrated with other sociological data into the explanatory framework. This, of course, was the fallacy of 'downwards conflation', and its presumption that the forces of socialisation simply imprinted themselves as beliefs (norms, values, attitudes etc.) upon agency, conceived of as 'indeterminate material'. It was fallacious in advancing a sociology in the third-person, because it denied properties and powers to the agent that could underpin any first-person authority. Consequently, this denial of personal emergent properties (PEPs) resulted in a precipitous slide into determinism.

Secondly and conversely, whenever there is acceptance of first-person authority and of its basic asymmetry with third-person accounts, then the problem of agency can never be by-passed. Those who accept this will not be found advancing 'hydraulic' accounts about the effects of social factors on people – classes, groups or collectivities. The danger, instead, is that many will be found advocating an individualist hermeneutics, which necessarily defies generalisation. Some will seek to escape this trap by positing 'typical individuals', their beliefs, desires, attitudes and so forth. Yet, this is basically incoherent, because such a process of generalisation substitutes third-person interpretations for first-person authoritative accounts. Then, the only alternative, which some like Hollis and Smith[55] advocate, is to accept that sociology will eternally be made up of 'two

[55] Martin Hollis and Steve Smith, 'Two Stories about Structure and Agency', *Review of International Studies*, 20, 1994.

stories', an 'internalist' account of individual hermeneutics and an 'externalist' account of structural properties, which can at best be presented in tandem but can never be merged.

What is distinctive about social realism, but needs to be developed, is that the reflexive deliberations of agents do indeed have their 'intrinsic' effects in modifying the lives of subjects themselves, but also 'extrinsic' effects, by mediating the cultural and structural properties (CEPs and SEPs) of their societies. There is only one story because we make our lives, at least in part, by deliberating *upon* the structural and cultural contexts in which we find ourselves, often involuntarily. It is our deliberations which determine what we will make of the constraints and enablements which we confront, what opportunity costs we are prepared to pay, and whether we consider it worthwhile joining others in the organised pursuit of change or the collective defence of the status quo. To a very important degree, agential subjectivity thus mediates socio-cultural objectivity.

This is not invariably the case. The significance of accepting that agents' knowledge of their own mental states is neither omniscient, infallible, indubitable nor incorrigible lies here. This is because it allows that there can indeed be social factors which affect our outlooks without the agent correctly diagnosing them, that is they know them under the wrong descriptions (such as over-despondency about the obstacles confronting a given course of action). However, even to establish this convincingly, one needs to know what is going on in the internal dialogue and what is 'missing' from it. In one way or the other, to explain how agency reproduces or transforms structures, we will not comprehend these processes unless we examine their internal conversations. The private life of the social subject holds the key to resolving the problem of structure and agency. This should not be such a surprising leap to make if the present chapter has succeeded in showing that the private lives of social subjects are indispensable to the very existence and working of society.

2 From introspection to internal conversation: an unfinished journey in three stages

Social theory, as a whole, is not rich in resources for modelling reflexivity, which is why the debate about introspection proved so long-lasting. However, without a substitute for introspection, there was a reluctance to abandon it, and therefore attempts to rescue it. For the most part, the debate ground to a halt at Kant's *impasse*: the acknowledgement that our self-knowledge was an 'indubitable fact', but one that we were unable to explain. Kant's problem with introspection was that it had to assume a split within the self such that we could simultaneously be both the observer and the observed, that is that we could be both subject and object at the same time. 'That I am conscious of myself is a thought that already contains a twofold self, the I as subject and that I as object. How it might be possible for the I that I think to be an object (of intuition) for me, one that enables me to distinguish me from myself, is absolutely impossible to explain, even though it is an indubitable fact.'[1] During the nineteenth century, introspection's detractors accentuated this *impasse*. Comte made a particularly forceful argument that introspection was 'null and void' on these Kantian grounds. 'The thinker cannot divide himself into two, of whom one reasons while the other observes him reason. The organ observed and the organ observing being, in this case, identical, how could observation take place?'[2]

To many, this seemed an irrefutable argument against introspection and, consequently, against our having any immediate knowledge of our mental activities. However, strictly speaking, it is an attack only upon the observational model of self-awareness and its fundamental assumption, namely that we can be both the observer and the observed at the same time. This principal point of criticism, which highlights the impossibility of our being simultaneously subject and object to ourselves, is only truly commanding with regard to perception. In fact, with most other mental

---

[1] Immanuel Kant, *What Real Progress has Metaphysics Made in Germany since the Time of Leibniz and Wolff?*, Abaris Books, New York, 1804/1983, p. 73.
[2] Auguste Comte, *Cours de Philosophie Positive*, Hermann, Paris, 1975 (vol. 1), pp. 34–8.

activities it has no force at all, as can be illustrated by considering our five senses. We are subject and object at the same time when we wash our faces, try out a new perfume, test our own cooking, hear our own voices or have a cold and feel dreadful. Of the five senses, it is only the eye that cannot see itself seeing, without the aid of a mirror to bring the subject (observer) and the object (observed) together. This needs to be strongly underlined, because Comte's objection would have no force in relation to conceptions of self-knowledge that did not depend upon self-perception. Much will be found to turn on this point because the notion of 'reflexive deliberation', which is being promoted here as the source of self-knowledge, rejects the observational model and replaces sight by hearing.

Nevertheless, John Stuart Mill's riposte to Comte had many takers because it preserved the 'indubitable fact' that we have knowledge of our own mental activities, and only required one revision to the notion of introspection, rather than involving its complete overhaul or overthrow. What he proposed was to solve the subject–object problem by inserting a small time gap, such that what we were engaging in was retrospection rather than introspection. Thus, 'a fact may be studied through the medium of memory, not at the very moment of our perceiving it, but the moment after: and this is really the mode in which our best knowledge of our intellectual acts is generally acquired. We reflect what we have been doing, when the act is past, but when its impression in the memory is still fresh. Unless in one of these ways, we could not have acquired the knowledge, which nobody denies us to have, of what passes in our minds. M. Comte would scarcely have affirmed that we are not aware of our own intellectual operations.'[3]

The nub of Mill's argument was that if the object of consciousness was suspended in memory, then no unacceptable split-consciousness attended the subject who inspected the recent past from the standpoint of the present. Yet, Mill's riposte was double-edged. On the one hand, it appeared to remove the major objection to introspection at a stroke, and hence to justify its adherents, especially the new and growing body of psychologists who sought to use introspective techniques as a method.[4] On the other hand, it served to make introspection less contentious, precisely because it made it anodyne and empty. Ultimately, did anything remain of introspection that could not be absorbed into an unobjectionable study of the memory? As Lyons puts it, 'What, if anything, can be the

[3] J. S. Mill, *Auguste Comte and Positivism* [1882], University of Michigan, Ann Arbor, 1973, p. 64.
[4] The most prominent being Wilhelm Wundt and E. B. Titchener.

difference between consciously introspecting something held statically . . . in memory and simply remembering in a very attentive manner? What evidence would make one believe that the former is not reducible to the latter, in the sense that the ordinary explanation in terms of memory ought to take precedence over an extraordinary explanation in terms of a highly controversial process of introspection?'[5] The two processes do indeed appear to be indistinguishable, and so studies of our memories could go forward, whilst the special claims of introspection, as either a personal resource or a scientific method, were quietly side-lined.

However, there was more to Mill's defence than the simple insertion of the retrospective moment into the introspective process. Mill reads directly on: we 'know of our observings and reasonings, either at the very time, or by memory the moment after; in either case, by direct knowledge'.[6] Three things are noteworthy here. Firstly, Mill is not un-equivocally defending the observational model, for under the rubric of introspection he includes both 'observings and reasonings'; the latter, of course, would embrace the 'reflexive deliberations' which are being defended here. Secondly, Mill is defending our capacity to have 'direct knowledge' of our mental activities 'in either case', that is by our 'ob-servings' or by our 'reasonings'. Thirdly, it is not unreasonable to suggest that it is the 'observings' which require the insertion of memory in order for us to perceive them and derive 'direct knowledge' from them, whilst the 'reasonings' do not depend upon such a time gap in order to be a source of direct self-knowledge. This interpretation derives support from the fact that at the start of the argument, memory was explicitly coupled with 'perceiving', whereas the introduction of 'reasonings' is coupled with the reassertion that we can have self-knowledge 'at the very time'.

In other words, Mill is not just advancing a simple defence in order to rescue introspection. Alongside this, and unfortunately intertwined with it, he seems to have begun speculating about 'reflexive deliberation', as a source of self-knowledge that is known to us at the very time it takes place. Since this is almost secreted in his text, he remains completely mute about how such deliberations could cope with the problem of our being both subject and object to ourselves at the same time. Failure to confront this issue proved to be long lasting and lastingly damaging to the conceptualisation of the internal conversation.

Whereas the vast majority contented themselves with the first and overt strand of Mill's defence of introspection, William James was exceptional

---

[5] William Lyons, *The Disappearance of Introspection*, MIT Press, Cambridge, Mass., 1986, p. 15.
[6] J. S. Mill, *Auguste Comte and Positivism.*

in incorporating both strands into his work. He was conversant with the Comte–Mill debate, which he cites in *The Principles of Psychology*.[7] There, he declares himself fully for Mill, although he never brought the two prongs of the argument together, any more than Mill himself did. However, in James's work devoted to thinking ('reasonings'), we can detect the origins of an alternative to the observational model of self-knowledge. In the convoluted history of American pragmatism,[8] it is possible to trace the germination of the notion that our mental activities take the alternative form of an 'internal conversation'. This will be examined here because it is the only sustained attempt to substitute a non-observational conception of the life of the mind. Our interior dialogues are not matters into which we *spect intra*, but rather conversations to which we are party, by speaking and by 'listening-in'. In other words, Kant's scantily developed notion of our 'eavesdropping' on ourselves (which implies that we are 'self-listeners' rather than 'self-observers') began to be tentatively fleshed out. James took the first step towards superseding the idea of 'introspection' as observation.

Although an alternative model of our mental activities as 'reflexive deliberations' never fully emerged as such in James's work, it is worth following his preliminary steps towards it, because this is the beginning of an attempt to supply a basis for self-knowledge which displaced introspection. Its particular interest lies in the fact that the earlier key thinkers (James and Peirce) were concerned to defend the same three features of the life of the mind which are regarded here as being the core properties of the 'internal conversation': interiority, subjectivity and causal efficacy. The ultimate failure of the pragmatist tradition to furnish a fully worked-out alternative to introspection can be traced directly to these properties later being abandoned. Eventually, our 'internal conversations' ceased to be considered as genuinely inner or ontologically subjective. As for their causal efficacy, what had been considered as a personal power was later construed as a social power: a personal emergent power (PEP) was replaced by a cultural emergent power (CEP).

In what follows, I will trace thematically the origins and the elaboration of the 'internal conversation' through the work of James, Peirce and Mead. The concern is with the unfolding of this one particular idea. Therefore I shall not pay any more attention than is required for explicating the internal dialogue to the history of pragmatist thought,

---

[7] William James, *The Principles of Psychology* (vol. 1), Macmillan, London, 1890, pp. 188–9.
[8] Edward C. Moore, *American Pragmatism*, Columbia University Press, New York, 1966; Morton White, *Pragmatism and the American Mind*, Oxford University Press, New York, 1973; J. David Lewis and Richard L. Smith, *American Sociology and Pragmatism*, University of Chicago Press, 1980.

and its various alliances with radical empiricism, semiotics or social be-haviourism. The three thinkers are presented as representing three mo-ments in the conceptualisation of the internal conversation: in James, the tentative departure; in Peirce its incomplete but basically sound de-velopment; and in Mead, the deflection which meant that its potential remained unrealised. It is because the potential still remains to be re-claimed for modelling our mental lives on the interior dialogue that this excursion is worthwhile.

Stage 1: William James's struggle with introspection: from 'looking' to 'listening'

'Psychology is the Science of Mental Life' are the opening words of James's opus, *The Principles of Psychology*, published in 1890. To discover his discontents with introspection, it is necessary to dig deeper than his manifest and frequently repeated proclamations. To unearth the seeds of the 'internal conversation', it is essential to come to grips with what he unswervingly considered to be the central feature of our mental lives, namely thinking. Putting together his 'discontents' with the old view and the 'seedlings' of a new conception, is what enables James to be seen as the harbinger of an alternative to introspection. However, it must be admit-ted that he himself never performed this juxtapositioning, nor conceived of initiating this conceptual shift.

The best-known William James is a forthright defender of introspec-tion, as a method of investigation: '*Introspective Observation is what we have to rely on first and foremost and always. The word introspection need hardly be defined – it means, of course, the looking into our own minds and re-porting what we there discover. Every one agrees that we there discover states of consciousness.*'[9] Equally, he cites Comte's objections (at greater length than above) and appears fully satisfied to repeat J. S. Mill's riposte.[10] That is, he explicitly accepts that retrospection solves the subject–object problem, by avoiding any need to postulate a split consciousness. Thus he readily concedes that for 'a feeling to be named, judged, or perceived [it] must be already past. No subjective state, whilst present, is its own object; its object is always something else.'[11] It is only, as he puts it, *post mortem* that the psychologist gets his prey, in the form of reports that should never be considered as infallible.

However, a very different view from this ready assent to introspection-as-retrospection emerges when James quits the domain of methodology

[9] William James, *The Principles of Psychology*, p. 185.
[10] Ibid, pp. 188–90.   [11] Ibid, p. 190.

and moves on to his central preoccupation with 'thought' itself. It is central because, although by 1905 James admitted that for 'twenty years I have mistrusted "consciousness" as an entity; for seven or eight years past I have suggested its non-existence to my students', still he never let go of the conviction that 'undeniably "thoughts" do exist'.[12] If his own retrospective report is trustworthy, then these doubts pervaded the writing of the *Principles* and give justification for paying particular attention to the sections on thought. Secondly, as James unfolded his theory of time, towards the end of volume 1, this does not sit happily with the linear representation of retrospection, and it casts real doubts on whether resort is being made to the memory as cold storage. In fact, when he asserts that the 'feeling of past time is a present feeling',[13] it is hard to resist the idea that recalled experiences have been re-inserted into the warm flow of the current stream of consciousness.[14] And if that is the case, then James is not availing himself of retrospection in Mill's sense of 'looking back'. Yet, if he is talking about 're-living' experiences in the present, then he re-confronts all the Comtean difficulties about introspection and how it can be done without positing split-consciousness.

In view of these changes and confusions, it strikes me as more fruitful to give close attention to the five principles of thought, which he enunciates in chapter IX of *The Principles of Psychology*. My contention will be that these contain the first tentative move away from mental activities being conceived of in terms of observation and towards their re-conceptualisation as conversation.

'Five characters of thought'

(1) Significantly, James prefaces this analysis with an ontological statement about the nature of thought. He is perfectly clear about the distinction between abstract ideas and particular thoughts; the former belong to the public domain whilst the latter are intrinsically private. There is no such thing as a disembodied thought. All thoughts have a subjective ontology because they are ineluctably linked to their bearers. Thus, it 'seems as if the elementary psychic fact were not *thought* or *this thought* or *that thought*, but *my thought*, every thought being *owned*'.[15] James immediately stresses that this means all thought has a first-person mode of existence; the 'universal conscious fact is not "feelings and thought exist", but

---

[12] William James, 'Does "Consciousness" Exist?', in his *Essays in Radical Empiricism*, Harvard University Press, Cambridge, Mass., 1976, p. 4.
[13] William James, *The Principles of Psychology*, p. 62.
[14] William Lyons, *The Disappearance of Introspection*, p. 14.
[15] William James, *The Principles of Psychology*, p. 225.

"I think" and "I feel" '.[16] That this is a statement about the ontology of thought, rather than about the phenomenology of mind, is beyond doubt when James insists, with his own emphasis, that '*every thought is part of a personal consciousness*'.[17] By corollary, James explicitly accepts that this means that our thoughts, being inner, represent a private domain of mental activity. 'Each of these minds keeps its own thoughts to itself. There is no giving or bartering between them. No thought even comes into direct *sight* of a thought in another personal consciousness than its own ... Neither contemporaneity, nor proximity in space, nor similarity of quality and content are able to fuse thoughts together which are sundered by this barrier of belonging to different personal minds.'[18] This is James's principle of 'absolute insulation',[19] the strongest possible version of the *private* life of the mind.

Thus, in the *Principles*, James begins his examination of our thinking by subscribing to the same three ontological principles of thought (namely, interiority, subjectivity and personal causal efficacy) as were defended in the last chapter. This is important, because as he begins to dwell upon the process of thinking and of how we know our thoughts, he increasingly deviates from introspection as an epistemology. Of course, there is no logical incompatibility at all between a subjective ontology of thought and epistemic introspection. On the contrary, it was their compatibility that was the credo of Cartesians, amongst whom James can be numbered. This probably accounts for his overt endorsement of introspection. Nevertheless, when James began to consider what was taking place in the privacy of our own minds, he became convinced empirically that we did not find out what was going on by 'looking in' on the process. That is, he began to recognise the deficiencies of the observational model and to grope towards an alternative.

(2) As James continued his explication of thought processes, this cumulatively amounted to a critique, not only of introspection but also of its reconstrual as retrospection, following J. S. Mill – which we have seen him endorse forthrightly, earlier on in the *Principles*. In this context, the crux of the second characteristic of thought that he considers is the impossibility of any thought recurring in identical form. Hence, the 'change which I have more particularly in view is that which takes place in sensible intervals of time; and the result on which I wish to lay stress is this, that *no state once gone can recur and be identical with what it was before*'.[20] To use his later terminology, the 'thing' experienced will indeed remain a constant feature of reality, but our 'thought' experiences (i.e. recollection) of it,

[16] Ibid., p. 226.   [17] Ibid., p. 225.   [18] Ibid., p. 226.
[19] Ibid., p. 21.   [20] Ibid., p. 230.

at different times, will vary with a host of factors: age, tiredness, mood, familiarity and so forth. Thus our thoughts are not immutable repetitions of Lockean 'simple ideas'. The life of the mind is fundamentally Heraclitan, for it never descends twice into the same stream. Because we ourselves change over time, so does our outlook or our thinking about the same items. 'Experience is remoulding us every moment, and our mental reaction on every given thing is really a resultant of our experience of the whole world up to that date.'[21] No two thoughts are exactly the same, on two different occasions, about the same subject. Conversely, the Lockean or Humean doctrine, namely that we house permanent 'ideas' which make their 'appearance before the footlights of consciousness at periodic intervals, is as mythological an entity as the Jack of Spades'.[22]

Yet, if this is the case, then retrospection is simply not viable as a means of rescuing introspection. Even after a short interval, that which is recalled will have subtly changed from how it was in the past. James himself does draw out the implications of this view of memory, which cannot be conceived of as a stable observatory, and thus cannot play the role which Mill assigned to it in the introspective process. Indeed, his next consideration shows a growing awareness of the impossibility of employing the observational model at all.

(3) This section is pivotal, because in it James steadily elaborates the incompatibilities between his conception of the 'stream of consciousness', of thought streaming over time, and the fundamental introspective notion of being able to 'look at it'. In part, their irreconcilability derives from the simple proposition that to see anything, that something must be clearly visible; and this, he maintains, is not the case with many of our thoughts, which are vague, cloudy and unformed. In part, it stems from the fact that many of our thoughtful activities consist precisely in non-observables, namely, swift thoughts that are incapable of inspection, which render the observational model wholly inappropriate. Here, James is fully explicit that this conception of thought also constitutes a critique of introspection as a means of knowing it. His ontology of thought is not compatible with an observational epistemology. This is not the banal point that thoughts cannot be seen (even as mental images), but the radical one that the whole analogy between 'grasping' a thought and 'looking' inwards at ourselves thinking is entirely misplaced.

Despite discontinuities in our thoughts, produced by things like sleep or distraction by a clap of thunder, James insists that they constitute a stream of consciousness that is our subjective life. What overrides such discontinuities and assures the continuity of the stream is the 'community

---

[21] Ibid., p. 234.   [22] Ibid., p. 236.

of the self'.[23] This feels itself to be continuous with its past, and the 'natural name for it is *myself, I*, or *me*'.[24] (Note that the reflexive, the subject and the object are being used interchangeably.) Because our embodiment underpins our thinking, then if 'the thinking be *our* thinking, it must be suffused through all its parts with that peculiar warmth and intimacy that makes it come as ours'.[25] Already, phenomenal feel and emotionality (both unobservable) are presented as binding together the life of every mind.

Each stream of thought has its rushes (transitive parts) and its sluggish stretches (substantive parts). It is especially the transitive 'darting thoughts' that defy introspection. His critique is worth reproducing because he clearly emphasises the deficiencies of 'looking-in' as a means of capturing them.

Now it is very difficult, introspectively, to see the transitive parts for what they really are. If they are but flights to a conclusion, stopping them to look at them before the conclusion is reached is really annihilating them. Whilst if we wait till the conclusion *be* reached, it so exceeds them in vigor and stability that is quite eclipses and swallows them up in its glare. Let anyone try to cut a thought across its middle and get a look at its section, and he will see how difficult the introspective observation of the transitive tracts is . . . The attempt at introspective analysis in these cases is in fact like seizing a spinning top to catch its motion, or trying to turn up the gas quickly enough to see how the darkness looks . . . The results of this introspective difficulty are baleful. If to hold fast and observe the transitive parts of thought's stream be so hard, then the great blunder, to which all schools are liable must be the failure to register them, and the undue emphasising of the more substantive parts of the stream.[26]

The upshot is that the observational model will only afford us, at best, an array of unrepresentative snapshots, which feature the bird (thought) perching at rest. When the bird is in flight, then the process of introspective observation can only disrupt or distort the thought process.

The case becomes worse if thinking is so vague and unfocused that there is nothing to look at. Here James dwells upon our 'premonitionary perspective', the mental fact of our having an intention to say a thing, before we have said it; a feeling about what thoughts are going to arise next, before they have arisen. In short, we are often aware of our thought tendencies before they have developed, and yet, prior to their development, there is nothing to observe. However, such tendencies are considered real, for ' "tendencies" are not only descriptions from without, but they are among the *objects* of the stream, which is thus aware of them from within'.[27] That these unobservable feelings are not delusory is something

---

[23] Ibid., p. 239.   [24] Ibid., p. 238.   [25] Ibid., p. 242.
[26] Ibid., pp. 243–4.   [27] Ibid., p. 254.

that only the 'I' can check from its inner life as it articulates a thought, by welcoming certain words which arrive and do express it and reject-ing those words which do not. In our awareness and monitoring of our inchoate thinking, James thus stresses the antinomy between the subjec-tivity of our inner lives, as domains of privacy, and the notion of 'looking inwards' to find out what is going on. Even were we possessors of the putative 'inward eye', much that really takes place is literally invisible to us ourselves; these are matters of internal *awareness*, but our being aware of them has nothing to do with *self-observation*.

(4) When James moves on to clarify the objects of our thoughts and their articulation, two things happen. Firstly, he reaches the climacteric of his critique of introspection-as-retrospection. Secondly, he presents a rudimentary shift from the notion of knowing our own thoughts, on the model of 'looking' inwards at them, towards an alternative model based upon 'listening' to ourselves. The critique arises from the assertion that the 'object of every thought... is neither more nor less than all the thought thinks'. [28] Thus, if either the investigator, or the subject himself, examines the statement that 'Columbus discovered America in 1492' and declares that the mind's object was either 'Columbus', or 'America', or 'the discovery of America', they are in error. It is a vicious error to extract some substantive kernel and to substitute it for the whole, which is the complete thought, as it has been thought. Thus as lay people, we 'have the inveterate [bad] habit, whenever we try introspectively to describe one of our thoughts, of dropping the thought as it is in itself and talk-ing of something else'.[29] Such 'bad habits' must also necessarily attend introspection-as-retrospection. If the object of a thought is identical with its precise articulation, which is 'exactly as the thought thinks it', then only perfect verbal repetition can perfectly replicate that exact object. Here James stresses that it 'is needless to say that memory can seldom accurately reproduce such an object, when once it has passed from before the mind... The mass of our thinking vanishes for ever, beyond hope of recovery, and psychology only gathers up a few of the crumbs that fall from the feast.'[30]

If introspection-as-retrospection has been relegated to dealing with crumbs, then an alternative method is obviously required by which we can know what our thoughts are about. It is here that 'listening' to ourselves is ventured in place of 'looking' inwards (and backwards) at ourselves. It is not developed as an alternative model, but nevertheless the first step towards the internal conversation has effectively been mooted – with the notion that thinking is a matter of interior speaking and listening.

[28] Ibid., p. 276.   [29] Ibid., p. 278.   [30] Ibid., p. 276.

Here James stresses that it takes time for the internal articulation of a simple thought, such as 'the pack of cards is on the table'. Although the total idea is present, with different degrees of clarity before and after this internal utterance, James draws our attention to how we 'feel its meaning as it passes',[31] word by word. The thought content which is first most prominent is that of 'the pack', and 'we hear the echo of the words as we catch their meaning'.[32] Prominence or awareness then shifts sequentially through 'being upon' to 'the table'. In short, we listen to ourselves as we move through the internal utterance, which is how we fully grasp the contents of our own thoughts, because our consciousness and our words are simultaneous. Hence, James is emphatic that although we may have 'premonitionary' notions prior to utterance, and clearer ones after it, nevertheless, the 'consciousness of the "Idea" and that of the words are thus consubstantial'.[33] If this is the case, then we can and do only fully understand our own thinking as attentive listeners to our own internal articulation of our thoughts, from the simple example given to the most abstract. In insisting upon this simultaneity, James distances himself yet further from the retrieval of introspection-as-retrospection.

(5) Crucially, in his final point, James underlines that this is neither passive listening nor the passive acquisition of minute increments of self-knowledge. Instead, it is an active process of self-monitoring. Thus the subject 'is always interested more in one part of its object than another, and welcomes and rejects, or chooses, all the while it thinks'.[34] In other words, there is an inner life, an intra-active process that consists in moment-by-moment deliberation, evaluation and selection, which is constitutive of thought and is possible because all thinking takes place over time. A few pages earlier, he had explicitly called this intra-action 'reflexivity', and deemed it part of the mature human condition. 'A mind which has become conscious of its own cognitive function, plays what we have called "the psychologist" upon itself. It not only knows the things that appear before it; it knows that it knows them. This stage of reflective condition is, more or less explicitly, our habitual adult state of mind.'[35]

Yet, this internal reflexive deliberation, as constitutive of thought, was as close as James came to the internal conversation. He had assembled most of the necessary elements. Firstly, the notion of thought as internal speech; a movement from inchoate premonitions to articulate utterances. Secondly, the insight that to accomplish this we have to listen to ourselves as we phrase our thoughts. Thirdly, the appreciation that the articulation of what we mean entails self-monitoring, in which some words are

[31] Ibid., p. 281.   [32] Ibid., p. 181n.   [33] Ibid., pp. 281–2.
[34] Ibid., p. 284.   [35] Ibid., p. 273.

welcomed as appropriate and others rejected as inapposite expressions. This latter undoubtedly implies a reflexive and intra-active sifting mechanism, which is where James left the matter. He did not take the final step and conceptualise this mechanism as *dialogical*. What he accentuated was thought as 'speaking' and 'listening'; what was missing was the notion of 'responding' internally. Yet, that is all that was wanting for James to advance the inner conversation as an alternative model of *self-awareness*, as opposed to the observational model of introspection, with which we have seen him become increasingly critical.

Thus, James had initiated the important move from 'looking' to 'listening' to ourselves as internal speakers, but not to our conversing inwardly. The simplest way of summarising his position is that James conceptualised thought as an inner monologue, but never as a dialogue. It follows that even though our material possessions and social standing were aspects of the empirical 'Me',[36] and hence known to the 'I', they could be voiced monologically, but could not constitute *topics of conversation* because he did not conceptualise inner dialogue at all. Consequently, James leaves us well short of a model of internal deliberations through which the reflexive agent could actively mediate his or her objective social structure.

Stage 2: Charles Sanders Peirce: opening-up the internal conversation

Peirce represents the fulcrum between James and Mead in his presentation of the life of the mind. His thought is poised mid-way between James's traditional individualism and Mead's exorbitation of our sociality. Peirce balances a full acknowledgement of our personal properties and powers against a full acceptance of the properties and powers pertaining to society. By carefully avoiding both an under-socialised and over-socialised conception of humankind, he is much closer to realism's concerns about how to link structure and agency than are the other two thinkers. Since my ultimate interest in the internal conversation is as a mechanism linking agency to social structure (and vice versa), then his recognition of the autonomous powers of the two elements should also be reflected in his treatment of the inner dialogue – as is indeed the case. The internal conversation is neither confined to individual psychology, as were James's preliminaries, nor absorbed into social psychology, as were Mead's developments of it.

---

[36] The Empirical Me 'is an empirical aggregate of all things objectively known' to the I. Ibid., p. 400.

Peirce was the first in the Western world[37] to take up the classical insights into silent speech and to transform them into a theory of the internal conversation. Simultaneously, he was quite aware that he was presenting an alternative model to that of introspection, a model of how we come by self-knowledge of our mental activities. What he developed, or more strictly what can be put together from scattered excursions from his principal concerns with logic and semiotics, represents a high point in the context of the present argument. Not only did he advance the internal conversation as modelling our thinking, but also endorsed the three principles of the life of the mind which were defended in chapter 1 – interiority, subjectivity and causal efficacy. Preserving these three properties and powers of our mental activities involved a strenuous effort to combine our concrete singularity with our undoubted sociality, without allowing the one to swallow-up the other. His contribution is therefore of considerable intrinsic interest, all the more so because it is Mead's thinking which now thoroughly overshadows references to the internal conversation within social theory.

Before he was thirty, Peirce had recognised the importance of inner dialogue and hinted at its implications. In 1868, he remarked, 'Thought, says Plato, is a silent speech of the soul with itself. If this be admitted, immense consequences follow; quite unrecognised, I believe, hitherto.'[38] Its particular consequence for his own thought was that, unlike James, he did not become caught up in the toils of the debate over introspection. No tension between admitting its indispensability whilst acknowledging its deficiencies arose to dog his work. He readily admitted that we cannot catch our own thinking in flight, that introspection is necessarily retrospection, but that, as such, it is vitiated by all the defects of imperfect recall.[39] As someone who did not regard introspection as being methodologically indispensable, he could acknowledge the reduction of the introspective process to a study of memory, and do so without regret. On the contrary, he saw remembering as a 'stock-taking' approach, which missed the mark about the inherent nature of our mental activities. Instead, as Colapietro notes, to Peirce, 'the principle function of internal reflection does not reside in taking stock of what we have already thought or in attempting to view what we are presently thinking; it resides in engaging in

[37] A little later, in 1881, M. V. Egger published his *La Parole Intérieure* in Paris. Although William James was familiar with this work and quotes from it in the *Principles*, there is no evidence that Peirce had encountered it.

[38] *Writings of Charles S. Peirce: A Chronological Edition* (vol. 2), 1867–71, Bloomington, Indiana University Press, p. 172.

[39] *Collected Papers of Charles Sanders Peirce*, vol. 7 (ed. Arthur W. Burks), Belknap Press of Harvard University Press, Cambridge, Mass., 1958, p. 420.

an inner dialogue – indeed an inner drama – and in judging the outcome of that dialogue or drama'.[40]

The alternative to the observational model was ready to be substituted. Instead of our being split into an elusive observer (subject) and the observed (object), the change was from passive 'looking in' to active participation: to speaking, listening *and responding*, which now constituted the life of the mind. Obviously, this meant that Peirce had re-posed the subject–object problem for himself; namely who was the speaker and who the listener and respondent? To this he proposed his own solution, as will be seen. Crucially, because turn-taking is intrinsic to conversation, because speaking and responding are sequential rather than simultaneous, the intractable problem of having to posit a split consciousness did not arise. However, this requires a little more work upon it, which will be undertaken in the next chapter.

The key to this transition was Peirce's conviction that thought itself was quintessentially dialogical, an insight which he consistently repeated. 'Thinking always proceeds in the form of a dialogue';[41] 'All thinking is dialogic in form';[42] 'meditation is dialogue. "I says to myself says I" is a vernacular account of it; and the most minute and tireless study of logic only fortifies this conception';[43] 'deliberations that really and sincerely agitate our breasts always assume a dialogic form'.[44] These quotations cover the whole gamut of 'thought', from the abstract mental operations of the logician to the mental anguish of the moral deliberator. Yet, if thought is really conversation, then it must employ language and logic, which are public media. Does this not, in turn, throw into question the interiority, subjectivity and personal causal efficacy which I maintained that Peirce upheld? In other words, does not this central reliance upon the public linguistic medium introduce our sociality, which would then invade us and thus discountenance the accrediting of mental features to us in our concrete singularity? Specifically, does it not undermine a domain of mental privacy, a subjective ontology for our thoughts and any personal causal powers derived from our mentation? These are far from being necessary conclusions, but they do represent a case to be answered.

Answering them is again part of Peirce's balancing act. He sought to insist *both* that it is utterly basic to us, as human beings, to be in

---

[40] Vincent M. Colapietro, *Peirce's Approach to the Self: A Semiotic Perspective on Human Subjectivity*, State University of New York Press, Albany, NY, 1989, p. 117.

[41] *Collected Papers of Charles Sanders Peirce*, vol. 4 (ed. C. Hartshorne and P. Weiss), 1933, p. 6.

[42] Ibid., vol. 6 (ed. C. Hartshorne and P. Weiss), 1934–5, p. 338.

[43] Vincent M. Colapietro, *Peirce's Approach to the Self*, p. xiv.

[44] Cited in Ibid., p. 118 from the unpublished manuscripts in the Houghton Library, Harvard University MS 318, 3.

communication with other beings, but equally that our inner lives are not swamped by our sociality. Instead, the life of the mind retains relative autonomy and relatively autonomous properties and powers. If the first part of this reasoning is taken in isolation, as it often has been, then it appears simply as though Peirce denigrates our individuality. This interpretation derives from his undoubted rejection of Cartesian subjectivism and from his direct attack upon James's principle of 'absolute insulation'; that is, that each individual mind 'keeps its own thoughts to itself'.[45] Specifically, Peirce objected to James's assertion that the 'deepest thing in our nature is . . . this *dumb* region of the heart in which we dwell alone with our willingnesses and unwillingnesses, our faiths and fears'.[46] To Peirce, we were not dumb, but internally vocal, indeed conversational about such reflexive matters.

In his earlier work, Peirce had made certain dramatic assertions, which prompted some to draw two conclusions. His statement that 'my language is the sum total of myself',[47] when taken alone, certainly permitted the inference that our communicative skills obliterated our individual uniqueness. Then again, he maintained that our consciousness, meaning our thought, 'it is more without us than within'. Instead, 'it is we that are in it, rather than it in any of us'.[48] This could license one to conclude that here is a social externalist who allows our sociality to override our personal autonomy. The first statement appears to be a direct denial of our subjectivity and the second of our interiority. Without these properties it is difficult to see how the individual has the wherewithal to exercise her own reflexive powers of self-control, which are obviously intrinsic causal powers – yet this became the *leitmotif* of his later work.[49] How then can the internal conversation retain personal causal efficacy, as he maintains, and how can he reject an epiphenomenal status for our interior deliberations,[50] as he firmly does?

---

[45] Cited in Ibid., p. 62, from MS 1099.

[46] William James, *Essays on Faith and Morals* (ed. R. Barton Perry), New American Library, New York, 1974, pp. 30–1.

[47] *Collected Papers of Charles Sanders Peirce*, vol. 5 (ed. C. Hartshorne and P. Weiss), pp. 134–5, p. 5.

[48] Cited in Colapietro, *Peirce's Approach to the Self*, p. 54.

[49] From such assertions as the above, certain critics claimed that Peirce's conception of the self was not one that could sustain his later views on our autonomous powers of self-control. See Richard J. Bernstein, *Praxis and Action*, University of Pennsylvania Press, Philadelphia, 1971, pp. 198f. and Manley Thompson, *The Pragmatic Philosophy of C. S. Peirce*, University of Chicago Press, 1953. However, see also Patricia Muoio, 'Peirce on the Person', *Transactions of the Charles S. Peirce Society*, 1984, 20, no. 2: 169–81. For the opposite view, see Colapietro, *Peirce's Approach to the Self*, ch. 4. However, I will not go down these exegetical by-ways.

[50] C. F. Delaney, 'Peirce's Account of Mental Activity', *Synthese*, 1979, 41, pp. 25–36.

The contradictions in his thought are only apparent, for what Peirce gives us is a *developmental* account of how interiority emerges from externality and how a subjective perspective is elaborated from the objective affordances of language, to endow the private domain of the inner conversation with causal powers. Colapietro gives the same overall interpretation: for Peirce 'we must start with the public world (including language and the laws which govern its use) and, then, try to explain how active beings in that public world come to acquire private worlds. In this context, to acquire a private world means to come to know the difference between the inner realm of imagination and the outer realm of actuality; moreover, it means to come to utilise the ability of withdrawing from the outer world into the inner world. The capacity to retreat into inwardness creates the possibility of performing imaginary experiments (i.e. experiments in the imagination).'[51]

Let us examine more clearly how the apparent contradictions dissolve. To begin with, it is *Cartesian* subjectivism, in the form of Jamesian 'absolute insulation', which Peirce repudiates, rather than human subjectivity itself. What he condemns is the subjectivist viewpoint in which consciousness confers meaning upon signs rather than signs being intrinsically meaningful. To subjectivists, thought is conceived of as primitive to the symbols expressing it, and, although these are necessary for communication with others, they are not necessary conditions of thought itself. Peirce rejects this subjectivist insularity because he holds that thought is dependent upon the use of inter-subjective signs: language, logic, visual forms and numerical symbols. This is one meaning of his saying that we are not 'shut up in a box of flesh and blood'.[52] The potential for inward thought is instinctual, indeed it is the main thing that separates us from 'the brutes', and it is gradually learned by children as they start to refrain from spontaneous action and begin to stop and think instead.

This learning is the effect of our necessary interaction with the world, given the way in which we are constituted and the way the world is. The objective constitution of the world can never be reduced to what we subjectively take it to be. The world's objectivity is quite '*independent of his thinking it to be so*, or any man's opinion on that subject'.[53] Thus, the development of self-consciousness itself is presented in realist terms; it is attributed to the 'primacy of practice' in the world and the dawning recognition of our human properties and powers in relation to worldly properties and powers. This referential detachment of the self-conscious

[51] Vincent M. Colapietro, *Peirce's Approach to the Self*, p. 102.

[52] *Writings of Charles S. Peirce: A Chronological Edition*, vol. 1, 1857–66, Indiana University Press, Bloomington, 1982, p. 498.

[53] *Collected Papers of Charles Sanders Peirce*, vol. 5, p. 211.

individual thus requires *no* social mediation. Instead, 'Peirce uses his famous argument that self-consciousness grows from an increasing awareness of ourselves as centres of ignorance and error. If everything always
went our way . . . if our merest wish served to accomplish the most amaz-
ing feats, we might never come to distinguish ourselves from the world . . .
As it is, our failures and errors teach us about our separate existence.'[54]

Thus, Peirce gives us a self-consciousness that is not suffused by sociality and a being who is sufficiently robust to make genuine *personal use*
of the Cultural System. Our reliance upon the public domain of culture
for thinking can be upheld, without this determining what we do with
it – that is the contents of our mental activities. Thus, the crucial point
about the full realisation of the inner world is that it depends upon the
private use of the public media. 'When I enter into the inner world, I take
with me the booty from my exploits in the outer world, such things as my
native language, any other languages I might know, a boundless number
of visual forms, numerical systems and so on. The more booty I take to
that secret hiding place, the more spacious that hiding place becomes . . .
the domain of inwardness is not fixed in its limits; the power and wealth
of signs that I borrow from others and create for myself determine the
dimensions of my inwardness.'[55] The reference to creativity relates to the
importance that Peirce assigned to our imaginations and the inestimable
role which they play in the inner life of the mind.

Since the inner world is emergent from the outer world, there is no
contradiction between Peirce's externalism and his sturdy advocacy of our
interiority. With his 'inner world' we find exactly that domain of privacy
that I have been defending from the beginning. What then of its second
property, its subjectivity or more precisely its first-person ontology? In
the statement that the mind's 'theatre is the plastic inner world',[56] he
leaves us in no doubts about this; my own theatre is plastic to me, it is
dependent upon my imaginative construction and use. That is its mode
of existence; one that means it has none apart from me. The inner world
is necessarily a first-person world. Moreover, it is the home of my own
unique subjectivity, because Peirce asserts that 'the true definition of
consciousness is connection with the internal world'.

The inner world is real and has real causal powers. In other words the
triad of interiority, subjectivity and causal efficacy is upheld. The latter
takes the usual form of defending personal emergent properties (PEPs)
with their two distinct powers: the capacity to modify ourselves and the capacity to modify our social environment. Under self-modification, Peirce

[54] William H. Davis, *Peirce's Epistemology*, Martinus Nijhoff, The Hague, 1972, p. 12.
[55] Colapietro, *Peirce's Approach to the Self*, pp. 115–16.
[56] Cited in Ibid., p. 85, from MS 318, 44.

includes the interrelated powers of self-consciousness, self-criticism and, above all, self-control. All are exercised through the medium of the internal conversation. Our inner dialogue is the modality through which our personal autonomy is explored, is directed to particular ends, affirms specific ideals, and is then realised in terms of our commitments. In turn, the modified self, as the embodiment of its ultimate concerns, stands forth as a sign to society, and the effects of this exemplary agency constitute its external causal powers.

I have here expressed the causal efficacy of the internal conversation in the terminology of social realism. Of course, Peirce himself employed and developed the conceptual framework of semiosis, with its three categories of 'object, sign and interpretant'. In this context, at least, it seems possible to translate backwards and forwards between the frameworks of realism and of semiotics. Thus, in relation to our extrinsic causal powers, which are rooted in the internal conversation, semiosis would designate the internal dialogue itself as the 'object', the resulting, modified self as the 'sign,'[57] and the future society as the 'interpretant', upon which the effect of the 'sign' is exerted. Where our intrinsic powers to modify ourselves are concerned, the same kind of translation between the frameworks is possible, as will be examined shortly.

It is important, in this connection, to note Peirce's views about the role of language in the internal conversation and its relationship to self-modification. As Colapietro interprets him, 'Language is not something *to* which I conform myself; it is something *by* which I transform myself.'[58] This expression of his later thought stands as a corrective to his earlier and excessive externalism and its claim that 'my language is the sum total of myself'. The latter cannot be the case, because transformation from within is distinctive of complex semiotic systems (as it is of morphogenesis). Further, authentic transformation is always much more than novel permutations upon something which is externally given. The private and innovative *use* of the public linguistic medium is just as significant as the fact that the public language is an indispensable tool for the emergence of the private inner world.

Let us now turn to a closer examination of the intrinsic causal powers and the detailed process by which the internal conversation is a vehicle for self-transformation. Obviously, any conversation requires its

---

[57] This emphatically does not mean some form of symbolism; 'when one understands Peirce's realism one understands that just as a chair *is* the *laws* of its behaviour, so a man (or better, a man's character) *is* the habits, tendencies and dispositions which he embodies. Thus a man, taken as a self, a personality, a "spiritual" being, is the unity of his sign activity.' William H. Davis, *Peirce's Epistemology*, p. 18.

[58] Ibid., p. 110.

interlocutors. If this is an inner dialogue, then is it predicated upon an internal differentiation of the self such that different parts of it can converse with one another? If the answer is thought to be 'yes', then this requirement could not be met from within the Cartesian framework adopted by William James, as has already been seen. Descartes had maintained that it was impossible to distinguish any internal parts to the self,[59] which, in turn, deprived him of one source of the interlocutors who could sustain a conversation. At variance with this conception is Peirce's stratified view of the self which he believed enabled him to conceptualise 'a dialogue between different phases of the *ego*'.[60]

Thus to Peirce, 'the past represents those events over which we have no control; the future, those over which we have a measure of control; and the present, those which we are endeavouring to control'.[61] The differentiation of 'phases' is clearly dependent upon temporality; that is, upon recognising that different 'parts' of the self operate over different tracts of time. Temporality is what makes it possible to distinguish them *analytically*. The differentiation of such 'phases' does not entail reification, because the ego itself is continuous. To stress temporal separability does not involve philosophical dualism in relation to the self. It is only, but very usefully, to specify the properties and powers that stand in relations of priority and posteriority to one another. Thus, in Peirce's conceptualisation, as with analytical dualism in general, the argument that different phases of the self operate over different time periods is based upon two simple propositions:[62] that a pre-existing self necessarily predates the (dialogical) activities which transform it, and that the elaborated self necessarily post-dates those activities. None of this is to deny the unbroken continuity of the temporal process, to which Peirce attached considerable importance as his principle of 'synechism'; it is merely to insist that this is perfectly compatible with the introduction of *analytical* distinctions.[63]

This is to express the procedure in the terminology of social realism. Such a conception then allows analytical cycles to be disengaged over time; ones made up of prior conditioning -> interaction -> posterior

---

[59] In the sixth Meditation, Descartes stated, 'inasmuch as I am only a thinking thing, I cannot distinguish in myself any parts, but apprehend myself to be clearly one and entire', *The Philosophical Works of Descartes*, Cambridge University Press, 1972.

[60] *Collected Papers of Charles Sanders Peirce*, vol. 4, 1933, p. 6.

[61] William H. Davis, *Peirce's Epistemology*, p. 57.

[62] See Margaret S. Archer, *Realist Social Theory: The Morphogenetic Approach*, Cambridge University Press, 1995, ch. 3.

[63] Since there is 'no cognition not determined by previous cognitions, it follows that the striking in of a new experience is never an instantaneous affair, but is an *event* occupying time, and coming to pass by a continuous process'. *Collected Papers of Charles Sanders Peirce*, vol. 5, p. 284.

elaboration. Peirce himself, of course, uses the language of semiosis instead; indeed, to him, the subject in its innermost being is itself a form of semiosis.[64] Nevertheless, this leads to a very similar triadic conception of the self, distinguished according to the same three temporal phases. It is also similar in placing the emphasis upon the middle element 'interaction' (in the guise of the internal conversation) for mediating prior conditioning and being responsible for the subsequent elaboration of the self. Although his insights are scattered and never fully developed, they can be synthesised and summarised as follows.

Fundamentally, semiosis advances a general three-part scheme, involving an 'object' (back-referent), a 'sign' (which represents it to something else) and an 'interpretant' (that upon which an effect is exerted). In the current context, the 'different phases of the ego' readily fit into this general scheme: the past 'Me' would stand as 'object', the present 'I' as 'sign' and the future 'You' as interpretant. Certainly, Peirce did not proffer this schematisation and admittedly he never uses the term 'Me' for the historic phase of the ego, but he does have the concept of the 'critical self', which occupies exactly the same role.[65] Let us now move on to the triadic scheme, and especially to how Peirce sees the inner conversation as being embedded within it. The crucial question is who is talking to whom?

'A dialogue between different phases of the ego'   Peirce's past 'Me', or what he calls the 'critical self', is fundamentally made up of habits, that is dispositions to respond in a given manner to given circumstances. Such ingrained pre-dispositions towards habitual action are largely experienced by the subject as constraints (that is, do this rather than that). Yet, Peirce is at pains to stress that habits are also enablements (that is, we know how to act rather than being perpetually at sea). Thus, he says that 'undisciplined young persons may have come to think of acquired human habits chiefly as constraints, and undoubtedly they all are so in a measure. But good habits are in much higher measure powers than they are limitations.'[66] The 'critical self' is thus a summation of the past, which provides us with an orientation to the future, from its deposition in the present.

It is the summation of the past because it represents the finishing point of anterior cycles of semiosis. That is, our acquired habits are the outcome of our interpretative efforts in previous contexts, which also represent the means of orientating ourselves to a new sequence of action in the newly arrived present. Here it is significant that Peirce associates the

---

[64] Ibid., vol. 5, p. 313.

[65] Norbert Wiley, *The Semiotic Self*, Polity Press, Oxford, 1994, chs. 2 and 3. Wiley interprets Peirce as differentiating only an 'I' and a 'You', but Peirce himself appeared to endorse the triadic scheme.

[66] Cited in Colapietro, *Peirce's Approach to the Self*, p. 112 from MS 930, 31.

'critical self' with the individual's conscience; in self-questioning about what is to be done, it supplies the answers which have been honed by past experience. The 'Me' is able to respond because it is alive in the present as a disposition to act in particular ways.[67] The Peircian 'Me', as the personal conscience which is regularly consulted, is thus very different from Mead's 'Me', as the 'generalized other', which furnishes society's guidelines to action. The former is a personalised sediment, the latter a socialised deposit.

However, if the 'critical self' always ruled, we would all be stable conventionalists, committed to routinised, habitual thought and action. Instead, Peirce maintains that our 'moral natures' (should) result in the systematic self-monitoring of our habits rather than their uncritical replication: 'you are well aware that the exercise of control over your own habits, if not the most important business of life, is at least very near to being so'.[68] To ask how this process of self-transformation takes place, involves introducing the 'I' and broaching the inner conversation between 'I' and 'Me' which is part of the mechanism through which human reflexivity is realised, according to Peirce.

The 'I', as the present self and the only one capable of action, is seen as a source of creativity and innovation, involving both intrinsic and extrinsic powers of transformation. In asking where this innovativeness comes from, we obtain a very clear distinction between the Peircian 'I' and the Freudian 'id'. The 'I' is no seething cauldron of primal urges, but rather its creativity is a response to the challenges posed by the socio-cultural environment to an intelligent being. It is here that Peirce is at his most delicate in balancing our individuality (which includes the 'critical self', distilled from our biographic experiences) with our ineluctable sociality. Specifically, he pinpoints two features of life in society, as an open system, which serve as stimuli to innovation.

On the one hand, structurally, we may be stimulated to creative conjectures when habitual action encounters some external impediment, presumably because of changed circumstances. Equally, he allows that such obstacles may exist only in the imagination and sees the detection of problems, to which others are oblivious, as indicating mental sophistication. Above all, however, it is precisely the open nature of society, which consistently enables us to conceive of alternative futures for ourselves. Were our ends antecedently fixed, 'there would be no room for development, for growth, for life; and consequently there would be no personality. The

---

[67] 'The immediate continuity of mental processes means that the past is never really past to a mind, but still really alive and present, only infinitesimally dying out.' William H. Davis, *Peirce's Epistemology*, p. 16. See also, *Collected Papers of Charles Sanders Peirce*, vol. 6, p. 134.

[68] Ibid., p. 111, from MS 614, 3.

mere carrying out of pre-determined purposes is mechanical.'[69] However, the very contingencies of life in an open system defy such programmatic responses. But our innovations are not conceived *ex nihilo*. On the other hand, there are the resources of culture, which is not conceived of according to the 'myth of cultural integration'[70] (as was Mead's tendency), but rather as an armoury of multifarious ideals. As intelligent beings, we have the power to ponder and meditate upon these ideals internally, to daydream about their realisation, to entertain and to endorse passionate aspirations. Thus, 'what most influences men to self-government is intense disgust with one kind of life and warm admiration for another'.[71]

It is from this process that the progressively transformed 'You' comes into being; a determinate 'You', which has been delineated and actualised from the array of potential future selves. As a disciple of the ideal that has been adopted, this new 'You' moves down the time-line and assumes the position of the acting 'I'. This commitment to an ideal entails the surrender of our egotism, but the self-transcendence then taking place results in self-possession. The achievement of this autonomy represents the zenith of our intrinsic powers of self-modification. Simultaneously, people also express their extrinsic powers, because by actualising an ideal, they become a sign to society. As living embodiments of ideals, they challenge the world, their interpretant, and the real influence of their exemplary living has causal efficacy, which is counterposed to that of force and coercion. This, of course, is an ideal transformatory scenario; not all will accomplish it and its full achievement would take more than a lifetime, which is why death is always tragic to Peirce. However, what most concerns us here are the dialogical dynamics upon which the realisation of our personal emergent powers ultimately rest – whatever the degree to which they are indeed realised.

The internal conversation and the transformatory process   Peirce's agent is both active and passive; someone who makes things happen as well as someone to whom things happen. It is the active aspect upon which he concentrates and the modality through which self-transformation comes about is the internal conversation. The internal dialogue is pictured as a process of self-cultivation in which we seek to conform ourselves to our ultimate concerns or ideals 'by cherishing and tending them as I would the flowers in my garden'.[72] Unique as the following analysis

[69] *Collected Papers of Charles Sanders Peirce*, vol. 6, p. 157.
[70] Margaret S. Archer, *Culture and Agency: The Place of Culture in Social Theory*, 1998, Cambridge University Press, ch. 1.
[71] Cited in Colapietro, *Peirce's Approach to the Self*, p. 111 from MS 675, 15–16.
[72] *Collected Papers of Charles Sanders Peirce*, vol. 6, p. 289.

of self-talk turns out to be, it is important to be aware of its focal concern and especially of what is correspondingly omitted. This is because there are two crucial issues that are allowed to fall outside the ambit of the internal conversation.

On the one hand, there is that large tract of life in which things do happen to us involuntarily, such as our initial social placement, the life chances 'assigned' to us, and the opportunity costs attaching to various courses of action. By omission, Peirce treats agents as completely passive in the face of the 'force of circumstances'. Yet, it is precisely what actors do when the projects they have conceived encounter social constraints (and enablements) which is the concern of this book. Peirce does not give consideration to the inner conversation as the means through which actors review their personal projects in the light of their social circumstances and vice versa. Through reflexive deliberations they elaborate various courses of action, even when they confront stringent constraints, of which compliance is only one such course. Evasion, circumvention or subversion are alternative responses.

On the other hand, Peirce was not a sociologist and his second omission reflects his lack of sociological concern. The dynamics of the internal conversation focus almost entirely upon the process of realising or failing to realise our *intrinsic* personal powers of self-transformation. What is largely left out of account are our *extrinsic* powers for social transformation or reproduction. These tend to be confined to our exemplary influence, and thus omit crucial dialogical deliberations about how best to act *collectively* in furtherance of social transformation or defence of (some aspect of) the status quo. That being said, Peirce does provide the analytical framework for the internal conversation about such matters; one which can later be extended and slid into a more prominent social context.

The power of acting at all is necessarily identified with the present 'I', but action itself is first mediated by a necessary detour through the inner world. Analytically, this involves two successive moments of the internal conversation: the first is concerned with ' "I" – "Me" ' relations and the second with the ' "I" – "You" ' relationship. In practice, of course, these will be overlapping and intertwined. They are only *analytical devices*, hence the inverted commas, because I only talk to myself and the internal conversation is not between three reified people inside me. They are indeed *aspects* of the ego, aspects which are alive in the present or being formed there, aspects of one thing, one person. Nevertheless, there is an important difference between them, because the first moment is concerned with arriving at a 'determination' in which the 'I' seeks to overcome the inertia of the routinised 'Me'. The second moment concerns deliberations of the 'I' about the 'You', which are preparatory to the realisation of any new commitment which has been arrived at intra-personally.

The 'discussion' between the 'I' and the 'Me' starts with the 'I' seeking to persuade the routinised 'Me' that habitual responses should give way to innovative action: 'when one reasons, it is that critical self that one is trying to persuade'.[73] Peirce employs the analogy of the courtroom to capture this phase of the internal conversation. The 'I' is effectively the Counsel for the Prosecution of change, who argumentatively marshals his case. Since this is a Court of Appeal, then the 'critical self', as one's conscience and the seat of the deepest underlying dispositions that one has developed biographically, has to be convinced, for it cannot be over-ruled. 'Although the court of conscience . . . is deeply committed to the preservation of judgements and present statutes, it is, nonetheless, a court in which earlier decisions and even criteria of judgement may be revised in the light of a convincing case by some innovative self.'[74] It is a matter for regret that Peirce is not more forthcoming than this; he gives us the substance of the dialogue, but none of its flavour. We are given no illustrations and no hint as to how far courtroom analogy should be pushed. The outline is tantalising, but what needs to be filled in is the actual deliberative process itself – the real inner conversation. Specifically, we need to know if the 'I' and the 'Me' are to be taken as literally speaking to one another, or if this is merely a metaphorical device.

Peirce is somewhat more specific about the second moment, which concerns the 'I' and the 'You', where an individual's 'thoughts are what he is "saying to himself"; that is saying to that other self which is just coming into life in the flow of time'.[75] What is crucial here is how the 'I', through self-talk, prepares the ground for a new transformed 'You' to succeed it. This is what Peirce called 'the power of preparatory meditation'.[76] In it, the 'I' uses its imagination to project what it would be like to be otherwise and how it would have to act otherwise, thus giving shape to this future *modus vivendi* within the mind. Not everything is talk, there is also the visual imagery of daydreaming, of mentally projecting the self into new situations, such that the mind rehearses and thus acclimatises itself to the new patterns of action it would then adopt. Peirce is emphatic about the efficacy of these musings, or what he called 'musement'.[77] 'People

---

[73] Ibid., vol. 5, p. 421.
[74] Vincent M. Colapietro, *Peirce's Approach to the Self*, pp. 94–5.
[75] *Collected Papers of Charles Sanders Peirce*, Ibid., vol. 5, p. 421.
[76] Ibid., vol. 6, p. 286.
[77] 'Peirce elaborates on musement, saying that he does not mean by it what we would call reverie – an aimless, imbecilic wandering of the mind. But rather a more or less careful thought, lacking only a *determined* direction or purpose.' William H. Davis, *Peirce's Epistemology*, p. 63.

who build castles in the air do not, for the most part accomplish much, it is true; but every man who does accomplish great things is given to building elaborate castles in the air and then playfully copying them on solid ground . . . Mere imagination would indeed be mere trifling; only no imagination is *mere*. "More than all that is in thy custody, watch over thy fantasy," said Solomon. "For out of it are the issues of life." '[78]

The power of this internal 'preparatory meditation' operates through the formation of new habits, that is forms of readiness for action. Thus, in imaginative anticipation, we review and rehearse how we would act under novel circumstances and these action plans prepare the future self to execute them when a similar real conjuncture arises. Here, he tells an anecdote about his brother's prompt action in extinguishing a fire from a spirit burner when the family was at table, and how the brother had previously run-over in his imagination what should be done in just such an emergency. At this point, it is appropriate to note that rather surprisingly, neither Peirce, nor Mead after him, gives us one line of dialogue from an internal conversation. It is as if, because thought itself is held to be dialogical, we can all be expected to furnish our own examples, by reference to our own internal conversations. This begs a big question, which will be examined in Part II of this book, namely how similar in fact are our inner dialogues?

So far I have stressed, as Peirce himself does, the effect of the internal conversation upon the emergence of our intrinsic personal powers, those of self-modification. Although more sketchily treated, the effects of our extrinsic powers in modifying the external environment are at least introduced. One down-to-earth example Peirce gives is of a man whose general purpose is to decorate his new house. Within his inner world he designs and reviews colour schemes and arrangements. Some he judges worthy of execution, others he contemplates and then scraps or modifies, but in the process he has clarified his objective – the external effect that he intends to create. This is an instance where the agent appears to have maximum degrees of freedom to bring the outer world into conformity with his inner world. Yet, it is only necessary to presume that he must work within his budget in order to raise some of the most crucial questions about structure and agency, and then about how these are handled within the inner conversation. In short, what does go on conversationally, as we seek to 'realise our designs' whilst 'living within our means'? Answering this question would involve laying bare those internal deliberations, by virtue of which we mediate social constraints. This entails thinking about our priorities, and deliberating how we weigh costs and benefits and in what

[78] Ibid.

currency; and it involves considerations about trade-offs, compromises and concessions in relation to our ultimate concerns.

The fundamental reason why a synthesis between Peirce and realist social theory can be entertained, is precisely because of his non-reductionist treatment of the 'outer' and 'inner' worlds, coupled with his insistence upon their interplay. On the one hand, the direct effect of the outer world upon the inner consists in *experience*, much of which impinges involuntarily upon the subject. On the other hand, the indirect effect of the inner world upon the outer consists in mental *deliberation*, whose resultant actions impinge upon the world voluntaristically. However, it is exactly this insistence by Peirce upon giving both structure and agency their due weight, which renders his thought compatible with realism, but simultaneously sets him apart from the subsequent handling of the 'internal conversation' by later American pragmatists.

Mention was made at the start of Peirce's careful balancing act between our external lives in society and our internal life of the mind – a balance which he succeeded in maintaining until the end. This stemmed from his conjoint refusal to countenance either the 'under-socialised' (Jamesian) model of agency or what was to become the 'over-socialised' (Meadian) model of the agent. Instead, to Peirce, 'to be human is to exist in the tension *between* solitude and solidarity'.[79] This brave and necessary attempt to walk the tightrope between the 'outer' and the 'inner', that is between 'externalism' and 'internalism' was abandoned by Mead. Incomplete as Peirce's theorising of the 'internal conversation' undoubtedly was, and unusual as it may be to present him as the central thinker in this respect, he is seen here as representing its climacteric. His better-known successor, George Herbert Mead, whose name is almost synonymous with the 'internal conversation' in sociology, will be examined in order to trace his undermining of the three key features of inner dialogue – interiority, subjectivity and personal causal efficacy. This explains why Mead cannot be the keystone in any endeavour to link structure and agency by means of the internal conversation.

Stage 3: George Herbert Mead: the over-socialisation of the internal conversation

If Peirce had nicely balanced 'externalism' and 'internalism', that is the outer world with the inner world, to use his own terminology, Mead is an almost uncompromising externalist. In this he swings to the opposite pole from James's trenchant subjectivism. Mead, as the latest of the three thinkers, takes James as his (negative) reference point, and there is

---

[79] Vincent M. Colapietro, *Peirce's Approach to the Self*, p. 118.

no engagement with Peirce in Mead's work. However, we cannot evade an encounter with Mead as the most celebrated exponent of the 'inner conversation'.

In fact, this encounter will be devoted to showing how Mead negated the three features of the internal dialogue which are being defended here: its interiority, subjectivity and causal efficacy. Another way of putting this, is to argue that to Mead, the internal conversation is the exact antithesis of what that notion seems to mean. It is *not* a dialogue with *oneself*; it is a conversation with society. Furthermore, it will be maintained that Mead's version of the internal dialogue is a non-starter as the process that mediates between structure and agency. On the face of it, the opposite seems to be the case. *Prima facie* there is no reason why an inner conversation between the self and society should not fulfil this mediatory role; indeed it sounds as though this is just what it does!

On the contrary, it is argued that structure dominates agency in a typically 'downward conflationary' manner, except that the mechanisms involve a distinctive detour through the life of the mind – which later became vulgarised under that portmanteau term, 'socialisation'. It is in this context that the three features of the internal conversation – interiority, subjectivity and causal efficacy were lost as attributes of the individual. My overall thesis, then, is that Mead over-socialised the internal conversation by subtracting from it those three features intrinsic to the mental activities of the reflexive agent. Perhaps it was because his name became virtually synonymous with the internal conversation, that the interior dialogue was never again taken up by those defending robust versions of both structure and of agency, as a potential linking mechanism between them.

However, these assertions require substantiation. In particular, because it is pivotal to the conclusions stated above, it is necessary to demonstrate that Mead's internal conversation was not a conversation with oneself. This involves scrutinising his concepts of the 'Me' and of the 'I'. Firstly, it is necessary to recall that his best-known 'Me', which stands as the interlocutor of the 'I', is no part of the first-person at all, but rather represents the second-person plural: the 'Me' is really the 'We' – what Mead called the 'generalized other'. Since 'I' talk inwardly to the 'generalized other', then my internal conversation is with society rather than with myself. Secondly, and much more contentiously, the aim is to show that his 'I' does not speak *for itself*, but for another 'We', that of a different community.

How society takes over the internal conversation

Here, the concern will be specifically with *how* the internal conversation is stripped of those three features – interiority, subjectivity and personal causal efficacy – which were previously held to link it directly to our mental activities as *self*-reflexive agents.

The loss of 'Interiority': absenting the private domain of thought
Mead's central credo is 'Thinking is the same as talking to other people.'[80] This is open to two interpretations. It could be an analogical assertion that private mental activities can be conceptualised in the same terms as public conversations, upon which they could thus be modelled. Taken in this way, it would not be too far removed from Peirce's view that intra-personal dialogues, which have to use public language in the privacy of the 'inner world', are therefore analogous to ordinary inter-personal conversations. This, of course, would not be to presume that the *contents* of our thoughts are the same as those that we would disclose when 'talking to other people'. Peirce could thus preserve privacy because our daydreams and ideals, our internal criticisms and running commentaries may never enter the public domain; they can be withheld from it and inaudibly accompany conversation in the outer world. Alternatively, Mead can be taken literally; thinking is the same as talking to other people because it really is conversing with these others inside one's head. In that case, the dialogue is not with ourselves, and the outer world invades the inner, to use Peirce's terminology. The burden of Mead's work is conducive to taking him literally and thus to the conclusion that the life of the mind is not a private domain of thought.

This is central to Mead's conception of what makes human reflexivity possible at all. Uncontroversially, Mead asserts that reflexivity requires not only a conscious subject, but also a self-conscious object – someone who can take 'an objective, impersonal attitude towards himself'. Controversially, he maintains that we can only experience ourselves as objects *indirectly* from the perspective of others. 'The individual experiences himself as such, not directly, but only indirectly, from the particular standpoints of other individual members of the same social group, or from the generalized standpoint of the social group as a whole to which he belongs . . . he first becomes an object to himself just as other individuals are objects to him or in his experience; and he becomes an object to himself only by taking the attitudes of other individuals towards himself within a social environment or context of experience and behavior in which both he and they are involved.'[81] In this way, society is built into our very self-constitution; its impersonality becomes part of our personality.

---

[80] G. H. Mead, '1927 Class Lectures in Social Psychology', in D. L. Miller (ed.), *The Individual and the Social Self*, University of Chicago Press, 1982, p. 155.
[81] G. H. Mead, *Mind, Self and Society* [1934] University of Chicago Press, 1974, p. 138.

This is a contentious move, because it explicitly rules out environmental relations through which we can develop conceptions of ourselves as objects – that is, both natural and practical relations. This is in clear opposition to those of us (including Merleau-Ponty and Piaget) who endorse 'the primacy of practice',[82] as the process through which we learn to distinguish our own properties and powers from those of other things, including other people. This view allows one to become an object to oneself, regardless of social input; for instance, I am that being who is insufficiently strong to swim or row against the current.

Conversely, the best-known part of Mead's work concerns the social constitution of the individual,[83] and it is in this context that his re-working of the internal conversation, as both the 'mechanism of thought' and the 'mechanism of introspection', needs to be understood. This context is made up of a quartet of familiar propositions, whose combined force is the claim that the self 'is a gift to the individual from society and always remains part of the social process'.[84] Elsewhere, I have argued at length against construing the agent in this way, that is as 'Society's Being'.[85] This critique will not be repeated. Instead, the four propositions are simply summarised to show how they ineluctably deprive the internal conversation of substantive *interiority*.

Firstly, Mead insists that society is prior to the individual and that our sociality is primitive to our self-consciousness – 'What I want particularly to emphasise is the temporal and logical pre-existence of the social process to the self-conscious individual that arises in it.'[86] Secondly, self-formation entails a process of the internalisation from others of 'significant symbols'. These furnish the stuff of our inner dialogues and are thus the only medium through which we can know ourselves. The third proposition details the dynamics of this process; namely, by 'role taking' we hear ourselves speak and react to significant symbols as others do. Thus we acquire an objective perspective, as if standing outside ourselves and hearing from the role of the other – 'Other selves in a social environment logically antedate the consciousness of self which introspection analyses.'[87] Fourthly, as 'role taking' extends to team 'games', so the

[82] See Margaret S. Archer, *Being Human: The Problem of Agency*, Cambridge University Press, 2000, ch. 4. For a defence of Mead against Piaget see, Hans Joas, *G.H. Mead: A Contemporary Re-Examination of his Thought*, Polity Press, Cambridge, 1985, pp. 162–6.
[83] G. H. Mead, 'The Social Self' [1913], in Andrew J. Reck (ed.), *Selected Writings: George Herbert Mead*, Bobbs Merrill, NY, 1964, p. 146.
[84] John D. Baldwin, *George Herbert Mead*, Sage, London, 1986, p. 107.
[85] Margaret S. Archer, *Being Human*, Ibid., ch. 3.
[86] G. H. Mead, *Mind, Self and Society*, p. 186.
[87] G. H. Mead, 'What Social Objects must Psychology Presuppose?' [1910], in Andrew R. Reck, *Selected Writings*, p. 111.

whole community enters into the individual's thinking, and she can then see herself from the composite perspective of society. To Mead, this perspective is that of the 'generalized other', and in it we do not just gain the gift 'to see ourselves as others see us' (that is, ourselves as objects), but acquire the interlocutor in our inner conversations. Thus the subject, the 'I', has acquired an object, the socialised 'Me', with whom to converse. Hence, the inner *dialogue* is not with ourselves, but between ourselves and society – in the form of the 'generalized other'. For, as Mead states, our 'thinking is an inner conversation in which we may be taking the roles of specific acquaintances, *but usually it is with what I have termed the "generalized other"* that we converse, and so obtain to the levels of abstract thinking, and that impersonality, that so-called objectivity that we cherish'.[88]

What does this then mean for the *inner* dialogue? It involves nothing less than a complete loss of all but formal interiority. Mead is a strong 'externalist', forcefully convinced that all internal psychological events are organised from the outside to the inside. We are quintessentially social and this sociality permeates the lives of our minds: 'We have a social consciousness which is organised from the periphery to the centre.'[89] Individualistic, subjectivist and solipsistic philosophy (for which read Cartesianism) 'had stolen qualities and meanings from the world and placed them in a mind that is entirely suppositious'.[90] Thus, Mead's aim is to restore these 'stolen goods' to the world, but a world in which the social overwhelmingly predominates. What he substitutes is a 'social theory of mind'. From there, it would indeed follow that if 'mind is socially constituted, then the field or locus for any given individual mind must extend as far as the social activity or apparatus or social relations which constitutes it extends; and hence that field cannot be bounded by the skin of the individual organism to which it belongs'.[91] That, however, must go for thinking too; it cannot then be *intra-personal*. Consequently, our inner conversations must properly be conceived as *inter-personal*, and, if they are, then their true interiority has vanished.

What I am defending, and what Peirce upheld, namely a domain of mental privacy, has been lost through its social colonisation. As Miller puts the matter, for Mead, thinking 'is a phase of a social act, and in that sense it cannot be private. Every individual must have, within his

[88] G. H. Mead, 'The Genesis of the Self and Social Control' (1924–5), in Andrew R. Reck, *Selected Writings*, p. 288; my italics.

[89] G. H. Mead, '1914 Class Lectures in Social Psychology', in D. L. Miller, *The Individual and the Social Self*, p. 55.

[90] G. H. Mead, '1927 Class Lectures', in ibid., p. 154.

[91] G. H. Mead, *Mind, Self and Society*, p. 223n.

make-up, a social component, in order to be able to think. No individual can indicate anything to himself or think about anything unless what he thinks about can also be indicated to another. In this sense, also, thinking cannot be private.'[92] This radical denial of mental privacy is light years away from Peirce's notion of our making private use of the public linguistic medium. And, if there is no privacy, then real interiority has been nullified.

The loss of subjectivity: denying the subjective ontology of thought
The repudiation of a subjective ontology for thought is a corollary of nullifying interiority, which has just been examined. However, Mead's full argument proceeds in three stages; the first two are ground-clearing operations, since they are intended to dispose of socially independent sources of thought. This paves the way for privileging language in our thinking, which, for Mead, leads to the social dependency of thought itself. This is not necessarily the case, as was seen for Peirce's private uses of the public linguistic medium, but it is necessary for Mead, precisely because he has rejected privacy.

To Mead, the key feature of human language is that it encodes 'significant symbols', meaning that such symbols are not only heard in the same way by sender and by receiver, but also elicit the same response in both speaker and listener. 'In a human society, a language gesture is a stimulus that reverberates and calls out the same attitude in the individual who makes it as it does in others who respond to it.'[93] Thus, the medium that is indispensable to the articulation of our own thoughts is one which is external, objective and shared. To frame a thought, we have to draw upon it, and having framed a thought, it will, by definition, summon up the same response in others. Thought thus has an *objective ontology* because it is dependent upon the anterior stock of communal meanings which have evolved, and is in no way dependent upon the subjectivity of the individual, since all will respond to the common stock in the same way as speakers of the same language. This is because there is no self, sufficiently autonomous from society to exercise an independent subjectivity over the public 'booty', as Peirce put it, through use of the imagination. One way of expressing this is that to Mead, individual thinking is part of society's conversation. Another way is that, whereas I maintained (chapter 1) that we could share our ideas but not our thoughts (because of their ontological subjectivity), to Mead there is no difference between a thought and an

---

[92] David L. Miller, *George Herbert Mead: Self, Language, and the World*, University of Texas Press, Austin, 1973, p. 158.
[93] G. H. Mead, '1927 Class Lectures', p. 136.

idea; all thoughts are potentially the common (and thus non-subjective) property of the language group. However, to assert this dependence of thought upon society, he has first to eliminate socially *un*mediated sources of thinking.

As has been seen, Mead is a radical anti-subjectivist. Because to him, there can be no separate self apart from others, and because the development of mind depends upon a social environment, Mead is diametrically opposed to the Cartesian and Jamesian notion that individual thought begins from 'subjective contents', ones of which we alone are directly aware – with introspective certainty and without external mediation. To him, this 'phenomenological fallacy' led directly to solipsism and 'solipsism is an absurdity. The self has reality only as other selves have reality, and comes in fact later.'[94] Hence there can be no *direct* self-awareness, because the very self which might claim such subjective knowledge is itself derivative from society.

Mead totally repudiates any 'self-feelings', as claimants to a subjective ontological status. There are no experiences which are inextricably tied to the first-person as their mode of existence. Thus, even something like toothache, which seems to be undeniably personal, cannot be a matter of direct self-consciousness, because to be reflexively aware that the toothache belongs to one's self, then the self must be there in advance, and can only be so as a gift of society. Therefore, the toothache is only known indirectly, after a social detour has been made. Hence, even 'phenomenal feel' is ruled out as a subjective resource for direct self-knowledge. This results in a complete rejection of any mental item having a subjective ontology since, through our mental equipment alone, we are incapable of having the necessary self-consciousness of it. 'According to Mead, the self is part of a social process . . . It is conscious of the objective, the shareable, *but not conscious of subjective states*. Of necessity, it has a social component, which precludes knowledge of a separate self, a self existing apart from others.'[95]

If Mead denies that 'what it feels like' (in Nagel's well-known argument[96]) is an unmediated subjective matter, his next concern in this ground-clearing, is to deny that our direct and practical involvement with the non-social environment, is a source of knowledge and thought which are independent of society. This is, of course, in opposition to protagonists of the 'primacy of practice'. Those of us who defend it also maintain

---

[94] G. H. Mead, '1914 Class Lectures' p. 55.
[95] David L. Miller, *George Herbert Mead*, p. 47; my italics.
[96] Thomas Nagel, 'What Is it Like to be a Bat?', reprinted in David M. Rosenthal, *The Nature of Mind*, Oxford University Press, 1991.

that the self/other distinction emerges from our interactions with the natural and practical orders of reality. A 'referential detachment' of ourselves from the world develops, which is based upon recognition of our own powers in relation to and in contradistinction from those which pertain to things (natural and artefactual).

Conversely, since for Mead self-awareness is predicated upon sociality and this turns upon the individual's ability to take the role of the other, then in a natural context, the equivalent is the ability to take 'the attitude of physical things'. Inflicting this social model upon nature can only end in anthropomorphism; the treating of physical objects as though they were social beings. Hence, he writes, the 'physical object is an abstraction which we make from the social response to nature. We talk to nature; we address the clouds, the sea, the tree, and objects about us.'[97] Other objections apart, early humans must have established working relations between humanity and nature for them to have survived long enough to evolve speech. Matters are not improved by the additional suggestion that even 'scientific man', the engineer, when calculating a bridge's tolerance of various loads, 'is taking the attitude of physical things'.[98] Why? The civil engineer assesses his own design in relation to his own purposes; when he has built a bridge correctly, he has incorporated certain load-bearing tolerances into its construction. This has nothing to do with attributing attitudes to inanimate objects. In so doing, Mead over-extends the social model of 'taking the role of the other' to the rest of the world.

Mead was attempting to establish an objective ontology for thought, by maintaining that it depends upon taking the role of other people (and things) *before* we can become an object to ourselves, and only then become able to think about other things. Neither subjective feelings nor direct first-person encounters with nature can be sources of thought to the subject without social mediation. Mead dismisses both these contenders on the same grounds; there can be no 'naked' contact between either of them and the individual. Instead, the precondition for either entering into thought is the subject's prior awareness of his or her self, which is socially derived and dependent. The insertion of this condition makes all thinking a matter of social mediation. Therefore, what is communal and objective is accorded precedence in our thinking, as a matter of necessity. Subjectivity can thus never circumvent objectivity, since it is always filtered through it. There can be no genuine first-person mode in which a thought exists because all thinking depends upon a preliminary detour through the second-person plural. We may voice a thought in the first-person only as a gift of society, which has given us a self to

[97] G. H. Mead, *Mind, Self and Society*, p. 184.   [98] Ibid., p. 185.

articulate it and the symbols in which it is articulated. In this, Mead clearly pre-figures Vygotsky.

The inner conversation: depriving it of personal causal powers   On the face of it, the very notion of an internal conversation seems extremely personal, for who can get inside our heads to discover our secret dreams, subversive notions and sardonic reflections? Freud's heritage reinforced folk convictions that the inner life was a domain for the violation of taboos, unbridled libidinal fantasies, and iconoclasm towards conventions, all of which threatened the thin overlay of civilisation. Less dramatically, the popular cartoon often expresses the same antinomy, with the balloon representing 'thinks' being opposed to the conventionalism of 'says' or 'does'. All of this implies personal powers that have the potential to burst through social restraints.

Mead went much further towards the demolition of this folk conviction, and a close examination of his interlocutors shows that *both* are socially permeated. As he often comments, he is no believer in the thin cranial membrane as a dividing line between the personal and the social, the private and the public domains. Nor, is it a wall behind which we can plot our personal schemes. On the contrary, as a fully permeable membrane, the life of the mind is just as intensively social as all that can be seen to go on outside it. The main result of this is that the causal efficacy of the internal conversation is not attributable to personal causal powers, but constitutes the powers of society working through the medium of the individual person.

We have already seen that one party to the internal dialogue, the 'Me' or 'generalized other', is society's representative in the parliament of the mind. However, are the procedures 'democratic', such that the 'I' can effect the course of events? It does at first sight seem as though the 'I' makes discursive contributions that significantly affect policy-making and the actions executed. Thus, confronted with the basic problem of what to do next, the 'I' can dialogically examine alternative responses, can review their feasibility through the use of 'reflective intelligence',[99] and can monitor its own capacities. All of this looks like the active, efficacious personal agent whose causal powers of reflective innovation make a real difference to the ensuing action. However, if the dynamics of the

---

[99] Ibid., pp. 90–109. It should be noted that Mead never explains where the 'I's innovative potential comes from. Wiley goes further and maintains that 'In fact, the genesis of Mead's I cannot be explained in his system at all.' Norbert Wiley, 'Notes on Self Genesis: From the Me to We to I', in Peter Hamilton (ed.), *George Herbert Mead: Critical Assessments*, vol. 4, Routledge, London, 1992, p. 115.

internal conversation are inspected more closely, the exchanges with the 'generalized other' are rather more autocratic than democratic.

The concept of the 'I', as the spontaneous (though unexplained) source of innovation, is moderated not only by the fact that 'I' am confined to use the public currency of 'significant symbols' in which to articulate novelty, but also by the necessity of conversational negotiation with the 'generalized other'. Since Mead's 'Me' or 'generalized other' is both an integral and indispensable part of a self-conscious human being, it exercises social control by means of self-control. Thus, the 'Me's' conversational role is not sternly to repress a wildly impulsive 'I'. Although Mead gives us no snippet of the sound-track from their dialogue, he makes it clear that conversations are not matters of frenzied clamourings by the 'I', which are verbally slapped-down by the 'Me'. Rather, the 'Me' functions as a social sounding-board, which gives verbal feed-back in the form of its evaluations of the innovations which the 'I' ventures. These can be either condemnatory or congratulatory. In the former, as Mead admits, 'the "me" is in a certain sense a censor'.[100] His qualification is meant to rule out blunt authoritarianism. In other words, the 'generalized other' does not say, 'You just can't do that.' Instead its censorship must invite and entail self-reflexivity, perhaps soliciting the 'I' to consider responses like the following: 'They wouldn't wear it – think of the opprobrium', or, 'You could get away with a modified version – isn't it worth toning it down?' Nevertheless, Mead is explicit, that, within the internal forum, '(s)ocial control is the expression of the "me" over against the expression of the "I". *It sets the limits.*'[101]

Conversely, the commendatory 'Me', which has positively evaluated an innovation as publicly acceptable, encourages the 'I' in its venture. As the previous quotation reads on, 'it gives the determination that enables the "I", so to speak, to use the "me" as the means of carrying out what is the undertaking that all are interested in'. The positive controls of the 'Me' (like the negative ones) are held to depend upon self-control for their efficacy. 'We are in possession of selves just in so far as we can and do take the attitudes of others towards ourselves and respond to those attitudes. We approve of ourselves and condemn ourselves. We pat ourselves upon the back and in blind fury attack ourselves.'[102]

So far, we have not been deprived of our personal causal powers; we, after all, remain the sources of innovation, even though the 'generalized other' severely edits the expression of the tendential powers of the 'I'.

[100] G. H. Mead, *Mind, Self and Society*, p. 210.   [101] Ibid., p. 210.
[102] G. H. Mead, 'The Genesis of the Self and Social Control', p. 288; my italics.

However, there are two further steps taken, whose eventual effect is the transference of causal powers from the individual to society.

Firstly, there is the important question as to who or what sets the conversational agenda in our own minds – an agenda such that the 'I' can venture innovative courses of action, of which the 'Me' might approve? The lay reaction, that since this is my mind, then obviously I can entertain what I will, is not Mead's response. It is not so because of his neo-evolutionary concern with adjustment and adaptation on both a micro-social and a macro-societal level. Thought is initiated because our first responses are obstructed[103] by circumstances, such that neither habitual behaviour nor truly impulsive actions will answer. The thinking process is therefore directed towards bringing about a better fit between us, as members of society, and our social environment. It is environmental checks that prompt internal conversations. As Miller puts it, 'thinking is a phase, the first phase, in the process of intelligent conduct, functionally related to conduct and having no function apart from it'.[104] In other words, 'I' do not set the dialogical agenda for my own mind. It is small wonder that Mead did not include day dreaming or reverie under the rubric of 'thinking', for these are imaginative activities, in which I can allow my mind to wander where it chooses.[105] Yet 'I' do not have this freedom if the life of the mind is confined to adducing cognitive solutions which are functionally related to social adaptation. What Lukes termed 'second-dimensional' power,[106] which is exercised by controlling the agenda and keeping items off it, is clearly operative here over our mental activities. Through it, our personal causal powers of thought have been severely confined and exclusively harnessed to solving problems about society's functional adaptation. Nevertheless, they remain our personal powers, even though we have undoubtedly lost power over the occupations of our own minds.

Finally, the point is reached where the personal causal powers of thought are transferred from the individual to the collectivity. It is also at precisely this point that the 'I' is deprived of its ability to speak for itself, but can only be the mouthpiece of another community. This represents the exertion of 'third-dimensional power', where the individual

---

103 'Reflective thinking arises in testing the means which are presented for carrying out some hypothetical way of continuing an action which has been checked', G. H. Mead, *The Philosophy of the Act*, p. 79.

104 David L. Miller, *George Herbert Mead*, p. 151.

105 As Collins rightly objects, 'But much more of our inner lives are made up of thinking which is not practical: reminiscences, ruminations, worries, fantasies, sometimes intellectual productions', Randall Collins, 'Towards a Neo-Meadian Sociology of Mind', in Peter Hamilton (ed.), *George Herbert Mead: Critical Assessments*, p. 288.

106 Steven Lukes, *Power: A Radical View*, Macmillan, London, 1974.

is 'mobilised out' of his own mind! The 'Me' component of the self, the 'generalized other', had always stood for 'society'; now the 'I' is evacuated of all that is personal and comes to stand as the *träger* for another 'society' and its values. Thus, while Mead allows that the 'I' can be the locus of demands for 'freedom from conventions, from given laws', such demands can only express a desire to move 'from a narrow and restricted community to a larger one, that is, larger in the logical sense of having rights which are not restricted'.[107] Does this really mean that no one can even think to contravene the 'generalized other' without simultaneously endorsing another 'generalized other' which is pitted against it in thought? It seems so.

Here one could object that this nullifies the individual conscience, that can prompt us to 'small' and spontaneous acts of altruism or self-denial, which are neither enjoined by the values of one's community nor entail the ethical consequentialism of anticipating a new society. Yet, Mead endorses this nullification; he denies that the conscience is an 'inner sense' of the individual, and he has already ruled out any possibility that the subject could place personal ethical considerations on his or her own mental agenda for deliberation. On the contrary, to qualify *as ethical deliberations* there must be a recognition of the *social impact* of the actions to which they lead, for without this consequentialism, no act can be moral – the personal is equated with the selfish. Mead's position seems correctly summarised as follows; if someone acts 'in good conscience it is only because he is appealing to a higher community or to a hoped-for community in which shared values can be realised, values whose attainment and sustenance are impossible under present circumstances and customs. No one claims to exercise his conscience for a selfish, purely personal end. Conscience emerges only in an individual who recognises the social import of his action, and exercising one's conscience is also a request for a community whose members will institute new practices and organise their roles in such a way as to effect and maintain the values at issue.'[108]

'I', as a person, come to play a diminishingly small part in my own mental life. Because of this, the internal conversation is not a medium through which personal causal powers are realised: causal efficacy has been transferred to the social. From the start it was clear that Mead's interior dialogue was not Peirce's internal forum in which converse was

---

[107] G. H. Mead, *Mind, Self and Society*, p. 199. This, as would be expected, is approvingly endorsed by Habermas. 'A Post conventional ego-identity can only stabilize itself in the anticipation of symmetrical relations of unforced reciprocal recognition.' J. Habermas, 'Individuation through Socialisation: On George Herbert Mead's Theory of Subjectivity', in his *Postmetaphysical Thinking*, Polity Press, Oxford, 1992, p. 188.

[108] David L. Miller, *George Herbert Mead*, p. 243.

between 'different phases of the ego'. From the start, too, one interlocutor, the 'Me' as the 'generalized other', stood for society. By the end, the other dialogical partner, the 'I', does not speak in its own voice but voices the values of an alternative society. Effectively, the internal conversation becomes an arena in which one 'generalized other' is pitted against another 'generalized other'. Individual minds and thoughts are simply the media through which this takes place. The causal powers that are exercised are all societal; they are the generative mechanism tending towards evolutionary functional adaptation at the macroscopic level. The one thing that Mead's internal conversation is not is an inner dialogue with oneself.

Conclusion

Finally, it is important to highlight why it is *impossible* for Mead to allow that we could indeed talk to *ourselves*. Mead remained at exactly the same point where William James ground to a halt – the fundamental inability to conceptualise how we are capable of any form of internal conversation with *ourselves*. Mead does indeed distinguish a second 'Me', which is not the 'generalized other', but is part of our (strictly) personal constitution. However, this 'Me' cannot stand as an object to the 'I' as subject, which is one way in which the subject/object requirements of reflexivity could be met. In an argument which echoes James's, this 'Me' is merely the past tense of the evanescent 'I', and the 'I' cannot be known in itself, but only through the 'Me'.[109] This is because 'the "I" of this moment is present in the "me" of the next moment. There again I cannot turn around quick enough to catch myself. I become a "me" in so far as I remember what I said.' The ever vanishing 'I' therefore does not stay around long enough to complete a sentence reflecting upon the 'Me'. Hence, 'if you ask, then, where directly in your own experience the "I" comes in, the answer is that it comes in as a historical figure.'[110] Because the 'I' fades so quickly into the 'Me',[111] they literally do not have the time in which to stand as subject

---

[109] Maurice Natanson draws from this the conclusion that 'The distinction between the "I" and the "me" is, for Mead, a methodological one.' If so, it would certainly preclude a subject/object relationship between them. *The Social Dynamics of George H. Mead*, Martinus Nijhoff, The Hague, 1973, p. 17. Similarly, behaviourist interpretations, eliminate the idea of conversation. Thus J. David Lewis substituted feedback mechanisms to unpack what Mead means by 'communication with oneself', J. David Lewis, 'A Social Behaviourist Interpretation of the Median "I"', *American Journal of Sociology*, 1979, 85: 2, p. 277.

[110] G. H. Mead, *Mind, Self and Society*, p. 174.

[111] Mead goes even further. 'Such an "I" is a presupposition, but never a presentation of conscious experience, for the moment it is presented it has passed into the objective case' and becomes a 'me', in Andrew J. Reck, *Selected Writings*, p. 142.

and object towards one another, thus enabling the exercise of personal reflexivity.[112] The 'I' known-as-the-'me', may be a 'spokesman', but its interlocutor is not itself but the 'generalized other'.

There is a second reason why *personal* reflexivity is precluded. This is because *both* present and past aspects of the 'I'/'Me' are too volatile to function as subject and object, both of which require some determinacy in order to permit of reflexive deliberation. Yet, the evanescent 'I' is also unpredictable and surprising – even to itself. The unpredictability of the current 'I' is such that it acts first and then, secondarily, this 'gets into his experience only after he has carried out the act. Then he is aware of it.'[113] Thus, logically action *cannot be deliberatively planned*. Mead explicitly admits that future action cannot be the subject of what Peirce called 'preparatory meditation'. For, 'it *is this living act which never gets into reflective experience*', because the subject 'is never sure about himself, and he astonishes himself by his conduct'.[114] Thus, the future cannot be deliberatively planned, for reasons beyond the spanner that the contingency of life in an open system throws into our best-laid plans.

Yet, neither can the past be the object of reflexive evaluation. This is because the 'I-as-Me' also lacks the *requisite stability* to constitute a determinate object of our reflections. It is fundamentally unlike Peirce's 'Me' (the 'critical self'), the stable repository of habitual responses, which can be challenged for their contemporary inappropriateness. Instead, the past 'me' is as mutable as any historical narrative. By this, Mead means something more radical than the unobjectionable historiographical observation that 'each generation re-writes its history',[115] which is merely an admission of our epistemological fallibility. Instead, his whole theory of the past[116] exemplifies the 'epistemic fallacy', by substituting how we take things to have been, for how they in fact were. Hence, his statement that all 'reality exists in a present'[117] means that the 'Me' is also volatile, because it can be endlessly re-made by *current* interpretations. Therefore, there are no such things as 'the way I was' or the 'things I did' to furnish topics for reflexive deliberation – leading to remorse and resolution

---

[112] 'The "I" appears in our experience in memory. It is only after we have acted that we know what we have done; it is only after we have spoken that we know what we have said.' G. H. Mead, *Mind, Self and Society*, p. 196.

[113] Ibid., p. 175.   [114] Ibid., pp. 203–4.

[115] G. H. Mead, *The Philosophy of the Act*, p. 487.

[116] See Harold N. Lee, 'Mead's Doctrine of the Past', *Tulane Studies in Philosophy*, 12, 1963, pp. 52–75, which shows how 'the world which is there' is for Mead, the world we take for granted epistemically.

[117] G. H. Mead, *The Philosophy of the Present* (ed. Arthur E. Murphy), Open Court, Chicago, 1932, p. 1. Randall Collins comments, 'this theory of time (1932) is so human-centred as to make history a subjective construction', 'Towards a Neo-Meadian Sociology of Mind', p. 278.

about amendment, or approval and renewed determination. Whereas the Peircian 'Me' is alive in the present as habitual action orientations and can be condemned there for its hidebound 'bad habits', the Meadian 'Me' is no 'old Adam', but merely a contemporary construct.

In sum, the internal conversation with oneself is doubly impossible in Mead's thinking. Firstly, this is because there is no way in which we can be both subject and object to ourselves, and secondly it is because the inner forum is denied the two main topics of reflexive deliberation – planning for the future or evaluating the past.

Thus, it is unsurprising that Mead's version of the inner conversation leads nowhere in terms of the *intra-personal* exploration of the agent's own life of the mind. It is understandable because his prime concern was our symbolic interaction with the 'generalized other' and hence was fundamentally *inter-personal*. What his thought fuelled was symbolic interactionism,[118] which increasingly focused exclusively on cultural networks of meanings, to the detriment of structural and agential properties alike. It seems highly likely that this is why the internal conversation was never taken up as a tool for elucidating the interplay between structure and agency. For it to do so, the respective causal powers of both structures and agents needed to be acknowledged. This is perfectly possible within Peirce's conception of the interior dialogue which allows both the external and internal their due, and thus invites examination of their interplay. It is quite impossible within Mead's version of the internal conversation, since the 'inner world' lacks real autonomy from the 'outer world'.

---

[118] Herbert Blumer, 'Mead and Blumer: The Convergent Methodological Perspectives of Social Behaviourism and Symbolic Interactions', *American Sociological Review*, 1980: 45, pp. 409–19. B. N. Meltzer, J. W. Petras and L. T. Reynolds, *Symbolic Interactionism: Genesis, Varieties and Criticism*, Routledge and Kegan Paul, London, 1975. For a somewhat contrary view, see J. David Lewis, 'The Classical American Pragmatists as Forerunners to Symbolic Interactionism', *The Sociological Quarterly*, 17, Summer, 1976, pp. 347–59.

3   Reclaiming the internal conversation

The aim of this chapter is to re-shape the concept of the internal conversation. This is necessary before it can even be considered as the process through which structure is mediated by agency. The achievement of Peirce was to cut the umbilical cord between self-knowledge and introspection. However, the observational model, by which supposedly we 'looked in' on our own thoughts was never completely abandoned in American pragmatism. Thus, Mead was still found repeating that he could not turn around fast enough to catch *sight* of himself in the act. Yet, to the social realist, introspective *observation* could never be an acceptable model for obtaining self-knowledge, because this perceptual criterion limits one to the level of empirical events. It thus precludes causality from being attributed to unobservable generative mechanisms. Introspection is incorrigibly Humean and irredeemably actualist. Thus, whatever realists *might* be willing to entertain about the mediatory role of human reflexivity, they could not countenance our reflexive mental activities being conceptualised in observational terms.

Although the pragmatists supplied good supporting reasons for abandoning introspection, they could put forward no alternative model of how we gained self-knowledge. The notion of the 'internal conversation', as a concept which defends the interiority, subjectivity and causal efficacy of the life of the mind, never fully emerged in their work. It reached its highest point of development in the thought of Peirce, only to be stripped of these three key (PEP) features by Mead. It thus lost any potential role as a mediator between structure and agency, and has remained in this position ever since. If the inner dialogue has any home today, it is within Symbolic Interactionism. The task ahead is to re-claim it and to refit it for use by the realist opponents of all forms of social constructionism.

To do so involves solving three major problems, which were raised but not resolved by the pragmatists. Each of the authors examined in the last chapter mooted a key issue. Before itemising these problems and proceeding to propose solutions to them, let it be clear what kind of concept will be ventured to replace introspection. The 'internal conversation' is a personal emergent property (a PEP) rather than a psychological 'faculty' of people, meaning some intrinsic human disposition. This is because inner conversations are *relational properties*, and the relations in question are those which obtain between the mind and the world. All emergent properties are relational in kind, but they pertain to different kinds of entities. Thus emergents like 'capital', 'rent', 'inflation', or an 'educational system' belong to the structural domain because of their primary dependence upon material components. Other emergents, like 'Buddhism', 'neo-liberalism', or the recipe for popcorn, belong to the cultural domain because of their primary dependence upon ideational components. As emergents, our 'reflexive deliberations' belong to the personal domain because of their primary dependence upon components of our mental activities, especially our continuous sense of self. Without our individual minds, they would not exist, just as there could be no culture without ideas and no structure without resources.

Because the properties and powers of 'internal deliberations' pertain to people, they cannot be expropriated from them and rendered as something impersonal. This would be to destroy their status as a *personal* emergent property (PEP). Thus the 'interiority' of the internal conversation cannot be exteriorised as 'behaviour', which could be impersonally understood by all. Similarly, the 'subjectivity' of inner dialogue cannot be transmuted into 'objectivity', as if first-person thoughts could be replaced by third-person ideas. Finally, the personal causal efficacy of our deliberations cannot be taken over by the forces of 'socialisation': this would be to replace the power of the person by the power of society. This latter manoeuvre transfers causal efficacy to the social; we become the *träger* of society rather than active and deliberative agents who are ultimately the makers of society. Thus, in tackling the three residual problems surrounding the 'internal conversation', the aim is to conceptualise a personal emergent power. Only as such can it possibly play a significant part in linking structure, culture and agency together.

The three residual problems can be detailed as follows:

(1) First, there is the *generic problem*, which so exercised William James, namely, how can the self be both subject and object at the same time? This is the central difficulty with introspection, as an observational model from which we purportedly gain self-knowledge, because it must necessarily postulate that we can simultaneously be both the 'see-er' and the 'seen'. A solution would be one which does indeed allow us to be both subject and object to ourselves, without simply building in a time-gap such that the only self-as-object we can know

is the one preserved in memory – and thus is at the mercy of faulty recall. Moreover, memories cannot be interlocutors, so James leaves us with an interior monologue rather than conceptualising an internal conversation.

(2) Next, there is the *analytic problem*, raised by Peirce's development of the notion of thought as internal dialogue, namely who is speaking to whom? Peirce had added 'responding' to James's discussion of 'speaking and listening'. However, since he never supplied a sample of the interior sound-track, the identity of the respondent remains ambiguous. In the course of his work he refers to a 'critical self' or 'Me', whose habitual action orientations are alive and active in the present, and also to a future 'You'. If these are *analytical* distinctions (between the past 'Me', present 'I', and future 'You') they are un-problematic. Yet Peirce uses a Courtroom analogy to capture how deliberations are conducted. The problem he leaves us with is 'Who is speaking and who is responding', because an analytical distinction can do neither. Nor, it would seem, can either a past or a future self!

(3) Lastly, there is the *explanatory problem*, which was Mead's bequest; namely, if our reflections do concern society, even *inter alia*, how does the societal get into the conversational process? Mead's manoeuvre was effectively to turn society into our internalised interlocutor. This undoubtedly gives us a dialogical partner within the inner conversa-tion, but at the high price that it ceases to be ourselves to whom we are talking. The problem here is to retrieve a strong enough person (who is also a social self) such that she can conceive of projects within society and also deliberate about the conditions of their realisation, without society orchestrating the discussion from within. Of course, if the 'generalized other' ceases to be our discussant, then we come full-circle back to (1), the generic problem of how we can be subject and object to ourselves and to (2), the analytical problem of whether or not 'aspects of the ego' can speak to one another.

How can the self be simultaneously subject and object?

In the interests of clarity this problem will be briefly restated. In a nutshell, if I am to have any self-knowledge, I have to be both the one who knows something (e.g. 'it is 8 May'), but also the one who knows that she knows that – and can thus 'report' it to herself. This is because the peculiarity of obtaining knowledge about oneself is that the roles of the investigator and the investigated, which are occupied by separate people in social re-search, are held here by one and the same individual. If we could not fulfil both roles, then we would be self-blind like Sydney Shoemaker's George[1] (ch. 1. pp. 28–31), who believed and desired certain things but was incapable of knowing that he did so. This makes him non-functioning because he cannot shape the thought 'I want X' to himself – he can only produce such a sentence by imitating others. Without the capacity to be both subject and object to himself, he becomes his own worst enemy, since he cannot know his own wants and thus pursue them. However, it was submitted that George was abnormal. To Kant, it was an 'indubitable fact' that all normal people do have self-knowledge and to William James, it was simply a fact about 'our habitual adult state of mind' that this entailed reflexivity.

How we obtain this self-knowledge is the problem. For centuries 'introspection' was held to be the answer. We looked inward and caught ourselves in our mental activities. Yet, if the observer and the observed are one and the same person, then a split-consciousness has to be invoked to account for the self being able to occupy both roles. Since this split involved perception, such that we were simultaneously held to be the 'seen' and the 'see-er', it was simply not on because we cannot do both at once. As both James and Mead agreed, we could not turn our gaze around fast enough to catch ourselves in the mental act. Thus, the simultaneity of our being both observer and observed had to go. John Stuart Mill attempted to rescue the observational model by dropping simultaneity. As subjects, we could observe ourselves a little later as objects by inspecting our memories. Yet now, both simultaneity and introspection had fallen together, because retrospection was later in time and entailed memory rather than observation.

As has been seen, James was rightly unhappy with both introspection and also with substituting retrospection for it. As far as introspection was concerned, if one tries to catch a thought in flight, one necessarily destroys it. As far as retrospection was concerned, then if you wait until after a thought is completed, you distort it in recall. His dissatisfaction went so far as a round condemnation of the possibility of 'looking in' upon ourselves. On the observational model we could not be both subject and object. Tentatively, he then began to explore the alternative notion of 'listening-in' to ourselves. This had the obvious advantage that we can indeed both speak and listen to ourselves speaking, internally just as externally. When we utter something we are the subject; when we hear our utterance, we listen to ourselves as object. Thus we can be both subject

---

[1] Sydney Shoemaker, 'On Knowing One's Own Mind', in his *The First Person Perspective and Other Essays*, Cambridge University Press, 1996.

and object at the same time. Perversely, sight is the only one of our senses that precludes this, and yet introspection was based upon it.

However, James pushed his alternative to introspection no further than this. What he left us with is what could be called a solution to simple reflexivity; I am the subject who holds it to be the 8 May because I am also the listener who has heard that I do so. Therefore I know *what* I know and also *that* I know that I know it. I have called this solution 'monological', because subject and object are forever frozen in these roles of speaker and listener. The speaker proposes and the listener registers or records. The difficulty is that these frozen roles cannot deal with the more extended forms of reflexivity in which we engage, as in cases of self-doubt, self-criticism and self-correction. For in such deliberations, subject and object *interact*, and the self-knowledge that is *generated* is not just a matter of passive listening and recording.

The monologue works adequately if we do no more than consider the (object) self as registering statements that the (subject) self holds to be unproblematic (which may or may not be the case). Thus, I state that 'it's now raining here' (as speaker or subject) and, in listening, I register that I myself am the object that holds it to be raining – for that moment we are simultaneously subject and object. However, our internal speech is not confined to the issuing of statements, which we regard as being incontrovertible, whilst simultaneously recording that we do so.

Instead, we often ask ourselves questions. Indeed, all of those extended reflexive activities already mentioned, and any number more which could be added, such as self-clarification, self-appraisal or self-monitoring, all involve self-questioning. Now simple reflexivity can only go as far as the first (monological) question, such that it can be registered that I myself am unsure whether today is 8 May. But questions invite answers and we appear to have no difficulty in supplying ourselves with (fallible) answers. This means that we are now having a conversation with ourselves. Like all conversations, it is one that takes place over time. Moreover, this dialogue can be even more long-drawn-out than inter-personal conversations be-cause we cannot go away or put the phone down on ourselves. Thus, the simple question, 'What shall I have for dinner tonight?' could lead to a long dialogue about personal preferences, availability of items, shopping patterns, healthy eating, budgetary constraints, organic food production, animal rights . . . Although hunger will probably cut short the issue for tonight, nothing prevents us from later resuming this conversation with ourselves.

The everyday ability we all possess, namely to respond to our own questions, was not something that James introduced. Hence he did not proceed from the internal monologue to the interior dialogue. Yet, when we do think of questioning and answering in the internal conversation, then such dialogues are like all others in one crucial respect, namely any conversation involves turn-taking. Therefore, it is argued, when we talk to ourselves *we alternate between subject and object* in the turn-taking process – but a moment of simultaneity between them is still maintained.

How is it possible to think of such alternation? After all, the thought that I produce (as subject) is identical to the one that I simultaneously hear (as object). Therefore, how can we logically entertain an alternation between two identical things? Obviously, that would be meaningless. To make sense of the idea of an alternation between subject and object, it is useful to recall and develop James's insight into 'thought tendencies', that is of thought as a tendential process on the part of the subject. The subject, he insisted, has a 'premonitionary perspective' on what she is about to think. This means, I take it, that she has both a blurred notion of an uncrystallised thought, and some inchoate awareness of what its thrust should be. Then, James argues, to express a thought tendency, we review the words that can articulate it, welcoming the felicitous ones and rejecting the inappropriate ones (pp. 61–2). What is crucial here for the subject is that there is a two-stage process, which consists firstly of dimly conceiving a notion and secondly of selecting the words to express it. That is to say that our intimations and our verbal formulations are not coterminous. Premonitions do not automatically and instantaneously become formulated into ready made and fully fledged sentences.

The important implication of this for the subject is that her thought tendency and its crystallisation into words are not identical. We all are familiar with this in everyday life, when we say to ourselves or to others 'I didn't mean to put it that way', or even, 'I didn't really mean what I just said.' By crystallising a notion in words, we thus create an object, an utterance. We concretise a thought, whose wording is 'exactly as the thought thinks it' (p. 62). The 'thought' is therefore different from the 'premonitionary' notion. Confronted (by listening) to the articulated thought, the subject confronts her object. She may then find it wanting in different ways. Perhaps she is aware that it does not properly capture her tendential notion and wants to reformulate it. Perhaps what she hears she immediately realises cannot be correct, because listening to the utterance also brings counterfactuals to mind. Perhaps its starkness shocks her and she wishes to moderate it or add shade and nuance. These are some of the ways in which subject and object interact. We can regard this as alternation because first there is the subject's 'premonitory' notion, then her articulated thought-object, followed by the subject's reactions and then revisions. The process of revision will again go through the same cycle,

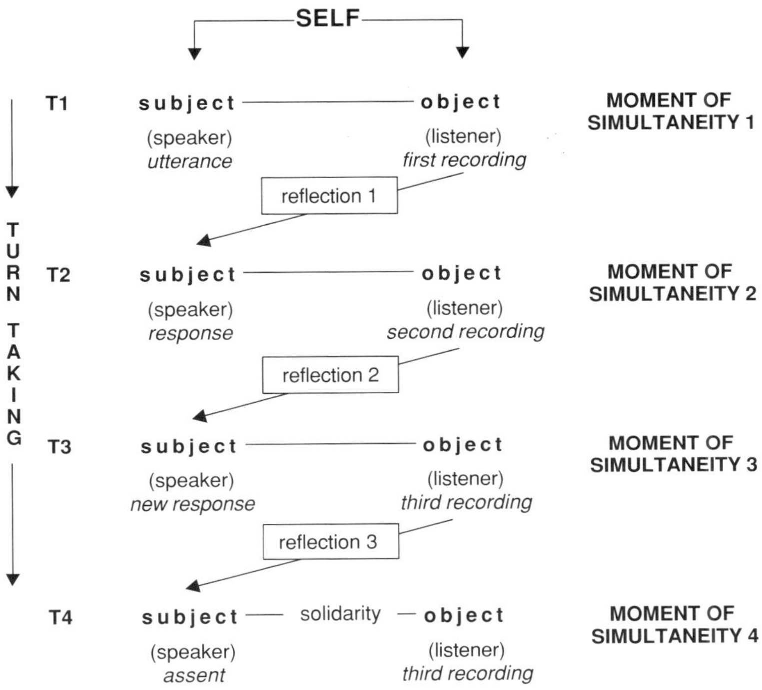

Figure 3.1 The internal conversation.

from tendency to crystallisation, to critique, to reformulation and so on. The sequence ends only when subject reaches solidarity with object. This is represented in figure 3.1. In other words, I reflexively agree with myself that a particular formulation fittingly expresses that which I have in mind. Of course, this process can be abandoned because the subject may deem her notion to be ineffable, even defying circumlocution and metaphor. She can say to herself, 'I just can't put it into words.' This would be unacceptable to those who hold that our 'thoughts are our words', as will this whole argument which depends upon rejecting the linguistic fallacy.

However, for those who will accept this processural and tendential account of thinking, which enables us to distinguish between subject and object within the same thoughtful self, there are further ways in which the two can alternate. Consider the everyday activity of questioning and answering ourselves. I am the subject who internally voices a question, but that utterance is also an object to which I, as subject, can then respond. My response is also an object which, on hearing it, can be re-questioned by me the subject and again be answered, with this new answer representing a novel object which the subject may then still doubt. The two will go on alternating until solidarity is reached or the issue is postponed or abandoned. All that is being done here is to extend James's basic insight into how the subject, the utterer, upon hearing her own utterance, registers herself as the object who stated that X was the case, which she as subject then doubts and questions. This is what enables us to say to ourselves, as we commonly do, 'No, you're wrong' – and then proceed to correct ourselves.

This extension of James only consists in allowing the subject to question her own object indefinitely. This alternation entails nothing more problematic than our ability to question internally (correct, evaluate or reject) what we have just said. We do it all the time, for this capacity to alternate between subject and object is exactly what takes place when we check our arithmetic or our conclusions. The following example of an internal conversation illustrates the *alternation* between the subject-self (SS) and the object-self (OS). These are terms of convenience, which must not be reified; they differentiate between the self as speaker and the self as listener, but both refer to the same being – a single person. What have largely been edited out are the moments of *simultaneity*, where what the subject utters is simply registered by herself as an utterance, an object.

SS   'What's today's date?'
OS   'I'm unsure of today's date.'
SS   'Oh, it's 8 May.'
OS   'Today is 8 May.'
SS   'But it can't be, that was yesterday.'
OS   'Yesterday was 8 May.'
SS   'No, yesterday was Bank Holiday, 7 May.'
OS   'Yesterday was Bank Holiday, 7 May.'
SS   'I'm getting lost; better check the newspaper.'
OS   'Checking the paper will decide the date.'
SS   'Yes, today is 8 May.'

The conclusion of this snippet is as fallible as is all our knowledge, because the individual may simply have got hold of the wrong newspaper. Nevertheless, it is how we come by self-knowledge, which has never been held to be a matter of infallibility, omniscience, indubitability or incorrigibility in the course of this text.

Questioning and answering form a central part of those internal deliberations that make up the inner conversation, but they are by no means the only one. Now that the idea of alternation has been clarified, it can also be introduced into what Peirce called 'musement'. Our musings can range far and wide to include daydreams or fantasies. Some person, situation, or idea that has been encountered may prompt them, or they may be triggered by the task in hand. Musings are exploratory; they are ways of clarifying our aspirations and ambitions, our hopes and our fears, our orientations and intentions. Increased self-understanding is their product. These explorations are very much part of our private lives because they are unobservable, have no necessary behavioural outcomes and the understanding we achieve may be of precisely the kind that we do not wish to communicate to others. Nevertheless, through our musings certain goals can be privately scratched from our personal agendas or they can internally reinforce our determination to see something through. The following illustration was jotted down a couple of weeks ago, when planning this chapter. I suspect it is just what we do *not* usually reveal to our readers or students because we prefer them to think that our books are produced with ease and élan. Yet without this kind of inner dialogue, how many books would get finished? In this conversation the moments of simultaneity between subject (speaker) and object (recorder) have been suppressed, except for the first two lines, in order to capture the thrust of the conversational sequence. The object-self is presented as recording the gist of the subject-self's utterance, upon which the latter reflects and then responds as subject to object.[2]

SS	I'm stuck over this chapter.
OS	I'm stuck over this chapter.
SS	I always think that, but it passes.
OS	This stage always comes and then passes.
SS	Yes, but this time I'm really stuck.
OS	This is a new situation.
SS	They always feel that way.
OS	This is really an action-replay.
SS	Possibly, but I'm too tired.
OS	I'm too tired to do it again.
SS	Maybe if I took a break.
OS	Taking a break might help.
SS	OK, I'll finish painting the kitchen.
OS	This weekend I'll decorate the kitchen.
SS	Call that a break!
OS	That's not a real break.
SS	Why don't you just shut-up and get on.

Finally, we should at least touch upon the long-running internal conversation that shapes our life projects. Peirce, it will be recalled, termed this

---

[2] For exemplification the inner conversation has been represented as made up of utterances, which are usually propositional. However, any utterance can be accompanied by affect. This is not an attempt to make the lives of our minds purely sentential.

the 'power of preparatory meditation' and I have presented it elsewhere as a dialogical scheme (DDD) entailing 'discernment', 'deliberation' and 'dedication'.[3] In it we are trying to prioritise our 'ultimate concerns' and to accommodate other necessary concerns to them in the form of a *modus vivendi* with which we think we can live. One of the key points to underline is that this is not just a cognitive matter of determining what is worthy of our dedication. Equally, it is an emotional matter of finding the particular project attractive enough to see it through and to bear the costs of subordinating other interests to it. This is important because it would be a serious error to present the internal conversation as over-cerebral, one that takes place in purely cognitive terms.

What does this have to do with the alternation between subject and object selves? In brief, each of the three stages in the DDD scheme represents a different phase of 'preparatory meditation' in which subject and object alternate in the process of designating our 'ultimate concerns' and in designing a congruent *modus vivendi*. Fundamentally, 'discernment' consists in the subject-self surveying those enterprises in the natural, practical and social orders to which it feels drawn, in terms of their worth and attractiveness. It then crystallises these projects (usually in the plural) into clear conceptions of them as ways of life. The object-self 'holds up' these scenarios, unfurled in detail and embellished with imagery, drawn from direct past experience or from the public domain, as an attempted concretisation of what these ways of life would be like and feel like. Since these are thought-experiments, nothing ensures their reliability or validity. They are best guesses, fleshed out by the imagination. The subject self then reviews its own projections of possible futures as objects, warming more to some and flinching, on closer inspection, from others. This constitutes a sifting process, in which the subject eventually sorts and logs those projects which she cares enough about to live with.

During the next stage of 'deliberation', the object-self re-presents recordings of the selected scenarios, which are now provided with greater detail by the subject to stress their positive and negative implications for her other concerns, located in the other two domains. The subject-self engages in intense questioning about the terms and conditions of endorsing any of these scenarios, which it has already deemed worthwhile, with the aim of determining whether or not she has the wherewithal to see through the one to which she is most drawn. Finally, in the course of 'dedication', the object-self records a mental balance sheet of what is involved in adopting a particular 'ultimate concern', in terms of what will

---

[3] Margaret S. Archer, *Being Human: The Problem of Agency*, Cambridge University Press, 2000, pp. 230–41.

have to be accommodated to it or subordinated because of it. Inspecting it, the subject-self may withdraw (indicating the start of a renewed conversation), may pause for supplementary questioning, or may say 'So be it' (thus terminating this particular round of the internal dialogue). Of course, such decisions are open to revision and internal dialogue is continuous, if only about how then to live out the commitment wholeheartedly.

This has been a very abbreviated account, partly intended to show how right Peirce was in closely associating the imagination with 'preparatory meditations' but, above all, to indicate how the same alternation between subject and object characterises how we arrive at our life projects. The latter can be schematised as follows:

SS-> 'discernment' ->OS->SS 'deliberation' ->OS->SS-> 'dedication' -> OS->SS

That inconstancy and contingency can de-rail any such life-project is indubitable, but this only signals a new round of the internal conversation in which the self does its imaginative best again to concretise its thought-experiments and then reacts to these mental objectifications of its own tendential thinking.

All of the above is commonly known as 'making up our minds' – from trivia like ascertaining today's date to decisions about our major commitments. As a phrase, it has much to recommend it. This section has been devoted to how we can be both subject and object to ourselves. It has been maintained that we can do this through the inner conversation by formulating our thoughts and then inspecting and responding to these utterances, as subject to object. This process *is itself* the practice of reflexivity; it is how we do all those things like self-monitoring, self-evaluation and self-commitment. Being reflexive is a human practice; it is something that we do rather than some mysterious faculty that we exercise. Internal dialogue is the practice through which we 'make up our minds' by questioning ourselves, clarifying our beliefs and inclinations, diagnosing our situations, deliberating about our concerns and defining our own projects.

There is another sense in which the notion of 'making up our minds' is particularly apt. Through the internal conversation we do literally make or produce self-knowledge – whether this is to be sure of the date, of our readiness to go on writing, or about the nature of our 'ultimate concerns'. Self-knowledge is something that we *produce* internally and dialogically; it is not something that we *discover* 'lying inside us'. There is no 'hidden self' secreted within us for the microscope of introspection to detect, no

Jamesian 'self of selves', covertly directing operations, and no internal 'citadel' which is our redoubt, protecting us from the world.

Self-knowledge is an accomplishment not a discovery. It is a relational property, emergent from our reflexive trafficking with the world, which is much broader than society. And it is there, *outside* in the world, that the discoveries are to be made, in our natural, practical and social relations – which supply the topics of our internal conversations. Thus it would be entirely wrong to construe us as the 'Discursive Selves'[4] of social constructionism, for we are not free to define ourselves discursively as we please. As ever, we make ourselves and our history, but not under the times and circumstances of our own choosing.

The self-knowledge which 'makes up our minds' is therefore something that we talk ourselves into. It is a matter of self-warranted belief, not infallibility, omniscience, indubitability or incorrigibility. Yet why do we talk ourselves into it, why do we engage in internal dialogue at all? The basic answer to this is because we are trying to talk ourselves out of something, namely being unsure. Because of the way humans are constituted and the way the world is made, their interaction is inescapable. We need to understand our powers and liabilities, to know where we stand, to determine what we want and value, and then to consider our activities in these lights. This is as true for getting up in the morning as it is for entertaining a moral career. Some of this becomes embodied knowledge or practical knowledge, which are quintessentially wordless,[5] but when we are unsure about ourselves in relation to our circumstances then we converse with ourselves to achieve understanding. This is not certainty, because all our understandings are fallible, but it is what makes us active individuals rather than passive *homunculi*.

In conclusion, where does this conception of the self as subject and object engaging in an internal conversation leave the status of this interior dialogue? First, it is genuinely interior. The subject shapes its thought-tendencies into internal utterances to which it then responds as to objects. None of this is observable and there is no constant conjuncture between its occurrence and manifest behaviour. The internal conversation is our private life in which we can, for instance, privately ruminate upon their competence whilst politely conversing with our doctors. Secondly, it is genuinely subjective. I have first-person authority about my inner utterances for I am not in doubt about what they mean; in my reflexive deliberations, I draw directly upon meanings known to me, which could

---

[4] Cf. Rom Harré and Grant Gillett, *The Discursive Mind*, Sage, London and Beverly Hills, 1994.

[5] Margaret S. Archer, *Being Human*, ch. 5.

only be known indirectly by others through interpretation.[6] My thoughts, my reactions to my thoughts and my conversational conclusions retain a subjective ontology. They have their first-person mode of existence that only I can transform into the third-person mode by publishing my utterances as ideas. Finally, these inner conversations have causal efficacy; they can lead to the re-setting of watches with the (putative) correct date; the continued writing of this chapter and to our determined commitment to life-projects. These examples show that through internal dialogue we can modify ourselves reflexively and we can also modify the world as a consequence of our internal deliberations about it.

Who is speaking to whom?

'I says to myself says I' is the popular rendering of the internal conversation. By and large this is correct, but it is not complete. By focusing upon 'saying' and, by implication, listening, this old saw leaves matters at exactly the same point as did William James. We are the source of a stream of inner monologues, internal running commentaries upon our own lives, stimulated by occurrences and amplified by associations. This is not a conversation. What prevents it from being one is that there is no interior response, which would transform monologue into dialogue.

The significance of the last section was that it sought to remedy the situation by conceptualising how we could respond to ourselves and thus host a genuine interior conversation. The solution turned on resolving the old bugbear of introspection, namely how could we be both subject and object to ourselves at the same time? It consisted in differentiating between ourselves as thinkers, that is as subjects who issue internal utterances which are intended to capture their thoughts, and as self-auditors, that is as objects who simply register those thoughtful utterances, as they have been formulated. Since speaking and listening are coterminous, distinguishing between these activities provided an answer to how we could be both simultaneously subject and object. Yet, issuing an utterance and registering it was not the end of the story, but rather the beginning of the conversational sequence, for the subject could then respond to the object. The subject could query the adequacy and accuracy of the object-statement, could supply answers to its own questions, comment upon its own commentaries, seek clarification of its own assertions, check its own conclusions and so forth. This is why it was called the 'generic solution'; because this subject/object distinction allowed of the internal conversation. We could engage in dialogue with ourselves as subject to object in

---

[6] Donald Davidson, 'First-Person Authority', *Dialectica*, 38: 2–3, 1984.

a process of 'internal deliberation' which was necessarily self-reflexive. (Therefore, this resolution of the subject/object problem did not leave our powers of reflexivity as a separate issue to address, but incorporated them into the solution of how we could talk to ourselves.) Internal conversations are reflexive through and through because they could not occur without our capacity to reflect upon our own utterances which we know to be our own. Quite simply, it is reflexivity which gives us our ability to respond to ourselves by examining our own sayings (bending them back upon ourselves) and thus of entering into inner conversations, rather than being confined to the monologue.

Since a dialogue entails repeated turn-taking between subject and object, it is *ipso facto* a sequential process in time. Indeed, where our 'ultimate concerns' and commitments to them are concerned, this conversation goes on over a lifetime. This does not abrogate the principle that speaking and listening to what is said, that is uttering and registering an utterance, are always simultaneous subject/object activities. Nor does the present specification of this principle need to invoke the Jamesian 'specious present'. After all, it was James who insisted that we register the enunciation of a thought on the 'knife edge' of time, by shifting our attentive listening from word to word. It is responding which 'starts the clock ticking', and this may be a lengthy process.

In it we have to inspect, interrogate and evaluate the object in relation to a premonitory thought tendency towards it, and then formulate a new utterance in response to it. All of this can take a long time, longer in fact than in inter-personal dialogue, where, if we are not ready to take our turn, we either bow out, muttering 'I'm not sure', or initiate a postponement by saying 'I'll need time to think about that.' Internally, our time is our own. I can spend half an hour deliberating about the next sentence because I am accountable only to myself and have none of the responsibilities associated with sustaining an inter-personal exchange. Certainly, I can be guilty of (inner) distraction and inattention, but these are matters of internal indiscipline and not of external bad manners. During this time, the subject is contemplating the object and they are therefore separate, which means nothing more than that I can distance myself from what I have just said. I can inspect my own internal utterances, be they statements or questions. Once the response is forthcoming, the new utterance and its registration bring subject and object back together again at the same time.

In all of this, I have been conversing with myself. Differentiating between the premonitory intentionality of the utterer and the objective properties of the utterance is a real distinction, as is the distinction between the first thought-object and later reflections upon it. These make it possible to conceptualise the internal conversation. However, they are not distinctions between different 'parts' of the self or between different interlocutors. There are no postulated inner entities and no reified components of the self. First and last, I do nothing other than speak to myself. All the previous considerations pertain to *how* I do it and not to *who* is conversing with *whom*. 'I says to myself says I' cannot be bettered, although it has needed extending to include 'I responds to myself responds I.'

Now we come to the problem of other potential internal interlocutors. This probably originates from another piece of folk wisdom, namely that we do hold dialogues with other people within our own heads. These can be specific individuals and may involve what we should have said to them, what we will say to them and what we would dearly like to say to them (and have them say to us). Alternatively, the others can be abstract authority figures, with whom I discuss such matters as why I should be given promotion or not be given a parking ticket. They may be role-holders in an institutional setting, such as a Court or a Confessional, where I mentally protest my innocence or profess my guilt. They can be personifications of standards, such as the neighbours, the family or senior members of the firm, whose verdicts I try to pronounce imaginatively on what I have done or are contemplating doing. Now all of this is perfectly compatible with 'I says to myself says I.' Much of our internal conversation is about things we (think we) know, including people, but the utterances we put in their mouths are still ours and not theirs. That we can be highly imaginative and engage in discursive wish-fulfilment (or dread-rehearsal) is neither here nor there as far as the question of interlocutors is concerned. We can readily hold internal conversations, conversations that we have with ourselves alone, about being a billionaire, a best seller or a Nobel Prize Winner (or being paralysed, unemployed or disgraced).

However, in terms of 'who speaks to whom', it was seen in the last chapter that Peirce was ambiguous. It is Peirce's ambiguity that will now be examined because he does raise the important issue as to whether or not the internal conversation can be conducted between 'different aspects of the ego'. This, of course, would be an inner dialogue in which I speak to myself. Conversely, Mead's inner dialogue is socialised through and through, *not* because we imaginatively converse with others (we do), but rather because the individual has no self with whom to talk that is not a social self. This equally important question about how society gets in on the internal dialogue is the subject of the third section.

How many internal voices?

The current issue is about 'parts' of the self and whether they can legitimately be conceptualised as interlocutors. The ambiguity arises in Peirce's work because he refers to the 'Critical self' (or what I have called the 'Me'), the repository of habitual behaviour, procedures and protocols. He also refers to a present-tense 'I', the only part of the subject who can act, but one which may not want to follow old habits and, in seeking to shake them off, often appeals to the future 'You' that it wishes to become. These different 'aspects of the ego' may simply be analytical distinctions (in which case we have to ask what work they do) or they may be the names of real referents (in which case we have to ask whether this can really be so).

The question becomes more pointed when Peirce proffers his famous Courtroom analogy. Here, the 'Critical self' (or 'Me') is presented as the Counsel for the Defence of habitual action and the 'I' as the Counsel for the Prosecution of change. To all of us, such a Courtroom image will summon up a place of intense dialogue, but how are we meant to take the analogy? Crucially, can the different 'aspects of the ego' talk to one another? Can the 'I', 'Me' and 'You' do things like marshalling arguments, demolishing evidence and entering pleas? There are some reasons why we should at least entertain this. On the other hand, does the analogy merely mean that there will be intense inner deliberation; discussion about abiding with action-orientations which have proved 'tried and true' compared with trying out an innovative approach, particularly if the latter promotes a future state of affairs deemed attractive and worthwhile? This second interpretation is fully compatible with the conception of the internal conversation presented so far. What would then need consideration is the analytical utility of making distinctions between the 'I', 'Me' and 'You'. Since Peirce provided no snatch of any internal conversation, which would have resolved the interpretative problem, there is no alternative but to consider the two possible meanings of his analogy on their merits.

Perhaps the reason why most of us would be prepared at least to entertain the proposition that different aspects of the self speak with their own distinctive voices is phenomenological. Not only do we undoubtedly hear voices inside our heads, but also they may sound distinctive, both in tone and content. Historically it has been quite common to associate these with different 'personas', such as the stern voice of Duty or the prudential voice of Experience. Similarly, in addressing ourselves we tend to use a variety of pronouns, which appear to refer to different 'parts' of the self. For example, most of us find ourselves saying things like 'I think it's time I went to bed', but also 'You should get to bed now', or 'It's bedtime for me.' Are these really indicative of different inner referents?

Phenomenologically, do we feel as if we address different aspects of the self in our utterances and do they seem to answer back? Of course, phenomenology is not the arbiter of what is in fact the case; for example, some young children do sustain long conversations with friends who are purely imaginary but seem real enough at the time. Nevertheless, personal experience is a reasonable and respectable grounding for beliefs, unless experiences can conclusively be shown to be illusory, as in the case of experiencing the sun revolving around the earth. However, since everyone has a past, present and a future, we should expect to establish a degree of consensus about whether people do feel as though they talk and listen to different 'aspects of the ego', before concluding that it is reasonable to pursue the matter further.

Let us first consider to whom we feel we are talking in our inner conversations. To begin with, pronominal use within self-talk is so interchangeable as to indicate nothing, phenomenologically or otherwise. For example, when shopping, I quickly discard bright red items on the clothes-rails. If sometimes, in all other respects they are just the kind of suit that I was wanting,[7] I can find myself saying one of three things internally:

(a) 'Red has never suited me.'
(b) 'I can't wear red.'
(c) 'You'll never look any good in red.'

All of these are self-referential statements, which refer to the past, present and future self. If these utterances had been considered in isolation, then they might have seemed (weakly) indicative of our addressing different selves. However, if these are, in some sense, distinct 'aspects', then discontinuities should be expected between the utterances that reflect this distinctiveness. Instead, in this example, it is much more plausible that the 'I' is simply drawing upon its past experience in (a), to confirm its present judgement in (b), which it reinforces by reference to its future expectations in (c). The fact that these pronouns are used interchangeably, in practice, strengthens the impression of a continuous self to whom all the utterances are equally applicable, rather than a discontinuous one to whose different 'parts' we would address different statements. In the latter case (a) would not be echoed by (b), but by the assertion of a difference between them; for example, 'Red never suited me, but I can wear it now I've gone grey.'

---

[7] It would be the desirability of the suit in all other respects which causes a pause and leads to an utterance. Otherwise red items would be immediately discarded, due to embodied knowledge, without a 'second thought'.

Yet perhaps that example is badly chosen since interchangeability is only possible between the three sayings because *there is* continuity in this (trivial) respect. What about instances where people firmly distance themselves from some past (unregenerate, naive, traumatised, dependent or unsuccessful) 'me', who has been 'put behind them'; or look forward to a 'you', transformed in virtue, confidence, accomplishments and so forth? Certainly, we can publicly speak *about* ourselves in this dichotomous manner, and the form of testimony fostered by evangelical revivals or meetings of Alcoholics Anonymous favours this self-presentation. But do we speak *to* ourselves like this? Well, we can do it in an act of attempted dissociation in which we try to personify the past as that of some disgusting, fixated or sinful 'other'. Yet, is this not really a device we use because we doubt that our present otherness is truly proofed against the resurgence of these tendencies? It seems rather that it is *because* the 'old Adam' is still alive in the present, because the alcoholic knows that his reform only lasts until the next drink, that we tell him he is not going to prevail again. Yet when we do so, we are talking to ourselves about what we recognise as an enduring possibility in the present, and not *to* an imperfect, or better still, pluperfect, 'me'. We can reify the 'me' in private as in public, but what is real is that the 'I' simply looks backwards and talks to itself *about* its own past. In short, our phenomenology provides no persuasive indication that we even believe that we address distinct aspects of the self.

However, what about hearing them? Is there any better phenomenal evidence that we listen to a plurality of inner voices emanating from different aspects of the self? Certainly, some utterances do sound as if they were addressed by one aspect of the self to another. Consider the following three statements, which could seem as though they were utterances of the 'Me', drawing upon its experiences, when talking to the 'I':

> You can't go through that again.
> But you promised to do x.
> You can do it; you've done it before.

Firstly, the pronoun 'you' should not be taken seriously, as addressing another, because in every statement, it could be replaced by the pronoun 'I'. If it can, then it is perfectly possible to avoid the unnecessary proliferation of posited entities by regarding the present self (the 'I') as drawing upon its experience and issuing respectively a warning, a reproach and an encouragement to itself. It would be reificatory to turn this into the Voice of Experience – something like the Voice of Christmas Past, which is acceptable only as a literary device. Certainly, the past is alive and influential in the present as memories, routines, inclinations and orientations. However, these can only form part of the inner conversation in so far as the 'I' is aware of them and draws upon them positively or negatively or simply reflectively – in its dialogue with itself.

The point is even sharper if we consider utterances which sound as if they could be addressed by the present 'I' to the future 'You', such as the following three examples:

I won't let you do that.

You won't make that mistake again.

You'll soon get over it.

The issue is clearer cut because how can we even conceive of a self which does not yet exist as being able to hear anything whatsoever? Undoubtedly we can all have aspirations about the self we would like to become, but it is the present self who harbours and husbands these ideals. What it is doing here is voicing its determination and resolution, so that the future it desires to have is being fostered in the here and now. Once again, every reference to the 'you' can be replaced by the words 'I' or 'Myself', without loss or distortion.

Phenomenology is a fallible guide to reality, but it can be a useful pointer. Here, however, it has not given the slightest indication that our everyday internal locutions seemingly purport to come from different voices. Variations in tonality do not serve to mitigate this judgement. Think of the many intonations that one can employ in saying 'I'm such an idiot', without questioning that this is a comment of the present self upon itself. Interestingly, in Latin, this utterance would necessarily be in the vocative, although ironically it is invocative – for the person whom I am invoking is myself! Pronominal use tells us a great deal more about the grammatical rules of different languages than it does about persons proper.

To entertain the notion of different voices issuing from different 'aspects of the ego' is tempting only because it is indeed necessary to allow for past experience and future aspirations being influential. Yet it is essential to hang on to the fact that the only 'aspect' which *can* be influenced is the present self. This 'I' is indubitably constrained and enabled by the past, and its reproductory or transformatory future begins to be forged in the present, but these processes should not be reified by endowing the past 'Me' or the 'You'-to-be with the power of speech or of hearing.

In short, I am my own and only interlocutor. Therefore, Peirce's Court-room analogy should not be 'cashed-in' literally. There are many senses in which old habits die hard, which require exploration within the internal conversation, but not by reifying the 'critical self' and turning it into a dialogical partner. There are many ways in which we have to convince ourselves about the desirability and feasibility of innovation, but not by personalising an 'innovative self' to voice its own case. At best, these are literary devices, which are used to capture the past-alive-in-the-present and the future-which-is-being-made. At worst, they entail the fallacy of misplaced concreteness and, moreover, distract attention from how past and future are dealt with in our real internal deliberations, which are always present tense but take place over time. In reality, the 'I' only speaks to itself by alternating as subject and object.

Having maintained that Peirce's Courtroom analogy is not to be taken literally, the suggestion is that the alternative is to regard the distinctions between the 'I', 'Me' and 'You' as analytical ones. Whether or not this was Peirce's intention cannot now be determined, although his references to the different 'aspects' of the self 'moving down the time line' are highly suggestive of this. In any case the analytical solution can be considered on its merits. However, in order for it to be evaluated, two matters require prior clarification: first, why is an analytical distinction called for at all, and, secondly, in what way does making it help to answer the basic question of who is speaking to whom in the internal conversation? These will be dealt with in turn.

Aspects of the self are only useful analytical distinctions

The first question can be given a straightforward answer. An analytical distinction between the 'Me', the 'I' and the 'You' is important because all of these 'aspects of the ego' change over time and therefore these three pronouns, which remain constant, in fact point to changing referents in all three cases. Today's 'I' is not the same as that of last week, last year or of our adolescence or childhood. Thus the 'I' alters as it moves along the time-line which is also the 'life-line' of each individual. Corresponding to the same movement, the past-self or 'Me' also changes, if only because it accumulates over the life-course, and the future-self or 'You' changes simultaneously, if only because its potential attenuates. Moreover, as the three alter in synchrony with one another, so do the relations between them.

If the 'I', the 'Me' and the 'You' are quintessentially temporal concepts, then they defy fixed definitions. Even the constancy of the 'I', its reflexive sense that it is the same continuous being over time, does not mean that it is substantively unchanging. For example, the 'I' who has recently been bereaved, knows itself to be continuous with the previously married self, but the fact of the bereavement necessarily makes an objective difference and, in most cases, it will also make a subjective one. Beyond this continuous sense of self, any constancy of the 'I' over time (beyond some of its biological characteristics) is its own accomplishment. It is due to the individual sustaining a recognisable life-project rather than to invariable and involuntary characteristics that are held to define it. Similarly, it will be obvious how the 'Me' and the 'You' also change accordingly. To pursue the same example, the past self of the recent widower is now one to which has been added the experience of losing his wife, and the future self of the same individual has accrued the new potential for re-marrying.

Thus, if we wish to grasp the internal conversation, this cannot be done by conceiving of it as the mental activity of a constant 'I'. Moreover, since inner dialogue is self-reflexive, its references to its past and its future cannot be constant either. This is not because we can construe or construct the past and future at will, as Mead and the constructionists would have it, but rather because these are really changing. Internal conversations are continuous; they always take place in the present tense but that, of course, is always situated at some specific historical time, and it passes. If mental dialogues truly exercise one of the causal powers which has been associated with them, namely the power to bring about self-transformation, then accordingly both our biographies and our prospects will also manifest the same changeability. How, then do we distinguish between aspects of what is in fact continuous?

The answer has to be analytically, that is by making a cut at some point in time and for some purpose in hand, so that the activities of the acting 'I', and its dialogue with itself can be examined at a given T1, wherever that is situated historically. The justification for doing so is identical to that for employing 'analytical dualism' in order to distinguish between 'structure' and 'agency', which are also continuous phenomena. Firstly, this is justified because although the cut is methodological, wherever it is made those things which pre-date it and those which post-date it are real. Secondly, it is only by separating them in this way that the influences of the past upon the present can be identified and the effects of the present upon the future can be determined. Exactly the same is maintained here. The 'Me', the 'I' and the 'You' are analytical distinctions; project the 'I' forwards and backwards over time and it is continuous. However, to examine the interplay between them, in the course of any given internal conversation, use is made of the fact that the 'Me' must pre-date the 'I' and conditions its doings, whereas the 'You' necessarily post-dates the 'I' and is shaped by its doings. Without this, it is impossible to understand the bearing of the past upon any current internal dialogue or the effects of that inner exchange upon the future. This is why an 'analytical solution' is indispensable.

Perhaps this is easier to grasp if it is thought of over the life-span of an individual, as in the following diagram. In turn, figure 3.2 will serve to complete the answer to our second question, 'who is talking to whom?'

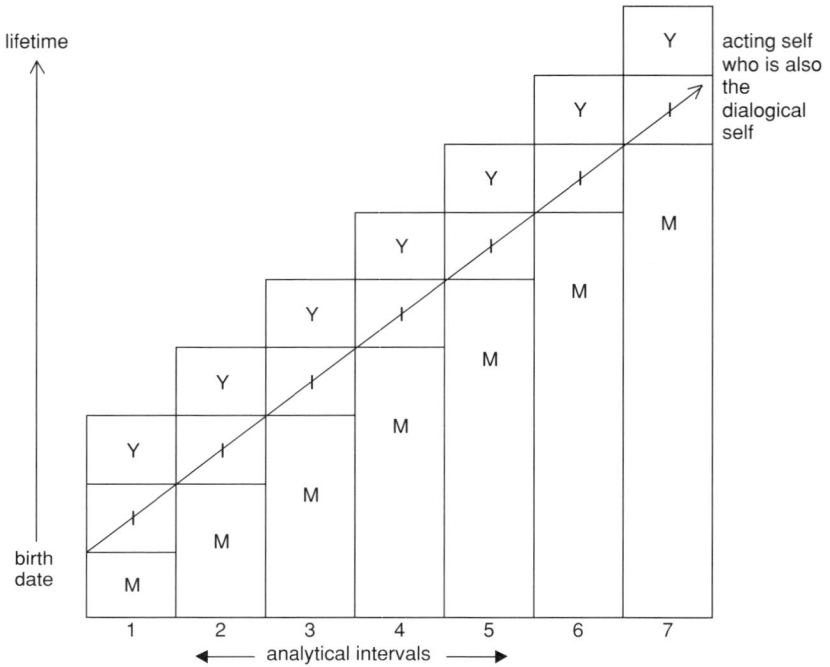

Figure 3.2 The analytical solution.

The life course has been divided into seven completely arbitrary analytical intervals for purposes of illustration, although with a nod to Shakespeare. There are several things that should be noted about the acting self or the 'I', which is represented by the diagonal arrow. Firstly, this manifestly changes over time; in part as the consequences (including the unintended) of its own past life-projects, and in part because of involuntary occurrences, attributable to life in an open system. Secondly, during any given analytical interval, that 'I', and that 'I' alone, is the one holding internal conversations with itself. Additionally, the arrow gives us two very good reasons why the internal conversation should be life-long and non-repetitious; the self itself is undergoing transformation and so too are the circumstances that it confronts. Thirdly, since our inner dialogues are at least partly self-referential, then the 'I' of any particular analytical interval will have a different past self and future self to whom it will refer. The analytical solution denies 'voices' to the 'You' and the 'Me'; since they are not acting selves, then neither can they be speaking selves. But that does nothing to prevent the 'I' from taking them into account

```
            the conditioning 'me'
T1                                          T2


                  the conversational 'I'
                                            T3


                              the elaborated 'you'
                                                    T4
```

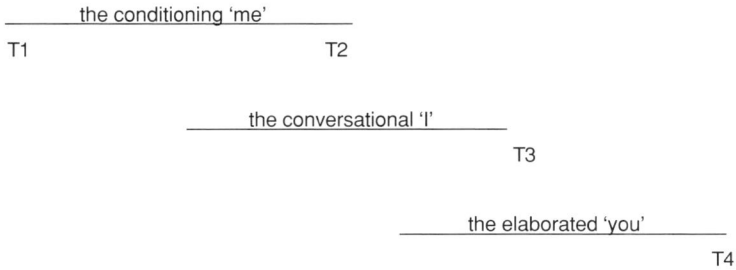

Figure 3.3 The morphogenesis of the person.

referentially – prospectively and retrospectively. Indeed, an 'I' who conversed with itself as if it had no past and no future would be in an abnormal mental condition – one of real denial.

The analytical solution thus consists of examining the internal conversation, in which the 'I' alone speaks to itself, as the pivotal process through which projects for the future self (the 'You') are articulated, but also conditioned by the past self (the 'Me'). This is the utility of the analytical solution; it permits us to understand how the succession of internal deliberations (which always look both forward and back) reflexively shape the trajectory of the 'I' across the life-course. This can be represented as a morphogenetic process, taking place over the life-span of each person, as in figure 3.3, which represents only one cycle of this process.

At any given time, the future will seem open, which accounts for our sense of freedom, but it is being made in the present by the projects that we discursively endorse and the activities in which we engage accordingly. Of course, in an open system, future contingencies can intervene to disrupt and distort such a trajectory. Nevertheless, the fact that we are made as we are as human beings and self-made as persons, who have acquired a personal identity,[8] means that we are also and necessarily project-makers. The future may seem more truncated for some, such as the aged, the severely ill, those in extreme poverty or undergoing political persecution, but surviving tomorrow is always a strategic project. For the rest of us, who celebrate our birthdays but are oblivious that our deathdays also pass by each year, we have our unique configuration of concerns to pursue – the projects that derive from and consolidate our personal identities. Yet these are not conceived of *de novo* in the present; elements of them are already deposited there as the heritage of the past 'Me'. They are there as the outcomes of its previous projects, as the enduring consequences of earlier *commitments* made by a person before any given T1.

[8] See Margaret S. Archer, *Being Human*, ch. 7.

Obviously, these outcomes were not defined under circumstances of the subject's own making. As the self which is now in the past, the 'Me' is made up of the things which have happened to it and the things that previous 'I's have made happen. Those features of the 'Me', which are alive in the present, represent objective restrictions upon the array of future projects which are entertained by the 'I' for the 'You'. During every segment of the present, the 'I' has reflexively to re-monitor its 'ultimate concerns' and to re-evaluate the opportunity costs that it is willing to pay for their furtherance. This is where the internal conversation is crucial. It is the process through which the 'I' re-dedicates itself to continuing with a project or rescinds a commitment and re-directs the 'You' along different lines. The analytical solution enables this process to be unpacked and the interplay between its component elements to be examined. Without attending to this mediatory mechanism, which is the internal dialogue, it is impossible to grasp *how* the individual can be an active subject in shaping his or her own life. For, literally, we talk our future selves into being – namely into being 'so' rather than 'otherwise'.

Talking to society or about society?

'Persons' who can talk about society

In discussing the analytical solution to how we can examine the internal conversation as the process through which our life-courses are shaped, two important caveats were inserted throughout. On the one hand, it was insisted that no subject could ever conceive or formulate a project except under circumstances that were not of her making; on the other, our human fallibility was emphasised. Not only can we get things wrong, including ourselves (our commitments, staying power and so forth), but also we cannot know anything at all except under particular descriptions. Both the circumstances that we encounter and the descriptions that we employ derive from the context of society. Therefore, it is undeniable that society plays a significant part in our internal deliberations. The last question to answer is 'what part'?

Two responses are traditionally given here. The extreme individualism of 'Modernity's Man'[9] presents society as a wholly external context, the direct equivalent of the physical environment. Within it, 'rational man' seeks to optimise his self-defined preference schedule, sometimes having to confront contextual obstacles and sometimes meeting with facilitation.

[9] For a discussion of the two strands of theorising, represented by 'Modernity's Man' and 'Society's Being', see Margaret S. Archer, *Being Human*, chs. 1, 2, 3.

Conversely, the profound socialisation of 'Society's Being' internalises society within the self, such that the properties, powers and projects of the singular self are always already those of the social self. In what follows, both of these positions are eschewed. However, there is a danger that the present conceptualisation of the internal conversation could be hijacked from either side. Thus it is important to signal why it is fundamentally incompatible with both.

On the one hand, it could be readily appropriated by the atomistic individualists, for example, by those of Rational Choice Theory persuasion. This would be done by accentuating that our private deliberations are conducted quite apart from society, which is reduced to being the aggregate product of individual 'choices' and deeds. This should be firmly resisted because, as the persons who engage in internal conversations, we are already, *inter alia*, social beings; we would be unrecognisable if we were not and we would lack the public language medium in which to exercise our reflexivity in interior dialogue. In other words, society is a necessary precondition for and an indispensable part of our internal deliberations – in much the way that Peirce suggested. Without nullifying the privacy of our inner lives, our sociality is there inside them because it is there inside us. Hence the inner conversation cannot be portrayed as the fully independent activity of the isolated monad, who only takes cognisance of his external social context in the same way that he consults the weather.

Conversely, the internal conversation can too readily be colonised by the social, such that its causal powers are expropriated from the person and are reassigned to society. This was Mead's path, since he firmly disavowed that the internal dialogue was a conversation with oneself. To him, our conversation was *with* society, in the form of the 'generalized other', and ultimately it was also on *behalf* of society, since the only way of contesting the censorship of community values was to align oneself with a countervailing form of social normativity. Sociality was foundational to our personal constitution because, for Mead, there could be no 'self' except one predicated upon prior concourse with other social beings. Consequently, his mysterious 'I' may somehow have been accorded the potential for innovative thought, but the power of in-built social control meant that such spontaneity could never be a relatively autonomous source for the design of society or for the subject to design her own life within society.

However, it is perfectly possible to allow for our sociality (contra Modernity's Man), without our being engulfed by it (contra Society's Being). Indeed, this is necessary if the objective is to present the internal conversation as a personal emergent power (PEP), which mediates the impact of the causal powers of society (SEPs and CEPs) upon each one of us. The key to this solution consists in making a distinction between the individual person and the social agent and Actor. Thus far in the text I have gone along with using 'agency' as the generic term for referring to people (as in the phrase, 'the problem of structure and agency'). From this point onwards, however, it is necessary to distinguish between *persons*, with their strict numerical identity, who are also *Actors*, as incumbents of roles, and *agents* too, through their determinate relationship to the distributions of society's scarce resources. In other words, it is time to introduce realism's stratified conception of the human being.

'Agents' are defined as *collectivities* sharing the same *life-chances*. Because of this, (i) everyone is necessarily an agent, since being an agent is simply to occupy a position on society's distributions of scarce resources. However, (ii) simply to be part of a collectivity that is similarly placed *vis à vis* resource distributions cannot give strict identity, because it only makes one part of a group of those who are equally privileged or underprivileged. Agency is therefore a term which is always and only employed in the plural. By contrast, it is 'Actors' who properly exist in the singular and who do meet the strict criteria for possessing a unique social identity. Actors derive their social identities from the way in which subjects personify the roles they choose to occupy. However, what array of roles is open to them, at any given time, strongly conditions who may become an Actor at that time, and thus who may acquire a social identity. Unlike agency, which is universal to members of society, not everyone can succeed in becoming an Actor – that is in finding a role(s) in which they feel they can invest themselves, such that the accompanying social identity is expressive of who they are.

On the one hand, everyone is *involuntarily* placed in a collectivity of (primary) agents[10] who share the same life-chances. However successful an agent may be in distancing herself from her original context of social placement *vis à vis* scarce resources, it will only be to find herself as a different (primary) agent in a new context with its own *involuntary* features. (Primary) agency is inescapable; all we can do is to move in one direction or the other along the continuum between highly privileged placements and grossly underprivileged ones. On the other hand, at any given time, society has an array of roles, incumbency of which makes Actors of us. Although the type of (primary) agent we become at birth conditions that segment of the total role array which is most readily accessible, becoming one kind of Actor rather than another is for most people a *voluntaristic*

---

[10] As distinct from 'Corporate Agents' who have articulated their aims and organised for their pursuit.

act. The aim is to occupy a role(s) which expresses our concerns – that which we value most and are readiest to live out.

However, in already talking about people who can do such things as distancing themselves from one kind of (primary) agency, or aiming to become a certain type of Actor, it is implicit that a third concept is required to capture *who* it is that conceives of and executes such projects. This is the person. It is by being persons that we not only strive for new placements and for roles, but also reflexively deliberate upon them once they are ours. A necessary condition for such reflexivity is not eliding the person with the agent or Actor. Only in this way can the subject consider his or her object status in society, deliberate upon it and have the possibility of determining to do something about it.

Moreover, the sufficient conditions for reflexive deliberation require a self-conscious person to do the deliberating and these conditions could never be fulfilled if our very self-consciousness was itself a gift of society – as Mead maintained. If that were the case, then the involuntary products of socialisation would supposedly reflect upon their equally involuntary social placements. Reflexivity itself would become over-socialised and mean something more akin to seeing oneself reflected in society's mirror than having the power reflexively to deliberate upon the circumstances in which one finds oneself. In other words, a fully social epistemology could not furnish the tools for a critique of our social ontology. Such an epistemology is a formula for acquiescence, which precludes the reflexive determination to challenge and change one's social circumstances. That formula would also exclude the deliberative project of becoming the kind of Actor who is rare from a given agential background. Ultimately, any version of this position would have insuperable difficulties in accounting for why and how D. H. Lawrence's mother determined that her son should not go down the mine.

Being Human was devoted to the problem of accounting for our personhood, that is for sequentially explaining the emergence of self-consciousness, the emergence of personal identity and the emergence of social identity, as properties and powers of the person, which could not be reduced to those of society. The key points for the present argument contra Mead are the following:

(i) Self-consciousness, as the central feature upon which the development of all other human *potentia* depended (including language learning) is the prime PEP. It is a relational property, emergent from our relations with the world, with which our physical constitutions dictate that we must interact if we are to survive. Yet the world is broader than society and our practical engagement with its objects (which include people since their differentiation from inanimate objects and animals is a learned distinction) is ineluctable. Through our earliest practical activities onwards, we begin to distinguish our properties and powers from those pertaining to the world. 'Self' becomes differentiated from 'otherness' as we learn the extent and limitations of our powers in relation to the affordances and restrictions presented by the world. The realisation of our referential detachment (from objects and from others) and of the transfactual efficacy of things (independently of us) result from physical practice and are inscribed in us as embodied knowledge. This is both prior to language acquisition and a predicate of it, because the sense of self and its differentiation from other things is primitive to any conception of linguistic referents. In other words, the primacy of practice is the anchorage of self-consciousness, as Piaget maintained, rather than the primacy of language bestowing this as a social gift, which Vygotsky upheld.

(ii) Personal identity is the achievement of subjects themselves in relation to their environment and is thus a personal emergent property (a PEP). It emerges from our inescapable involvement with the three orders of natural reality – nature, practice and society – and is therefore relational. Given our human constitution, the way the world is made and the necessity of interaction between them, subjects cannot avoid having concerns, which are vested in the three different orders. These are concerns about our *physical well-being* in the natural order, about our *performative achievement* in the practical order and about our *self-worth* in the social order. However, although all three are inescapable, nothing determines that different subjects prioritise them in the same way. Ineluctability only means that no type of concern can be entirely repudiated, but this does not prevent it from being subordinated and accommodated to that which the subject reflexively endorses as her 'ultimate concern'. It is the precise configuration of this triad of concerns which represents our strict *personal identity* – above and beyond our concrete singularity as organic parcels, which are also self-conscious beings. In short, who we are is a matter of what we care about most and the commitments we make accordingly.

(iii) Social identity is necessarily a sub-set of personal identity. This has to be the case if our self-worth in society is something that we evaluate in relation to other concerns and can assign to any position on our list of personal priorities. By viewing the social self as a sub-set, it then becomes possible to answer some crucial questions about the behaviour or comportment of the person in society. Specifically, what will be known is *how much* of themselves different persons invest in the social roles that they hold. Even more importantly, a crucial gap can be filled in; namely *who* is actively personifying any social role in a particularistic manner and thus participating in active role-making rather than passive role-taking. This is the key to what different *persons* make of their initial involuntary placement as *social agents* and to what they do as voluntary *social Actors*.

This realist conception of the self, summarised under (i) – (iii), presents us as the bearers of emergent personal powers (PEPs) which are neither derived exclusively from society nor are reducible to society. In contradistinction to Mead, whose model left the innovative 'I' completely mysterious in its origins and objectives, yet also insisted that our perpetual interlocutor was the 'generalized other' of society, the realist conception can avoid both of these problems. On the one hand, it enables us to hold genuine inner conversations with ourselves because our self-consciousness and powers of deliberation are personal properties and not gifts of society. On the other hand, who the 'I' is receives an answer in terms of strict personal identity, which enables us to examine the person's own project(s) in the world and to give due weight to her intentionality. This replaces Mead's procedure, which assimilates personal aspirations and outcomes to the process of functional social adaptation, under the hegemonic internalised control of the 'generalized other'. This is the point where an alternative explanation can be advanced for how society gets in on the internal conversation, without allowing the social to orchestrate the interior dialogue. To avoid doing so is crucial, because it was by permitting society to dominate the internal conversation that Mead stripped it of its interiority, subjectivity and personal causal powers. In consequence, our internal deliberations lost the ability to be the process that mediated between structure and agency.

Society enters the internal conversation in an entirely different way in the present approach, compared with that of Mead. Whereas to Mead, we talked *to* society, in the realist conception we talk *about* society. Because, on the present argument, our inner dialogues are with ourselves, we are not short of a conversational partner. Instead, by alternating as subject and object, we can genuinely engage in self-talk and can set our own dialogical agendas. Because the self who does the talking, listening and responding is not 'Society's Being', this relatively autonomous person is free to reflect upon society. Therefore, things social are amongst the *topics* of our internal deliberations, rather than society being our (censorious) interlocutor, as Mead represents it.

One of the great drawbacks of Mead's approach was that he had effectively transferred the intractable problem of how to be both subject and object from introspection to society. If society was a participant in internal conversations, that is a subject in the form of the 'generalized other', then how could it also be the object of our (critical) deliberations? It could not. Our minds were too close, colonised and controlled to exercise social critique, which is why we could only do so by putting ourselves under the protective wing of another society. Yet this effectively reduced us to *träger*, the carriers of an inter-societal debate. We were not persons with the capacity to reflect upon our own objective social circumstances and the relationship of these circumstances to our personal projects. The subject status accorded to society constantly stood in the way, obscuring and distorting its object status.

The approach developed here reinstates sufficient distance between person and society for the subject to relate to her society as an object, thus restoring to her the personal power of social critique. It can do this without in any way denying that society enters into her constitution. Here lies the significance of distinguishing between the person and the agent. This distinction is always there, although both elements can change over the life-course. Our agential status is entirely *objective*, it is ever significantly *involuntary* and its causal power is always to attach *opportunity costs* to the Actors that we can become in society at any given time. Throughout our lives we cannot slough off the parental influence of agency, although, like any parent–child relationship, this too undergoes biographical transformations. Our agency, the fact that we can never evade being an agent of some kind, accounts for how society is consistently part of our constitution.

Yet from our agential placement, at any time, we have the personal powers to make something of ourselves, because the influence of involuntary placement is not deterministic. What we make of ourselves, through the 'ultimate concerns' that we endorse and the projects we conceive of in order to realise them, represents the other part of our self-constitution. This process of becoming the kind of Actor whose role is the social expression of our personal identities, though not accomplished under circumstances of our choosing, is *voluntaristic*; it is an expression of our activity rather than passivity. Personal identity also has *causal efficacy*, an important instance of which is the power to transform our initial agential placement and to modify subsequent placements, without however being able to nullify the fact that we always have an agential status. As persons we also have the causal power to personify our roles as Actors in a unique manner, to modify them incrementally, or to find a role personally wanting once we have come to occupy it.

The importance of distinguishing between agents and persons can now be made clear. In a nutshell, the person can deliberate *upon* her objective status as a social agent. In other words, when we talk to ourselves, one of the things that we talk *about* is our agential placement. An important topic of our internal conversations is an attempt to understand where we do stand socially, to diagnose those objective properties that characterise us willy nilly, and to grasp their implications. In short, there are many discoveries to be made about our objective statuses as agents in society. Thus, contra the introspectionists, the crucial discoveries we can make are not about our inner being, in a journey to disclose a hidden 'self of selves'. On the contrary, the real discoveries are to be made outside in society, in exactly the same way that our external natural environment is a place of limitless exploration and discovery for any one of us.

The further important pre-occupation of our reflexive deliberations is with what we can do about our personal concerns in the light of these objective discoveries. Thus, contra Mead, our social selfhood does not consist in the internalisation of the 'generalized other' with whom we converse, as with an inner mentor, about the normative rectitude of the projects we conceive – thus permitting them to be censored by society's expectations before they have seen the light of day. On the contrary, our internal dialogue, which now includes the discoveries we have made about our objective status as agents, is exercised about what is to be done. We survey our circumstances discursively (although always fallibly) and our reflexive inclinations are not silenced by society's inner voice before they have even been tried in practice. Instead, they are the source of practical experiments in the outside social world. We conceive of our projects, which may well involve bucking society's laws, as well as cocking a snook at its expectations, because as persons we will not tamely endorse the goals or means associated with our agential status. The only way that this tension between personal aspirations and social expectations can be resolved is by practical action. Such action can be seen as the person's own feasibility study. This, of course, is another source of discovery. When once we have reflexively determined what is to be done, meaning which Actors we wish to become, we then have to take on board the objective lessons about what we can and cannot get away with doing in society.

All of this bears a close resemblance to Peirce's portrayal of how external experiences interact with internal deliberations to co-determinate our life-courses. It has nothing whatsoever in common with Mead's depiction of the innovative individual being internally mentored and often censored by the 'generalized other'.

The inner conversation and self-transformation

Now that a completely different explanation has been put forward to account for how society is both part of our constitution and part of our

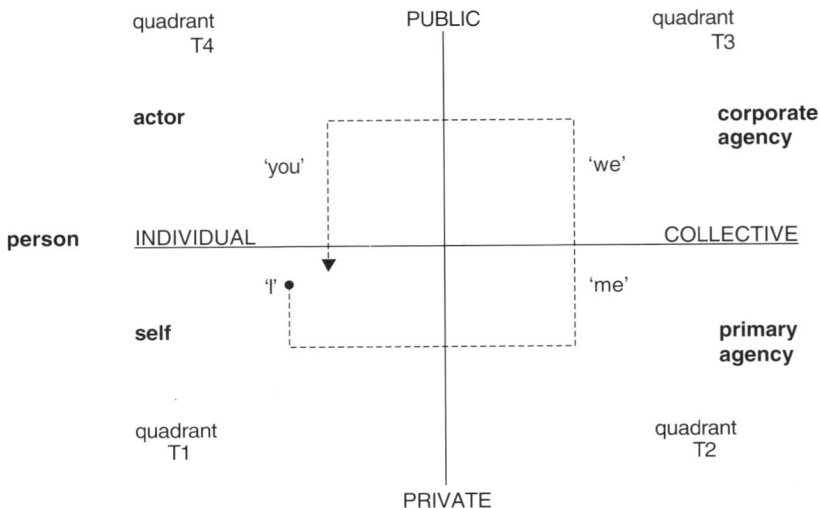

Figure 3.4 How the subject reviews itself as social object.

internal conversations, this can be linked-up with the analytical solution, advanced in the last section. The argument is summarised in figure 3.4.

The life-course of any person is pictured by the dotted line. The first round of the circuit represents the period from birth to maturity. During T1, the 'I', experienced as a continuous sense of self, is disengaged from other things and other people. This self then encounters and begins to learn about her involuntary social characteristics at T2. These are her 'object' properties as a (primary) social agent, acquired involuntarily from her family and proximate social background. They are represented by her life-chances and shared by the collectivity of those similarly placed in society. The collective action in which she may engage at T3 is largely omitted here because of its interpersonal nature. Finally, at T4, the subject becomes an Actor by taking on those roles that are most expressive of her dawning concerns.

Analytically, the life course consists of perpetually circulating around this square. Each circuit represents a new personal morphogenetic or morphostatic cycle. What figure 3.4 is intended to accentuate are the generic transformations which our powers as persons can induce as we 'revisit', as it were, each quadrant in turn and engage in inner conversation about it. In this sense, the mature emergent person (at T4 which is also start of the new T1′), inspects the 'I', the 'Me', the 'We', and the 'You', which have been part of her personal morphogenesis. She then applies her personal powers to pursue replication or transformation, by endorsing old projects or devising new, revised projects after reflexive deliberation. To talk about re-visiting the four quadrants is obviously an analytical contrivance, which is justified because each presents distinct problems and we have the personal powers to give them our selective attention. Let us now link up the solution to the generic problem, the analytical problem, and the explanatory problem, in order to clarify the nature of self-talk *about* society.

(A)   At any given T1′, the self consists of those things that have happened to it, together with those which it has made happen. The past is alive in the present in terms of those objective properties that are carried-over and, as it were, deposited there as modifications to the current 'I'. The most important of such features are the *commitments* that have been made at maturity, because they carry over from the old T4 to be deposited at the new T1′. The results of prior commitments can include marriage and family; an established career or vocation; membership of organisations, associations and social movements; the skills and knowledge acquired during the pursuit of earlier projects; and distinctive lifestyles such as celibacy or vegetarianism, which are the practices resulting from subjects' preceding attempts to live in accordance with their 'ultimate concerns'.

This group of features has two important things in common. On the one hand, they are *objective*. Either I have an apprenticeship or degree to complete, or I do not; either I have acquired a skill, such as speaking a foreign language, being computer literate or the ability to play a musical instrument, or I have not; either I have children, am in vows, have a work contract, or I do not. On the other hand, they are all relatively enduring, though some would be much easier to shed than others. What unites them is that action would have to be taken in the present in order to dispossess the current self of them. Not only may this be impossible (how do you stop being a mother), but it may also take considerable time (to get retrained or to become laicised). Meanwhile, these remain properties of the 'I', unless and until it seeks and gradually succeeds in changing over time, as in figure 3.2. Of course, it is always open to the 'I' to re-affirm its 'ultimate concerns' and to re-endorse those commitments, which were and still are the concrete expressions of them. Indeed, the 'I' will be facilitated in such a project because it is easier to build upon what exists than it is to start from scratch. Whether the subject eventually opts for a project representing personal morphogenesis or morphostasis, the contemporary round of the internal conversation will necessarily deliberate about these object-features of the self.

To see the results of our previous commitments as objective carry-overs from the past into the present, which ineluctably feature as considerations in current inner dialogues, is at complete variance with Mead's treatment of the past. To begin with, we are not subjectively free to make what we will of the past, constructing our biographies along such story lines as we please. The 'deposited' features are real and impose serious limitations upon narrative freedom because any re-telling of the past has to account for them. More importantly, however we try to re-tell it, we are still shackled to our old commitments *pro tem*. Even those that can be shed, as in ending a marriage, take practical action in order to do so. They also continue to have consequences which are projected from the present into the future, for example, the subject then becomes a divorcee, probably with divided assets and possibly with alimony to pay.

Next, it should be evident that these enduring characteristics cannot be rendered simply as 'habits' or habitual action orientations, as Mead considers them to be. Firstly, and perhaps most importantly, ongoing commitments are continuing expressions of our past 'ultimate concerns', which may (or may not) be re-affirmed in the present. Whether they are or not, it makes no sense of the very meaning of 'commitments' to construe them merely as habits, and it is equally nonsensical to view disavowing a commitment simply as the interruption of habitual action. Secondly, legal obligations are entailed by some of the elements mentioned, and disembarrassing ourselves of them involves more than kicking a habit. Thirdly, opportunity costs are involved in self-transformation (and some opportunities will have to be foregone as part of the re-affirmation of commitments). Yet, these are deliberative matters, which cannot be assimilated to the habitual repertoire of the subject because the outcome of his or her reflexive deliberations could go either way.

(B)   'Re-entering' the T2' quadrant, now as a person, that is someone with both a personal identity and also a social identity as an Actor, I find 'I' have a place, and perhaps a new position, upon society's distribution of resources. The mature 'Me' has been assigned her own life-chances and these are not entirely involuntary because anyone who has become an Actor has actively collaborated in making themselves *what* they are, even though this was accomplished from the context of his or her initial involuntary placement as (primary) agent. Yet now, 'I' can reflect upon 'my' positioning, as subject reflecting upon object, and can compare 'my' life-chances with those of other people. Even more, 'I' can reflect about the nature of the resource distributions themselves. 'I' can deem 'myself' fortunate or unfortunate, a victim or a victor. Because of *what* 'I' am and *whom* 'I' have become, 'I' will also evaluate these distributions as fair or unfair. As persons we can judge distributions to be too steep, or too flat, or too skewed. However, in 're-visiting' the T2′ quadrant, the 'Me' whom they encounter there is again a Primary Agent – one amongst others similarly placed. *Qua* Primary Agents we are still confined to unitary acts which may or may not aggregate into something consequential. It is at this point that subjects will internally review the desirability of collective action in quadrant 3′.

One action, however, which can have immediate effects stems from the personal judgement passed on the placement of the 'Me'. 'I' can be content or acceptant that 'I' now have these resources – remuneration, representation and repute – at my disposal, or resent where 'I' now find 'myself'. 'I' can regret the combination of circumstances and delibera-tions, which have placed 'Me' there or resent the exclusion or discrimi-nation that have left 'Me' there. Provided the subject does not see herself as condemned to passivity, this inspection can trigger a new cycle of the internal conversation, in which she strives to narrow the gap between that which she has become and that which she would be. From this nexus orig-inates the mature student, the career change, the late vocation, certain 'elderly prima gravidas' and many who divorce early in marriage. How they will fare depends on the projects they design in conjunction with the constraints and enablements they then encounter.

(C)   At T4′, the continuity of personal and of social identity alike is scrutinised. It is not hyperbole to say that each day we revisit our role commitments and have to make an act of re-commitment, because our daily wakening confronts us with yesterday's on-going concerns. These we not only have (effectively) to re-endorse, but also (effectively) to re-determine how this re-endorsement will be personified. The 'I' has the day-to-day task of determining what kind of 'You' will be projected for-ward into the future. Today can always be the day of either reversal or renewal of our commitments to the social identities that were assumed in becoming Actors. Inexorably, each day is one or the other, precisely because personification has to be an active and reflexive process of invest-ing ourselves in our existing roles, which involves novel and unscripted performances, hour by hour. We are our own script writers, since even the smallest print, which spells out our formal role obligations, cannot tell us how to greet our partners, breakfast the children, get down to a day's research, acknowledge God, or let the dog out.

Conversely, a subject may consider that the Actor that she has become by T4 is one with which she no longer reflexively identifies herself. Ei-ther her role has changed or she has. Roles are dynamic because the activities of (corporate) agents transform the role array and because the un-scripted personifications of Actors also cumulatively transform the normative expectations associated with positions. Nothing guarantees that such transformations are consensual, much less that every Actor is somehow 'consulted'. Necessarily then, role changes will leave some people stranded in positions that they had originally assumed as vehicles for the expression of their social identity, but which no longer operate in this way. Yet we cannot change most social identities at the drop of a hat or like changing hats. There are questions of preparation, of training and of acceptability and there are considerations of 'sunk costs' in the role(s) we occupy, which come in a variety of currencies. However, when our personal identity can no longer be expressed through our social roles, then only bad faith characterises the continuing role incumbent. Others will resign their role(s) and seek to become different kinds of Actors. In this quest for a new 'You', taking a cut in social salary may well be the price of maintaining personal integrity.

Much the same is true of persons whose own concerns shift and change even though the roles they occupy do not undergo substantial or significant modification. Particularly through our agential involvement in social movements (in quadrant 3), certain concerns will increase in personal salience, whilst other get demoted through disillusionment. This is only one common process; there are many other ways in which love can grow cold or new fires ignite. Here the key question is whether or not the new personal concern can be combined with an existing role. The subject will deliberate about this, for some roles are more flexible than others, but may have to conclude that she should seek to become a different Actor in another part of the role array.

To conclude this section, the 'I' can only devise projects for the future 'You' it seeks to become because it possesses personal emergent properties (PEPs): its self-consciousness, personal identity and capacity for reflexive deliberations. Without these, it would lack the powers either to envisage self-modification through its projects or actively to confront structural and cultural properties and powers (SEPs and CEPs) in its attempts to realise its future designs. Self-modification and social transformation are always allied, even though they are not identical. Thus the key point about the internal conversation is that it is necessarily preoccupied with how 'I' can promote my concerns by becoming the kind of 'You' which advances that about which 'I' care most, and thus embodies who 'I' want to become. These are my aspirations as a person, but I can only practically express my concerns within a social context in which 'I' bear a status as an agent and as an Actor. The inner dialogue cannot but address and assess the relationship between the former and the latter. This is how and why society inevitably gets in on the internal conversation – as *something* about which we cannot but deliberate. This is a very different explanatory solution from that advanced by Mead, who has us talking to society and our projects being internally censored by social normativity. The most crucial factor which his model disallows is our own (PEP) powers to deliberate about our 'ultimate concerns' and reflexively to design projects for their realisation – projects which involve self-modification but which are also expressions of social critique and quests for social transformation.

Conclusion

This chapter has been concerned firstly with 'James's problem', namely how can we be both subject and object to ourselves, which the observational model of introspection could not incorporate? The 'generic solution' to this was that we were subjects as we formulated our internal utterances, but that simultaneously, in listening to ourselves, we acted as registering objects, with the subject then responding to the object in a typical turn-taking conversation. Secondly came 'Peirce's problem', namely 'who was talking to whom' and whether or not 'different aspects of the ego' could converse? The 'analytical solution' to this was to resist reifying the 'Me', the 'I' and the 'You', and to insist that I only ever could be speaking to myself. However, as analytical distinctions, at any given time the prior 'Me' and the posterior 'You' enabled the examination of the influence of the past self upon the present self and the present self upon the future self. Finally, 'Mead's problem', namely how did society become a party to the conversation, was treated to a very different 'explanatory solution' from the one he advanced. Instead of our talking internally *to* society, in the guise of the internalised expectations of the 'generalized other', it was maintained that we necessarily talk *about* society. This is because whatever we wish to achieve as particular persons, the conception and conduct of our projects always has to take into account our objective status as social agents and our objective roles as social Actors.

Until the generic, analytical and explanatory solutions had been introduced in this chapter, in order to complete the unfinished journey from introspection to the internal conversation, our inner deliberations could have no claim to mediate between us as persons and our social circumstances. At last we are in a position from which properly to consider the potentialities of our reflexive deliberations as the process which mediates between 'structure and agency'.

4   The process of mediation between structure and agency

Drawing the threads together

What is advanced throughout this book is a concept of the 'internal conversation', by which agents reflexively deliberate upon the social circumstances that they confront. Because they possess personal identity, as defined by their individual configuration of concerns, they know what they care about most and what they seek to realise in society. Because they are capable of internally deliberating about themselves in relation to their social circumstances, they are the authors of projects that they (fallibly) believe will achieve something of what they want from and in society. Because pursuit of a social project generally spells an encounter with social powers, in the form of constraints and enablements, then the ongoing 'internal conversation' will mediate agents' receptions of these structural and cultural influences. In other words, our personal powers are exercised through reflexive interior dialogue and are causally accountable for the delineation of our concerns, the definition of our projects, the diagnosis of our circumstances and, ultimately, the determination of our practices in society. Reflexive deliberations constitute the mediatory process between 'structure and agency', they represent the subjective element which is always in interplay with the causal powers of objective social forms.

Since two sets of causal powers are necessary to account for agential doings, then those pertaining to the agent cannot be neglected. On the contrary, it is agential reflexivity that actively mediates between our structurally shaped circumstances and what we deliberatively make of them. There is no question of our making exactly what we please out of our circumstances, which would be to endorse the 'epistemic fallacy'. If that were the case, then the concepts of constraints and enablements would be redundant. We would fall back onto the opposite mono-causal account, namely the idealist and individualist one, which attends only to the causal powers of agents. On the contrary, the interplay between socio-cultural properties and the exercise of agential reflexivity is essential to explanation. Fundamentally, we cannot account for any outcome unless we understand the agent's project in relation to her social context. And we cannot understand her project without entering into her reflexive deliberations about her personal concerns in conjunction with the objective social context that she confronts.

Indeed, it is what agents seek to do, the precise projects that they pursue, which are responsible for the activation of the causal powers of constraint and enablement; otherwise, structural and cultural properties which are constitutive of situations remain real, but their causal powers are unexercised. Yet once an agential project has activated a constraint or an enablement, there is no single answer about what is to be done, and therefore no one predictable outcome. Conditional influences may be agentially evaded, endorsed, repudiated or contravened. Which will be the case and what will be the outcome only become intelligible by reference to the agent's own reflexive and therefore internal deliberations.

However, considerably more effort has been devoted to conceptualising how structural and cultural properties are transmitted to agents, and potentially work as conditional influences upon them, than has been given to the other side of the equation, namely, how they are received and responded to by agents in return. It is this one-sidedness that I seek to redress. The generic process by which structural and cultural emergent properties are held to impinge upon agents derives from the acknowledgement that all social action is necessarily contextualised and that all contexts embody social forms. Initially, the process of conditioning is transmitted to the agent by structural and cultural properties shaping the situations in which agents find themselves involuntarily – by moulding their circumstances, which were not of their making. This was formulated as follows in *Realist Social Theory*, and I reproduce it in order to re-endorse it.

Given their pre-existence, structural and cultural emergents shape the social environment to be inhabited. These results of past actions are deposited in the form of current situations. They account for what there is (structurally and culturally) to be distributed and also for the shape of such distributions; for the nature of the extant role array, the proportion of positions available at any time and the advantages/disadvantages associated with them; for the institutional configuration present and for those second order emergent properties of compatibility and incompatibility, that is whether the respective operations of institutions are matters of obstruction or assistance to one another. In these ways, situations are objectively defined for their subsequent occupants or incumbents.[1]

---

[1] Margaret S. Archer, *Realist Social Theory*, Cambridge University Press, 1995, p. 201.

The stress is the same at all levels of society – the distributional, positional, organisational, and the institutional – and it is firmly upon the shaping of the *objective* social contexts that agents necessarily and involuntarily encounter. This seems correct, because agents do not confront structural or cultural properties 'head on'; it is features of their situations that are encountered. The same is true of emergent properties of a physical kind; we do not and cannot confront 'two atoms of hydrogen plus one of oxygen' in themselves, because they have already combined to make water. It is the causal powers of H_2O which impinge upon us, including those of being able to be seen, whereas its constituents are invisible gases, and of being liable to drown in it, whereas we can breathe oxygen and become air-bound in a hydrogen balloon.

Different kinds of emergent properties impinge upon us quite differently: water works upon our embodied liabilities and potentialities whereas a cultural contradiction works upon the ideas that we hold. In all cases where structure influences agency, an interaction of two sets of powers is involved. Often this is not specified since the relevant human projects are so universal that they are taken for granted: no one (except the suicide) wishes to drown, and everyone (except the hunger striker) wishes to drink. Yet, the existence of these exceptions shows that it is indeed a human project to avoid drowning and to slake thirst – however general these may be and however automatically they *seem* to work as human responses. However, the creation of a vast number of artefacts to convey water to us and away from us reveal these to be very active human projects indeed.

Mediating social conditioning: the internal conversation

Thus the first stage in the conceptualisation of the mediation of structure to agency consists in specification of how the powers of structural and cultural emergent properties impinge upon us; namely by shaping our situations such that they have the capacity to operate as constraints and enablements. These structural and cultural properties only become causally efficacious in relation to human projects in society. In other words, there is a distinct second stage in the mediatory process during which our general potentialities and liabilities as human agents, necessarily inhabiting a social environment, are transformed into specific projects which agents, both individual and collective, seek to realise in society. Thus it is not agential properties that interact directly with social powers, rather, it is the projects formulated by agents, in exercising their subjective and reflexive mental powers that do so. In sum, structural and cultural factors do not exert causal powers in relation to human beings, but rather in relation to our emergent powers to formulate social objectives. This is the logical implication of the fact that one level of properties does not directly affect another level of properties, but that this is always a matter of the interplay between their causal powers.

Yet, if this is the case, then it also follows that there is necessarily a third stage to the mediation process. This is the stage, commonly ignored, where agents, in virtue of their powers of reflexivity, do indeed deliberate about their circumstances in relation to their own concerns. Agential subjectivity reflects upon societal objectivity. Since constraints and enablements work automatically, whereas agents work reflexively and can monitor their own ways of monitoring society, the third stage consists in the elaboration of *strategy* by self-conscious social subjects *towards* non-reflexive social powers. In everyday terms, we examine our social contexts, asking and answering ourselves (fallibly) about how we can best realise the concerns, which we determine ourselves, in circumstances that were not of our choosing. This final stage which completes the mediatory process is conducted through the internal conversation. We survey constraints and enablements, under our own descriptions (which is the only way we can know anything); we consult our projects which were deliberatively defined to realise our concerns; and we strategically adjust them into those practices which we conclude internally (and always fallibly) will enable us to do (and be) what we care about most in society. Thus, the progressive specification of concrete courses of action, which involves the trajectory **concerns**→ **projects**→ **practices**→, is accomplished through internal conversations. Primary agents do this for themselves; Corporate agents[2] pool these intra-personal deliberations and then subject them to inter-personal scrutiny.

This final stage of mediation is indispensable because *without it we can have no explanatory purchase upon what exactly agents do*. Deprived of such explanations, sociology has to settle for empirical generalisations about 'what most of the people do most of the time'. Indeed, without a real explanatory handle, sociologists often settle for much less: 'under circumstances x, a statistically significant number of agents do y'. These, of course, are not real explanations at all. They are a retreat into Humean 'constant conjunctions', from which a causal mechanism linking the two cannot be derived. Methodologically, this means that efficient causation will always be lacking, whilst ever the subjective powers of agents are excluded from research designs.

---

[2] Primary agents are defined as collectivities sharing the same life chances, which makes everyone an agent. They are distinguished from corporate agents which have articulated their aims and developed some form of organisation for their pursuit. See *Realist Social Theory*, ch. 8.

In reports of empirical work it is frequently found that the effect of structure upon agency is represented as a *two-stage process*, which is held to work directly rather than requiring agential mediation. It is presented as a wholly objective process because what is dropped from consideration is the reflexivity of agents that is intrinsic to their concerns, projects and actual doings. The elimination of the subjective contribution to mediation often occurs because constraints and enablements are not treated as transitive, that is requiring something determinate to constrain or enable. Instead they are confused with 'advantages' or 'disadvantages', which have the appearance of being intransitive. The assumption here is that no one will look a gift horse in the mouth or that everyone gets down to cutting their coats to suit their cloth. Yet, 'advantages' are not properly intransitive because they have to be positively evaluated by the agent for some purpose. This is particularly relevant where the luck of having been dealt better life-chances than others is then presumed to entail that the advantages of 'keeping ahead' will dominate the activities of all who are so placed. This may be a common concern, but if it is, then it must have been subjectively adopted, for it is not one that can blandly be imputed to everyone. What these considerations point to is the impossibility of any discussion about how structure conditions agency without *some* reference to agential subjectivity, however flawed, as in those cases where it is either taken for granted or imputed.

The common deficiency of these procedures is the failure to acknowledge that agential intentions are neither uniform, nor static, nor passive. Instead, our mental powers of reflexive deliberation firstly secure our unique personal identities through our singular constellation of concerns, meaning that we are radically heterogeneous as people, rather than having common ends. Secondly, our subjectivity is dynamic rather than static because we modify our own goals in terms of their contextual feasibility, as we see it. Finally, by virtue of our internal dialogues, we are active rather than passive because we can adjust and adapt our projects to those practices that we consider have a better chance of realisation.

Unless these three points are acknowledged, what is omitted are *agential evaluations of their situations in the light of their concerns, and their evaluation of their projects in the light of their situations*. Without the two, it is impossible to explain what the agent will actually do in practice, for the subjective agent is the ultimate and effective cause of social practice. Therefore, the process of mediation between structure and agency must be considered as entailing three stages, which capture the interplay between objectivity and subjectivity, as follows:

(i) Structural and cultural properties *objectively* shape the situations which agents confront involuntarily, and possess generative powers of constraint and enablement in relation to

(ii) Agents' own configurations of concerns, as *subjectively* defined in relation to the three orders of natural reality – nature, practice and society.

(iii) Courses of action are produced through the reflexive deliberations of agents who *subjectively* determine their practical projects in relation to their *objective* circumstances.

Taken together, these three propositions seek to capture the interplay between the objective and subjective components of the mediatory process, whereby structural and cultural influences condition agential doings. Obviously, the last thing that such an account attempts to do is to transcend the difference between objectivism and subjectivism, precisely because it respects the independent causal powers possessed by both structures and agents, and usually exercised by each to some degree. In interplay with one another they determine the practical courses of action adopted by agents (both Primary and Corporate), whose own interaction is ultimately responsible for the reproduction or transformation of society – or a sector of it.

At the latter and second-order level of Corporate interaction, a whole new range of factors come into play, such as coalition, compromise and concession between Corporate agents themselves and Corporate agency in relation to unorganised but not therefore uninfluential Primary agents. Consequently, it must be remembered that these are of both kinds and that further interaction is involved between them. However, space precludes giving due attention to collective influences in this text.

The three stages will now be examined in turn, with most attention being given to the third, since (i) has already been examined in *Realist Social Theory* (ch. 7) and (ii) in *Being Human* (ch. 7).

The three-stage process of mediation

Structural and cultural properties objectively *shape the situations which agents confront involuntarily and possess generative powers of constraint and enablement in relation to (agents' concerns as subjectively defined)*

The fundamental and wholly objective manner in which structural properties (be they distributional, positional, organisational or institutional) and cultural properties (be they propositional, theoretical or doctrinal) impinge upon agents is involuntary, namely by structuring the *situations* in which they find themselves. Involuntary placement is most evident for the new-born, who immediately become privileged/under-privileged in relation to resource distributions, and some of whose biological charac-teristics, like gender and skin-colour, receive positive and negative cul-tural evaluations. Nevertheless, the same involuntarism is true of those whose role incumbency enmeshes them in conflicting expectations, the researcher embroiled in contradictory theories and findings, and of those involved in institutions whose operations are obstructed or promoted by the systemic configuration in which they are embedded.[3] This involun-tary placement of agents is a direct consequence of the *temporal priority* of structure and culture to any 'generation' of agents.

The significance of such involuntary placement is that the situations encountered by agents endow different sections of society with different vested interests. Such vested interests are also wholly objective, which means they cannot be dissolved into subjective constructs. Either agents enjoy distributive privileges, rewarding roles or institutional facilitations or their opposites. Nothing binds them to supporting the former and op-posing the latter. But objective opportunity costs are associated with the repudiation of privileges, rewards and facilitations, meaning there is a real price to be paid for the pursuit of projects that are antipathetic to vested interests. Conversely, bonuses accrue to those who successfully extricate themselves from under-privileged or problematic positions. These repre-sent objective social inducements to different courses of action by those differently placed. Whether the agents recognise it or not (including being induced to misrecognise it), they pay a forfeit if they traduce their vested interests by endorsing projects hostile to them. Similarly, their different placements and the different privileges associated with them mean that the same course of action is differentially costly to groups in dissimilar situations. Therefore the 'same' project (such as undertaking a Univer-sity degree) involves a higher outlay from some agents than from others. Such pricing is again objective and failure to allow for it can simply derail strategic action.

Nevertheless, society may supply these situational reasons or motives, incentives or disincentives, and bonuses or penalties, but it is agents who have to find them good, which means better than any other course of action that they may have been inclined to adopt. Equally, the effects of opportunity costs are real, but it is the agents themselves who have to weigh them (fallibly under their own descriptions) and to decide how to

[3] For the latter, see Margaret S. Archer, *Social Origins of Educational Systems*, Sage, London and Beverly Hills, 1979.

act in view of their own weightings. The agent holds the scales of worth and establishes her own weights and measures, which tilt the balance one way or the other. However, she has to do this *within* her situational environment. There she does indeed remain the arbiter of 'worth', but has to allow for or counter-balance certain fixed costs which were not of her making or minting. But only she can establish the exchange rates payable between these objectively non-convertible currencies.

Thus, as was argued earlier, there can be no assumption that the involuntary acquisition of vested interests in the maintenance of privileges or the transformation of deprivation will automatically be translated into the corresponding courses of action. Agents have to find these interests subjectively worthwhile, which does not depend upon their simply being objectively privileged or objectively deprived. In short, we can have properly delineated all the above ways in which our situations transmit structural and cultural distributional properties to us, without having much idea what agents (primary or corporate) will actually do in these circumstances.

This can be quickly illustrated by considering the effects of different distributional placements of agents and the impossibility of deducing determinate courses of action for them. Suppose a collectivity of agents is well placed in terms of remuneration, representation and repute. These positionings cannot in themselves be assumed to foster reproductory projects, despite all having much to lose objectively. To begin with the most obvious reason, not all agents are guided by their objective interests; they can choose to marry downwards, to take vows of poverty, to renounce titles or to chuck it all up for subsistence living. Thus, at best, this leaves a probability statement about the doings of 'most people most of the time', but to what actual courses of action do these probabilities attach?

Furthermore, allowance has to be made for the fact that, for all normal agents, these distributional positions never feature amongst their ultimate concerns *per se*, but are used to further some other concern. Indeed, logically, money is valued for 'x', power for 'y' and repute for 'z'. (Only pathologically, as in the case of the miser, is money valued for itself.) It is these unknown 'x's, 'y's and 'z's which constitute the ultimate concerns of agents, and it is a matter of contingency whether these are internally related, externally related or fundamentally unrelated to any of the three resources. Until these ultimate concerns are themselves defined and until their relationship to resources is rendered determinate, then no probabilities whatsoever can be attached to protective courses of action, let alone to any precise course of action. What is clear is that no explanatory power derives from popular banalities about 'no one likes to lose out', nor from such a sociological reification as would have people exerting themselves to reproduce distributional positions for the sake of a position upon a distribution.

Once again, the time seems to have come at which to 'let the men back in' (individually and collectively) in order to render determinate that which otherwise remains indeterminate. In short, tell us your concerns and then we can understand your costings – and mis-costings. All of the above is simply intended to illustrate the fact that social properties like distributions *may* exert constraining and enabling powers. However, it is impossible to know *whether* or not this is the case until it is known upon which agential powers they impinge – in this case, agents' projects designed to realise their concerns.

> *(Constraints and enablements become activated in association with) agents' own constellations of concerns, as subjectively defined in relation to the three orders of natural reality – nature, practice and society*

By virtue of our human constitution in relation to natural reality, agents ineluctably inhabit its three constituent orders, those of nature, practice and society, and must establish working relationships with all three. Failure to do so threatens physical well-being in the natural order, endangers the performative achievement that is essential to work in the practical order, and imperils the achievement of self-worth in the social order. In other words, the establishment of satisfactory practices in the three orders is the inescapable condition for human beings to survive or thrive. Consequently, it is necessary that all agents conceive of projects with respect to each order of reality, whose pursuit is at least minimally successful in protecting and providing for the body, ensuring subsistence through work, and generating positive self-worth for the social subject.

Objectively necessary as the establishment of all three sets of practices is for everyone, there is nothing that compels each individual to evaluate them equally or which prevents different individuals from conceiving and carrying out more ambitious projects in one order compared with the others. Indeed, a central argument of *Being Human*[4] was that people reflexively survey these three clusters of ineluctable concerns and determine their relative importance to them. This entails the definition of their 'ultimate concerns' and the subordination, but also accommodation of other concerns to them, since subordinate ones cannot be repudiated entirely. Through a lengthy process of inner dialogue, involving the conversational phases of 'discrimination', 'deliberation' and 'dedication',

---

[4] Margaret S. Archer, *Being Human*, Cambridge University Press, 2000, p. 232–41.

individuals prioritise their concerns, in terms of what they care about most, and then accommodate others. Prioritisation and accommodation subjectivity produce a personal pattern. This both accentuates pursuit of the ultimate concern and adjusts other inescapable concerns into a *modus vivendi*; one with which the individual believes she can live. This constellation of concerns constitutes her unique *personal identity* and is the expression of her most important personal emergent power – her own reflexivity in relation to reality.

What is crucial to the present argument is that if personal identity is delineated with reference to the whole of natural reality, then social identity is a sub-set of it. All who achieve a personal identity, which is not everyone (and a stable identity is impossible until maturity), do indeed entertain social projects. We cannot but be socially engaged because this is the source of one of our ineluctable concerns *qua* agents. However, the direct implication is that we cannot simply be socially determined, because part of us has to be vested in and responsive to the prompts and restraints of the other two orders. Also and more radically, it follows that there can be considerable agential autonomy from society because that which concerns us most, and therefore that to which we are most responsive, may not lie in the social order at all.

Even if it does, personal identity is an emergent property whose powers include the designation and design of specific projects in society, their strategic pursuit through self-monitoring and a commitment to the successful establishment of practices which express a particular over-riding concern. Self-knowledge and self-commitment are the two factors conducive to suspending the causal powers of constraints through strategic circumvention and subversion based upon willingness to pay the price. They are also the factors responsible for enlarging the scope of enablements, through the reflexive elastication of projects, which enlarge the range of enterprises upon which propitious circumstances can be brought to bear.

In other words, our subjectively defined concerns, and especially our ultimate concerns, act as a sounding board for our reception of and response to the objective situations that we confront. Situations do not directly impact upon us; they are reflexively mediated via our own concerns and according to how well we know our circumstances, under our own descriptions. This means that agents will evaluate the same situations quite differently and their responses will vary accordingly. This statement makes no concessions to social constructionism. Objective situations, as shaped by socio-cultural properties are real; we cannot make what we will of them with impunity. If the descriptions under which they are known are wildly divergent from reality, then reality will have its revenge, because the strategy for pursuing a project will be defective. Nevertheless, the ontological status of something real is not impugned by allowing that it can be valued differently by different subjects.

Thus, an 'ultimate concern', which has been reflexively defined, acts as a prism which refracts the exercise of objective constraints and enablements. Here, vested interests (for example, in distributional privileges) may translate into enablements, provided they are commensurate with those projects which agents have defined to realise their concerns and provided that they have also been strategically appropriated by the same agents. Conversely, the pursuit of divergent concerns can effectively suspend the causal powers of distributional enablements. Their repudiation will represent an objective loss in relation to the benefits that harnessing them could have yielded, but agents have the power to pay the price if the projects that would have been advanced are matters of low concern to them – or, better, are negatively evaluated by them. This was presumably the understanding of Tony Benn when he renounced his peerage. Exactly the same points can be made about a willingness to pay the price in relation to constraints.

Moreover, any attempts to co-operate with enablements or to circumvent constraints are nothing but attempts. Both involve creativity, for there are few routinised templates for courses of action which ensure that vested interests are protected and projected onwards. Enablements are powers which, when intelligently used, help agents to 'stay ahead', in terms of the distributional example being used; they are not guarantees that people can 'stay put'. Life in an open system precludes such behavioural assurances and life in a morphogenetic system quickly renders habitual action obsolete. Even more obviously, the attempt to circumvent constraints has few established patterns to follow. Therefore, circumvention demands a greater use of personal powers than dogged commitment alone. Commitment, determination and endurance have to walk hand in hand with acuity. Part of this acumen is a realistic knowledge of what one can live with and the strategic planning of projects in this light. *Jude the Obscure* had all the powers of dogged commitment in abundance, but miscalculated both his circumstances and his own staying power, when he conceived his grandiose project to breach Oxford University.

The significance of the last paragraph lies in showing that *effective* structural and cultural conditioning *always* need a reflexive agent. Enablements require *intelligent* co-operation, which can only be supplied by agents drawing upon their own powers of creative deliberation. Similarly, constraints need *considered* compliance in order to be effective, because their own powers are jeopardised once agents consider circumvention instead. In short, the reflexive agent is an indispensable character when accounting for *either* successful socio-cultural conditioning, *or* for its repudiation, *or* for its contravention. The reason is the same in all three cases, namely that the process by which objective structural influences becomes mediated to agents *always* involves agential subjectivity.[5]

> *Courses of action are produced through the reflexive deliberations of agents who* subjectively *determine their practical projects in relation to their* objective *circumstances*

The fundamental concern here is to account for a process, namely by what means do active agents reflexively forge a sustainable, and ideally satisfying, *modus vivendi* for themselves from out of the objective social circumstances they confront, but that were not of their making? Of course, the very fact of envisaging such a process at all is predicated upon rejecting determinism and allowing that agents play a highly significant part in shaping their own lives. In fact, it is to go much further and to allow that the properties and powers of human agents actively mediate their own social conditioning (by structural and cultural emergent properties). This is the corollary of rejecting that social factors ever operate as hydraulic pressures, as 'pushes' and 'pulls' upon 'indeterminate matter'.

Although such factors and the situations they shape are entirely objective, their causal efficacy is mediated through subjective agential evaluation. Certainly, the objective opportunity costs which their circumstances attach to different courses of action have reflexively to be taken into account by agents, but it is they who have to evaluate them, because conditioning is not compelling. Certainly, too, agents are always fallible and can misjudge both the 'costs' and 'benefits' of pursuing a given course of action. They can also misjudge their own capacity to sustain it – in which case they will pay the objective 'price' regardless and may thus be later induced to revise or redefine their projects. There is a life-long dialectic between objectivity and subjectivity because circumstances can change (necessarily or contingently) and so can we (again necessarily, as we move through the life cycle, and contingently because we can re-assess our concerns).

In short, we are what Charles Taylor calls 'strong evaluators'[6]; for, as social subjects, unlike other animate beings, we have the capacity to find

---

[5] This has nothing to do with agents infallibly 'getting reality right', which would entail the 'ontic fallacy'. Nor can how they take matters to be subjectively, ever be substituted for how things are – which would entail the 'epistemic fallacy'. It is merely to assert that (fallible) reflexive mediation is indispensable in explaining the causal efficacy of structural and cultural emergent properties and also to account for the suspension of their powers.

[6] Charles Taylor, 'Self-Interpreting Animals', in his *Human Agency and Language*, esp. pp. 65–8.

different 'significance features'[7] in different parts of natural reality. The suggestion here is that the mediatory process entails our putting together that which is of over-riding significance to us, namely our 'ultimate concerns', with the 'imports' that our particular social placements convey about them. This is how we work out a *modus vivendi* for ourselves and the process is evaluative and reflexive through and through.

Through reflexive deliberation, we accomplish three things. Firstly, we delineate and prioritise our concerns, which is what enables us to achieve strict personal identity, as previously discussed. Secondly, we have to survey our objective circumstances and make discretionary judgements about the courses of action that we both deem to be desirable and with which we think it feasible that we can live. In contradistinction to Mead, this is the stage when our internal conversations are *about* society, rather than being conducted *with* society in the form of the 'generalized other'. Indeed, some of our internal deliberations will be precisely about *whether* to evaluate (positively or negatively) the expectations of given 'others'. Since society is a good deal less normatively homogeneous than the concept of a 'generalized other' implies, the subject has more degrees of freedom and therefore also carries the burden of determining *whose* expectations to endorse personally and to what extent. For example, I believe I lived up to my school's expectations by being a high academic performer in the Sixth form, but the school's historic mission was to maximise its numbers going to Oxford or Cambridge. From the age of eleven, we sat in morning Assembly surrounded by huge panels listing the names of Oxbridge entrants since the 1890s. So, when I declared my first preference to be the London School of Economics, there was a summons to the Head, an unpleasant lecture about how I was letting the school down, coupled with strong exhortations to reconsider becoming a 'Girton girl'.

That anecdote serves to introduce the third point. Reflexively, the evaluation of our concerns and the assessment of the courses of action we believe are feasible in our particular circumstances, have to come together and come to a point. That point is, what specifically do we intend to do? In other words, which precise activities do we believe are both expressive of our ultimate concerns, yet are also within our means? Again, internal deliberations will engage to define our actual doings with some precision. This is inevitable because at various stages of life we are confronted with decisions – to leave school or to continue, to enrol in further education or not, to have children before it is too late or not, to take early retirement

---

[7] 'Beings which have the significance feature are to be explained, at least for part of their behaviour, in terms which have no role in explaining inanimate things', e.g. interests, desires and purposes. Charles Taylor, 'Consciousness', in Paul F. Secord (ed.), *Explaining Human Behaviour: Human Action and Social Structure*, Sage, London, 1982, p. 50.

as soon as eligible or not. And of course, non-decisions are also decisions; pupils who go on to University with no particular aim in view have postponed this matter, but since most of them will emerge with a degree, they have also changed matters because of the new array of openings then available to them.

It is in relation to explaining these precise 'doings' that reference to our internal deliberations is indispensable. Without it, sociology is a blunt instrument, which settles for informing us that, for example, 'graduates have better occupational opportunities'. This is another way of saying that not only social realism, but also many other approaches, are stronger at conceptualising macroscopic influences upon the behavioural trends of collectivities than they are at reaching down and giving explanatory purchase upon actual agential doings. This is effectively to concede that a mediatory mechanism cannot be adduced. It is an admission that despite considerable sophistication in the conceptualisation of socio-cultural properties and powers, the explanatory pay-off is no greater than what are essentially Humean correlation or regression analyses, which can never produce a real linking mechanism between 'cause' and 'effect'.

Yet if agential properties and powers are given their due, then the mediatory process ceases to be elusive. If it is known what projects agents entertain, because they *are* 'strong evaluators' about their own ultimate concerns, then this is the sounding board against which the 'imports' of structural and cultural factors will reverberate. It cannot be a mechanical process because agents themselves must deliberate upon a precise course of action in view of their concerns and in the light of the circumstances they confront. But reference to their internal deliberations about this gives an explanatory handle upon what they reflexively decide to do.

This can best be illustrated by an example. Consider those upon whom the structural influence of inflation impinges severely; that is those living upon fixed incomes whose purchasing power is inexorably reduced. To explain their actual doings necessarily means resorting to their internal deliberations. Otherwise, accounts will be tautological; that is they will consist only of references to 'being worse off', which is not a doing. Alternatively, to escape tautology, taken-for-granted assumptions about ineluctable human concerns will be imported to produce generalisations, such as 'pensioners will be driven to trade-offs between heating and eating'. In other words, bodily necessities are first presumed and then assumed to acquire automatic priority under these circumstances. Now firstly, this is not necessarily the case for everyone, and, secondly, this abstract term 'trade-off' reveals nothing about actual doings without reference to the agents' own subjectively defined 'terms of trade'.

Firstly then, the presumption that bodily concerns automatically predominate in these circumstances will simply be false for some people. For instance, it implies that 'luxuries' like the telephone will uniformly be sacrificed. Yet for those whose ultimate concern is maintaining contact with their families, keeping the telephone could well be defined as an 'essential', which takes precedence over eating and heating. Of course, it remains true that such pensioners still need to eat and keep warm, but how they do it is a matter of reflexive ingenuity.

So, secondly, reference has to be made here to their own 'terms of trade' in order to explain courses of action which become established practices. For example, the cost of warm or suitable clothing can be drastically reduced, providing this is reflexively acceptable. Mrs Gaskell's *Cranford* gives the exchange between two impoverished old sisters who concur that their threadbare wardrobe will do for going away, 'because nobody will know us', and can serve equally well at home 'because everybody knows us' – their poverty is known and accepted, by themselves and their community. Yet for some, this acceptance would not be the case. To be seen foraging around jumble sales or using the Charity shops would represent a damage to their self-worth which outweighed the objective saving. Without reference to reflexivity, it might then be concluded that a group foregoing cheap clothing must necessarily be cutting back severely upon their food. Yet even this does not follow, if the same pensioners are prepared to use drop-in centres or Church lunches, perhaps saying, 'I really come for the company.' In short, intense internal deliberations will consider how to make ends meet and the ensuing doings and different patterning of practices will remain inexplicable without reference to its mediatory role.

What we are all trying to do is to establish a *modus vivendi* in which our concerns always play a role, even under stringently restrictive circumstances. Of course, the practices expressive of these concerns may well be severely limited in comparison with their ideal expression; those above who kept their phones may be grudgingly parsimonious about their calls, because of the need to pay the rental. Equally, people can only know their circumstances and its constraints and enablements under their own descriptions, which are always fallible. Too great a discrepancy between how they take things to be, compared with how they actually are, and the price is paid. The *modus vivendi* that is sought turns out to be untenable in practice, frequently with tragic consequences, as for those pensioners who do succumb to malnutrition or hypothermia.

Nevertheless, it must also be underlined that the deliberative development of stable practices is independent of a fully accurate discursive understanding of objective circumstances. Those pensioners who successfully define a sustaining *modus vivendi* may be entirely ignorant of inflation. They might even advance a completely erroneous diagnosis of their reduced purchasing power, attributing it, for example, to decimalisation. They may never have heard of the term 'index linked'. Their development of sustainable practices can rest purely upon a pragmatic interpretation of their circumstances, namely, that 'money doesn't go as far as it used to'. There are many unacknowledged conditions of action, such as inflation to many pensioners. Yet there is no need for them to be recognised as such in order for them to be influential. This in no way conflicts with the earlier assertion that the process by which objective influences become mediated to agents always involves agential subjectivity. It is their *situations*, as moulded by structural and cultural emergent properties, which are reflexively taken into account. And that requires no knowledge of the generative mechanisms which have helped to shape these situations.

In other words, the realisation of satisfactory practices has to be one which meets both connotations of this term: they must be ones which are found to be subjectively liveable (which does not mean maximally satisfying) and they must be ones which are objectively workable. Neither of these conditions depends upon a state approximating to full and accurate discursive penetration of reality – its natural, practical or social orders. Logically, this could not be the case, for that would mean no practice whatsoever could be established in the absence of a fully adequate theory. Yet none of our theories can ever claim such a status; they are, at best, temporary approximations, which will be progressively superseded. In that case, no practices at all could ever have become established, yet counterfactuals are readily found in all three orders of reality.

Although it is the case that instrumental rules of thumb can always be improved by more advanced theorisation, it is also the case that in everyday life we can get by, and also get a long way, on the basis of practical instrumentality. After all, many of us are competent motorists without having even a rudimentary knowledge about what goes on under the bonnet. Similarly, Polynesian flat-earthers could successfully navigate for 2,500 miles on their system of dead reckoning. In exact parallel, a sustainable *modus vivendi* may be far removed from the 'best conceivable practice' or the 'most theoretically informed practice'.

That there is an indubitable dialectic between theory and practice, I have defended elsewhere.[8] But it is a long-term process, during which humanity lives by yesterday's proven practices rather than awaiting tomorrow's theoretical advances. Therefore, no workable *modus vivendi*

---

[8] See Margaret S. Archer, *Being Human*, ch. 5.

depends upon our endowing the agents concerned with full discursive understanding or the properties of 'the good sociologist'. Pensioners on fixed incomes can work out how to get by in complete ignorance of the mechanisms of inflation; and it is their own deliberations that will determine how they actually live. That, of course, is not to deny that if they do achieve and articulate some theoretical understanding of their situation, they will be more prone to support corporate movements promoting better pensions – as seems to be coming to pass amongst the retired population in Britain.

Provided that the subject can endorse projects and blend these into a way of life that yields a fair degree of personal satisfaction, then her projects will remain within the parameters of her socio-cultural context. Conversely, subjective dissatisfaction, deriving from an internal inability to design a personal *modus vivendi*, will be a powerful agential (as opposed to institutional) prompt towards pushing back the cultural parameters with which agents were involuntarily endowed. In these subjective circumstances, the young in particular may seek to lift the objective veil, but they can burst the bounds of their *milieu* in different directions; with very different and often unintended consequences. Young people who leave home can move laterally, for example, by hoping to acquire a better life in a bigger town, or 'downwards' by spiralling into homelessness, or 'upwards', perhaps by enrolling at a college which then furthers their aspirations. Yet, in each case, they will interrogate the possibility of squaring subjective satisfaction with the new objective context. Inner deliberation will intensify because the new information acquired has to be mentally assimilated to personal concerns and then harnessed to the elaboration of projects that can be realised as practices with which the subject believes he or she can live.

For those who make no such radical break from their initial and involuntary context of placement, nevertheless, experience can gradually elasticate or contract their projects. In the case of elastication, let us take the case of a man who begins his occupational life in a relatively modest job, but whose proven ability leads to incremental promotions. If work was his ultimate concern, he could then begin to aspire to more distant horizons, including such elements as the kind of house he had never dreamed of, a better education for his children and so forth. All of this has come objectively within his grasp. But let us also assume that he married young, that commitment to his wife is another of his concerns, yet that she herself is increasingly uncomfortable with the finer house, the geographical mobility and the fear that the children are drifting beyond her ken. This hypothetical man then has to engage in serious internal deliberation about his constellation of concerns. Does he continue his upward occupational mobility, see his marriage break down and risk losing his children? Maybe he does, especially if a more 'suitable' new partner is around and one who is willing to try to make an amalgamated family work. Maybe, instead, he curbs his careerism, settles for some compromise on housing and locality and retains his marital stability. In the former case, he stretches elastication to its limit; in the latter, he compromises on limited expansion.

In the two cases, the objective occupational opportunities were identical; it is his subjective concerns which make the difference and the quality of his internal deliberations will play a vital role in whether he can establish a *modus vivendi* in either case. Once again, this is an instance of someone thinking to himself *about* society; his reflexive conclusions cannot be decisive because he lives in an open system (and could die in a traffic accident tomorrow). Nevertheless, it is the form of mediation which differentiates between the model of the person as someone to whom things just happen and the model of man as one who seeks to shape the contours of his own life by balancing his enablements and constraints with his concerns.

Conversely, one can imagine a woman who married and became a mother before her training was complete, but who retained the intention of finishing it once the children were at school. Meanwhile, the marriage breaks down and, as a dedicated single parent, she takes on part-time work, commensurate with her existing skills and convenient for nursery school hours. Gradually, she builds up a supportive network of friends at work and is also offered full-time employment there, as and when she can take it. When she finally escorts the last child to the reception class, she has subjectively to review that postponed completion of training. She has to be the evaluator. Maybe it is now her 'turn' at last, maybe she will readily meet with a cohort of mature women in the same position, and maybe the course itself will be a welcome challenge. However, she has now something definite to lose: a job she can cope with easily, relatively free evenings and a proven friendship network. Nothing compels her to contract her original aspirations; she is counsel for the prosecution, counsel for the defence as well as being judge and jury.

What she has to evaluate is forfeiting a *modus vivendi* that is assuredly manageable, in exchange for the prospect of re-making a new, more demanding and more rewarding one. As a mature woman, she also knows that she is likely to have regrets either way; so perhaps her dialogue is inconclusive and issues in a further postponement. Years later, her non-decision-making will have come to represent contraction. Objective constraints are not necessarily like boulders in someone's pathway; subjectively they can be mediated by gradually eroding one's projects. Only retrospectively may we acknowledge that we have almost imperceptibly curtailed our concerns in the light of our circumstances.

The *modus vivendi* – a matter of establishing practices

The establishment of a successful practice is taken to mean the realisation of a particular project by an agent in the relevant part of his or her environment. However, it needs to be acknowledged that any single project is only part of each agent's total enterprise and that the significance of a given project can only be assessed in relation to the totality. This is often a major difference between investigators and their subjects. Frequently, sociological specialisation means that researchers are only interested in one domain of agential practice, be it work, the family, education, religion, health and so forth. Such can never be the case for agents themselves.

Even if people have one dominant ultimate concern, this cannot be their sole concern. Because of the way we are humanly constituted, because of the way the world is, and because of the necessity of interaction between the two, then ineluctably we have concerns in each of the three domains of natural reality – nature, practice and society. To these correspond generic concerns about our physical well being, performative competence and social self-worth. A complete failure to attend to any one of these necessarily and severely threatens the other two. It makes the establishment of successful practices in the remaining orders both tenuous and temporary. Unlike the specialist researcher, the agent must be a generalist in her own life.

Certainly, every (normal) agent can and does prioritise her concerns, which usually involves accentuating one of the three orders over others, but she must also accommodate meeting those of each other order to some degree – they can be subordinated but cannot be repudiated. We may, for example, neglect our health, but we cannot entirely ignore our physical well being, if only because its serious deterioration imperils the achievement of what we care about most. Together, prioritisation and accommodation define the constellation of concerns which give us our personal identities. Although it will be the nature of our priorities which marks us as distinctive individuals to others, then equally, it is the nature of our accommodations which ensure that we can sustain such priorities, because they underwrite our surviving and thriving. In short, each and every agent has a multiplicity of projects, ultimately grounded in their three ineluctable concerns; and this is the case regardless of the differential importance which individuals assign to their projects in any particular order.

Consequently, their aim can never be the establishment of a *single* successful practice that realises one project alone and reflects a concern solely with one order of reality. On the contrary, because we must necessarily have a constellation of concerns, then we must also seek to establish a plurality of successful practices – compatible with one another and coherent with the ranking which we ourselves have assigned to them. In short, each and every agent strives to delineate a *modus vivendi*; a *set* of practices which, in combination, both respects that which is ineluctable but also privileges that which matters most to the person concerned. This is no bromide about the 'well rounded life', for any number of the most bizarre life-styles can constitute the necessary plurality of successful practices; it is simply to maintain that the development of such a *modus vivendi* is required by the human condition.

Yet, this cluster of successful practices may fail to be established for two basic reasons, besides the intervention of contingencies which derive from life in an open system and which can play havoc with the most careful deliberations and nullify the best-laid plans. The two fundamental reasons are fallibility about us ourselves and about our circumstances. Throughout our reflexive deliberations, we are evaluating ourselves, our natural environment and the relations between them. And we may be wrong on each of these counts. Since these are the building blocks of every *modus vivendi*, as reflexively defined by an agent, then the design may simply be unsound.

On the one hand, agents may discover that they are wrong that progress towards the realisation of their projects yields them increasing satisfaction. They may be wrong about their ability to sustain the commitments they have made. They may be wrong about the concerns they believed they could severely subordinate; just as they may be wrong about the objective prices they thought they could pay or their capacity to circumvent constraints or to repudiate enablements. Why do priests who renounce their celibacy in order to marry, General Practitioners who succumb to breakdowns, or academics who take very early retirement to do something else, attract so much attention from their colleagues and immediate circle? Perhaps this is because these represent public 'declarations' that the individual in question had got it wrong; because these constitute private reminders about our own self-doubts; because they show that the stability of any *modus vivendi* rests upon the fragility of our commitments and the fallibility of our self-knowledge.

On the other hand, agents, under their own descriptions, may have seriously misread their situations. What they had reflexively deemed to be a feasible course of action may prove not to be the case, however strenuous their personal exertions. This is most obvious for those whose projects entailed the circumvention of constraints and who may have grossly underestimated the costs of the enterprise. *Jude the Obscure* shocks because his own death and that of his children signals not only the self-confessed failure of his aspirations, but because there can be no future *modus vivendi* for any of the characters. Yet the quiet abandonment of training courses, the failure of one-person businesses, the retreat from an insoluble research problem, or the break up of a long relationship are all part of the same confession. The difference of course is that the possibility for establishing a new but perhaps less ambitious *modus vivendi* remains open. Less obviously, on the other hand, an equally gross over-estimate of enablements can lead to an equally untenable position. Thus, John Durbeyfield learns of his descent from the extinct line of d'Urbervilles. Later, he seeks to establish a connection with an eponymous family as an enablement. Consequently, he deprives Tess of whatever rural *modus vivendi* she might have achieved and precipitates those events which end with Tess hanged as a murderess. The *leitmotif* of Hardy's tragic view of life is the epistemic fallacy; substitute how we would have things be for how they are, and reality always has its revenge.

The establishment of those successful practices, which together constitute a *modus vivendi*, involve both a realistic recognition of the multiple needs of the human condition and an intelligent, though fallible, interaction with those constraints and enablements which are activated during the pursuit of our concerns. To repeat, for the last time, it is not by transcending the divide between subjectivity and objectivity that we can account for the practices out of which patterns of life in society are woven. Such accounts can only be advanced by exploring the nexus between the causal powers pertaining to social forms and the very different, because reflexive, causal powers belonging to and exercised by agents. This nexus consists of our internal conversations.

Part II

Modes of reflexivity and stances towards society

5   Investigating internal conversations

Substantively we know very little about the internal conversation. The American pragmatists alone took a sustained interest in it and yet they were less than generous with examples of it. Since they held the phenomenon of inner dialogue to be universal, because it represented thought itself, they assumed that all readers could and would furnish their own instances. This both entails and also secretes the presumption that our inner dialogues are similar in kind. Yet there is no warrant for presupposing such uniformity. Even if the exercise of dialogical reflexivity is essential to the normal functioning of human beings, and even if it is a transcendentally necessary condition for the existence of society (both of these propositions being endorsed here), it does not follow that we converse with ourselves in a common way.

Similarly, in its quest for general principles of thought, experimental psychology has extended and secreted the same presumption about the common form taken by human reflexivity. Since the main potential sources of variation in people's thinking to have received sustained investigation are those broadly associated with either brain damage (various) or stages of mental development, both overtly appeal to norms and thus again presume universal processes. Moreover, within the psychology of thought, its typical experimental designs reinforce this presumption of universalism by setting the same laboratory task for all subjects and then registering the effects of imposing secondary tasks, introducing controlled stimuli and other environmental variations. Thus the general thrust of psychological research has entirely begged the question – are our internal conversations, in fact so very alike, so similar that inter-personal differences are uninteresting?

However, here it is 'natural' internal conversation that is of interest, and some very basic questions are at stake. Do different people devote their self-talk to different matters? Do all people engage in the same range of mental activities, as described in folk terms? Do subjects conduct their internal conversations in the same way, or can one speak of different modes of reflexivity? Is the private life of their minds associated with their social positions or backgrounds? Structuralism and neo-structuralists have tried to usurp the answers to these questions by positing unconscious mental grids as common mechanisms governing the lives of all our minds. However, these are reductionist accounts which nullify the personal causal powers of our internal deliberations by subordinating them to control by the 'hidden hand' of unconscious processes – which are again presumed to be universal.

In my attempt (a) to uphold the *private* life of the social subject, and (b) to defend subjective reflexivity as a *personal power*, the only recourse is to investigation in order to discover what warrant there is for these two key propositions. If such investigation is feasible, both the presumption of universalism and the possibility of reductionism can be questioned empirically.

The enterprise

What was undertaken was a very small, in-depth, and entirely exploratory study. It had only one expectation, namely that because all the participants were functioning members of society (with greater or lesser problems), then all would have a life of the mind. Furthermore, it was assumed that subjects would be able to tell something about the nature of their own internal conversations, a hope founded upon the belief that consciousness is indeed self-consciousness.[1] In asking interviewees to find the words in which to discuss their internal dialogues, in entering into discussion about self-talk with them, and in writing the next four chapters on these exchanges, all the problems of the 'double hermeneutic' are encountered. Ineluctably, the whole enterprise involves the interpretation of interpreting subjects. Since all knowledge is conceptually formed, then how interviewees interpret their own internal conversations, under their own descriptions, is necessarily theory-laden. Equally, how I interpreted their interpretations, under my own conceptual descriptions, is also inescapably theory-laden.

The double hermeneutic is unavoidable, but cannot be an intransigent barrier to investigation. Indeed, to hold it to be such is not possible, because it would entail a radical performative contradiction. However great the difficulties may be in one person conveying a subjective meaning, and another comprehending (something of) it, the process must at least be *imperfectly successful* to account for such durable practices as talking and teaching. Whatever their differences, every proponent of hermeneutics, *verstehen*, or interpretative understanding has to start from this one

---

[1] Following Harry G. Frankfurt, see ch. 1, p. 39 and n 35.

'given' – that of imperfectly successful communication. The fact of this being a 'given' also underwrites social investigation in general. Most obviously, taking imperfectly successful communication as 'given' necessarily underpins every form of 'question and answer' research in the social sciences. Less obviously, so too does the construction of a seemingly objective index, like GNP.

Rather than engaging with any of these methodological debates, the only point it is sought to establish is that the undoubted problems involved in investigating the 'internal conversation' are generically no different from those which always attend interview or survey research. This may strike many as counter-intuitive. It may do so precisely because our inner conversations are indeed private and the thinker has a special personal warrant to know better than anyone else the meaning of what she thinks and of what she says about her thinking (as defended in chapter 1). Therefore, the investigator, who is necessarily an interpreter, is likely to err in his or her third person construal of anyone's private meanings. However, that is also the case for interpreting any of an individual's answers to a fixed-choice questionnaire about, for example, voting intentions. There, it is commonplace to recognise the heterogeneity of meanings which are compatible with ticking the box for a particular party, or, for that matter, placing a tick by 'none of the above'.

I suspect that counter-intuitive resistance to the public investigation of the private 'inner conversation' may lie deeper and consist in people's gut-reaction that they have the greatest difficulties in representing their inner dialogues to *themselves*, let alone to another. Thus it might (rightly) be held that nobody could successfully reproduce their intra-personal exchanges, taking place over the course of one hour (in the form of intra-locutions, as illustrated in chapter 3). We lack the capacity for such prolonged self-monitoring and genuinely doubt our ability to reproduce what has passed with any accuracy. This is correct, but would not exactly the same be the case for reproducing an hour's worth of our contributions to a busy inter-personal conversation? In either case, we store only the gist of past exchanges and produce only some current synthesis of its outcome, both of which are interpretative. More importantly, for parallels within the investigative process, are not the opinions and attitudes that we venture in any interview also 'digests' of a long and imperfectly self-analysed process of their formation?

In other words, it is suggested that the relationship between our internal conversations and their investigation is fundamentally no different from the relationship between our 'attitudes' and 'attitudinal research'. Suppose an investigation was concerned to elicit our 'political outlooks' as opposed to our 'voting intentions', precisely because researchers accepted that a declared intention to 'vote for X' could represent anything from high personal commitment to Party X, to 'strategic voting', 'deferential voting' or 'protest voting'. Any honest internal attempt to represent to *ourselves*, let alone to the investigator, what exact sequence of events, discussions, readings and ruminations had led to our current 'political outlooks', would not entail their exact mental reproduction. We would produce a 'digest' *both* for internal consumption and for external reporting (which are also unlikely to be identical). In short, we have to interpret ourselves synthetically before we can furnish any statement for external interpretation. All this is undeniable because we are indeed 'self interpreting animals';[2] but we interpret ourselves by means of our current syntheses and not by relying upon imperfect recourse to our memories.

The argument is simply that there is no difference in kind about reporting upon our internal conversations and doing the same about our political outlooks. Both entail subjects' current interpretative 'syntheses' of reflexive acts of self-knowledge, and neither summary statement is equivalent to an exercise of memory. In other words, this exploratory study does not minimise the interpretative and 'shorthand' nature of subjects' reports upon their inner conversational activities, but neither does it maximise the investigative difficulties entailed, such that they are regarded as being different in kind. All research touching upon our 'attitudes', 'beliefs', 'outlooks' or 'intentions' taps into syntheses of our mental activities; to explore the 'internal conversation' does not entail qualitatively different difficulties. That it is difficult is undeniable, but if it is deemed impossible, then so must all the research topics with which it has just been bracketed.

A parallel argument can be advanced about the other face of the 'double hermeneutic' – that which concerns the investigator. As researchers we are always and ineluctably engaged in another interpretative act. This fact remains intransigent, whether it pre-dates the investigation, by imposing fixed response categories, or post-dates it when reporting on unstructured interviews. There is no circumventing this state of affairs. Consequently, in this small and exploratory study, it is no defence against my own inevitable interpretative incursion to plead that this was 'pure' exploration, approached without an 'interpretative repertoire' on my part. Formally, the absence of an articulated repertoire was indeed the case, but no one's protestations of neutrality free their analysis from informal concept-ladenness. As investigators, we all lack an epistemic vantage

---

[2] Charles Taylor, 'Self-Interpreting Animals', in his *Human Agency and Language*, Cambridge University Press, 1985, pp. 65f.

point from which to be a 'pure visitor'. Only the 'usual' kind of defensive protestations can be made, and they are now offered.

Firstly, in explicitly exploring the nature of people's (reported) forms of internal conversation, there was openness to the discovery of difference. This has to be preferable to the unwarranted presumption of a universal and homogeneous phenomenon, as mentioned at the start of this introduction, even if differences can indeed be known only under my proffered descriptions. Secondly, such an investigation also has to be preferable to lay understandings and folk psychology, since every interviewee was found to endorse an inductive fallacy, namely that all other subjects exercised reflexivity in much the same way that he or she did. Again, my discovery of differences in modes of reflexivity can only be known under my own descriptions, in all their concept-ladenness. Thirdly, however, cross-checks were not lacking. The interpreted accounts were handed back to eight (previously known) subjects for comment. Nevertheless, their lack of dissent only witnesses to inter-personal accord, which is not auto-veridical since not proofed against the selection of subjects or their 'affirmation bias' – otherwise known as good manners. Conversely, it could be argued that there is no good reason why eight people, who readily disagree with me about many matters, should become excessively deferential, especially when it is their own inner lives that are being portrayed. If they each individually claimed to recognise their own internal conversations under my descriptions, then this does supply additional ammunition against the 'intuitive fallacy of sameness' – because my characterisation of their 'internal conversations' in fact portrayed different modes of reflexivity for different subjects. Finally, the results presented come before the open court of collegial critique, or what realists would call the exercise of 'judgemental rationality', and the findings themselves stand at the bar of replicability. These are all very 'usual' methodological comments, but that is the only point that is being made, namely that there is nothing really 'unusual' about undertaking this research project.

The decision to investigate a very small group in depth was jointly prompted by the topic itself and by feasibility. Since the aim was exploratory and the means dialogical, there was no way of preparing a formal interview schedule for administration by others. The themes introduced by subjects themselves were (to prove) far more valuable than my prompt sheet, as was the discursive elaboration of points, which could not have been scheduled. Since it quickly emerged that these taped interviews could be over three hours in length (sometimes representing thirty pages of transcript), it was concluded that twenty subjects (or approximately 500 pages of transcript) was the most this one person could handle.

Table 5.1 *Socio–economic background of subjects interviewed*

Subject	Age	Father's occupation (or mother's if head of house*)	Registrar General's social class	Subject's current occupation	Registrar General's social class
Andy(m)	29	Heating engineer	IIIM	University lecturer (scale A)	I
Angie(f)	37	Telecommunications engineer	IIIM	Secretary (university grade II)	IIINM
Anna(f)	65	Analytical chemist (in industry)	I	General-secretary to religious order (Ret. deputy sec. school head)	II
Cass(f)	55	Foreman: wood factory	IIIM	Ret. social worker	II
Eliot(m)	57	Grammar school head	II	Antiquarian bookseller (sole trader)	II
Farat(f)	37	Labourer	V	Secretary (university grade II)	IIINM
Graham(m)	62	Pattern maker: iron industry	IIIM	Building site foreman	IIIM
Gwen(f)	58	Bus driver	IIIM	Ret. school secretary	IIINM
Ivan(m)	32	*Not in employment	–	University lecturer (scale A)	I
Jason(m)	17	Train driver	IIIM	Unemployed – part-time HE (GNVQ)	IV
Keith(m)	45	Tanker driver	IIIM	Electrical site foreman	IIIM
Kevin(m)	43	Factory worker	IV	Porter (of building)	IV
Kim(f)	17	Salesperson (retail)	IIINM	Hairdressing apprentice	IIIM
Lara(f)	18	*Factory worker (unskilled)	V	Full-time HE (GNVQ)	IV
Lawrence(m)	31	Head coach: women's NFL, USA	II	Full-time HE (GNVQ)	IV
Mel(f)	18	*Not in employment	–	Hairdressing apprentice	IIIM
Michael(m)	16	Electrician	IIIM	Electrical apprentice (construction industry)	IIIM
Paul(m)	56	Electrician	IIIM	Chartered engineer	I
Trish(f)	18	Warehouseman	V	Hairdressing apprentice	IIINM
Vincent(m)	67	Industrial chemist (research)	I	Roman Catholic priest (University chaplain)	I

Source: Registrar General 1990

Note: M = manual, NM = non-manual

I was encouraged about the fruitfulness of small-scale qualitative research by the impact of two impressive exemplars. One was Elizabeth
Bott's 'old' study of twenty families in *Family and Social Network*, encountered in my undergraduate days. Certainly she and her colleagues
investigated these families at much greater length and in much greater
depth in order to establish the links between conjugal roles and social
networks, but they were animated by the same aims and objectives as
my own. As she puts it: 'We were engaged in an exploratory study. We
started with no well-defined hypotheses or interpretations and no ready-
made methodology and field techniques . . . Our task was not to test hypotheses but to develop them.'[3] Even closer in spirit is Doug Porpora's
rich 'new' study of forty diverse interviewees in *Landscapes of the Soul*.
Although, at certain points, Porpora was able to cross-reference some of
his findings with national data or with his own more extensive local data,
his remarkable dissection of 'the loss of moral meaning in American life'
is based upon treating his forty interviewees as both data and conversational partners. For both of us, 'the point of the in-depth interviews
is not to establish the proportional representativeness of views . . . but to
elicit an illustrative sample of the different ways differently situated people
think about life's ultimate questions. The point of the interviews, in other
words, is to identify inner mechanisms of thought on ultimate matters.'[4]
Only the last three words reflect a difference in purpose – my own being
to identify inner mechanisms of thought on what is of most concern to
subjects, according to their own definitions.

The subjects

The twenty interviewees were not randomly selected, nor are they representative, for it could not then have been said what or whom they were
meant to represent. The only objective was to make these twenty people
as *diverse* as possible, with regard to class, age, gender and occupational activity. Their demographic details are found in table 5.1. Subjects
ranged from a sixteen-year-old electrical apprentice, who had been in
work for ten days, to a sixty-seven year old priest and member of a religious order; from three teenage hairdressers, employed in the same salon,
to an antiquarian bookseller, working from home as a sole trader; and
from two homeless young people to a volunteer social worker in Southern

---

[3] Elizabeth Bott, *Family and Social Network*, Tavistock, London [1957], 1971, pp. 8–9.
[4] Douglas V. Porpora, *Landscapes of the Soul*, Oxford University Press, 2001, p. 6.

Africa. In between are found construction workers (various), young academics, secretaries, a porter, a chartered surveyor and a missionary nun. In terms of known national distributions, the nine women subjects should obviously have included one more, the one member of an ethnic minority should have been two, and the three Catholics should have been one less.

The first eight subjects to be interviewed were personal friends or acquaintances, known to me in either a professional or a residential capacity. The main reason for approaching them was the need to have subjects to whom I could later return and who would be willing to comment freely upon what I eventually wrote about the lives of their minds. However, to have completed the constitution of the exploratory group in this manner would have greatly reduced its diversity by concentrating upon older, middle-class professionals. Therefore, the remaining twelve subjects came from other sources. A firm of contract builders, working on campus, was approached through visiting the site manager. He, in turn, supplied four construction workers of very different levels, who were willing to be interviewed during work time. Since these were all male and three of them were over forty, they were counterbalanced by three young, female hairdressing apprentices from a salon in the market town, six miles from my home. Personal contacts furnished the one interviewee belonging to an ethnic minority and the one male, working-class employee in the service sector.

Because, with one exception, these seventeen subjects were all in steady employment, and because choice of occupation and the nature of working life were thought likely to be of significance, it seemed useful to complete the exploratory group by three interviewees who were in search of work. Consequently, I approached the Jobcentre in the market town, once again seeking young people. Unfortunately, after discussion of the project, it was deemed that it would be inappropriate for me to interview job-seekers in case the purpose was misunderstood as relating to benefit entitlements. However, the Jobcentre personnel wished to be helpful, took me very literally about wanting young people who were not making the transition from school to work smoothly, and introduced me to a residential project for those who had found this particularly problematic, often to the point of having become homeless. In some ways, the inclusion of these last three subjects might be viewed as controversial, since they were known to be people with problems. Conversely, and in view of the sole aim being to maximise diversity, this seemed justified in order to offset the number of (seemingly) 'well-established' professionals with whom I had begun.

The interviews

The interviews themselves fell into two parts, although open-ended responses and a dialogical approach meant that equivalent amounts of time were not devoted to each for everyone. Part 1 was the more structured, since its objectives were to ascertain subjects' reactions to the notion of the 'internal conversation' and then to explore their own ranges of inner dialogue with them. Therefore, the same opening question was always used. Having stressed that 'we are all different' and that 'there are no right answers', in order to legitimate any response, it was put to interviewees that some people were aware that quite often they were having a conversation with themselves, silently in their heads. They were then asked whether or not this was the case for them. Each was encouraged to discuss this theme, under their own descriptions, for as long as they appeared to have more to say. Significantly, no subject had difficulties with the concept and no one disavowed the activity. Very interestingly, most interviewees volunteered that they themselves assumed the practice of interior dialogue to be universal, and, even more importantly, that they presumed we all did it in much the same way. As the next four chapters show, the latter was far from being the case. Following that discussion, subjects were presented with ten mental activities, derived from discussion with an informal pilot group. Items from this prompt list were put sequentially to each interviewee, prefaced by an assurance, gleaned from piloting, that not everyone engages in self-talk about each item:

> *Planning* (the day, the week or much longer ahead)
> *Rehearsing* (practising what you will say or do)
> *Mulling-over* (dwelling upon a problem, a situation or a relationship)
> *Deciding* (debating what to do, what is for the best)
> *Re-living* (some event, period or relationship)
> *Prioritising* (working out what matters most, next, or at all to you)
> *Imagining* (the future, including 'what would happen if...')
> *Clarifying* (sorting out what you think about some issue, person or problem)
> *Imaginary conversations* (held with people known to you or whom you know of)
> *Budgeting* (estimating whether or not you can afford to do something in terms of money, time or effort)

Afterwards, all were asked if there were any other themes upon which their own internal conversations dwelt. One subject volunteered 'self-monitoring', but said that she saw this as a common denominator rather than a separate item, and another mentioned what he called 'mental diversions', such as puzzling over crossword clues or 'brain teasers'.

The second part of the interview was much more loosely structured and focused on two main areas. Firstly, subjects were asked about their current concerns, that is which areas of their lives mattered most to them at the moment. They were encouraged to talk freely around this issue, whilst I used a check-list to ensure that the following aspects were addressed:

whether or not these had long been the subjects' concerns;

whether or not their (open-ended) listings of concerns were ones that dovetailed smoothly;

whether or not subjects spent time in thinking out exactly what they should do in the light of their concerns;

whether or not they saw (or had seen) anything in their back-grounds which was helpful or obstructive in relation to realis-ing their concerns.

Within this broad framework, I was happy for subjects to dwell on what they pleased and in all cases a biography emerged, which was developed by supplementary questions if it seemed to have a bearing on the above four issues.

Secondly, once subjects had outlined their configurations of concerns and how these had developed, they were encouraged to look forward and to discuss how their 'life-projects' related to remuneration, repute and re-sponsibility (class, status and power); to sacrifices and regrets; to support and satisfaction; and to ambitions, commitments or re-orientations. Since the main interest was in how each subject internally deliberated about his or her own future, every time they hit this note they were prompted to go on talking, to give illustrations, or to supply anecdotes.

Because I was entirely dependent upon conversational collaboration throughout these interviews, I made no attempt to play the role of inter-viewer-as-cipher. In any case, this would have been impossible with the eight known subjects. With the other twelve, I felt these dialogical partners deserved human reciprocity. Thus, whilst attempting to remain receptive and never intentionally to be evaluative, I was quite ready to participate in non-directive exchanges. For example, these ranged over childcare, the domestic division of labour, commuting to work, or writing books, and, on certain occasions, sports cars, make-up, abseiling, the 'baby blues', whether or not one can love one's dog, or why buy *The Big Issue*.

The analysis

Data never speak for themselves and their patterning is not self-revelatory. Even an exploratory study is guided by questions, as have already been listed. To recapitulate, these twenty diverse subjects were interviewed to provide preliminary answers to the following four summary questions:

(1) Do different people devote their self-talk to different matters?
(2) Do all people engage in the same range of deliberative mental activities?
(3) Do people conduct their internal conversations in much the same way, or can one speak of different modes of reflexivity?
(4) Are people's internal dialogues associated with their original or acquired social positioning?

During the course of the interviews, I became increasingly preoccupied with (3), the idea that there were indeed different modes of practising reflexivity, something which was intensified by the interviewees' shared conviction that everyone else's internal conversation was much the same as their own! During the six weeks in which I played and replayed the tapes, this impression was reinforced, as three clusters of subjects increasingly appeared to exercise very different modes of conducting their inner conversations. Once these modes had been identified, further internal support was forthcoming. The answers given to questions (1), about the substance of interior dialogue, and (2), the range of mental activities constitutive of self-talk, were so closely related to the three 'modes of reflexivity', now tentatively designated, that they appeared to be aspects of a particular type of life of the mind. Equally importantly, the three 'modes of reflexivity' bore very close relationships to the material contained in part 2 of the interviews. These different forms of interior dialogue were closely related to central aspects of subjects' life-projects: (a) to the nature of their ultimate concerns; (b) to the ease or difficulty they experienced in dovetailing their plurality of concerns; and (c) to the establishment of a *modus vivendi* that was felt to be both satisfying and sustainable.

Moreover, as my interest increasingly focused upon the three modes of reflexivity (question (3) now subsuming questions (1) and (2)), then connections with question (4), about the relationship between different forms of internal conversation and original or acquired social positioning, also became increasingly apparent. On the one hand, 'contextual continuity' or 'contextual discontinuity' with subjects' original and involuntary social placement appeared to be far more important than social origins *per se* for fostering and sustaining different modes of reflexivity. On the other hand, the most exciting finding of all was that those practising the three modes of reflexivity also assumed different 'stances' towards society and particularly *vis à vis* its constraints and enablements. The detection of this *differentiated* mechanism, mediating between structure and agency, is regarded as the most important hypothesis to emerge from the exploratory study. Its operation is explained in the course of the four following chapters and is summarised in their conclusions.

Obviously, all of the above is open to the charge of verificationist induction, which only broader investigation could dispel. Nevertheless, there is one defence against the charge that the analysis was simply nudging people into a typology. This is that only fifteen of the twenty subjects could be clustered into one of the three modes of reflexivity. The remaining five interviewees simply did not fit. They were also distinctive in being people with overt problems, though their difficulties were very different in kind and in origin. After re-listening to their five tapes, what became clear for all was that their internal conversations were doing very little indeed to help resolve their problems, since inner dialogue augmented emotional distress without contributing instrumentally to a way forward. The effect was to induce agential passivity. These became people to whom things happened, rather than active agents who could make things happen, by assuming some governance in their own lives. As damaged people (*pro tem*), part of what had sustained damage or disruption was their reflexivity itself. The process by which the sequence 'concerns → projects → practices' is internally monitored seemed to have become distorted by external assaults upon subjects' ultimate concerns. Hence the notion of 'fractured reflexivity' was explored for this group, as an extension of the general conviction that the life of the mind is not a fixed, psychological faculty, but is an emergent, and therefore relational property, which is open to mutation. The eventual outcome of such potential mutations would require longitudinal investigation.

One of these five subjects was a young man with the barest possible life of the mind, which approximated to near non-reflexivity – making him the most 'fractured' of reflexives. He also had the most appalling background of family rejection and had been living rough on the streets since he was thirteen years old. His reflexive limitations made him the most 'passive' of agents, because his virtual inability to converse with himself deprived him of active control over his own life and the circumstances he confronted. His existence invites much further consideration of the background conditions which restrict the development of that most central of personal emergent powers, our reflexivity, and of the social consequences of conceptualising oneself as an object towards which things merely happen.

The results of this analysis and the order in which the three modes of reflexivity are examined are presented in figure 5.2.

[near non-reflexive]
Jason

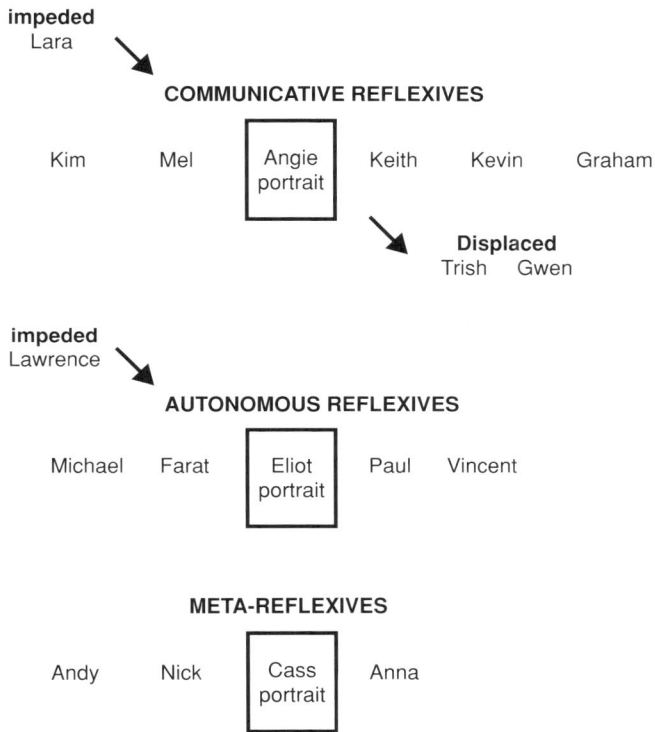

impeded
Lara

COMMUNICATIVE REFLEXIVES

Kim   Mel   Angie   Keith   Kevin   Graham
                      portrait

                                      Displaced
                                      Trish   Gwen

impeded
Lawrence

AUTONOMOUS REFLEXIVES

Michael   Farat   Eliot   Paul   Vincent
                            portrait

META-REFLEXIVES

Andy   Nick   Cass   Anna
                        portrait

Figure 5.2 Modes of reflexivity: guide to twenty subjects.

The limits of exploration

Each of the following four chapters constitutes a hypothesis in its own right. Chapters 6, 7 and 8 suggest that there are such different modes of reflexivity as to warrant distinguishing between 'communicative reflexives', 'autonomous reflexives' and 'meta-reflexives'. In chapter 9, the argument is advanced that 'fractured reflexivity' frequently results from an 'impediment' to, or a 'displacement' from, one of the above modes. The implications (also hypothetical) of the most significant finding – that the three modes of reflexivity mediate socio-cultural constraints and enablements in quite distinctive ways and represent entirely different 'stances' towards social structures and cultural systems – will be taken up in the Conclusion.

However promising one's hypotheses might seem to be, and that is what is self-consciously promoted in the next four chapters, it is well to be clear about the matters upon which one is bound to be mute. These are the limits of exploration, which are objective, rather than matters of subjective self-deprecation. So, what we cannot know from this exploratory venture are the following:

- The distribution of the different modes of reflexivity throughout the population, including the possibility that further modes may be identified.
- The causal contribution of quantitative and qualitative aspects of 'contextual continuity/discontinuity' to the emergence of each of the three modes of reflexivity.
- The distributions of 'impeded', 'displaced' and 'under-developed' reflexivity among the population and whether a radical transformation of one's type of inner conversation can be successfully accomplished.
- How the different *individual* modes of reflexivity, which mediate constraints and enablements in quite distinctive ways, are also related to *collective* action. Even were all else to be substantiated, this would remain the missing link in a complete account of the interplay between structure and agency as responsible for morphostasis and morphogenesis in society or part of it.

6   Communicative reflexives

Everyone is a reflexive being. This means that we deliberate about our circumstances in relation to ourselves and, in the light of these deliberations, we determine our own personal courses of action in society. Nevertheless we do not all exercise our reflexivity in the same way. Everyone has a domain of mental privacy from which they subjectively survey and evaluate their external circumstances, within which they savour their satisfactions or nurture their discontents, and through which they monitor their future doings. The vehicle for all of this is the internal conversation. However, the nature of our internal conversations is far from being identical and such differences exceed personal idiosyncrasies. These varying types of internal conversation are important because they are inextricably related to different forms of deliberations and, ultimately, to the kind of *modus vivendi* which an agent seeks to establish in the world.

Even within the small group which was interviewed, one sub-group could readily be distinguished as 'communicative reflexives'. These are people who do indeed initiate internal dialogues in the privacy of their own minds, but that is not where they complete them. Instead, their pattern is one of 'thought and talk'. Having raised an issue intra-personally, they seek to resolve it inter-personally. They share their problems, discuss decisions and thus externalise much of what, to other interviewees, remains intrinsically an internal deliberative process. For the 'communicative reflexive', subsequent decisions about what to do, how to act and, ultimately, who to be, are held open to the dialogical influences of those with whom they share their concerns. In other words, the membrane between the life of the mind and the life of the group is highly permeable and there is regular two-way trafficking between them.

'Communicative reflexives' share two distinctive sets of characteristics. On the one hand, as individual people, they all admit to considerable doubt that a fully autonomous internal conversation could lead them to right action. It is not that they suspect that it would lead them to wrong action, but rather they are profoundly unsure that internal dialogue, conducted entirely alone, could complete the process and culminate in self-resolution. Instead, the fear is that without external consultation, their internal conversations would revolve inconclusively. As we will see, this external reliance is closely coupled with a mistrustful dismissiveness about private mental deliberations. That these take place, this sub-group never denies. They plan, imagine and rehearse through self-talk, as do all others, but are convinced that 'things never work out as they planned'. This greater awareness of contingency itself, or of their own inability to factor all the necessary considerations into their solitary deliberations, seems to be what precipitates them to supplement their interior dialogues with exterior ones. Because inter-personal exchanges are regarded as being more trustworthy, the consequence is to regard their own internal conversations with suspicion, if not negativity. Flights of fancy, consideration of 'deep matters', or dwelling on possibilities rather than probabilities, all may be simultaneously avowed yet treated dismissively. In all likelihood, they 'mean nothing' and thus do not merit much attention from these subjects themselves. Since the lone self, or rather the self alone, is not considered to be a trustworthy guide, then there is self-censorship; above all keep your feet on the ground and do not let the internal conversation take you into rarefied reaches where its fallibility would only be greater.

Secondly, the six core 'communicative reflexives' share three salient characteristics which are associated with their pattern of using external consultation to complete their inner deliberations. To begin with, since this is their deliberative pattern, they must have other people with whom they can share. Although we have all heard of those chance meetings on trains, when people supposedly bare their souls to a complete stranger, precisely because they will never see him or her again, such brief encounters do not resonate with the needs of our present group. If self-mistrust prompts them to communication, then their interlocutors have to have earned the trust placed in them. The first feature, common to the group, ensured that they all had such dialogical partners in plenty. All six people possessed an exceptionally high degree of 'contextual continuity', compared with the other two types of reflexives. They defied both modernistic tenets about the breakdown of the extended family and also post-modern notions of fragmented human relations, ones where we engage in 'kibitzing' upon, rather than commitment to any form of social interaction. Instead, this sub-group has shown little geographical mobility, has retained dense and intense relationships with family and friends, and maintains considerable occupational continuity with both. As interlocutors, this close circle of family and friends were 'tested and true'. Moreover, they not only knew our subjects 'inside out', as the saying goes, but were closely acquainted with their past and present

circumstances and intimately involved with their current contexts, because these were commonly their own too.

Of course there is an immediate temptation to suggest that the 'communicative reflexive' is such precisely because of this biography of 'contextual
continuity', which has never left them to their own mental devices alone.
This would be premature, because there are members of both other sub-
groups who had reached maturity and begun working life with the same
biographical background. It would also be too deterministic, because it
is not the case that once a 'communicative reflexive', this remains one's
deliberative style for life. Examination of our two 'displaced persons' will
reveal that this is not the case; forms of reflexivity are mutable as well as
being susceptible of 'fragmentation'. Finally, it would be over-simplistic
because the contextual facility of being able to share thoughts with close
others is not the only feature that 'communicative reflexives' have in
common.

Their next characteristic is a smooth dovetailing of their multiple concerns. This group of six all unequivocally designated their 'family and
friends' as being their ultimate concern, and one that greatly outdistanced
other concerns in every single case. They were the only respondents to
name 'people' as what they cared about most, if we also include the two
individuals 'displaced' from this sub-group. Equally importantly, at the
time of interview, none reported anything other than the ease with which
their other concerns, particularly those of work and leisure, were harmo-
niously accommodated to their prime concern. Not one of the six foresaw
future dovetailing to be problematic, unlike the 'meta-reflexives', who,
though unhesitant in designating their ultimate concerns, had difficulties in subordinating their other concerns and thus in achieving a stable
pattern of accommodation. Dovetailing is a reflexive achievement and
for two respondents in particular, it had been hard won through painful
learning and deliberative self-monitoring. These were both men whose
first marriages had broken down and whose determination to make a
success of their re-partnerings had entailed bringing other concerns into
line and ensuring that they continued to be accommodated in due order.

The final feature, shared by all six 'communicative reflexives' was a
marked degree of contentment with the *modus vivendi* which each had
established. This was not a failure to imagine how things could be better;
indeed most were quite specific about changes in their circumstances that
would improve their lot. Yet this was what was distinctive about them; it
was circumstantial change which would make a difference, rather than any
form of self-change. In this, they were utterly unlike the 'meta-reflexives'
whose questing self-critique demanded more change in themselves than
in their surroundings, even if these would ideally change too. They were

also dissimilar from the 'autonomous reflexives' who believed that a constant self-monitoring always had been and always would be necessary for the achievement of their goals or the meeting of their commitments. It was not that members of the latter two sub-groups lacked their 'quantum of solace' or lived in deep existential angst. That was the poignant condition of the two individuals who were impeded from fully exercising the different types of reflexivity towards which they strongly tended. It was rather that those who fully exemplified either 'autonomous' or 'meta-' reflexivity were, in a fundamental sense, still travellers towards a goal – the realisation of their ultimate concerns. By contrast, the 'communicative reflexives' had fundamentally reached their objectives or, if very young, nevertheless saw the goal as being within reach. In this they expressed a literal self-satisfaction which, being largely devoid of pride or self-congratulation, is probably best represented as simple contentment.

Before exploring these three features – 'contextual continuity', 'dove-tailing of concerns' and 'contentment' with the *modi vivendi* established, it seems essential to breathe some life into that dry term, 'communicative reflexive'. Without some hermeneutic grasp of this kind of life of the mind, it is impossible to understand how those who deliberate in this way also pilot themselves through society – since it is not everyone's way and it is not the only way through the world. What I hope to show is that 'communicative reflexives' have a very special relationship indeed to structural (and cultural) constraints and enablements. This is by virtue of the projects that they entertain, the manner in which they monitor their circumstances and the practices which they establish. Yet before any of this can carry conviction, we need to come as close as we can to someone whose personal reflexivity is of this kind.

Angie Fletcher: a picture of a 'communicative reflexive'

Angie, a full-time secretary, was picked for this 'close-up' because at the age of thirty-seven she is in the middle of the sub-group. She has both a pattern of established practices behind her and the expectation of a large portion of her life before her, which could mean the time in which to pursue new and different life-projects. I began by establishing that Angie does engage in internal dialogue and we started to probe it together. Immediately the matter of decision-making arose and Angie's response was a clear intimation of her 'thought and talk' procedure. 'If it's a major decision, I'll talk to somebody about it. But if it's sort of a relatively minor decision, I'll probably just sort of "umm and aah" in my head to myself a little bit, and then formulate the right decision. A big decision, I would discuss with people. It's a reassurance really, isn't it? You've done the right thing. Sometimes I take different things from a different point of view then. I never thought of that sort of thing.' Angie trusts her own deliberations only for minor matters, but seeks the reassurance of others when larger issues are at stake. Incidentally she reveals that she has never reflected upon herself as having this pattern of deliberation – her last sentence came after a pause, whilst the distinction she made between major and minor decisions was spoken very readily.

If Angie mistrusts herself in big matters, whom would she trust and turn to in order to talk things through? She answers, 'Friends really, I suppose – friends or my Mum and boyfriend or whoever's around at the time really. Everyone thinks – if someone's been there, done that, got the T-shirt, been through what the decision involves, I'll go to them. It just depends, really – whoever's around, I suppose.' Angie seems confident that her close circle would possess the necessary experience or expertise, but equally she repeats that whichever friend is around could serve as her interlocutor.

Not only does Angie trust them more than she trusts herself, but also she is correspondingly negative about her inner conversation, when conducted alone. I ask her if she can give any idea about the frequency of lone inner dialogue – does she talk to herself most days? 'No', she replied, 'not most days. If something's playing on my mind I will think about it all day, but, on the whole I'm not too bad, I don't think really – I'm not a worrier.' This close association between self-talk and worrying rather surprised me, but less so than the feeling she expressed that it was rather a good thing not to have too much inner conversation. One reason for this emerged when we discussed 'practising' or 'rehearsing' for a testing encounter, such as an important job interview or a difficult meeting with a friend. Angie maintained that when she was going to an interview, 'No I don't [rehearse]. Not really, because at the end of the day you don't know what you're going to be asked anyway. I'd probably think of the points I want to try to get across, but no, I don't, not really.' Angie believes that there are too many uncertainties involved for her mental rehearsal to be of utility. Her respect for contingency, popularly known as 'sod's law', is common to this sub-group. Yet there is more behind her reaction than pragmatic considerations. Angie does not engage in any of the freer forms of mental activity, such as 're-living', holding 'imaginary conversations', 'daydreaming' or speculation. She does not consider herself to be imaginative or to go in for thinking 'what if . . . ?' 'No, only when the alarm clock goes off in the morning and, "Oh, I wish I could win the lottery and didn't have to get up today". But nothing, just sort of silly things really.' Thus Angie is very dismissive of her intra-personal ruminations because they are not seen as serious explorations of real possibilities; they are just 'sillinesses'. They are 'silly', not merely because the contingency is so un-likely, but rather because such intra-personal thoughts are so much less important to Angie than her inter-personal considerations.

What was marked was that those types of inner deliberations, such as 'mulling over', 'deciding' or 'clarifying', which could very well be taken to apply to abstract matters, were systematically interpreted and exemplified by Angie in an inter-personal manner. 'Mulling over' or 'dwelling upon', I suggested, could involve a problem, a relationship or an event. Angie seized on the personal: 'If I've done something that I've not got right, I think, "Oh gosh, I wish I hadn't done that." Or if I've really embarrassed myself and done something really stupid, that will play on my mind for a bit, yes, definitely. I won't be happy until I'm like – if it involves somebody else, that I apologise or something... I think once I've apologised and know people have sort of either laughed it off or forgotten about it, yeah, I can relax a bit more about it then. I can't relax about it myself until after I've apologised.' Similarly, 'decisions' always affected other people, who had in consequence to be taken into account, and 'clarifying' was about what people might have meant or if they could have taken something the wrong way.

Angie's inner conversation clearly reflects her priorities, which are 'Definitely family and friends – I'm very conscious about things like that.' She is not only conscious but also considerate, thoughtful and generous towards them in her mental life. In fact, consideration of them is rarely absent from her internal conversation. As she goes out and about, she is monitoring experiences, not just for herself, but for them too. 'If I'm out, I'll think, "Oh, you know, my Mum would like it here, like to come here", or "Oh, I don't like it here; Mum wouldn't like it." That sort of thing. I sometimes think, "Oh so and so would like it here, we'll have to do that" and bear things in mind.' These mental deliberations directly com-plement the nature, intensity and above all the continuity of her social life.

To appreciate the extent of this 'contextual continuity' we have to go back to Angie's earliest years, whose key figures then continue to be central today. Had Angie generally received support from her family? Her response anticipated the third theme common to 'communicative reflexives' – that of contentment. At home, Angie 'always felt secure. My Mum and Dad were happily married and I was brought up in a loving environment. They've got lots of friends who are always around.' This is an interesting slip into the present tense, for Angie's father is now dead; it might even be that the similarity between past and present patterns of sociability blurs the divide. Be that as it may, 'There's always lots going on. And I was quite happy at school. I think what you hear about some people going through, I was very lucky, definitely. I lived quite a sheltered childhood, I think really. Protected.' A number of Angie's friends go back to these earliest days. She met the woman who has remained her best friend at the age of two, school friends were always welcome around the house and the building up of the rest of her dense network is continuous with her biography.

What is important here is that her life to date by choice and by history is also one of '*contextual* continuity' – devoid of breaks. At eleven or twelve, Angie considered a career in nursing. Then, 'I decided I was a bit too squeamish, so I didn't. Then I decided I liked clerical work, I liked typing and that, so just sort of went from there.' Although she remarks that one of the attractions of secretarial work was that 'it wasn't a mucky job', even more significant was the 'contextual continuity'. 'I know lots of people that were secretaries. My Mum was a secretary and my Auntie was a secretary. Lots of my Mum's friends were secretaries. Just the sort of environment I've grown up in really.' Angie proceeded to replicate this environment. After taking her 'O'-levels, she went on to college and gained a business diploma, underwent a spell of work experience and then took up full-time secretarial employment with a large electrical company. College yielded a group of seven friends, who are still in close regular contact nearly twenty years later, and the electrical company another cluster, who have become interwoven with the former. This friendship group has readily enfolded boyfriends, who now have their own 'lads' nights', and is resilient enough to accommodate the children of married members, who even come on some of their many holidays. Obviously, the female members of this friendship network not only share the same socio-economic status, but precisely the same occupational context as Angie herself, so the environment in which she grew up continues to be her environment.

It reaches backward and forward, reinforcing its continuity by the intensity of contact: 'I see my Mum about twice a week I suppose, and I see my Auntie about once a month, and then cousins and that – I don't see my cousins very often. I see my uncles probably about once a month. It just depends what's going on. Not a regular sort of set pattern. I don't tend to speak to them on the phone – my relatives – as much as my friends, but I speak to my Mum, I suppose, not every day, but certainly every other day I'm on the phone.' She continues in the same vein about her friends. Angie usually meets her best friend (the one of thirty-five years' standing) once a week and, with others in her network, always does 'something on a Friday or Saturday with them, and then probably a couple of nights in the week. Probably four nights I'd say ... depending on what's going on.' Since there is so much going on, little time or space is found or created for extraneous people. Moreover, all the novel experiences, which the group shares, through its hectic programme, are filtered through the friendship network. Even if she marries, as she hopes, Angie does not see this as threatening a break-up of her network. 'I mean perhaps we wouldn't see each other as much, but we'd always be there for each other, I'd like to think. And still sort of go out and do things and not forget about each other.'

This presumption about future dovetailing is an extension of Angie's experience of how smoothly her concerns have always dovetailed in the past. What are the most important areas of her life now? She not only volunteers a hierarchical list of her concerns but, without prompting, also stresses their harmoniousness: 'Sort of your family, your social life, your friends, your work. It's a combination of things isn't it really? I think because one sort of complements the other, doesn't it? It sort of builds up a pattern there really – definitely.' It never seems to have been problematic for Angie that this pattern does gel. She mentions how her parents used to like all her friends, so that this was not an area of conflict. Angie herself had introduced work as one of her subordinate concerns and I wonder after she was made redundant by the electrical company about seven years ago, how her subsequent job in a big educational institution has dovetailed with her ongoing concerns. 'Yeah, they work quite well together really. They sort of intermingle, you know.' I ask myself which of these two statements is the more accurate. Does Angie simply mean that her work and social life are mutually compatible, or does she mean that they are actually intertwined?

Angie has admitted that work is a subordinate concern, instrumental to her social life: 'if you didn't work you wouldn't be able to [enjoy yourself] would you? It's as simple as that.' Yet it turns out to be rather more important and complex. This is because Angie is actually looking for inter-personal satisfaction at work; she is actively working to enhance the dovetailing of this concern with others. Although she accentuates the importance of money, especially now that she has a mortgage to service, Angie volunteers the need to balance her salary against her ultimate and inter-personal concerns. 'Obviously it's important [money]. But I'd rather work in a nice, happy, friendly, environment for a lesser salary, than work in an environment and get a bit more money and absolutely dread it and hate it, and hate going into work and have the boss from hell – it's a case of balancing it out, isn't it really?'

This balancing or dovetailing is an active enterprise on Angie's part, because what she is looking for at work is again friendship and close personal relations. Her horror is meeting with unfriendliness at work, which would be discontinuous with her ultimate concern. 'I can think of nothing worse than having a job where your colleagues were horrible and couldn't bother to talk to you or stabbed you in the back and that. Oh, no, I couldn't be doing with that. I think you're at work for thirty-six hours a week, you know, and I think it makes it pleasanter if you're nice to each other.' Angie means what she says; she quit the only job where she ever experienced this unpleasantness, after one week. Conversely, her definition of a good colleague does stress some work qualities, but strongly emphasises their personal ones, which would literally make them working friends. Angie's ideal colleague is 'Someone that's nice and chatty and happy. Someone that, you know, will help you if necessary, the same as you would do for them . . . Just someone who's pleasant to be with really. Someone whose company you can enjoy – can have a bit of a laugh with. I know you come to work to work, but it's nice to have a laugh, isn't it.' Correspondingly, she herself puts in effort to make work a place of conviviality: first up with the Christmas decorations, always prepared to organise an office outing, and ever ready for a celebration. Dovetailing is not something that just happens, it is an accomplishment that has to be worked at by the subject.

From all of this, Angie appears to derive considerable contentment, something she herself puts down to 'being lucky'. She reports only one brief and miserable experience, temping at a large insurance company after her involuntary redundancy. 'It was awful. I could not have worked in that environment. There was four of us in the office and the minute one of the girls went off to the loo or went home or whatever, they'd all sort of say, "Her skirt's too tight" or "She slept with him last night". I'd think, I can't be doing with it. You got paranoid then; what are they going to be saying about me when I go, you know? I absolutely hate that.' She quickly left; this setting was far too dissonant with her desired *modus vivendi*. Now she says she is happy at work, has a boyfriend, her own home and a social life packed with droppings-in, meals out, theatre visits, trips and outings plus, on average, a couple of holidays a year. Is this entire whirl simply for variety and entertainment? The role of her friendship network seems to go much deeper; it is a source of support, which also fosters self-esteem and banishes the spectre of being socially unwanted. For Angie, 'I think you go out with your friends and you have a good laugh and it gives you a real good lift and makes you feel wanted and needed, I suppose. You have a good time and you get phone calls. And there's nothing more depressing than sort of being at home and thinking "Oh no one's phoned me tonight" and "I can't go out tonight", you know. Definitely, yeah, it all does help, doesn't it?'

The 'communicative reflexive' *needs* to communicate. Low value is attached to lone thinking and there is low tolerance of one's own company.

In this crowded network with its frequent contacts, Angie has no difficulty in exercising her 'thought and talk' mode of reflexivity. Integral to her, it pervaded the interview. Most of Angie's statements end with a question. These 'isn't it's?' and 'doesn't it's?' are syntactical invitations to me, as interviewer, to affirm the thought, to share experiences and to turn every utterance into the first move in a conversation. It is not that Angie lacks a private life of the mind, or fails to engage in silent self-monitoring, but she regards this as incomplete until supplemented by an inter-personal exchange. One way of expressing this is that for Angie, the private/public barrier is extremely thin: she wants and expects it to be constantly breached.

'Communicative reflexives' across the age-range

There are five other people whose internal deliberations conform to the 'thought and talk' pattern; two are women and three men. Their ages range from seventeen to sixty-two. The first question to answer is how closely their modes of reflexivity resemble those of Angie's? It will be recalled that she was selected as the portrait for the group because she fell in the middle of the age range. She had developed well-established practices, but could still look ahead to a future in which she might wish to adopt new life-projects. Part of the interest lies in how far the accumulation of experiences, over their life-courses, has tended to modify the internal conversations of the 'communicative reflexives' in any way. This entails the assumption that the three modes of inner dialogue which have been disengaged are not immutable; they are not psychologically reducible to something akin to fixed personality types. Without a longitudinal study, which could monitor such changes, reliance has to be placed upon interviewees' reported learning experiences and retrospective accounts of changes in their deliberative process.

This introduction to five new people will focus upon the nature of their deliberative processes, as individual variations upon this common type. Only then will the three characteristics associated with the communicative pattern be introduced. These three features will then be considered seriatim in relation to the theoretical considerations presented in chapter 4. The same format will be adopted for the 'autonomous reflexives' in chapter 7 and the 'meta-reflexives' in chapter 8.

Kim and Mel are two hairdressing apprentices, aged seventeen and eighteen, who work in the same salon. Kim is the most extreme example of 'communicative reflexivity'. She had no difficulty with the notion of holding an inner conversation, but she steadily maintained that as soon as something began to go through her head, she immediately precipitated herself into inter-personal dialogue. Her first reaction established this pattern: 'I just say things if I think of something.' I pressed her whether this was always the case; did she ever keep thoughts to herself? 'No' said Kim, 'I don't really because I just like say 'em out if I'm thinking of something. I don't really normally keep it in me. So I just say it outside.' She shows a remarkable consistency; in so far as she engages in any of the mental activities on the prompt list, they are always quickly comple-mented and completed by external conversations. Whether it be planning holidays or planning the next day, she will actually use other people as her *aides-mémoires*. She jots things down, but 'It's mainly like talking to him [her boyfriend] about holidays, or anybody if I've got to plan some-thing. To my Mum or somebody. I'll say "I've got to do this tomorrow, I've got to do that."' Similarly, when I ask her about 'clarifying' things to herself, her response is to externalise it: 'If me and my boyfriend have an argument – well I like to talk it out, you know, and speak about what happened and everything.'

It seems as if when Kim is alone and knows she cannot move onto talking then she barely deliberates at all, unless put on the spot. The one example she offered was about rehearsing her lines for a difficult conversation: 'I had to actually do something this morning and I was practising saying it in my head, what I had to say. Because I had to phone up for my boyfriend for his community service, because he didn't go in yesterday because he had got bad stomach cramps. And I was like saying in my head what I'd say to her [the case officer] and like I had to repeat it about three times because she didn't like understand me. So that made it worse for me, but I got it over in the end.' Kim is not confident about the value of rehearsing and displays Angie's familiar negativity towards such internal deliberations: 'Normally I get it wrong. So, I don't think it's a good idea to practise.' Kim also shows that she is not an acute self-monitor of herself on the job. Beyond carrying lists in her head of what to do next, she does not monitor her own performance, other than noting her boredom, nor does she monitor clients' moods or bearing and adapt accordingly.

Mel too is undoubtedly a 'communicative reflexive'. Early on she tells me about a big dispute with her boyfriend and the problem of being alone when this occurred. 'Two of my best friends – my friend Paula, she went away to Finland on a world challenge thing, and my other friend was away on holiday as well at the same time, when me and my boyfriend had this like huge argument. And I didn't think anything of it until I needed them, and then I was I suppose, you know, thinking, "I wish they were here" and things like that. Definitely, I'd have gone round to them and talked – yeah, or even just to get it off my chest you know – just shout at them. They can take it.' But Mel, who is deeply attached to her boyfriend/fiancé is clearly having difficulties because he does not complement her 'thought and talk' on some of the topics that genuinely concern her. She mentions that with her two best friends (the three of them grew up alongside one another), she would have 'deep conversations about why we're here and all that'. Then she would dwell upon this internally 'for ages' and another exchange would ensue. As far as considering the meaning of life is concerned, 'My boyfriend thinks I'm mad.' Is Mel now being thrown back more upon her internal resources and learning to sustain an autonomous internal conversation?

Certainly in some areas she does. Although when she 'plans', 'decides' and 're-lives', these are matters of 'thought and talk', Mel is definitely imaginative and assures me that she has always been that way, often engaging in 'what if' thoughts, both good (what if I became famous) and bad (or had a car accident). She confides an evocative little episode, whose concluding words reinforce my idea that circumstances are encouraging Mel to turn more inward and to forego the conversational complement. 'One time my Mum had gone away for the weekend and me and my boyfriend were in my house watching a video. I was lying on the sofa and he was in the chair, and I was just thinking, "Oh wouldn't this be nice if we were married", and I could imagine a little baby on my lap – cuddling my little baby. And he come and jumped on me and I nearly said to him, "Oh watch the baby", because I'd got so deep into it. Then I thought, "No I'd better not say that." '

Her self-monitoring goes much further than just biting off her words and it extends to work in the salon and difficult encounters. At the moment Mel is learning cutting and styling. She wants to be good at both: 'So I make sure all my attention's on that. And I do talk myself through it, thinking shall I cut this bit, you know. I always have a picture of what I want it to look like afterwards in my head.' Similarly, when we discuss 'rehearsing', Mel tells how she reflected upon going back to the dentist about a crown, which had already been replaced twice, unsatisfactorily. 'I don't like to go in there and cause a fuss, you know, because we get it here. We get like horrible clients that come back and they're not happy and they're really horrible about it. So I have like to figure out what I'm going to say because I don't want to go in there and sound like I'm being a pest.' It appears as if Mel's growing self-awareness is helping her towards greater occupational and social skills, as she talks to herself as subject in relation to her social environment as object.

Yet she herself is dubious about the value of self-talk and uneasy with the conundrum of 'who is talking to whom'. Sensing Mel might be starting self-contained inner conversations, above and beyond her childhood daydreaming. I finally press her about situations in which she has no interlocutor. We start discussing experimenting with make-up, alone in front of a mirror, and her opening words are revealing: 'It sounds a bit sad actually, if I'm just putting my make-up on, I'll have a conversation with me, you know. So I'll talk to me and talk to myself about that, or – I don't know if it's me or someone else that I'm thinking. But yeah, I always have conversations in my head. It could be about anything – stupid things.' To get away from the negativity, I suggest that since I've never been any good with eye-shadow, I think that my own self-talk would be a running commentary on my messy effects. Far from seconding this, Mel sticks to her dismissiveness: 'I don't know. I just come out with a load of crap really [laugh]. Which doesn't mean anything. It's just . . .' Mel at eighteen is a 'thinker and talker', with flashes of a different reflexive mode; any potential change to another mode would depend upon her coming to recognise positive advantages to autonomous internal conversation or continuing to dismiss it.

In turning now to two men in their early forties, I find with both Keith and Kevin that it is precisely their lasting mistrustfulness of their internal deliberations, as guides to action, which induces them to be 'communicative reflexives'. In the case of Keith, a forty-five year old electrical foreman, this is personal distrust which is reinforced occupationally by a need for double-checking in a job where mistakes could be dangerous. For Kevin, a forty-three year old deputy head-porter in a large institution, his distrust stems more from a learned respect for the growing contingencies of life. Significantly, the other feature they share, besides having their families and friends as their ultimate concern, like everyone else in this sub-group, is that they place far more emphasis upon the nuclear unit alone. Moreover, both deeply regret the breakdown of their first marriages and are correspondingly grateful for the success of their second ones. Therefore, one of the elements to explore is how far the intimate exchanges, which characterise their re-partnerings, have actually reinforced their 'communicative reflexivity'.

Keith has no shadow of doubt where his ultimate concern lies: 'Nearest and dearest, you know. They come first before everything. There'd be no hesitation about them. If there was a problem, then I'm there for them. They are your life aren't they?' He met his second wife eleven years ago, is evidently well pleased with their compatibility, and both work hard to blend her daughter and his son into a family unit. He admits to dwelling upon any threat to its smooth functioning, but this is very much a conjoint exercise that is dependent upon 'thought and talk'. 'Me and my wife can talk, you know. That's one good thing. So most of it gets aired out – sorted out.' Nevertheless, encouraging his wife into the complementary role takes effort: 'she's different, she does bottle a lot of things up. I do sort of have to force things out of her. Yeah, I do try to keep things smooth.' Much of the time, this effort seems to have worked, because when I tap various kinds of mental activity with Keith he does not respond in the first-person but answers in terms of how 'we' plan and dream. When a problem does come along, such as monitoring his sixteen-year old stepdaughter's dating, Keith has tried privately practising how in conversation to resolve this, but is unconvinced about the efficacy of solitary rehearsal. 'As much as it's in my head what I want to say to her, it doesn't come out. I don't know why.' Therefore his preferred mode of dealing with such situations is to talk them through. 'I think with family and friends a lot of the time I can actually say it rather than just be thinking it. You know you can get away with it with certain people – I tend to go and say it most of the time. It can be taken the right way without somebody sort of taking offence, rather than just keeping it in your head and thinking it.'

Yet at work, Keith has learned that he cannot spontaneously exercise his preferred pattern. Employed on an electrical sub-contract, he has to take part in building progress meetings in which 'we're sitting there and they say what they want [doing] and then it's going through your head thinking, "he doesn't know what he's talking about". But to them, you can't really say it; you have to be careful.' He expresses his frustration when the 'thought and talk' mode is unavailing, even with carefully self-monitored circumlocution, because 'they're sort of asking you to do something that can't really be done and you can't make it clear to them that you can't do it – it's not possible'. Yet far from abandoning his 'communicative reflexivity' in these circumstances, Keith takes a detour and then persists with it. He recognises that he has 'to sort of prove it at the end of the day', but is also very aware that lone deliberative decisiveness will not work on a site which requires co-operation between contractors. So, 'yeah, you have to do it and say, "look that's it, that's the best it gets". Just try and actually take them physically and see something to explain it and get it through to them.'

In general however, the demands of team-working on site and the necessity of ensuring the safety of electrical installations are factors which re-inforce his pattern of reflexivity. This becomes clear when we talk about 'clarification' in relation to technical problems. Keith needs to be sure that complex layouts of wiring are correct, and the best form of reassurance is inter-personal. 'Get support along the way . . . you think it works this way, but it may not, so you just want to phone somebody up or get somebody else's opinion, just to make sure it is right.' 'Communicative reflexivity' is an achievement which takes effort from Keith at home and at work, but effectively the two both reinforce the same pattern of deliberation for him.

Kevin has also been re-partnered for eleven years, but his job in an educational institution does not entail the kinds of technical problems which reinforced Keith's 'communicative reflexivity'. Rather, because he is constantly encountering people who are sources of new ideas and because his partner has recently enrolled on a psychology course, it is the nature of their very 'thought and talk' pattern which is put under some strain, since both are constantly assimilating new information and perspectives. One of the effects of 'contextual continuity' is that it provides shared settings, which effectively confine talk to familiar ground. Kevin has this background, but his foreground is more exposed. He admits that his re-partnering has always had its problems, perhaps because it has lacked a common context in which to anchor conversation, but this has been intensified since his partner started doing psychology. 'Really this psychology course armed her with different information, like body language and actually what you're saying and how...she was able then to dissect things, right, and come up with answers or reasons. But what I found is they weren't applicable.' It sounds as though they are in discursive difficulties.

Kevin gives a telling example about an uneasy pub-lunch. During this his partner seemed distracted and was constantly glancing around. When asked why she was not looking at him and chatting easily, she said that she was uncomfortable about infringing upon someone else's space in a busy pub and also countered that his continuous eye-contact indicated a 'super confidence'. Kevin denied it and explained that his father always insisted that 'you look at me when I'm talking to you, otherwise I'll clip you round the ear 'ole'. Matters are not helped because Kevin regards many of her new concepts as psychobabble: 'I think half of these things are garbage.' This might imply that his old background and the middle ground they have forged together are now seriously threatened by her new foreground.

Not necessarily, because Kevin too is a magpie with new ideas. He is particularly taken-up with exploring gender distinctions, to the point where he and his partner are willing to experiment together about whether a man can become as adept at interspersing cooking, ironing and clearing up as he admits most women to be. Kevin places a very high premium upon joint activities with his partner and son, having recognised that his first marriage probably broke down because, as a couple, they were simply too busy for one another. It could then be that he and his new partner might negotiate a broadened communicative repertoire. He remarks that there are stages in any relationship, from early lust to what he nicely terms 'growing comfortability', which he is working hard to foster. Yet his very manner of articulating his internal reflections, as subject upon his relationship as object, indicates that rather like young Mel, he is also being propelled towards a more autonomous inner conversation.

Graham, the oldest member of this sub-group at sixty-two, has been led to a certain amount of self-contained reflection by his work rather than by his stable marriage of nearly forty years' duration. Occupationally he has undergone considerable mobility, from starting out as a bricklaying apprentice to becoming the general foreman on a thirteen million-pound building project. Fundamentally he remains a 'communicative reflexive', as he shows in several ways. Firstly, he places considerable reliance upon staff meetings on site, often initiates them, and finds them very necessary for double-checking that nothing is overlooked. 'Well, this company now, we have staff meetings. We don't have an official time for it, but sometimes I'll say to Stephen [site manager], "It's time we had a staff meeting", so we all know which direction we're going in, and we find out our problems out there. You know, if one of your colleagues says "You haven't done this" or "You should have done that." ' He has no doubt about the value of these frequent public exchanges, not only for co-ordination, but error-detection. Some might wonder, 'is it necessary, this meeting, but it is. It may be that only two or three things develop out of this twenty minutes, but they're very important things – probably one that was forgotten.' Similarly, on an everyday basis, Graham will complete his own deliberations by inter-personal consultations: 'Well, lots of times I will just sit in my office there and I'll be mulling over something out there and then come back and ask Paul [project manager] or Stephen [site manager] what we ought to be doing – or say "we're not doing this, but we ought to be doing it now and not in two weeks' time." ' Finally, he sees extensive exchanges as being reciprocally beneficial, especially with the apprentices. He believes that much of his worth on site is his willingness to share his accumulated knowledge. 'Project managers, they like to see me on their job because I'm the life and soul of the job, you know, with past experience. So it's, "Graham, have you done that?" – "Yeah, I've done that." You have a vast range of experience that you can feed back to the young lads that are coming up in the market place.'

Nevertheless, Graham has huge responsibilities, keeping track of every man on site, ensuring that tasks on different levels do not endanger other workers, dovetailing delivery of material and machinery safely on a restricted site, monitoring safety standards and inducting new teams of contractors. As he describes his working life, this has gradually led him to engage in more and more autonomous internal conversation. He tells me that right now, it is going through his head 'there's a scaffler down there doing a table and another [man] doing an adaptation right inside, so what I'm saying is your mind is ticking. It doesn't shut off. Although we're talking, you're still ticking over. You can't shut off completely.' Graham welcomes this as 'being on the ball', he does it during his fifty-six mile journey to the site – 'You're driving, you're listening to music and you're listening to other things coming into your own head at the same time.' Only when he is busy at home can he switch it off.

By now, he knows that this non-communicative inner dialogue is necessary, that he has to 'plan', 'rehearse' and 'clarify' things in order to stay on top of the job. Nevertheless, he retains the old prejudice about people who talk to themselves, especially when he admits to imaginative practice: 'I'm not going daft or anything.' He seems mistrustful of himself in the context of new training courses and rehearsing for them: 'You're talking to yourself silent on what you're going to say and what he's going to say back to you, and when we go and deliver our presentation, it completely went the opposite way.' Graham is an old believer that sod's law can't be outdone mentally: 'The stupid things that people do – and you're thinking, "he can't do that." When you get there, he's doing that.' Work has made Graham no stranger to the self-contained inner dialogue; he acknowledges its necessity to him, but has he made a friend of it? Significantly, in his home-life and duties as a parish councillor he seemed to fall back upon his preferred dialogical mode of reflexivity, underpinned by huge amounts of shared experiences. When he retires in three years' time, his village activities will again permit pure 'communicative reflexivity', whilst the demands of work, which had nurtured a substantial amount of autonomous internal conversation, may well fade away.

Communicative reflexives and the mediation of social structure

Having introduced this group and its distinctive mode of reflexivity, we can now consider how these respondents subjectively mediate structural properties and powers, as discussed in chapter 4. It will be recalled that such mediation was conceptualised as a three-stage process. This begins with the objective and involuntary social placement of agents in different situations in relation to the distribution of society's scarce resources. The structural and cultural properties, which shape the situations that agents necessarily confront, possess generative powers of constraint and enablement. However, whether these are or are not activated and exercised is a question of their relationship to the configuration of concerns, which are subjectively defined by agents themselves. Ultimately, what courses of action are adopted and which social practices become established derives from the reflexive deliberation of agents, who subjectively determine their practical projects in relation to their objective circumstances. What is discovered here is that the 'communicative' pattern of reflexivity is tightly associated with a corresponding pattern of mediation.

At the beginning of this chapter, three features were highlighted as common to 'communicative reflexives': a remarkably high degree of 'contextual continuity', the 'unproblematic dovetailing' of their concerns, and a considerable 'contentment' with their established practices. It is now possible to show how one of these features stands in a determinate relationship to each of the three phases which make up the process of mediation. Such relationships are particular to this sub-group and clearly distinguish it from the manner in which the other types of reflexives mediate the properties and powers of their own involuntary social placement. By working through these three stages of the mediatory process, it is possible to demonstrate how 'communicative reflexivity' actively serves to protract the effects of the original and inegalitarian positioning of its practitioners.

Simultaneously, 'communicative reflexives' gain considerable satisfaction from the *modus vivendi* that they establish for themselves within the changing social structure. If this finding could be generalised to the population at large, then 'communicative reflexivity' would have far-reaching political implications. It would be a powerful subjective force, working conservatively for social stability, because the accommodations which 'communicative reflexives' achieve with contentment are inimical to calls for political radicalism. 'Communicative reflexives' are fundamentally apolitical, not because they are necessarily unaware of social injustice, and not because they necessarily fail to diagnose the manipulative pressures of market forces, but rather because of their underlying belief that they have succeeded in carving out a micro-life world whose intrinsic satisfactions outweigh any difference that extrinsic macro-political intervention could make to them.

Involuntary placement and contextual continuity

The central proposition about stage 1 of the mediatory process was that structural and cultural properties *objectively* shape the situations which agents confront involuntarily. It was significant in this connection that all of the 'communicative reflexives', including the impeded and displaced subjects, came from working-class backgrounds. Angie's father, once a telecommunications engineer, was the only one with a slightly higher socio-economic status. However, to avoid over-hasty, deterministic interpretations, it is equally important to note that half of the members of the other two sub-groups also had working-class origins. What this means is that fifteen of the twenty people interviewed initially shared and confronted the same type of objective situations. Therefore, for every one of these fifteen, a wholly objective bonus would have attached to extricating themselves from these modest backgrounds, by pursuing more ambitious projects, if these successfully resulted in social mobility. Yet, such extrication would necessarily have entailed high opportunity costs, since those of working-class origins are the worst placed for engaging in courses of action, usually entailing extended education and training, which lead to middle-class positions and better. Nevertheless, it is *always* the agent who has to weigh and evaluate these costs and find them worthwhile – and this is necessarily true of projects whose goal involves social mobility. It was the case that five out of the fifteen had found the price worth paying, and their project formation and trajectories will be traced in later chapters.

Conversely, all the 'communicative reflexives' had, at the time of interview, reproduced their social origins in socio-economic terms. The obvious questions are about why and how closely this particular mode of reflexivity is linked to social reproduction. This is where the 'contextual continuity', which is so marked in this sub-group, appears to be of considerable significance in aligning subjective orientations with objective circumstances, so that the two are mutually reinforcing.

However, I am not content with advancing some generic statement about the complementarity between (objective) social positions and (subjective) dispositional states – for several reasons. Firstly, as has already been noted, this association does not hold for several of those with working-class origins, that is the people who have developed a different type of reflexivity. Secondly, 'communicative reflexives' are doing something more precise than reproducing their parental social class position; more exactly they *are replicating their inherited context* – and projecting at least part of it onwards, over their own life-courses and often that of their children. Thirdly, there is nothing quasi-automatic about this; the process involved does not remotely resemble acquiring a mode of subjective deliberation through discursive osmosis. Instead, it is possible to be quite precise about the inter-personal processes which foster and sustain 'communicative reflexivity'.

Let us begin with these processes, which point directly to a more detailed consideration of 'contextual continuity'. The concept has two facets, which may themselves be intertwined, as was the case for Angie. On the one hand, there are close and continuous personal relationships between family members (often including extended family relations), supplemented, at least in youth, by a lasting friendship network. On the other hand, these personal relationships not only span the crucial transition from school to work, but are often directly instrumental in orchestrating this key move. Even when they are not so proximately involved, they operate as sources of information, contacts and support that facilitate occupational placement. Continuity of contact long outlasts this transitional point and tends towards a life-long 'mentoring'. Moreover, contextual intertwining can work in both directions over the generations. Thus, we have the example of Kevin finding part-time jobs, at his own place of work, for his parents in their retirement. Equally, two of the older members of this sub-group, Keith and Graham, are continuing the contextual pattern, having placed their own boys in the same trade as themselves.

It is necessary to appreciate the density of such contextual continuity for the 'communicative reflexive', because in many ways it appears like a historical survival to those of us who have become geographical migrants, socially mobile or direct participants in globalisation through our work. This time I will start with the oldest interviewee, Graham aged sixty-two, and work back to the two young apprentice hairdressers to see whether there has been any historical diminution in the pattern over the forty years that separates them in age.

Graham still lives in the rural village in which he was born, one where his mother's family-tree goes back two or three hundred years. He is actively rooted there, not only as parish councillor, but also as a tree warden and water bailiff for the parish as well as farming a little land. Graham is deeply concerned to protect the village, to keep its footpaths open and to defend it against the more rapacious property developers. He declares that 'city people to me are strangers. I call them nomads, because they roam around owned by banks and building societies. They make all the fuss and two or three years later they've gone somewhere else.' To him, these 'townies' 'are not likeable people' and he clearly wishes his village to remain dominated by those amongst whom he grew up. Although his father began life as a pattern maker in the iron industry, he later moved into the building trade, where uncles, cousins and second cousins had been employed 'for donkey's years'. Graham's own apprenticeship as a bricklayer was instigated through his uncle and, equally significantly, he married into the local farming community.

An urban version of similar density was sketched for thirty-seven year old Angie, who had replicated the secretarial job-context of her mother, aunt and many of their circle, telling me that this was 'the environment I've grown up in'. Since Angie is a quarter of a century younger than Graham, many of these people are still alive and active as part of her network. To it she has added a large complement of friends from home, secretarial college and work – their work being exactly the same as her own occupational context. Does any of this change if we drop back another two decades to Kim and Mel, who have only just entered the world of work?

It does not do so in the least. Of course it is unsurprising that on their limited apprentices' pay both still live at home, but also in the same houses in which they were born within the market town in which they now work. The first hint that geographical stability still underpins 'contextual continuity' comes from Kim, when I ask her whether she got any surprises upon starting work. Just a single one, she explained, which had caused her some alarm. The salon has a sister establishment, twenty minutes away by rail in a Spa town, where apprentices were expected to supply when there were staff shortages. 'That is quite a shock to me, because I'd never been on a train before on my own. It was a bit horrible.' But that was the only surprise, because for Kim 'everything else was what I expected'. This confirmation of their expectations was the *leitmotif* for both young women, which is understandable precisely because of their 'contextual continuity'.

Kim's aunt is a hairdresser too, and Kim is already very knowledgeable about salon work versus 'going mobile'. Mel had direct personal conversancy with the context since she had been a 'Saturday girl'. She had no surprises, because 'I was working here Saturdays before; so that was good because I definitely knew. I've always wanted to do it, but because I was here before I left school, I definitely knew that I could hack it.' Continuity was further reinforced since both Kim and Mel were at school with three fellow apprentices, all of whom went straight into the salon together. Both young women stress the importance of this friendship network, not only for easing the transition from school to work, but also for tension-management on the job. In busy periods, where tempers fray and some clients get irate over delays, the apprentice group, already intertwined from school, acts as its own buffer zone. As Mel puts it, 'we just talk about it between ourselves and we shout between ourselves about what we're going to say – which we never end up saying. But it's just getting it off your chest, because I mean there's five of us in the same boat. It's not as if I was here on my own.'

Perhaps the foregoing makes 'contextual continuity' sound like a conveyor belt, which transports these subjects from school to work and through their careers. Yet it is not deterministic; on the contrary it requires considerable voluntary collaboration and active maintenance on their part. In short, 'contextual continuity' is just as much the product of agential constitution as it is an involuntary given. The first clear indication of this comes from Kim and Mel, when they discuss their sisters who were reared with them and are close in age. These two sisters have gone on to higher education, have moved away and thus cut both aspects of 'contextual continuity'; interpersonally, there is no carry-over to university, where they must forge new friendship networks, and contextually there will be discontinuity between their backgrounds and eventual occupational placement.

This led me to explore how all the 'communicative reflexives' actively sustained 'contextual continuity' by designing career projects, early in life, which remained *within* their situational horizons. In short, were these people who had never seriously entertained any project which would have entailed extricating themselves from the environment constituted by their involuntary social placement? To explore this, I turned to their last couple of years at school and asked about their occupational aspirations then.

What becomes clear from this sub-group is a pattern, which perdures through half a century of educational changes. The pattern is one in which 'communicative reflexives' indeed never did conceive of projects that exceeded their contextual confines. The only whiff of awareness about social discrimination comes from Graham, who left school in 1954, after receiving what he recognised to be an inferior education in his secondary modern school. Compared with today, he sees that opportunity 'in my sort of village community was very limited. We still had the squires and we still has "them and us". So, um, education in [the village] was very limited too.' He adds that the Suez crisis and petrol shortage further limited available openings, so he did not entertain any particular occupational aspirations but simply followed the 'ongoing thing', in the male line of the family, and became an apprentice bricklayer. However, counterbalancing his retrospective class grievances, Graham regards it as a definite bonus that having worked for one of the nation's biggest building contractors for twenty years meant that 'the lads got an excellent trade there'. His sons, too, became building apprentices, thus carrying 'contextual continuity' onwards.

Again Kevin and Keith, both in their early forties, gave very similar responses. School was a place of boredom, truancy and irrelevance that did nothing to foster aspirations. Keith is particularly interesting because the one and only reported incidence of geographical discontinuity in this sub-group nearly de-railed him. When his family moved from one county to another on account of his father's work: 'It messed me up moving, and that knocked me back anyway, changing schools half way through. I was about twelve years old. I never really settled down into it. The third year, like, I did a lot of playing truant and suffered for it in the final year anyway... I never dreamt of actually leaving school and going to college. I was expecting just to be – probably what was in my mind was something like a car factory, the gas board or something like that.' At that point, his mate managed to have Keith taken on by the village electrical company, where he himself worked. This employer then set Keith back on course by offering a full apprenticeship, involving four

years of day-release at college. Once again we must be wary of hastily
invoking social constraints. Later on in the interview Keith admitted that
he had harboured an ambition during this period which he had voluntarily
squashed, namely 'I did want to be a lorry driver, and that was something
my first wife didn't want me to do. So I always felt like I'd sacrificed that.
Because it was what me Dad did and I did want to follow on. But it
never happened.' This anticipates the voluntary shedding or curtailment
of job aspirations, which turns out to play an important role in the smooth
dovetailing of concerns – the next theme to be examined. Remaining with
'contextual continuity', Keith who regretted not following his own father
and becoming a tanker driver, ensured continuity for his son and 'enjoyed
seeing him through his apprenticeship' – into the same trade as his own.

Angie, who has provided our portrait of continuity, also reported having
been rather indifferent to school. After being attracted to nursing, around
the age of twelve, she soon deemed herself 'too squeamish' and reverted to
the secretarial norm of the female-line of her family. Here she comments
revealingly and reflexively about her aspirations. 'I think I'm quite sort of
middle-of-the-road. I know what I want to do but I'm sensible enough to
know whether it's too big a goal or if I won't be able to do it.' This notion
of being sensibly down-to-earth, of taking no risks and of knowing one's
limitations, is also echoed by Kim. 'I did plan to be an airhostess for a
while, when I was younger. Well, it was between the two really. But then
I heard you have to learn a few languages, so that put me off because I
wasn't very good at French at school. So I thought, you know, if I've got
to learn more of that sort of thing – well I thought hairdressing would be,
you know, the easy option out of the two.' On the one hand, this 'modesty'
is self-imposed, on the other hand, education had done nothing to stretch
their horizons – and between the two nothing countered the influence of
'contextual continuity'.

This is equally clear for Mel, who like Angie gained a respectable clutch
of certificates at sixteen. Yet Mel's comment, apart from indicating the
importance of the friendship network at this juncture, raises 'the paradox
of aspirations' which is also the irony of voluntarism. To elucidate it we
have to follow her own account; 'I've always wanted to do hairdressing . . .
I had my job here as a Saturday girl and I always knew that I wanted to
do this. School wasn't really that important to me, you know. I mean I
did all right in my GCSEs and everything, but I wasn't top of the class,
you know, teacher's pet or anything. It was more like a social club really
[laugh] for me. I get to see my friends. So I think – I mean my sister, she
didn't have a clue what she wanted to do. So she did really well in her
GCSEs and then she went on to [the market town] College. And the same
with my friend Sarah. She doesn't know what she wants to do, so she's

getting all the qualifications she can get before she can make a decision.'
Mel is spelling out the irony of voluntarism; if you yourself conceive of a
project within your contextual bounds, then continuity will confirm you
in it, cushion you through it and counsel you about it. You have willingly
consigned yourself to a context, which welcomes you to its confines.

In contrast, there is the paradox of aspirations; namely, that if you do
not form any whilst at school and therefore cannot articulate an occupational project, you may well remain open to acquiring higher goals
and to achieving them. Not to collaborate readily, to be unable to designate a project within one's situational horizons, to gain further education
whilst remaining undecided, may well have the unintended consequence
of 'elastication'. What is supremely propitious to the development of
broader horizons is that the process of higher education engenders a
radical break in 'contextual continuity'. We will find this amongst those
in other sub-groups. As the old saying goes, 'friendships need to be kept
in good repair', but those who move on and away find that distance comes
to mean discontinuity. Conversely, those who stay within the boundaries
of their original context also reinforce inter-personal continuities and, in
turn, they themselves become agents in contextual replication.

This constancy of an objective contextual reference point and the continuous supply of tried and trusted interlocutors appear to be necessary
conditions for the making of a 'communicative reflexive'. I have insisted
that for this condition to be operative requires the voluntary co-operation
of agents. This is because, at rock bottom, they must be authors of their
own projects. Even if those surrounding them do encourage them to remain within the bounds of their involuntary placement, it is still the agent
who must specify a project inside these boundaries. And the concerns
which such projects express must be ones which agents both deem to
be desirable and also judge that they can live. These are quintessentially
first-person tasks because they entail reflexivity; any such project has to
be worthwhile to the agent herself and only she can assess the feasibility
of making such a commitment. There cannot be a third-person substitute
for the author of reflexive acts.

All that this defence of the necessity of a voluntary contribution by
agency categorically rejects is determinism. It resists any notion that our
internal deliberations are fully determined by our involuntary placement
and that the life of the mind is a mere reflection of a position in society.
Three kinds of substantive support were found for this within the small
exploratory group. Firstly only two-thirds of those with working-class origins were found to be 'communicative reflexives', that is people whose
deliberative practices were conducive to social reproduction. Secondly,
some of their siblings had been unable to articulate projects within the

horizons of their involuntary placement and this seemed propitious for social mobility. Thirdly, as will be examined in chapter 9, 'communicative reflexivity', and consequently its reproductive tendency, can 'fracture' if 'contextual continuity', 'dovetailing of concerns' and 'contentment' with established practices themselves break down. However, if we now move on to a consideration of the dovetailing of their concerns by 'communicative reflexives', it can also be shown that a further exercise of agential voluntarism is involved here which adds its own weight to social reproduction.

Dovetailing concerns and the active reduction of social horizons

The second proposition about the process of mediation between structure and agency stated that the generative powers of constraint and enablement, which stemmed from the *objective* situations which agents confronted, were only activated in relation to agents' own configurations of concerns, as *subjectively* defined. Now, it was argued at length in *Being Human* (chapters 6 and 7) that in order to survive and to thrive, no one can avoid having a concern with each of the three orders of natural reality. We must all have some concern about our *physical well-being* in relation to the natural order, about our *performative achievement* in relation to the practical order, and about our *self-worth* in relation to the social order. None of these concerns can be repudiated: any two can be subordinated to an over-riding ultimate concern, but they must nevertheless be accommodated to it.

This is a fundamental human dilemma; how can we give priority to that about which we care most whilst also giving our other necessary concerns their due? For unless we satisfactorily perform this accommodation, we jeopardise our prime concern. The development of such a *modus vivendi* (which both prioritises and accommodates) is a huge human achievement, which requires continuous reflexive deliberation, practical experimentation and a great deal of self-learning. Some never do achieve it, and others do so only to find that their achievement is destabilised by internal and external contingencies, such as health and redundancy.

The second distinctive feature of the 'communicative reflexives' was the success with which they had all performed this dovetailing exercise. Each had established a stable *modus vivendi*, meaning a set of practices that they themselves deemed worthwhile, workable and with which they felt they could live. Their subordinate concerns were clearly defined as such and were smoothly accommodated to their ultimate concern. Moreover this pattern of smooth dovetailing was already evident amongst those who were still in their late teens; and older subjects had manifested an extraordinary virtuosity in sustaining variations upon their pattern throughout the vicissitudes of their lives. Yet dovetailing is always hard won because some things have to give way if the ultimate concern is to retain its priority. It is also hard work because only the subject herself can maintain and monitor her own desired alignment between her concerns. This is where the next element of voluntarism comes in. It is possible to trace how each of the 'communicative reflexives' willingly, and with increasing self-awareness, performed these acts of self-adjustment.

Each of the 'communicative reflexives' had unequivocally named their 'family and friends' as their ultimate concern, though necessarily under their own descriptions ('they definitely come first', 'are the most important thing in my life', and so forth). However, all of these subjects also needed to work, which is the most crucial relationship that nearly everybody has to sustain with the practical order. Each one had experienced the tension between home and work in his or her own way. What is of particular interest is how each had solved the problem of subordinating work to family life, through anticipatory accommodation, through a rectification of their past 'mistakes', and through a resolve to keep matters that way. What will be highlighted is the voluntary reduction of social horizons this entailed, in terms of reduced occupational aspirations, reduced social mobility and an acceptance of 'living within one's means'. Although none of the sub-group considered that he or she had significant health problems, unlike one of the 'displaced people', nevertheless, the forms taken by leisure and relaxation displayed the same two features as was the case for work. Firstly, leisure activities were smoothly dovetailed with the ultimate concern and with the subordinate position assigned to work (and hence earnings). Secondly, even for Angie, Kim and Mel, as yet without their own children, some curtailment of leisure pursuits was a direct implication of maintaining the dovetailing achieved. Modifications in lifestyle as well as life-chances were entailed by their common ultimate concern.

What I shall be at pains to show is how much internal deliberation this smooth dovetailing took from these six people and what their particular style of 'communicative reflexivity' contributed to this process. In other words, attention will focus upon the subjective side of mediation, which entails both project-design and project-management. Such rationalistic terminology fails to do justice to the deep affectivity involved in making and sustaining a prime commitment to the welfare of other people. The vivacity of the subjects' own words and the poignancy of some of the situations they describe will counteract the commodified connotations of a term like 'trade-off' – which does, nevertheless, accurately characterise their actions. Only when these subjectively defined life-projects have been described will it be possible to introduce the objective side of mediation, and to ask how the 'communicative reflexive' fares in relation to constraints and enablements.

Before any of the above can be discussed, it is essential to put flesh on the bones of what a 'smooth dovetailing of concerns' means for a 'communicative reflexive'. None of these subjects had any hesitation about naming and ranking their major concerns. However, that is different from having achieved a workable accommodation of lower concerns to higher ones. Angie has already supplied us with the *leitmotif* of harmonious dovetailing, which is characteristic of this sub-group. Let us recall her statement; 'your family, your social life, your friends, your work, it's a combination of things isn't it really? I think it's because one sort of complements the other, doesn't it. It sort of builds up a pattern there.' However, this begs a question. Does this pattern just somehow build itself up, or does this building process entail reflexive work on the part of the subject?

Both of the youngest respondents initially imply that co-ordination of their concerns (family, boyfriend and job for Kim; boyfriend, family, job and friends for Mel) is a relatively easy matter of timetabling. As Kim puts it, accommodation is not problematic because 'my job gets involved with them, the other two – there's no problem when I work late or anything, because my boyfriend normally works late. That's it', meaning that she has plenty of time for her family on other evenings. To begin with, Mel too gives the impression of effortless co-ordination, requiring little if any reflexive effort on her part. 'I see my family really often, I see my boyfriend, my friends and I'm really happy here [in the salon]. So I don't really think about it that much. I think maybe if I wasn't happy then I would think.' She too attributes this to a felicitous timetable which obviates potential tensions. 'I live at home with my Mum. My sister comes down most weekends. My boyfriend's down at the weekends. And so, during the week when my boyfriend's away, I get to see my friends, my Nan, see my Dad. I see my Nan once a week; I see my Dad once a week. I get to do my training here. And then at weekends it's like all my time's mine then.'

However, as we pursue the subject, it emerges that the best of time-management alone does not fully achieve accommodation. Both deliberation and work are involved. Being 'communicative reflexives', it is unsurprising that this work entails face-to-face contact and talking things through. Thus Kim admits that her family and boyfriend do clash over the time Kim spends with him, but they get by through conversational negotiation. Mel is even more revealing about the personal effort it takes to meet the demands of her subordinate concerns, rather than repudiating them. She tells a story of a Thursday night when her friends wanted her to go out and celebrate a birthday. 'I went to bed late on the Wednesday and we worked until six on the Thursday and seven on the Friday, so I was already knackered in the middle of the week. And I couldn't afford to go and I was too tired to go. So I phoned them up and said, you know, I'm not going to come. I felt just awful saying no. I know they wouldn't take offence but... and then my Dad phoned me. He'd just got back from Ireland and I was absolutely knackered. He was like "are you going to come round", and I feel awful saying "Well, no, I'm tired", because I ain't seen him like – he doesn't live with me – so I hadn't seen him for a couple of weeks. So I went round there and ended up being knackered on Friday.' Here Mel was deliberately balancing the fact that her (higher priority) friends would not be offended, against her pattern of regular weekly meetings with her father. She puts herself out in order to maintain the established practice which accommodates the (lower priority) concern. This *vignette* presages the greater efforts expended by those in mid-life.

Keith and Kevin share the same hierarchy of concerns: family, work and leisure. Both, it will be recalled, had been through a divorce and were determined to make a success of their re-partnering. This, it transpires involved considerable deliberation about disordered priorities in the past. Both men had made a real commitment to not repeating the same mistakes, and accepted that this would involve self-monitoring supplemented by dialogue. Keith recognises that this is part of his desire for effective dovetailing. 'I like things nice and smooth and no problems, you know. That's life. I think you have to make it that way yourself.' Yet, as a 'communicative reflexive', the effort involved also entails interpersonal dialogue. 'You have to work at it, yeah, with your partner, wife or whatever. Oh yeah, you have to. It certainly has to be worked at – it's obvious – it's a joint thing to sort of come to an agreement.'

Keith attributes the breakdown of his first marriage to the tension between job demands and family needs and to his early failure to order his concerns; a lesson painfully acquired, but one that he is determined will serve to protect his second marriage. Splitting-up was attributed to 'working away from home and things like that, so there was big tension there. And I felt I was doing like my bit, but obviously I wasn't thinking enough of them. Yeah it [work] did sort of come between us then. No doubt about that, I mean I did always say that. But I won't let it happen again over working. Your priority, you know, your family being the priority – that would be it. If there was a problem between that and work, then that would kick in.' Keith's confidence is not just intra-personal.

His second wife also works, which helps, but more importantly they have reached a mutual understanding that 'we're basically doing it for each other to get what we want'.

Kevin's story is very similar, only he seems to have gone much further in his recognition that work and family and even leisure pursuits are constantly threatened by misalignment and that considerable work has to go into sustaining subordination so that the ultimate concern is undamaged. His marital breakdown is attributed to the same reasons as in Keith's case, and similar lessons were drawn from it. 'I mean I was working, she was working; we'd got a business that we were working as well. We'd got a lad who needed . . . and there was always something doing, always something on the go. And I think you get carried away with that . . . Although you're together and living together and everything else, it's that you don't build there. It's because your time's doing other things . . . I think, as you get older, you realise all that and you turn round and say "hold on a minute", I'm taking time out from all these things to give the relationship a bit of a boost.'

Nevertheless, Kevin still finds today that subconsciously his overtime hours can start creeping up again, that this is a habit which it is hard to change, but, 'it just takes a little jolt or something like that to stop you in your tracks. Just to think "Ah, I'd better cut down on all that now."' The jolt may well come from his partner, for unlike Keith, his re-partnering has not been smooth. As a 'communicative reflexive', there is always discussion, but as we have seen earlier, with this pair their terms of reference often conflict and so conversations are inconclusive. When this point arrives, then to preserve this important relationship, 'you, for want of a better word, capitulate for the sake of the other person'. Kevin has made a commitment to his partner, the word also used by Keith and Graham, and he is working hard to ensure that it has priority. Here he goes much further than Keith in monitoring all subordinate concerns in order to bring about continuous alignment. Television is censored to guarantee quality family time, and Kevin talks at length about how he has limited his current passion for golf, which he would gladly play every day, to once a fortnight and only at times when his family is otherwise engaged. He considers it as part of both his commitment and his self-learning that now, when someone asks him to play golf: 'then you've got to have the – I wouldn't say the bottle or anything, but you've got to have the awareness to turn round and say "No, I can't do that because I'm committed here", instead of saying, "Oh yeah, I'd love to go", so I'm going. You have to look at the situation.' Looking, learning, deliberating, discussing and then plenty of effort are what make dovetailing possible for Kevin.

Perhaps this sounds such a strenuous business that it may come as a relief that Graham, at sixty-two, and still committed to his wife of forty years' standing, now finds that his concerns (family, work, and his village involvements) 'all dovetail nicely'. As he puts matters, 'Once you've made a commitment, stick by it. The family definitely first.' Yet now, Graham seems to have been able to revert to time-management to preclude tensions. He made it clear to the construction company that Wednesday nights were sacrosanct to parish council meetings, at which he manages to arrive punctually. He leaves home at 6.20 am which does not trouble his wife who is still farming, but his weekends are free for home and village concerns. Future dovetailing does not sound problematic. Although Graham regrets his retirement in three years' time, he has plenty of shared and shareable activities to take up the slack.

Alignment of their concerns is an achievement for these 'communicative reflexives'. This is doubly so, because their mode of reflexivity also entails successful inter-personal negotiation. In this respect, they stand in direct contrast to 'autonomous reflexives', the other sub-group to accomplish a smooth dovetailing of their concerns, but for whom this achievement requires a more elaborate and less concessionary 'ethic of accommodation'. 'Meta-reflexives' never arrive at a stable accommodation of their subordinate concerns with their ultimate concern. They question their prioritisation itself, or are repeatedly dissatisfied with their accommodative practices, which give either too much or too little to other concerns that also matter.

However, the 'communicative reflexives' go further still, because their accommodations involve a radical subordination, so that the ultimate concern is accorded an unassailable primacy. This is the case with both work and leisure. Since work entails our performative skills, this means a relegation of the practical order. Since many forms of leisure are related to our physical well-being, this often spells a parallel relegation of the natural order. None of this is surprising, of course, because the 'communicative reflexive' is supremely concerned with the social order. Their inner deliberations, personal evaluations and inter-personal practices are all centred upon the social domain. Yet, where work and leisure are concerned, they pay a high price for this in terms of intensifying the unequal distribution of scarce resources in society. As has been seen, all 'communicative reflexives' started out life as subjects who had been involuntarily placed in the working class. Now what emerges is that they not only reproduce their social positions, but *actually reduce their potential for occupational mobility*. In a voluntary and often anticipatory manner they actively curtail their work aspirations and limit their own opportunities for advancement in the employment market. This is one of the prices they willingly pay in

order to bring about a smooth dovetailing of their concerns. Its immediate corollary is the adoption of a highly instrumental relation to work;
although work may provide a source of satisfaction, its fundamental purpose is to provide the money to service their ultimate concern. In turn
there are the further consequences, namely that this sub-group alone
becomes heavily pre-occupied with 'living within its means' and almost
fixated upon 'budgeting'.

Before this chain-reaction can be understood it is necessary to appreciate quite how the subordination of work to a common prime concern
('family and friends') also constitutes a self-imposed curtailment of work
horizons – as part and parcel of the 'dovetailing' process. When I ask Kim
about her ambitions, it is clear that at seventeen, she is already mentally
reducing their scope because the effort and dedication involved could
conflict with the shared life she anticipates with her boyfriend. 'At first,
I don't know any more, but I was going to go mobile. I think it's just a
bit – it's not hard work, it's just a lot of things you've got to take in to it
and do yourself and everything – but it just depends how much money
you've got to do it – you've got to buy all that stuff. You've just got to
do it all yourself, haven't you really? It's just not like here – here you just
come to work and get your money.' There are many small and affluent
villages surrounding the market town, so 'going mobile' could be an advancement for Kim, once she finishes her training. She is making several
points. Certainly there would be the initial outlay, but Kim already has
a savings policy that will yield £5,000, soon after her apprenticeship is
complete. However, mentally Kim has already allocated this to tide her
over the arrival of her children. Next there is the responsibility and she
knows from her Aunt, a successful mobile hairdresser who uses an ac-
countant, about the paperwork involved. Why shoulder this, thinks Kim,
as well as the effort of keeping her own appointment system, when all that
is done for you in the salon and with regular hours thrown in? Finally,
there is a refrain about having to do the job alone, which is not offset
by the close inter-personal relations that develop with regular clients. We
talk over the pros and cons and I ask her what she now reckons she will
be most likely to do. 'Stay in the salon, yeah, and work my way up to
be a good stylist.' Deliberately and in anticipation, Kim is reducing her
aspirations, by blocking-off the avenue to self-employment, and turning
herself into a financial instrumentalist – here, in the salon, 'you just come
to work and get your money'.

Mel's account of her ambitions echoes the theme of early and voluntary
truncation, for exactly the same reason. 'I've always wanted, um, I used
to want to do cruise liners and stuff, but I don't want to do that anymore.'
This would not fit in with settling down with her boyfriend. Mel has killed

one ambition, because of its incongruity, but not yet all of them. 'I'd like to go into theatre or something – do hair for theatre, just styling it. But I'll just have to see when it comes.' Yet even if she does attempt this, Mel only thinks of it as an interlude, lasting about five years, before achieving her real ambition; 'I think family more than anything would be my one big dream.' When the children do arrive, she can already foresee that they would be compatible with gradually building up a mobile clientele. In all of this, the one certainty to Mel is that 'I know that I'll be getting good money when I am there [qualified].'

We have already noted that Kevin attributed the breakdown of his first marriage to the demands of running a family business and also seen his resolve that his re-partnering must not be subjected to the same strain. Consequently, Kevin has taken employment for many years as a porter in an educational institution. Although he enjoys his work and takes pride in it, nevertheless, despite his years of good service, he does not look for promotion. 'I find that I'm not ambitious really. I mean work is a means to an end. The more you get on and go up, the more time you have to put in.' Work is not and must not become 'the be all and end all of things' and Kevin has already shown that he is wary of letting his overtime creep up. Working is necessary to provide the 'money to pay the bills and gas, and that means that if you want something extra, it's going to cost extra. You've got to work harder at work or do some overtime to get money to do that.' Kevin is not just an instrumentalist about work and money, he is a self-restrained instrumentalist, since he now restricts overtime in the interests of the family. It is very easy to see how his voluntary self-monitoring in this respect leads to the family unit's preoccupation with 'living within its means'.

We talk at greater length about Keith's period of self-employment, which significantly he regards as having been a period of aberration rather than of ambition, despite its success. The precipitating factor was his (then) employer putting the men on short time because of a fall in orders. Although very happy otherwise with the company, Keith believes that 'in your career, money is a major point in making your decisions to go from one job to another'. The sufficient condition for self-employment was that his first marriage had ended and he maintains that this affected his risk-assessment, enabling him to be less cautious. The 'going self-employed, um, didn't seem so much of a risk at the time because I was on me own and it was just for myself, you know. It didn't seem like I'd got any commitments in anything other than looking after myself at the time.' Keith is thus stating that his ambitions could expand when alone, but are voluntarily curtailed when he is not. Retrospectively, he looks on this period of self-employment, coinciding with the time between his two marriages, as a brief and belated chance to sow his wild oats. Note the contrast below between his own designation of this as an interlude of 'selfishness', when he starts the story, and the re-establishment of his 'normal' consideration for others, with which he concludes it. 'In the break between the first and the second marriage, I suppose I was selfish in that sense. It was a time when – I think I married quite young really – twenty, I missed out. So within that time from the first marriage splitting up to getting married the second time, it was my little free time, if you like. Living my youth again and just being myself. And meeting my [second wife-to-be] then, like in 1990, it changed again. That's when I started getting feelings for someone again, and that was it really. And back to my old self [laugh].' Returning to his 'old self' and making a new commitment spelt a return to the cautiousness of curtailment: Keith abandoned self-employment, even though he was doing well.

I question him about regrets and when he tells me that, 'it wasn't a problem to change back' to employee status: the reasons given are all ones of financial instrumentality. Coming 'back on the books' involved no drop in money, it obviated the nuisance of making tax-returns, made credit and mortgage facilities easier to obtain, and, as a great bonus, included holiday pay. Here Keith is concentrating upon the bright side; what he never mentions is that self-employment with the regular team he had successfully built up, could have been even more lucrative. To him, risk and commitment cannot go hand in hand; caution must rule when others are concerned. This *vignette* of the voluntary extension and willing contraction of occupational horizons illustrates very clearly the close connection between the family, as his ultimate concern, and its role in curtailing his aspirations. Suspend this ultimate concern and Keith's horizons expanded; reinstate it and they were immediately reduced.

Even Graham confesses to this influence, despite his rise from brick-layer to site foreman on large-scale construction projects, and admits that his cautious financial instrumentalism had actually held him back. Because of the perks accruing to the family, he considers that he remained far too long with one company. 'What mattered was always pay really in one respect. But with [a national construction company] which I worked for for twenty years, just over twenty years, what was most important there was I bought one of their [company] homes and lived on the site. And then they sponsored the daughter for a degree and the two lads did their apprenticeship with them. So that involvement kept me with [the company] for longer than I should have done really, but we saved money in lots of respects.' Again, his final words point to the last link in this chain of self-imposed curtailment. If you truncate your occupational mobility for the sake of the family, if your orientation to work is then financially instrumental, if the wages of not being ambitious are lower in consequence, then a preoccupation with 'living within your means' is an inevitable conclusion to the sequence.

When I try to talk about the mental activity of 'budgeting' to this sub-group, pointing out to each interviewee that we can budget not only in terms of money, but also in terms of time and effort, I receive a uniform reply from all. Budgeting is indeed about money and more specifically, it is about making ends meet. Thus Kim and Mel discuss the savings schemes into which they have entered on their very small apprentices' pay, and how this necessarily limits their social life. Angie adds the same reflection upon the decision to buy her own house. Kevin shows his caution in inspecting forty houses, before buying, and he and Keith both have in hand carefully detailed and costed programmes for home improvements. Graham sums up the attitude for the group. 'I'm very cautious in what we spend – I like to be right if I'm going to do something out there. And the caution is don't jump straight in. Just stand back and make what we've discussed earlier – plans. Stand back, don't stand forward.'

Standing back entails accepting the consequences of the self-imposed curtailment of one's horizons. For the 'communicative reflexive', it means embracing the *status quo* and editing one's hopes to that which is possible within it. Since ambition has been voluntarily renounced, only external factors outside the agent's control (such as changes in national pay scales) can alter their lot. Consequently, all internal attention shifts to how to make the best of it, by intensive budgeting. Only contingency rather than agency could change any of the terms in this equation. Significantly, the lottery was mentioned by everyone in this sub-group and by nobody in any other. Once you have made your bed, then lie on it economically, but if part of you persists in dreaming, then keep buying a lottery ticket. There appears to be nothing between a limited savings' scheme and hitting a lottery jackpot.

Beyond that common practice, living within one's means meant es-tablishing a *modus vivendi*, centred upon 'family and friends'. Within it, 'holidays' assumed an enormous importance for everyone. They were al-ways taken together, their planning was a joint exercise and part of the enjoyment – the event itself being both the celebration and vindication of 'good budgeting'. As Keith puts it, his aim, which could stand for the sub-group, is to 'make things so that you plod along nicely, you know. I don't want to be struggling. It's much easier to have an easy life, a bit of peace. Holidays [laugh], Oh we like our holidays.' Leisure has thus been somewhat paradoxically accommodated. In the form of the holiday, it is both exalted as 'the best of times' yet restricted to two or three weeks of the year. Nevertheless, it would be entirely wrong to view the holiday as the victory of 'budgeting' over drudgery. It may indeed be the high-point, but only of something that is highly prized all year round, namely the quality of life enjoyed by the family unit and friendship network. This then brings us to a discussion of the import of the third feature shared by all communicative reflexives. Since they express what I have simply called a high degree of 'contentment' with their *modi vivendi*, certain conclusions can now be drawn about what bearing their subjective outlook has upon their objective circumstances.

Contentment and the avoidance of constraints and enablements

The third proposition about mediation states that courses of action are produced through the reflexive deliberations of agents who *subjectively* determine their practical projects in relation to their *objective* circumstances. Courses of action refer to regular and therefore established practices. Discrete actions performed on special occasions, such as fire, threat or other emergencies fall outside the purview of the present argument. What is of concern is the *modus vivendi* which individuals develop reflexively and live out day-by-day as stable practices. Generically, the *modus vivendi* is the concretisation of how agents have determined to live in view of their concerns and in the light of their circumstances. It is the modality through which our subjective reflections about what we most care for intersect with our objective conditions of life, which have the potential to constrain or to enable different courses of action.

This is the culminating moment when agential reflexivity mediates socio-structural powers. Precisely *how* agents deliberately determine that they will live out their configurations of concerns is what is decisive for the activation of the causal powers of constraints and enablements or for these latter remaining unexercised. Hence the key question is does the specific mode of 'communicative reflexivity' have any bearing on the activation of constraints and enablements, or on their remaining unexercised? Obviously this will not be a direct relationship because it is agents' projects (the results of their reflexive deliberations) which are responsible for unleashing the causal powers of structures and cultures upon their protagonists. The *modus vivendi* represents the ensemble of projects which an agent has established as expressive of her concerns. All of our 'communicative reflexives' have 'family and friends' as their ultimate concern, and have dovetailed their subordinate concerns with that which they most care about. This was an achievement which, it has been seen, entailed self-awareness, self-monitoring and the self-conscious renunciation of pure self-interest through the curtailment of incongruent ambitions.

The question therefore becomes, how do the resultant *modi vivendi* of this sub-group stand in relation to constraints and enablements?

There is a very clear relationship indeed. The *modus vivendi* of each of the 'communicative reflexives' interviewed does not invoke constraints or enablements, but, on the contrary, it evades them. In structural terms, the life practices constitutive of these *modi vivendi* are *stable* and *sustainable*. On the one hand, they have considerable stability as established practices because their continuation is only at the mercy of contingent causes of disruption, and not of systemic ones. No enablements are invoked which would entail a change of practice, because an exceptionally high degree of 'contextual continuity' was found to be part of the make-up of the 'communicative reflexive'. On the other hand, their established practices were not ones whose sustainability was threatened by an uphill struggle against constraints. Here the combination of 'contextual continuity' and a 'smooth dovetailing', achieved through the voluntary reduction of subordinate aspirations, effectively evaded constraining powers. Put at its simplest, our 'society' places no obstacles in the way of those wishing to found a family and maintain a friendship network, especially when this is coupled with a commitment to providing for them, without any aspirations towards social advancement.

However, in chapter 4, two conditions were attached to a viable *modus vivendi*. For the component practices to become established ones, they were required to be not only *sustainable* but also *satisfying*. Sustainability has just been touched upon; no current social powers threaten the generation, continuation and even replication of these patterns of life. However, for them to be satisfying, then agents have to find satisfaction in or derive satisfaction from them. The priorities they have reflexively determined, and the projects they have deliberately defined to realise them, were ones conceived of within the horizons of their involuntary placement. Only if the agents themselves are content with this *modus vivendi* will they work for its maintenance rather than its transformation. An assessment of their reported 'contentment' is the last building block to be put in place to complete this review of the subjectivity of the 'communicative reflexive' and its relationship to objective causal powers.

'Contentment', like every other emotion is partly an affective matter and partly cognitive. In normal English usage, when someone states, 'I am content', this connotes an affectivity which is probably closer to being 'satisfied' rather than to exultant 'happiness'. That is precisely what 'communicative reflexives' express. Cognitively, 'contentment' entails a judgement by a subject that her present condition is acceptable – in the knowledge that both better and worse states are the lot of other people. It is therefore a comparative judgement, where on balance the individual makes a positive assessment of her condition, which lies somewhere comfortably above whatever she conceives the mid-way point to be.

Graham, the oldest respondent, reflecting on his current position in relation to his early beginnings and with retirement approaching, sums up his feelings economically: 'I'm quite happy with what I've achieved and what I've got and thoroughly enjoy it.' Effectively, this same 'enjoyment' is echoed by the rest of the sub-group. Cognitively, it becomes clear that this assessment is made against a background of modest aspirations. I discuss the question of wanting to exert influence in society with him because, as a parish councillor, he is the only member of the group who recorded the slightest interest in it. 'Oh yes' he responds, 'in a very quiet way. What I do, sometimes people say it don't matter. It's not looking for glory – it's just what I enjoy.' The same modesty characterises Keith's approach to life in general. Since he had mentioned the importance of 'being successful', I press him on what success represents to him and receive a response couched in terms of a comparative judgement. 'Do what I want to do successfully and be happy. I don't think that there's anything major occurring in my life – sort of around the world ballooning or something – not that sort of success. I mean generally, it's just being successful just to live your life the way you want to, or as close as possible.' In terms of class, status and power, the 'communicative reflexive' seeks comfort rather than affluence, personal respect rather than high esteem and, at most, a limited local influence rather than substantial power or authority. Their goals are attainable, so they can enjoy their fruits without this 'contentment' being vitiated by the knowledge that others are better off on all three dimensions.

I want to be sure how far these affective and cognitive judgements go and what lies behind them. After all, it could simply be a matter of pride not to denigrate one's own achievements, whatever these may be, and many people seem to comfort themselves with the thought that 'there's always somebody worse off'. Do matters go any deeper with these interviewees? Tackling affectivity first, I probed their 'contentment' slightly more obliquely in order to discover whether or not it was mitigated by the harbouring of 'regrets' or was inflated by the 'sacrifices' that achieving their present positions had entailed. Significantly, they collectively denied any deep regrets and those which were avowed were uniformly presented intra-punitively; they were 'my fault', they were inter-personal in nature and never reflections upon social injustice, distributive inequalities or negative features of their involuntary placement. Thus we have seen that the breakdown of their first marriages was both a serious source of regret to Keith and Kevin, but also one for which they took a large share of personal responsibility. Graham's only regret was staying too long with one company, but he admits freely that this was due to his decision to take advantage of the housing and educational benefits associated with the job. Once again, Angie sums up for the group. Her regrets are 'nothing really major – "What did I see in him?" or "I shouldn't have been so stupid and done that." But no, nothing major, I don't think.'

Similarly, our discussion of sacrifices yields nothing that would reduce 'contentment' to mere affective relief after strenuous self-denial. Instead, the making of sacrifices is either disavowed or is considered to carry its own reward. Thus sacrifice is in no way antipathetic to enjoyment. Mel, still in her teens, sets up her own balance and finds that it comes down on the positive side. There are moderate consolations in moderate self-denial: 'Have I had to make any sacrifices? No, not really. I mean last year I went on holiday which was nice, um, no I don't think I have. The only thing that – it's like most people of eighteen, they're going out clubbing all the time and everything, and I can't afford to do that. But then, like I said before, my boyfriend's home at weekends, so I like to spend quality time with him and I like it when I go out, because I don't go out all that often. When I do go out, I like to get all dressed up and, you know, it's different, isn't it? If you go out every week, you just get bored with it. So, no, I don't think I've had to make any sacrifices.' At the other end of the age range, Graham looks back on weeks of living out of a suitcase when engaged on distant sites, and voices much the same sentiment. 'They were sort of sacrifices, but you get the reward, don't you. So it's not an empty sacrifice, is it?'

In affective terms, expressions of 'contentment' seem genuine, but the last two comments indicate that cognitive assessments are integral to this, with one factor being balanced against another. Since 'contentment' implies comparisons and because weighing things entails weights and measures, such cognitive judgements cannot be understood without grasping the 'currency' in which worth is assigned. Here, for example, rational choice theorists engage in over-commodification when they suggest that all our 'utiles' can be expressed by some common measure of being 'better off'. Yet, as we have seen, these subjects talk readily about their 'commitments', which are expressive of who they are, rather than being a means to something else or the product of cost-benefit analysis. In other words, their ultimate concerns are the source of their measures of worth and, to them, what is worthwhile has nothing to do with being better off in monetary terms. Thus, if the 'coinage' in which they assess worth can be made explicit, this will serve to explain how cognitively they come up with positive judgements about their present situations.

In one sense, these 'currencies' are hard to articulate, unlike 'money', yet in another sense they pervade most things expressed in these interviews. 'Communicative reflexives' are not ambitious people, their satisfactions are intrinsic and expressive, and their currency is basically inter-personal fulfilment. If, subjectively, they have achieved enough of that, then their personal contentment is neither enhanced by privately gloating over those who are objectively worse off, nor is it diminished through envying those who are objectively better off. Just let me have a comfortable family of my own, Kim and Mel are saying. Angie's contentment pivots around having 'a full life' of socialising with her friends. Keith wants his family to 'plod along nicely', which represents 'an easy life'. Kevin, who is acutely aware of stressful external demands, says that for him 'relaxation is the big thing'. At home and at work, Graham simply 'likes it to be right', so his motto is 'stand back – just take it very steady and cautious'.

The 'communicative reflexives' are not social competitors. 'Contentment' is what they seek to cultivate within the micro-environment which is where worth is located – in a small life-world which has been carved out from the wider society. Certainly, the latter can intrude, especially if it damages personal dignity and self-esteem. Thus, at the two ends of the age range, Mel can fulminate against 'snobby clients' and their ungraciousness, but although it hurts, she deflects it by questioning their human values. 'I always see it as just because we're younger than you and we're doing skivvy jobs, it doesn't make us any less of a person. They're just so snobby and you think they're worrying about the littlest things, when you think "get your priorities right – think of all the bad things that are out there", and they're worrying about their nails or something.' Mel dismisses them for their misplaced sense of values and reassures herself that matters will change once she is a stylist. Similarly, the only anger Graham showed was towards the collective low esteem in which workers in the construction industry are held. 'You're "just" a builder. You're just one of those people that somebody calls to put on a few slates – frowned upon over the years as though we're some sort of idiots building a shed down here.' Yet he admits that recently the image has improved because of more entrants with engineering degrees, public awareness of safety standards and hazards, plus the same managerialism as in other big concerns. Again, the outside world has held wrong values, hurtful when they impugned Graham's own personal dignity, but matters are improving.

These flies in the ointment are points at which the impersonal macroworld can impinge upon the intimacy of the micro-environment by questioning personal worth. Yet 'society' cannot penetrate to the heart of the small unit, let alone 'colonise' it, because it is in the micro-world that the currency of personal fulfilment is minted, exchanged and accumulated, one which pays its dividends in the form of simple contentment. Kevin can have the last word, speaking as a contented man. 'I find it doesn't matter exactly what you're doing. Even if you're just in the garden, relaxing, reading a book, all together, the idle chat and that, it's such a relaxed atmosphere – we go on holidays to different places together and it's the nice relaxed atmosphere that we've got when we're all together – the laughing, the joking, taking fun out of each other. We're all together and everything else around is really something we're oblivious about.' Kevin's last sentence epitomises the relationship between their ultimate concern, their definition of worth, and the achievement of 'contentment' for the 'communicative reflexives'. His reference to being oblivious to the rest of the world is highly significant. 'Contentment' is generated and sustained inside a micro-unit that remains continuous with its original context of involuntary placement. Thus there are no discontents whose assuagement would systematically induce 'communicative reflexives' to seek major changes in their social positions.

Conclusion

The effect of structural and cultural emergent properties upon agency is a matter of the confluence of their causal powers. In other words, the powers of constraints and enablements are only exercised *in relation* to agential projects. The conception, formulation and pursuit of such projects is accomplished through the subjective deliberation of agents and is thus an expression of one of their irreducible human powers. Because two sets of *sui generis* powers are involved, they can stand in various relationships to one another. This is why agential mental activities, represented by their internal conversations, are held to play a mediatory role. It always depends upon the nature of the projects advanced by agents whether or not constraints and enablements are activated or remain unexercised. What has been examined in this chapter is a distinctive form of the inner conversation, one conducted through 'thought and talk', which was called 'communicative reflexivity'. It now remains to venture certain hypotheses about how and why this particular mode of subjective reflexivity mediates the objective socio-cultural structure in a distinctive manner – especially its constraining and enabling powers.

Firstly, the 'communicative reflexives' do not activate social constraints. This is because they conceive of their projects *within* the context of their involuntary placement. Achieving their aims is in no way dependent upon a change in social position. On the contrary, 'communicative reflexivity' depends upon a high level of 'contextual continuity', which, in turn, it not merely reproduces but more exactly tends to replicate.

It depends upon it because the 'thought and talk' mode of deliberation requires 'another', as interlocutor, to complement – in both senses of the word – the exercise of personal reflexivity. In one sense, 'the other' completes the thought process; in the second sense, 'the other' is also complementary because for others to act as public extensions of a private process, they have to be socially continuous with the subject. They must literally speak the same language, because the introduction of discordant notions would impede rather than foster completion. Thus, had one of our young apprentices externalised her boyfriend trouble to another person whose response was to dismiss it as trivial or to advise that she was too young to be 'going serious', this precludes completion because it denies her ultimate concern.

'Communicative reflexives' turn to others because they mistrust their lone internal dialogues, but this means that 'the other' must be deemed more trustworthy than oneself. Here, trust means that the subject places reliance upon what the other would do in a similar situation. For this to be possible, it must be very credible indeed that the other could find herself (or once had been) in such a situation, motivated by the same concerns and with much the same resources at her disposal. This very contextual dependency is itself responsible for the myriad interchanges out of which 'contextual continuity' is woven. In the process, the projects that are conceived within the context of involuntary social placement and which are acknowledged, reinforced and advanced by those who are similarly placed, remain within the contextual horizon and hence evade the activation of constraining powers.

This avoidance of constraints ultimately depends upon subjects conceiving of projects, which are of supreme importance to them, within their existing social horizons. At this point, some might be inclined to appeal to much more diffuse constraining influences, whose discursive or dispositional effect is to 'normalise' both projects and practices, thus serving to confine agents to their initial social position. Whilst I do not resist the notion that factors such as the differential social distribution of information, role models and practical experience may be conducive to this end, they must fall a long way short of explaining the phenomenon as a whole. These cannot be deterministic influences because several of the other working-class subjects interviewed had undergone social mobility and were pursuing projects that did indeed invoke constraining influences. Moreover, such individuals had also developed a different mode of reflexivity. This points to the fact that subjectivity is changeable. Such mutability is also underlined by the existence of those impeded from exercising the reflexive mode towards which they incline. Equally, those who are 'displaced' from their previous practice of a given mode, leads one to suspect those theories which advance a durable alignment between the 'positional' and the 'dispositional'. Finally, such theories necessarily curtail the contribution of agential voluntarism – of self-consciousness, self-monitoring and self-commitment, which are also crucial in explaining why 'communicative reflexives' avoid enablements, just as they evade constraints.

To remain continuous with one's initial and involuntary placement, involves the doings of an active agent; it is not the deterministic product of agential passivity. Among the small exploratory group investigated, there was plenty of evidence of the availability of enablements to social advancement, and equally much to indicate that these were voluntarily shunned. On the one hand, in terms of family background, the younger subjects both had same-sex siblings enrolled in higher education, which would disrupt their 'contextual continuity' and probably result in social mobility. Their inability to endorse a project within existing class confines was what differentiated them from their sisters, whose parents, they reported, would have been equally willing to enable them to undertake tertiary education, had they not already determined upon other projects. On the other hand, and even more important, was the role which the 'smooth dovetailing' of their concerns played in the voluntary curtailment of ambition and thus in the actual repudiation of enablements.

In one way or another, all the 'communicative reflexives' had self-consciously subordinated their occupational aspirations in order to give primacy to their ultimate concern. With some, this was an anticipatory renunciation, which precluded enablements from coming into play and confirmed their own confinement to their original social placement. With the two men who, in their prime, had successfully started their own businesses, which might have resulted in their socio-economic advancement, it was they themselves who determined not to continue, in the interests of their family life. This sub-group unanimously declared itself to be unambitious and, in so doing, they were also declaring themselves to be disinterested in and thus immune to any enablements that might come their way.

Lastly, their collective contentment with the *modi vivendi* that they had established put the capstone upon their unavailability to enabling influences. The established practices of 'communicative reflexives' involved an intense concentration upon and interaction with family and friends, whose effect was to insulate them against external stimuli or opportunities. If these did intrude, as with Kevin's partner undertaking a psychology course and introducing new notions into their relationship, then their destabilising potential was recognised and feared. Yet, generically, the focus of 'communicative reflexives' upon combined activities, shared plans and the celebration of togetherness, erected an effective barrier of contentment that kept them socially *in situ*.

The subjects whose interviews formed the basis of this chapter all happened to be working class in origin. Therefore it is a perfectly fair question for the reader to ask whether 'communicative reflexivity' is particular to this class. In empirical terms, it is one that I am incapable of answering. Nevertheless, I am prepared to venture that there is no reason *in principle* why it should be so restricted. Indeed it might be hazarded that the established upper classes could be just as propitious to the making and maintenance of 'communicative reflexivity' as might also be medium-sized rural communities with sufficient job opportunities for the young to remain there. Why then are the middle classes tentatively hypothe-sised to be hostile towards this mode of reflexivity? In the grossest terms, because middle-class life, despite its infinite variety, generally fosters discontinuities: geographically it is migratory, educationally it is experimental, occupationally it encourages mobility, diversity and novelty. I am thus venturing, as an entirely unsubstantiated hypothesis, that the mode of 'communicative reflexivity' is not restricted to any given social class. Conversely, there are factors which will be hostile to this type of life of the mind which can appear in all classes, and also ones which serve to foster 'communicative reflexivity' whose frequency may well be much greater in certain socio-economic groups.

'Communicative reflexivity' is a mode of mental deliberation whose exercise depends upon turning to *similar* others. As such it is not a fully private life of the mind, but one that exposes itself to its proximate environment. The better the inter-personal relationships involved, the broader the self-disclosure and the greater the permeability of the self to the surrounding context. In the process, this self-opening to similars and to familiars fosters reproductive continuity, even to the point of contextual replication. The other side of the coin is that it induces self-closure against external influences that could set in train an 'elastication' of horizons. Thus, in the making of a 'communicative reflexive' we should not expect to find seriously discordant family relationships or any severe incidence of contextual dislocation. The maintenance of 'communicative reflexivity' depends primarily upon sustaining 'thought and talk' and, as has been seen, the constitution of the subject's own micro-unit will powerfully reinforce it by promoting mutual *avidaya* – the joint preoccupation with the proximate. This 'comfortability' is equally inimical to an adventurous exposure to the outside world as it is to an inward withdrawal into solitude.

7 Autonomous reflexives

The internal conversation of 'autonomous reflexives' is precisely that. It is the lone exercise of a mental activity, which its practitioners recognise as being an internal dialogue with themselves and one which they do not need and do not want to be supplemented by external exchanges with other people. In other words, the life of their minds is a private domain, because to these subjects their inner deliberations are self-sufficient. 'Autonomous reflexives' are people who would subscribe to the view that 'no one can know my own mind as well as I do myself'. Only they can know exactly what they value, only they can define which projects constitute the pursuit of the worthwhile, and only they can design the life practices which embody such goals and then monitor them to establish whether or not these are ones with which they are able to live.

This self-sufficiency might easily be taken for, but is not, arrogance. 'Autonomous reflexives' acknowledge their personal limitations as readily as does anyone, but they define them in a distinctively technical manner. They will agree that they have many areas of sheer ignorance and they willingly seek those with the requisite expertise – be it in plumbing, dentistry, or information technology. These are all matters of specialist qualifications and relatively impersonal services. Conversely, as far as their inner lives are concerned, 'autonomous reflexives' take responsibility for themselves and for the conclusions drawn from their own interior deliberations. Since they are as fallible as the rest of us, they will often turn out to have been mistaken in the courses of action they have adopted. Indeed, this handful of interviewees provides some radical examples of wrong turnings and of re-direction during their life-courses. Nevertheless, these are their self-diagnosed errors, self-directed corrections and self-monitored revisions – all of which are grounded in a development of self-knowledge. While these subjects will readily call in the builder, I suspect that they would share a suspicious reluctance to call upon the psychotherapist.

Unlike the 'communicative reflexives', they would not make constant resort to 'friends and family' in order to complete their internal deliberations. For the 'autonomous reflexive', the internal conversation is indeed a matter of autonomy. It was seen that one reason why the 'communicative reflexives' engaged in their pattern of 'thought and talk' was because they mistrusted their own deliberative conclusions, unless these were supplemented or corroborated by others whom they trusted. In contrast, the 'autonomous reflexive' displays none of this self-mistrust and seems highly confident in the outcomes of his[1] lone inner conversations. Certainly, he often admits himself to have been wrong, but, conversely, he would not agree that he would have done any better by consulting others, and is more likely to assert that he would have fared much worse.

Given their self-confidence in their own internal conversations, it is not surprising that all 'autonomous reflexives' declare themselves to be decisive people, people who have no difficulty in coming to decisions. Equally, given the significant amount of time that all members of this sub-group declared that they devoted to inner dialogue, it is also congruent that they should engage in many more of the types of mental activities (from the prompt list) than was the case for the 'communicative reflexives'. These differences pervade the interviews. 'Autonomous reflexives' are economically articulate. Confident in their self-knowledge, they quickly delivered decisive responses, hardly ever availing themselves of my invitation to take as much time as they needed to formulate their replies. Moreover, they responded in the form of self-contained statements which usually lacked those final, interrogative 'isn't its', by which the 'communicative reflexive' sought confirmation or conversational engagement from me, as interviewer. The economy of their articulation does not imply a better command of English or a higher level of education. This group of five spanned three from working-class backgrounds (two skilled and one unskilled) to two from upper middle-class families (one with two graduate parents and the other whose father had undertaken a doctorate). Two subjects had qualifications which were indistinguishable from those in the previous sub-group, whilst the other three held higher degrees. It would thus be very difficult to attribute their common pattern of response – quick, clear and decisive – to social-class origins, elaborated language code, or educational level.

That was only the start of their differences and distinctiveness as a sub-group. Three features, in particular, set them apart from the 'communicative reflexives'. Firstly, in place of the remarkably high degree of 'contextual continuity', which we have seen to be characteristic of those whose deliberative pattern was 'thought and talk', the 'autonomous reflexives'

---

[1] Since four of the five interviewees in this sub-group are male, the masculine pronoun will be employed in this chapter, except for personal references to the one woman.

had all shown a readiness (if not a desire) to move away from their initial context of involuntary placement. In any case, the backgrounds of most had been much more discontinuous. Geographical moves were mentioned spontaneously in four of the five cases. Two subjects had attended boarding schools, and these, together with a third interviewee, had been to university. Thus a dense and continuous network of family and friends was absent from the backgrounds of all but one member of the sub-group (who volunteered nothing on this matter). Before over-hasty conclusions are drawn about the making of an 'autonomous reflexive' from the unavailability of this contextual resource, attention must also be focused upon their unanimous response to their backgrounds. Each and every one of them had early on (that is, before twenty-one for all, and much earlier for most) either sought to distance themselves, or accepted with equanimity that they were distancing themselves, from their initial context of involuntary placement. In no sense did this spell 'bad family relations', indeed all spoke quite warmly about their parents. It was rather that these people had conceived of projects whose realisation would firmly separate them from their initial context and would also represent a socio-economic break with it.

As the bearers of projects that were divergent from their original *milieux*, there is obviously no sense in which these subjects were engaged in contextual replication. Because they were not, then further differences came into play. On the one hand, to pursue a 'transformatory' project is also likely to activate social constraints and enablements. Among 'autonomous reflexives' it is thus unsurprising that considerably more of their internal conversation is about society – about the means, the 'costs' and the 'benefits' of seeking to realise one's ultimate concerns within it. On the other hand, this was a two-way relationship between structure and agency, which involved both 'elastication' and 'contraction' of their aspirations, for different subjects at different times. In turn this meant that these subjects did not remain unchanged over their life-courses. In so far as they succeeded with their original projects, they themselves came to occupy new social contexts, but ones that, as ever, carried their quota of involuntary features. They were then in novel positions, ones in which to learn new things about both themselves and society. In turn, this mobility prompted further distinctive cycles of the internal conversation, as subjects evaluated their new situations in the light of their concerns and simultaneously evaluated their old projects in the light of their new situations. Unlike the 'communicative reflexives', who remained faithful to a single project over their life-courses, and one which entailed a voluntary curtailment of their aspirations, the lives of 'autonomous reflexives' were considerably more eventful. In becoming detached from their original social moorings, the new contexts they confronted presented them with a different array of questions to answer. These ranged from whether or not to re-endorse their original projects, and if so, how to live them out in a changed setting, to whether or not their changed circumstances constituted good reasons for a re-examination of their projects, perhaps ones involving radical revisions. In short, their life-courses were much more varied and this had entailed a more intensive internal scrutiny of their ultimate concerns.

The second feature which characterises the 'autonomous reflexives' is one which they share with the 'communicative reflexives', but not with the 'meta-reflexives', namely an unproblematic dovetailing of their concerns. It will be recalled that all 'communicative reflexives' designated 'family and friends' as their ultimate concern. Other concerns were smoothly dovetailed by subordinating them to the welfare of this inner circle. In particular, the 'communicative reflexives' accommodated work by voluntarily reducing their occupational aspirations, whenever these clashed with the (perceived) needs of family and friendship. 'Autonomous reflexives' also achieve the same unproblematic dovetailing, but do so in relation to a totally different ultimate concern and by use of a quite different method. For all in this sub-group, 'work' was their priority (as a matter of fact, rather than of necessity[2]). Therefore inter-personal relations have to be subordinated to this ultimate concern. This is not done inconsiderately, because all members of the sub-group struggle to elaborate an accommodative 'ethic of fairness', which gives other people their due, whilst protecting their own ultimate concern. In so doing, they are probably harder on themselves than on others; they tend to go the extra miles to ensure that both concerns are served, but in due order. Other concerns, which are not defined as responsibilities, are given short shrift. These are not people who place much of a premium on hobbies, holidays or homes and gardens. Indeed, their own physical well-being is often rigorously subordinated, until it has to be given a modicum of attention lest its deterioration threatens the dovetailing achieved.

Their third common feature is individualism, with all its most salient connotations. These are independent people, whose self-sufficiency makes each of them something of a 'loner', regardless of whether they are married or, in one case, a member of a religious order. What this means quintessentially is that they are not dependent upon others, and this is reflected in the form of *modus vivendi* which they find satisfying and sustainable; not for them the simple contentment which the 'communicative

---

[2] This is an empirical finding. Nothing would prevent an 'autonomous reflexive' from nominating, for example, his sporting, artistic, or investment performance as his ultimate concern.

reflexives' derive from their familial conviviality. Next, they are philosophical individualists in their profound belief that they, and everyone else, must take personal responsibility for themselves. Hence the appropriate epigraph for them would be: 'I am the master of my fate: I am the captain of my soul.'[3] To be such entails disciplined self-monitoring, for the subject alone assumes responsibility for the projects which he has embraced and for living with their outcomes, but it does not involve self-doubt. It is congruent with such individualism that three of the five interviewees were self-employed or worked alone. Finally, they also show a marked tendency towards political individualism. Just as 'autonomous reflexives' are self-reliant in their personal lives, so their political tenets are non-interventionist. Personally, they can all be generous, charitable and compassionate, but this is a voluntary giving to other individuals; it is not a policy that they believe it would be beneficial to institutionalise.

Yet the individualist does not live in a world of social individualism. Because these are people with projects, especially ones whose accomplishment entails a shift away from their original and involuntary social placements, they confront constraints and enablements which are socially irreducible. Unlike the 'communicative reflexive', whose concerns and courses of action systematically evade the impact of these causal powers, the 'autonomous reflexive' will necessarily interact with them. As individualists they may be adept at self-monitoring, but how good are they at monitoring their circumstances – at circumventing constraints and at harnessing enablements? In other words, how good as strategists are our five individualists? This is the question that this chapter seeks to answer. First, however, we had better make the acquaintance of an 'autonomous reflexive'.

Eliot Wilson: a picture of an 'autonomous reflexive'

Eliot is fifty-seven years old and a self-employed antiquarian bookseller. He took up bookselling at the age of forty, after resigning his academic post in order to do so. The new *modus vivendi*, which he has established over the last seventeen years, is obviously of considerable interest in this 'portrait'. Eliot is married to a working professional, has two sons, now aged over twenty-one, and he works from home.

As usual, I begin by establishing that Eliot does engage in internal conversation and start to probe its frequency. He immediately links the question of the timing of his internal conversations to the interior dialogue being a mental activity that can only be exercised when alone: 'I think

---

[3] William Ernest Henley, 'Echoes for Invictors', *The Cornhill Magazine*, 1875.

I do it at distinct times, the times when I'm on my own.' Less than five minutes into the interview and Eliot has already pinpointed his major difference from the 'communicative reflexives'. There is no externalisation of his internal deliberations, no quest for conversational confirmation, corroboration or completion from others; rather there is confidence in the self-sufficiency of his own interior dialogue. He puts the capstone upon this when emphasising that he trusts himself, whilst his inclination is to mistrust others – and, the more they are agreed, the more misleading they would be. 'Yes, self-confidence, backing my own judgement . . . I just don't pay attention to what other people put value in. That doesn't seem to me to be the way forward – steer clear of the herd.'

As soon as we begin to work through the prompt list of internal mental activities, it is clear that Eliot engages in a wider range than was the case for 'communicative reflexives', but also that each one is channelled towards his work. We begin by discussing 'planning', which is obviously important to him: 'That's one of my major areas. How best to fill the time. How best to use the time – fill the time is the wrong word – how best to use the time. How to use the time to best effect.' As Eliot substitutes 'using' for 'filling', we have an interesting example 'out loud' of a Jamesian premonitory thought, which the subject, on hearing his own utterance as object, questions and proceeds to correct. In this short response, Eliot gives, as it were, a public demonstration of the form of his private inner dialogue. The continuation is equally significant. I ask him whether or not this statement refers to planning in general, meaning the planning of everything he has to do, and am told that he intended it as 'work related'. He continues: 'I think it is part of being self-employed that I need, or feel the need, to use my time most efficiently. I think it [planning] is mostly in terms of "office management" (ironic laugh). To put it more crudely, it's how the heck do I get it all done today. What have I got to do today? Where do I start?'

As we move through 'rehearsing', 'mulling over' and 'prioritising', these are all important mental activities for Eliot (the last of which is, 'what I do nearly the whole time'), and they are all interpreted in the same work-related manner. When we come to 'deciding', he says that, 'yes, it is central to my existence. I have to think through the pros and cons of everything I do.' Since Eliot himself has just spoken of 'everything', I wonder whether he is now speaking more broadly and so echo the word interrogatively. He replies: 'I don't think I've been able to get away from my work in anything that you've said so far, or the way that you've put it automatically suggests work to me. You would really have to jolt me away from what it is that I'm thinking about – tell me that I'm quite as limited as I am, in thinking along such narrow lines as I think you're suggesting that

I am doing. You can nudge me out of it, but it's you that'd be nudging.' This is perceptive about what I was trying to ascertain and equally it is confidently self-reflexive. Eliot owns his ready responses, as opposed to other reactions which could be elicited if I took the responsibility for enforcing an agenda. Not only was I trying hard to be non-directive but, more significantly, I had put exactly the same questions to Angie, in virtually the same words. Systematically, Angie had given them an interpersonal interpretation. Correspondingly, Eliot has just said that 'the way that you've put it automatically suggests work to me'. It seems hard to resist the conclusion that the subjects' own ultimate concerns do act as a sounding board which consistently directs their responses towards that about which they most care.

This is confirmed when we move on to the freer forms of mental activity. Where 'clarification' is concerned, which I suggest could involve an issue, a person, a problem or an event, Eliot says that, 'quite a lot of the thought is what I would call drafting for what I would put on paper'. Similarly, 'imaginary conversations' tend to be preparations for his forthcoming phone calls. At that point, he ruefully comments, 'I'm awfully sorry, it's business yet again.' I tell him there is no reason whatsoever to apologise for his own mental pre-occupations, which are precisely what are of interest, and then raise the topic of free imaginative play, including fantasy. This is the first and only negative response he gives to any heading on the prompt list. Its form is revealing. Eliot acknowledges this mental activity but says, 'I'm sure I've disciplined myself out of that. I would regard that as a waste of my time.' What this statement reveals is the tip of an iceberg. Self-discipline, or disciplined self-monitoring, turns out to play a major role in Eliot's autonomous internal conversation.

So far he has sounded very self-confident in his own mental judgements, and this remains unqualified during the rest of the interview. Yet, he now reveals that his uncertainties concern performance, or how to turn right judgement into right action. This comes to the surface as we discuss demanding tasks (ones which he designates as such), and whether or not he mentally talks himself through them. Eliot says, 'if I know that it's difficult, I try to give my full attention to it. The fear is that in not giving full attention, I will make some stupid error and curse myself for it. So there is discipline.' The self-discipline comes at the start of a task, in the form of enforced attentiveness, and the self-monitoring comes at the end, as a form of quality control. 'If I'm trying to prepare something that I know should be perfect in presentation, camera-ready, then I will be very cross with myself and regard myself as failing to have concentrated properly or cross because I know that I'm tired and not producing perfect copy. I could kick my own backside. I hate those moments when

I think this is just not up to standard – I can do better than that.' There is also meta-reflexivity in this comment, but it is entirely task-oriented; Eliot shows little interest in himself as subject *per se*.

Within his internal dialogue he is a hard task master on himself, constantly uncertain about the standard of his own performance, ever cognisant of his own fallibility, and never willing to give himself a pat on the back when things do go well. The most that he allows himself to think is, 'crikey, I haven't made a bog of it today. There is some relief in that, but I would never be more positive than that. Just blessed relief, not congratulation.' It is every kind of performance which comes in for this severe self-discipline, and that includes talking to people. Whilst 'communicative reflexives' concentrated upon monitoring the other, for mood, receptivity and so forth, Eliot monitors himself. 'When talking to other people, I'm normally aware of the correctness of my own contribution, that I haven't said precisely what I ought to have said. And I spend longer criticising my own performance to myself.' I ask whether these thoughts affect his behaviour towards his interlocutor and am told that, 'it has an immediate and obvious effect, that is to say how can I cut it short and get out of it without making even more banal statements and landing myself in a hole'. Thus, whilst Angie reaches out to others conversationally, to complete her own thoughts, Eliot is poised for withdrawal if conversation extracts what he deems to be an undesirable presentation of himself. The 'conversational reflexive' needs the other to complement her thoughts with their talk; the 'autonomous reflexive', with no such needs, is really evaluating whether another person stimulates a good, bad or indifferent performance from him.

We move on to a discussion of his main concerns in life and, having heard so much about work, I expect his bookselling to be immediately volunteered as his ultimate concern. Instead, Eliot tells me that, 'I wish to have the sense of being useful.' As somebody who takes full and sole responsibility for his activities and their outcomes, it is completely congruent that he should also need to find them justifiable – and that this can only be a matter of self-justification. Justifiability entails 'being busily fruitful' and this is what Eliot means by 'the centrality of my work' as his ultimate concern. I enquire directly whether work has always had this centrality for him. He replies with an indirect statement of his work ethic: 'The pattern was established pretty early on and certainly I think anyone who had known me as an undergraduate wouldn't have been the slightest bit surprised to know that. But there are emotions . . . there is control and there is discipline. Most of the time that control and discipline doesn't need to be seen – doesn't manifest itself. People just assume that I do my work because I love my work.' Here Eliot is stressing that the 'centrality' of his work cannot be understood by what he is seen to do, nor as something towards which he just happens to have an affinity, but that it is central because it engages so much of his inner life as well.

It is significant that Eliot has just dated the start of his recognisable pattern of mental activities to his undergraduate days. Prior to that his biography was one of considerable 'contextual discontinuity'. Both of his parents were graduates, his mother a teacher and his father a grammar school head; his aunt and uncle occupied the same respective roles and his older first cousin became head of a public school. Other relatives constituted a broader network of teachers – something whose replication Eliot was eventually to repudiate. Yet contextual discontinuities emerged early; first the death of his father, which prompted a move from north to south; secondly, his mother's re-marriage and another move, to East Anglia; third his dispatch to a boarding school, which he remembers with loathing as a mix of bullying and boorishness, with few saving graces; until he took up his place at an Oxbridge college. There had never been a pool of those contextually continuous with him to whom he could have 'thought and talked'. There had been much to drive him fairly miserably in upon himself, and he had already accumulated enough negative experiences to make him question the desirability of replicating the teaching line.

His eight years at Oxbridge (as undergraduate, doctoral student and research fellow) were a period of 'elastication'. After gaining a first-class degree, he was encouraged to continue and gradually embraced the project of becoming an academic himself. He was now mixing with those of a different socio-economic status, some of whom saw themselves as the intelligentsia of the establishment. In coming to be part of them, Eliot had distanced himself from his background of plain living, politically uninfluential, nonconformist teachers. Ironically, by assuming a higher academic role, his family could only applaud. He began to embed himself in his new context. His first life-long friends date from this time, for significantly and unlike Angie, Eliot makes no mention of friends prior to this period; he has none who are continuous with his beginnings, none from school.

Yet before he could forge a *modus vivendi* within his new context, another discontinuity intervened. When an appointment in his university, if not his own college, was not immediately forthcoming, Eliot took a lectureship at a redbrick university. For the first few years, he seems to have viewed this as an interregnum, a time in which to make Oxbridge applications and then to return from the cold. He is scathing about that nameless institution where he would lecture for thirteen years, and increasingly saw it as a huge disjunction which had ironically carried him back to teaching. As he describes it, 'the realisation came to me in my late thirties that I didn't wish to spend the rest of my life with twenty year olds – teaching twenty year olds'. As a subject, he had examined his redbrick context as an object, and had found it wanting. Only two things were logged on the positive side of his balance sheet. Firstly, for several years he had enjoyed doing a little bookselling, within his area of academic expertise. Secondly, on campus he had also met and married his wife, someone who was as committed to the academic life as he was now disenchanted with it. When Keith Joseph's 'golden handshake' scheme was introduced, Eliot took the voluntary redundancy package, and, when forty years old, adopted the new project of becoming an antiquarian bookseller.

We will return later to an assessment of what part constraints and enablements played in this decision and its execution. Meanwhile, Eliot had a wife, two young children and a dog, all of whom he lists as his concerns, though he has the courage of his self-knowledge to list them as subordinate ones. How could he have made such a dramatic change of career and yet still have achieved a smooth dovetailing of his concerns? As he answers, he begins to articulate what I have called the 'ethics of accommodation', as is common practice among 'autonomous reflexives'. 'Had I not had a salaried professional working wife, I probably wouldn't have dared to do what I did do. But I don't think that I threw on her any undue burden. And were I now looking back and to say, well those school fees, obviously I couldn't pay them out of my earnings – but we did share them the whole way through. I wouldn't now like to look at my children and say they could never have had that education but for my wife's contribution . . . If I didn't think that I'd paid my fair share, I would be pretty unhappy in looking back over what I have done, or been allowed to do, or enjoyed doing. It would be a pretty unpleasant stain on what I would regard as the enjoyment of the last seventeen years.'

In other words, accommodation is achieved by respecting the rightful expectations of others and making the appropriate contribution – in cash and in kind. This is predicated upon the other (in this case his wife) having her own concerns which were not harmed by Eliot pursuing his new project. In fact, this 'concordat' assumes much more. It presumes that his wife also conducts and concludes her own 'non-communicative' internal conversation, because their domestic *modus vivendi* is not arrived at by 'talking things through'. Indeed, Eliot relies upon an unvoiced consensus between two independent people who try to act fairly towards one another, to achieve dovetailing. Unlike the 'communicative reflexive', he is fearful that too much shared conversational analysis would prove destructive of the very balance they have achieved. 'The relationships that I have in my own house matter, but not in the way that most other people would assume they matter. But they do rest on respect for the other person's desire to get on in their own way with their own priorities. I think it's respect for other people's priorities, within the home. But maybe I deceive myself – maybe mine are the ones to which other people necessarily defer – in which case that's rather sad, but it works. And I suppose if it works, if something works as a relationship, then in large measure I don't question it. I don't take it for granted, but I don't want to upset it perhaps by questioning it or doing anything that might take it onto a slightly different basis.' Eliot is an individualist and he expects his wife to be independent and his children to grow up to be independent adults. Since this seems to be the case, then dovetailing remains unproblematic, and he is a great believer that 'if it ain't broke, then don't fix it', especially by conversational means which might challenge the terms of their unspoken 'concordat'.

Finally, I question him about how he looks back upon his change of direction seventeen years ago. He replies, 'I think you're asking me whether I'm happier with myself doing what I'm doing than I could possibly have been were I still pursuing that career which is the only career that I imagined for myself when I got into it, thirty something years ago – university lecturer. I'm happier doing what I'm doing.' Eliot finds his *modus vivendi* satisfying and sustainable. It would probably be so only to a tough individualist; one who is confident of his own judgement, in a business environment for which he has no training, who is indifferent to the opinions of others as to whether or not he has taken a step upwards, downwards or sideways, and above all, who is prepared to work from home, in considerable isolation. Some college friendships have endured, and many more than he expected have developed from bookselling – and now play a significant part in what he defines as his 'usefulness'. Yet, unlike Angie, he has never pursued friendship for friendship's sake. It is an ancillary benefit which comes from work, largely punctuating his solitude by the ringing of the phone, and leading to little outside social life. Work continues seven days a week, a rota of solitary invoicing, packing and the compilation of catalogues. It is difficult to imagine anyone other than an individualist being happy in this working environment: as a sole-trader whose employment is un-pensioned, whose market is ever unpredictable, and whose whole enterprise now has a huge electronic question mark over it. Perhaps the only certainty in his way of life is that it invites an endless amount of internal conversation and thus systematically reinforces his 'autonomous reflexivity'.

'Autonomous reflexives' across the age-range

Let us begin by comparing and contrasting 'autonomous reflexivity' with the previous mode of reflexivity to be examined. 'Communicative reflexivity' tends to remain a pattern of internal deliberation which, with very minor variations, lasts for life – on one condition. This is that life itself remains relatively unchanging. If the life-course displays considerable 'contextual continuity', from beginning to end, the pattern of 'thought and talk' seems to perdure throughout it. Not only did the six 'communicative reflexives' undergo no major shifts away from their original social placements, but also they themselves voluntarily contributed to the maintenance of their stasis in the society. In other words, their social stability was jointly attributable to structure (to no radical disruption of their circumstances) and to agency (to people conceiving of no radical change, working hard to maintain the *status quo*, and being content to 'live within their means'). 'Communicative reflexivity' was therefore a form of mental activity which subjectively endorsed involuntary social placement and also perpetuated objective social inequalities, by virtue of establishing *modi vivendi* which replicated them.

By comparison, 'autonomous reflexivity' is a more developmental pattern in which people have to learn how to sustain a self-contained life of the mind. They are helped in this because the pattern is self-reinforcing by virtue of its consequences. Those who begin to exercise some autonomous subjectivity are already subjects who can survey their social circumstances as objects and can conceive of how they would wish matters to be otherwise. This is what is meant by their articulating novel projects for a 'better' life. As they do so, these are not 'cut down to size' by offering them out for conversational comment by 'family and friends'. In so far as any such life-project begins to succeed, it introduces a 'contextual discontinuity' whose effect is to distance the subject from the commentaries of his original close circle. These people are no longer around on a day-to-day basis, such that parents and peer-groups can conduct a running commentary *with* the subject on his doings. Consequently, the subject becomes freer to develop his autonomous inner deliberations – and then to apply their conclusions in the world, by making use of all of those reflexive activities which begin with the prefix of 'self'.

Since this tiny sub-group of five has an age-range from sixteen to sixty-seven, it is possible to examine them as *vignettes* of how autonomous internal conversations develop. This is only to see how 'autonomous reflexivity' *may* develop; there can be no determinism here. Any particular person may do things, or things may happen to him, which arrest or even reverse such a development. For example, at sixteen, Michael shows all the makings of a fully 'autonomous reflexive'; but if a serious industrial injury threw him back upon family care, or if he fell deeply in love with a 'communicative reflexive', there is simply no knowing what his life of the mind might become. Methodologically, I can only 'take people as I find them', at a given point in their lives, so the trajectory traced is only indicative and not predicative.

Michael began work as an electrical apprentice ten days ago. He still lives with his mother, because he cannot afford to do otherwise, and drives to work with his father, because he is not yet eligible for a driving licence. In most other ways too, his background is indistinguishable from that of the 'communicative reflexive'. The difference is that he wants it to be different. Already he has plans which will distance him from his original social context. Already too, he manifests a difference which sets him apart from the group of 'communicative reflexives'. As was illustrated by Angie and echoed by all the others, 'communicative reflexives' do not maintain a strong boundary between the public and the private – and their need for interlocutors means that it is constantly breached. Michael is exactly the opposite.

In the interview, we had just established that he does hold inner conversations and I had begun probing their frequency by asking whether this was something he did most days, or only if he came across a problem in his personal life or... Here he broke in and interjected: 'If it's in my personal life, I try to keep it to myself like, you know. If it's personal you keep it to yourself, don't you? You don't want really to share it with anyone. You try and think it through yourself though. But then, if you think it's alright, then that's up to you. Do what you feel is right.' I am surprised by this, partly due to (unwarranted) expectations derived from his background, but partly also because of his form of expression, which appears to be very like that of a 'communicative reflexive'. However, as this short speech progressed, it gained in self-confidence and at the end it was eliciting no completion whatsoever.

As we start working down the prompt list, it becomes clear that Michael autonomously engages in all the mental activities, except for 'clarifying', to which we will return in a moment. When I question him about 'mulling over' or just 'dwelling on something', he reformulates this and asks, 'as in when something's bugging you, but you ain't really got time to think about it?' This is acceptable, so I ask if he tries to 'suss it out', when that is the case. His reply is intriguing because it hints at a public/private distinction, which he has introduced by interpreting the 'something that is bugging you' as being a personal matter. 'I do if I've got the time. But if I'm thinking about something else, I try to think about it later... If I'm at work and I've got a problem at work, I'd rather get that sorted out and then sort out something like that later on.'

In answer to when he would do this, he produces a series of statements, all of which confirm a marked tendency towards 'autonomous reflexivity'. The most telling of these is his repeated insistence upon the need to be alone. He does his 'mulling over' or 'sussing out' when listening to music. 'That always helps when I'm trying to think about something – or lying down listening to music, that's good. When you think about something, it clears your head – it's much better than sitting up. And I have to be on my own as well, to think about something. Because you've always got someone speaking to you, and you, like, can't think about it properly if you've got to answer their questions and things like that.' When we move on to discuss 'deciding', Michael repeats this need to be alone and reinforces the autonomous nature of this activity by stressing that decision-making is not a matter for sharing: 'If you can't get any music, you just sit somewhere on your own and think about it – run it through your head again. I don't really share with anybody. No, not these problems. I sort it out myself.'

By now I am puzzled why 'clarifying' is not an activity that he does autonomously. Why does he consider this to be different from 'sussing out'? Because, to him, 'clarification' pertains to the public domain, to the world of work, where as a very new apprentice he has a right to ask – and a duty to listen attentively. At work, he accepts his technical limitations: 'You've got to watch someone. You've got to pay real attention. You can't just listen to bits of what they're saying, you have to listen from like start to end of it like. Make sure you're listening, and if they're showing, make sure you're watching as well. Don't get looking at someone else or anything like that . . . If you just look away and then look back and you miss it, you won't be able to suss it out yourself.' Michael states his dilemma. If the demonstration gets complicated and he tries to work out the problem in his head, necessarily he becomes less attentive and thus still does not fully understand. At that point, it is appropriate to ask the demonstrator to provide 'clarification': 'If you're there and you pay attention you should really put your hand up and say, "look I didn't understand that". Get them to explain it, instead of trying to think it through myself.' Far from this being 'thought and talk', it is a strictly temporary division of labour – and Michael knows it. He has to master the technicalities of his job in order to think for himself at work, but the latter depends upon the former. He knows that he has to try to work things out, 'otherwise you won't learn to think for yourself. Because one day you're going to have to think for yourself. So I suppose it's a good thing in a way. But you've still got to ask when they've just said what you missed.' Here, Michael is accepting that during his apprenticeship he has to learn to think as autonomously about (public) work problems, as he already does about private matters. He himself accepts that acquiring full 'autonomous reflexivity' is a developmental process.

Farat, the only woman in this sub-group, would accept that too, for she has given plenty of details about her gradual acquisition of self-knowledge. But she would enter a caveat. The time and circumstances have to be right before 'autonomous reflexivity' can be put into effect to design one's future life-project. Farat is thirty-seven, she is Asian-British, married with two children, and working as a full-time secretary in a large institution. Like most working mothers, she is acutely aware of the difficulties of balancing the needs of childcare against the requirements of work. However, she is also reflexively aware that she walks this tightrope only because she wants social mobility for her children and for herself. She is not working to supply family 'extras', but as part of a plan; without the plan, there is no financial need for her to work. As far as the social placement of her boys is concerned, Farat says: 'I'd not like to think – this is it. I'd like to think beyond that. Because I want better for my children than I had. I want to say to them, "you are going to university and I will support you". And that's one of the reasons I'm working. Because otherwise I wouldn't have to work if I didn't think about it in that way.'

Because she does 'think about it in that way', she also deliberates about the whys and wherefores. Farat has invested in personal equity plans to enable her children to go through university without contracting debts, but when her younger child starts school, she sees no incompatibility between her occupational advancement and the children's interests. 'Then I can think of myself a bit more and not have to worry about the time. It would be like getting a better job to help them as well as myself to do something more interesting.' Farat is confident in the outcomes of her inner conversations and shows none of the self-mistrust, common amongst 'communicative reflexives'. Thus, where 'rehearsing' is concerned, if her 'practising' does not work out for a particular interview, she does not fatalistically conclude that contingency will always render it useless, but analyses her specific mistakes and seeks to learn from them. Congruent with this, Farat avows that, 'I do plan, try to plan for the future.' She is determined to be an active agent who makes things happen, rather than a passive one to whom things just happen. Moreover, she is an independent thinker. All of her responses are made in the first-person singular. Although she considers her relationship with her husband to be good, it is a good relationship between two independent people. Therefore her own reflections are never expressed in the first-person plural; 'we' do not think anything, because that is not how either of us thinks.

Like Eliot and Michael, she has a profound moral sense of what is due to other people, in relation to what rights and responsibilities she herself can and must assume. Whilst the 'communicative reflexive' is guided by traditional action, which is *ipso facto* justified, those who think autonomously have to legitimate their individualist plans and actions – and do so by appealing to a more abstract moral code.

Farat also displays the same self-discipline as other autonomous thinkers. In her case, this means a self-imposed delay before she can implement her plans for herself: 'So, the plan for me for my future is, as long as my children are okay, to get a better job and do something more for myself. Because I'm getting to the point in my life where I want a better life out there. Before, I wasn't too fussed – when you've got young children, you just get on with it. But now I think I'm ready for that... So I do plan ahead. It's all in your mind, you just think about it and it's there all the time. You act when the time comes.' Meanwhile, she is preparing herself practically for when work can become her ultimate concern, which is why so much of her internal conversation is preoccupied with planning for change. The conclusions she draws from her interior dialogue cannot yet be put into effect, but by virtue of her 'autonomous reflexivity', Farat, a good mother, does not seem likely then to become a disoriented person once the children's high dependency is over. She has acquired a great deal of self-knowledge about her own needs as she has gone along, and has already deliberated about their future fulfilment.

Paul, aged fifty-six and a chartered engineer, who is employed as project manager on a large building site, provides a good example of an 'autonomous reflexive' at work. He readily identified himself as a 'thinker' rather than a 'talker', volunteers that his internal conversation is continuous, unless he is fully absorbed, but states that his most effective and far-reaching deliberations are conducted before and after work. For example, when discussing 'mulling over', he contrasts his approach to that of an ex-business partner and concludes by emphasising the solitary nature of the autonomous inner conversation. 'Well. I used to work with a partner who'd say, "never do anything until you absolutely had to, and you make fewer mistakes". I'm a bit more pro-active than that... you do mull things over, generally after work to be honest – outside work – whether you could have done that better or, how can I achieve this next week. You do it all the time – certainly when I drive.'

Being pro-active is just one part of using the autonomous internal conversation to produce results. Paul engages in all of the mental activities on the prompt list, with the exception of holding 'imaginary conversations'. However, it would be more accurate to say that he employs each of these activities with the conscious aim of making some occurrence more likely to happen. The following examples give the flavour of his deliberations and their objectives. As far as 'planning' is concerned, this is something he does, 'all the time, in effect. Every day, even possibly at five o'clock in the morning before we start work, so that when you get to work, you know exactly what you've got to achieve.' 'Rehearsing' is quite common to Paul, 'especially when you know you're in for a difficult meeting. You take a step back and just jot down a few notes on what you need to achieve from the meeting – and then try to make sure that happens.' 'Clarifying' he sees as, 'problem-solving and setting yourself targets really. [Assessing] whether you can make progress and monitoring yourself to make sure you have achieved it.' Equally, inter-personal monitoring is involved: 'it's how you can juggle and get the result that you want'.

Work is centrally important to Paul, and his kind of work in the construction industry is one where tangible results must be produced – quickly, safely, and to a high standard, subject to external assessment. Therefore, given that his ultimate concern is to do well at it, he explicitly directs his internal conversation to this end. As an 'autonomous reflexive', he uses his interior dialogue for effective quality-control to meet not only his own standards but also the public standards to which he knows his work must conform. Paul maintains that his experience has taught him how to perform this disciplined self-monitoring efficiently. He thus confirms that 'autonomous reflexivity' entails a prolonged learning experience. However, his case also raises a question, namely is self-monitoring for quality-control accentuated by the nature of his work, and thus is shared by Michael and by Eliot, who also deal in tangible goods? Would someone who works predominantly with intangibles have acquired the same process, especially if their job is of a form that seems wholly unsuited to formal external assessment?

Vincent is the ideal subject to furnish an answer. He is a sixty-seven-year-old priest who has been a member of a religious order since he was nineteen. There is no doubt about his 'autonomous reflexivity'. When I first start probing the inner conversation with him, his ready response shows that this is a matter upon which he has deliberated independently and long beforehand: 'I think that is how a human being lives, in constant dialogue with himself. There is always a stream of consciousness and we are aware of ourselves thinking and doing all the time. One is conscious of oneself doing it, like driving the car and being aware of oneself driving and of other road users. I don't see how one can help being aware – and being aware of being aware.' He asks if I have heard the story about the old man sitting in church who, when questioned about what he is doing, replies, 'Well sometimes I sits and thinks and sometimes I just sits.' The point is that Vincent declares himself to be incapable of just sitting anywhere without thinking: 'I couldn't do that. Either I'm reading my book or watching my television or I am thinking – being aware of myself being aware.' Thus the internal conversation is continuous throughout the day, unless he is specifically absorbed in another activity. Moreover, like Paul, the only mental activity in which he declares he never engages is holding 'imaginary conversations'. 'No', he says categorically, 'my conversation is with myself.'

Almost every day since his ordination, nearly half a century ago, Vincent has celebrated Mass. He sees this as being quite central to his role, wherever he works – and this has covered schools, hospitals and universities. However, he himself volunteers that one of the intransigent problems is that the Mass is a ritual, and it is only too easy to slide into a routinised mode of presiding, which allows the mind to wander. I ask him how he deals with this and receive a reply about self-monitoring for quality-control, which is a transposition of Paul's statement into this entirely different context: 'I tell myself to keep my mind on the job. I say to myself, this is important, this is vital, do it to the best of your ability, so bring as much of you as you can to the celebration of the Mass.' Yet, I venture, there must be some days when he feels far from prayerful, indeed like cold porridge, so how does he then cope? He responds that he, again like Paul, uses his autonomous conversation to reinforce self-discipline: 'I remind myself internally that it's not "my Mass" – a detestable term – I hang on to it being a collective celebration, one which is in no sense solely dependent upon me, but one that I must not spoil by getting in the way between "the Boss" and his people.' In fact he *is* acutely aware that there is external assessment. If he presides without seriousness and con-centration, if he is negligent or an interference, then people will simply not come. Not only is there something he intensely dislikes about say-ing Mass on his own, but to have contributed to bringing that situation about would be the most serious failure he could commit in his work – and towards his ultimate concern.

Autonomous reflexives and the mediation of social structure

'Autonomous reflexives' have an entirely different relationship to their backgrounds of involuntary social placement from that of 'communicative reflexives'. This relationship involves an agential and a structural compo-nent. The agential element consists in subjects endorsing or distancing themselves from their original backgrounds. They do so by virtue of the first projects which they conceive, and the crucial factor is whether or not these enterprises fit comfortably within their original contextual con-fines. It was uniformly the case that 'communicative reflexives' adopted projects which re-endorsed their working-class backgrounds. Conversely, 'autonomous reflexives', who originate from a diversity of socio-economic positions, all distanced themselves by looking to broader social horizons. Well before they reached their majority, they had usually formulated projects which would burst their contextual bounds. The structural element consists in the extent to which the subjects' social backgrounds constituted a dense net of inter-personal relations. Such density profoundly affects whether or not members are retained within their initial context of placement. As was seen in the last chapter, 'contextual continuity' seemed to be a powerful influence which encouraged 'communicative reflexives' to reproduce and even to replicate the positions in which they had been involuntarily placed. Agential voluntarism, meaning here the readiness of individuals to embrace projects *within* their social contexts, and structural conditioning, that is the strength with which the social background enmeshed subjects in its confines, are mutually reinforcing.

By contrast, the 'autonomous reflexives' generally had backgrounds of 'contextual discontinuity', and thus structural influences to keep them socially immobile were weak. Agentially, what is distinctive about the 'autonomous reflexives' is their very early ability to articulate projects that would carry them away from their original social backgrounds – something which, in most cases, was reinforced by 'contextual discontinuity'. In turn, their relationship to social constraints and enablements is entirely different from that of 'communicative reflexives'.

Involuntary placement and contextual discontinuity

In many ways, sixteen-year-old Michael is the most intriguing member of this sub-group because, unlike the other four, his background was formally indistinguishable from that of the 'communicative reflexive'. He lived at home with his mother, went to work with his father, who had found him his job as an electrical apprentice, and has the typical circle of working-class 'mates'. Yet, throughout the interview, Michael made clear his desire to be different, and his indifference to the expectations of his peer group. When we first touch upon 'prioritisation' as a mental activity, it is Michael who volunteers that his wish to become a qualified electrician has nothing to do with contextual replication, as might well have been the case since that is his father's trade. Instead, he sees it as a springboard to doing things which the vast majority of his acquaintances would never do: 'I want to be able to ... I want to definitely be a qualified electrician. Do things I haven't done before. More than most people would do.' So, to him, getting a trade will open up the possibility of new projects and new experiences which have not been available to him: 'getting a good job behind me – a good trade. Not a dead-end job – just sort of like something I can fall back on if I want to try something else. Do things I haven't done before. I want to go to another country like and get a job there as an electrician so that I can see bits of the world and then move somewhere else and get another job.'

Michael shows his individualism here, meaning that if he wants to achieve something, he accepts that the responsibility for doing so is his alone. He construes this as 'selfishness', which seems harsh since he is talking only about being independent. Nevertheless, disengaging himself from his collectivist background probably does seem egotistical from his standpoint. Yet his standards are his own and not those of his context. What is 'good' is not when you fulfil the expectations of others but, 'when you do something you're really proud of. If you really wanted to do it and then you've done it – that's what it's all about, doing what you want to do. Really it's mainly about yourself. You've got to be selfish a bit.' Whenever Michael has wanted anything, it has been a matter of getting it for himself. To obtain pocket money, which his mother, as a cleaner, could not supply, he started valeting cars at the age of fourteen. Now that he wants to do parachuting and bungee jumping, he accepts that he must generate the necessary means.

When at school, he did not think beyond getting a trade, but replicating his father's position was not his intention. He was attracted to carpentry, but being left-handed, found this unexpectedly difficult. Whereas school had done nothing to elasticate Michael's horizons, evening college did. He now thinks that being so young, 'I could even get a couple of trades behind my back' and is seriously considering adding stonemasonry. This would facilitate his great urge to travel by increasing his armoury of transferable skills.

Since Michael's formal training is by evening courses, he has the opportunity to pace himself and to complete the requirements faster. This he is keen to do, even though it will reduce the time he can spend with his mates. Yet far from being regulated by these mates, and curtailing his aspirations to coincide with theirs, Michael thinks in competitive terms. If competition is the name of the game, he wants to come out ahead. 'Well, I want to get it done really fast . . . which means three nights a week for a couple of hours each. And I won't be able to knock about with my mates as much – but if I do it three nights a week, I'll have it done quicker, I'll probably have done it faster than them.' I ask him about their attitudes to his plans; not only does he distance himself from their expectations, but is effectively looking at distancing himself from them. 'They reckon I won't keep it up, but I think I will. When I'm on more money than them and they're still training, that'll be good. Then I'm carefree to do what I want. I'm not tied down by anything.' He is intimating that he knows that the consequences of his (planned) actions will reinforce his separation from his context, and he welcomes this discontinuity. Michael is a young man in a hurry to get to a better life than that described by his involuntary social placement. The project he has conceived, against 'flack' from his peers, will demand plenty of commitment, but could then bring about his geographical relocation and social advancement. 'You don't look for the bad things like, you look at what's got to be done. You just look on the bright side and just think, I'll get that done. There's something better to do then.'

Some, like Michael and Vincent, had defined life-projects, very early on, whose tendential effect was increasingly to distance them from their involuntary social positioning. For others, like Eliot and Farat, this is a much slower process, involving an initial 'contextual discontinuity' that is then followed by trial projects. These essays fail to satisfy, but are rich sources for acquiring self-knowledge and slowly culminate in revised projects – ones that incorporate a deeper knowledge of self and a more penetrating analysis of society. Their revised projects are mature syntheses of these two forms of knowledge, which are achieved through prolonged internal conversations. The long-term consequence is to re-situate both subjects in a new socio-economic context, but it took both Eliot and Farat until their mid-thirties even to conceive of such radical social re-positioning. The influence of social constraints and enablements and the manner in which subjects strategically took these into account will be assessed at the end of the chapter. This section concentrates upon project-formation, upon how it is related to 'contextual discontinuity' and on how it results in an intentional distancing of these agents from their original and involuntary social placements.

Farat's teenage years appear to have been ones of growing tension between her own aims and those promoted by her Asian family. In this first phase, we can see the effects of 'contextual discontinuity' as ones encouraging Farat to assert herself against familial expectations, especially those of her father, yet being unable to formulate a project which was fully satisfying to her. Farat's father is a labourer, with a great respect for education as a source of advancement for his three children. He was seeking social mobility for them, but had rather rigid notions about the route towards it. Initially, Farat had voiced the idea of becoming either a nurse or a beauty therapist, but these plans were firmly quashed. 'My Dad was not having that at all, because he just thought that a waste of time, you know. He didn't see that it was educational.' To her father, education meant taking the standard route; to Farat, who was keen to get out into the world with a qualification, it did not. 'I wanted to go on to college and do something, and he wanted me to go into the sixth form. So

I was very stubborn there and said, "Well, I'm not going to do anything then", and ended up with a job in a printing firm as a receptionist. And then I thought, "What am I doing? – wasting my life."' When the family moved from the north to the Midlands, a compromise was reached about further training. This compromise was on gendered lines: university for her elder brother and night school for Farat. She did not object because it allowed her some escape from the family orbit: 'So I stayed on working, but I went to evening classes about three or four times a week to get my secretarial qualifications, which for me at the time was good because it got me out of the house. Because my parents were very strict being Asian. You know, they didn't – years ago they didn't like their daughters going out too much. So in a way it gave me a bit of freedom really, so I quite enjoyed it.' Yet despite enjoying the taste of freedom and the further independence she could then attain in secretarial employment, the snag was the work itself – 'I haven't landed up in a job that I would have liked.'

By marrying early and having her first child before she was twenty-one, it seems that Farat then thought she could have her independence whilst assuming the one traditional role to which she was drawn. 'I always wanted children. I was brought up with them. My nephews are a bit younger than me – I've got an older brother myself and he had children and I always used to look after his children. Yes, I've always wanted children.' By that time she had a good job in the county court, with prospects she relished for training to enter social work, but she was determined to dedicate herself to the 'traditional' domestic role. When her first child arrived, 'I had a good job and I just packed it in. I said, "Oh no, I'm not going to come back – Oh, no way am I coming back." And that was the most stupid thing I'd ever done. I had a good job and, you know I would have done really well. But I just – it was set in my mind, when I have children this is what I'm going to do. I'll bring them up on my own, you know, I'm not going to have childminders and all that.' Then comes a very painful learning experience during which Farat acknowledges to herself that she is not a woman who can be fully satisfied by the maternal role alone. 'Some people are just made for kids and it doesn't matter what they do, they just seem to flow through with everything. But I'm not like that – things really irritate me . . . That's why I have to come out to work, even when I've got kids, because some people are quite happy to stay at home. I just couldn't do it . . . I'm not the type of person that can stay at home and look after kids and have no social contact with any other adults in the day. It's just not feasible for me.'

After two years of regrets about quitting her job, rather than combining it with childcare, Farat gradually eased herself back into secretarial work and later began voluntary youth work. She took a job with the city council which also enabled her to train as a full-time youth worker. Then, soon after she gained her qualification, her second son was born. Farat was sent back to her mental drawing board. She now had the self-knowledge that not working was no option for her, she also had a strong sense of what was due to her young child, which precluded youth work because of its evening requirements, and she has a husband who was strong on moral support but shorter on domestic help. The only way that she could devise to meet these incommensurate demands was to return to secretarial work, this time in a large educational institution.

Farat now occupies a new socio-economic position which is contextually discontinuous with that of her own background. Yet, as she surveys her current social placement, which is of her own making, she finds it wanting. What it lacks is job satisfaction: 'I mean at the moment the job I'm doing is fine, but I do tend to get quite bored with it. I need something a little bit more challenging. I think sort of perhaps like teaching.' She is discontented with her pattern of taking one step forward and then one step back. Now her family is complete, now she has proved to herself that she can combine it with full-time work, she is actively looking ahead to combining it with fulfilling work of a higher status. Although, like most working mothers, Farat runs from dawn to dusk and performs a running logistical exercise in her head, she has found or made time in which to begin a foundation course by distanced learning for university entry. At thirty-seven and after much learning about herself and her society, she has finally designed a project which would yield the intrinsic satisfaction she needs and also give her a social position with which she feels she will be satisfied to live.

If Eliot and Farat went through two decades of acquiring sufficient knowledge about self and society before they could even articulate the projects which would be the culmination of their 'contextual discontinuity', Paul was quite clear about his ambition as a sixteen year old at school. He was frustrated because his school was not equally clear in its advice. He had no desire whatsoever to follow his father into the electrical trade, but wanted to enter the merchant navy. He was advised to stay on until eighteen to gain his 'A'-levels, only then to be told that seventeen was the maximum age for entry to officer training school. 'And I'd have gone. That's what I'd have gone for, rather than university. But they said, "Oh you're too old now", so I went to university. And I didn't really know what I wanted to do. I wouldn't have minded going into teaching. I think I would probably have been good at it. I was probably better at the arts, back then, if you want the truth. But, I opted for civics [civil engineering] and did a degree in that.'

Paul had entertained a clear project which would have distanced him from his context, but when that was blocked, he could not substitute another. Yet, given that he now had good 'A'-levels, the 'paradox of aspirations' came into play. He proceeded to university, thus distancing himself from his *milieu*, although in an unintended manner, but was forced to pick a degree course. Once again, the school worked against his own inclinations – towards a teaching career – and he emerged with a degree in civil engineering. Now, at fifty-six, he consoles himself with the thought that merchant shipping is a dying industry in this country. Then, as a new graduate, he moved into the construction industry and quickly became subject to 'elastication'. He found his first job, planning the erection of power stations, to be unexpectedly enjoyable and was then picked for the team which would move from the south coast to the Midlands to design a new expressway. With it came the opportunity of gaining further professional qualifications, and Paul became a chartered engineer.

Although he did well over the next eight years and was steadily promoted, he found this job, which had probably chosen him as much as he had chosen it, to be stultifying. So, 'you're in a job and you think, well it's all right, but this is only a living. In thirty years, you'll be in the same boat. I didn't really like that.' The trouble was, 'I couldn't see a future – long term. I couldn't face going thirty-five years with them in the same job.' This is Paul speaking about himself at the age of thirty, the time at which he decided to take his future into his own hands. In stock-taking terms, he had already sunk a great deal of personal capital into engineering; some of the more varied and challenging assignments he found 'very enjoyable', compared with his present employment which was simply 'alright'; he was now married to a working wife, but they did not yet have a family. Against this background he formulated his new project, and a year later he successfully launched his own business. This had not been his life-project from the beginning, but it was one that his accumulated self-knowledge told him he could find satisfying.

By contrast, Vincent, now aged sixty-seven, is still living out the project which he conceived of at the age of twelve. He represents the clearest example in this sub-group of how 'contextual discontinuity' fostered autonomous project-formation, which then reinforced distancing from his original social *milieu*. To an even greater extent than Eliot, his family history was one of substantial discontinuities. At the age of six he was separated from his siblings and evacuated to relatives in Ireland for a couple of years. In itself, this seems to highlight a dissonance about 'where do I belong', which affected all five children. His parents were born in Scotland, Vincent himself in Greater London, and Ireland had entered the picture before he was seven. Vincent has always clung strongly to his English heritage, but this was clearly a matter of individual choice, with his older siblings identifying themselves with the Scottish roots and his young brother accentuating the Irish connection. Yet when the family was re-united, its post-war years were ones of geographical mobility as his father, an analytical chemist, moved from post to post. With this went a frequent change of schools, including boarding at a prep school when the family moved further north. All of this seems highly propitious for the making of an 'autonomous reflexive', because, as in Eliot's similar situation, there was simply insufficient 'contextual continuity' to have sustained 'communicative reflexivity'.

Indeed, there appears to have been only one continuous thread in his early and highly discontinuous biography. The family were committed Catholics and they steadfastly chose Catholic boarding schools for their children. Ironically, in picking up this thread, Vincent precipitated further discontinuities. When he was twelve, his headmaster entered the classroom and encouraged any boy who thought he might have a vocation to the [particular] teaching order to explore this with the visiting provincial. Vincent did so and, 'my family was appalled, "no, no, no, this is far too young to take a decision like that."' What the formulation of this life-project challenged was his father's notion of his paternal responsibilities, which he defined as seeing his children through university, so that all five would retain their position in the professional middle classes. 'My father has always said, "Right, these are my children, I work hard to earn the money to educate them, but I want all of them to be educated to degree-level and then I can wash my hands of them." He felt very strongly about this and was saying, "By all means go off and be a priest, but I would like you to get a degree first."' In fact, father did very well with his ambitions: the oldest son and daughter both became doctors, the younger daughter a headmistress, and the youngest son a lawyer.

Meanwhile, the parish priest, a friend of the family and respected by Vincent, was brought in to arbitrate on this dispute. Effectively he mooted a compromise: '"stay on and get a good education at school and then when you're finished at school, think about it."' After moving to another Catholic school, run by a different order, Vincent says, 'this is more or less what I did'. At the point of school-leaving, Vincent declares that, 'I stuck to my guns and said, "No, if at any stage I need a degree, then I'll get one in the Order."' Thus, at nineteen he entered the noviciate and soon propitiated his father by being sent to gain an Oxbridge degree. Since, potentially, he could have been deployed to work anywhere in the world, Vincent had both embraced and exacerbated 'contextual discontinuity'.

This section has concentrated upon how all five 'autonomous reflexives' sooner or later conceived of projects that burst the bounds of their original social *milieux*. Obviously, this owes much to agential voluntarism, because only agents themselves can articulate projects. However, in those cases where details were volunteered, the presence of 'contextual discontinuity' during their early years appears to have been associated with the development of 'autonomous reflexivity' itself. Retrospectively, this seems logical. Since the 'communicative reflexive' needs to be continuously surrounded by those who can complete and confirm their thought processes, a common contextual reference point serves to anchor the 'thought and talk' pattern. Without such moorings, without a continuous group of 'similars and familiars' as daily interlocutors, without such ongoing exchanges bridging crucial decision-making points, like the transition from school to work, these subjects were necessarily thrown back upon their own mental devices. This gave an early spur to the development of a self-contained life of the mind – to the making of an 'autonomous reflexive'.

Whether or not 'contextual discontinuity' is a necessary condition for 'autonomous reflexivity' is impossible to determine from this small exploratory study. Respondents were encouraged to share only that which they were comfortable to voice. Thus, the interviews did not probe the quality of family and background relations, as a different dimension of 'discontinuity', if subjects chose to remain silent about them. Conversely, there is no doubt that the emergence of 'autonomous reflexivity' subjectively led every member of this sub-group to embrace enterprises which eventually distanced them from their objective contexts of involuntary placement – regardless of the social class to which these pertained.

The dovetailing of concerns and the realisation of projects

In the last section, the biography of each 'autonomous reflexive' was examined up to the point, which came much sooner for some than for others, when life-projects had first been conceived. Their stories were temporarily frozen at that stage, to facilitate now introducing the second proposition about the process of mediation between structure and agency. This stated that the generative powers of constraint and enablement, which stemmed from the *objective* situations confronted by agents, were only activated in relation to agents' own configurations of concerns, as *subjectively* defined. Our 'autonomous reflexives' have been left at the point where they have all articulated their ultimate concern. Yet like everyone else they must have a plurality of concerns in order to survive and to thrive in the three orders of natural reality – nature, practice and society. By accentuating 'work' as being their prime concern, this subgroup has plumped upon *performative achievement* as that which it values most highly. Nevertheless, its members cannot entirely ignore consider-ations of *self-worth* in the social domain or of *physical well-being* in the natural order; these may be subordinated but they have to be accommo-dated.

The accommodative pattern of the 'communicative reflexives' was one in which they systematically reduced their 'work' aspirations in order to protect the quality of 'family relations', as their prime concern. In consequence, they voluntarily contributed to reproducing their own social *status quo*, thus activating neither constraints nor enablements. Since the 'autonomous reflexive' cannot confront the world with a single ultimate concern, it is necessary to discover whether there is an accommodative pattern which is common to them, and, if so, whether or not it has a similar reproductive effect?

The one feature that these two very different modes of reflexivity share is that practitioners of both achieve a smooth dovetailing of their multiple concerns. However, this is accomplished in a very different manner with very different results, although it is equally voluntaristic. Since all the interviewees in this sub-group nominated their 'families' or 'households' as being the second most important areas of their lives (except young Michael who put his 'mates' in third place), this permits a direct com-parison between them and the 'communicative reflexives'. What happens when inter-personal relations are subordinated to work, rather than vice versa?

As people who have usually been subjected to 'contextual discontinu-ity', but have also courted it, they cannot deal with inter-personal relations according to the mores which prevail in their background *milieux* – which is what 'communicative reflexives' do because of their social continuity. Yet neither can the 'autonomous reflexive' simply adopt the accepted pat-terns of behaviour which are characteristic of the new contexts into which they have moved (or are moving). If these are taken-over unreflectively, they may well be hostile to prioritising work. This was precisely Farat's dilemma. She was behaving impeccably, according to lower middle-class expectations, by suspending work in favour of full-time care for her pre-school child, yet that was just not feasible to her. Therefore, if habitual class patterns of behaviour cannot be taken-over unproblematically, the 'autonomous reflexive' is prevented from relying upon established cus-tom and practice. Their comportment will require a justification because it has kicked over the traces of self-legitimating traditionalism – twice over.

'Autonomous reflexives' solve this problem by appealing to abstract ethical systems to legitimate their courses of action. Specifically, they had all elaborated an 'ethic of accommodation' to justify the pursuit of their ultimate concern with work in relation to their treatment of others. The crucial point about such accommodative ethics is that they furnish a definition of 'fairness' – a justified demarcation between the rights and responsibilities of the subject and the rightful expectations of others. In every case the 'ethic of accommodation' delineated what was due to the self and what was due from the self to other people. These notions of 'fairness', which will be teased out for the five subjects, do show variations. However, this particular sub-group turned out to be morally very sensitive, and this itself raises a question. Is there anything that prevents an 'ethic of accommodation' from simply being an 'ethic of convenience'? Is there anything which precludes 'autonomous reflexives' from raiding the plethora of ethics, lodged in the cultural system, and simply coming up with one of those sets of ideas which have 'justified' unbridled self-interest (exploitation, discrimination and inhumanity)? Yes, there is; namely the very fact that what is sought is an *accommodative* ethic. Other people, that is 'families' and 'households', were the second concern of four of our subjects and his 'mates' were the third concern of our fifth. It is because inter-personal relations were *amongst* the concerns volunteered by this group that they adopt high standards of 'fairness'. In other words, their moral tone is not intrinsic to 'autonomous reflexivity', it is how these particular 'autonomous reflexives', who *are* concerned about others, succeed in dovetailing this subordinate concern with the top priority that they assign to work. Were this inter-personal concern to be completely lacking, there is nothing about 'autonomous reflexivity' *per se* to conjoin this life of the mind with a life of such moral rectitude towards other people.

It is striking that Michael, who puts his 'mates' third in his list of priorities, after his work and sporting activities, has a clearly articulated notion of fairness. Since many of his mates are those with whom he works, it seems justifiable to present his views here, even though their 'accommodation' is less important to him than to the four other interviewees. We have already heard Michael talking quite severely about his own duties of attentiveness as an apprentice. When we start discussing if he is 'put upon', as the youngest worker on the site, he quickly furnishes an ethical defence of normal working practices, in terms of reciprocity. As one of the new entrants, 'you think you're just going to be their skivvy. You're going to be running around for them, carrying everything, do all the dirty jobs and things like that. But it's not really like that. It's not as bad as everyone makes it out to be . . . If it's quicker for them to do it, they'll do it. But, like, if they're doing something and they need it quick, then I don't mind doing it because they'll do it for me. Which is fair enough. That's what it's all about really.'

This is quite a contrast with teenaged Mel's fulmination against 'skivvy jobs' and 'snobby clients' in the hairdressing salon. However, as a 'communicative reflexive', Mel was preoccupied with the quality of interpersonal relations and could only reflect that performing such tasks did not make her less of a person. Michael, who does not share this preoccupation, already seems able to stand back and find fairness in the division of labour, provided that it is not abused. Abuse is if work-mates ask him to do things merely because they cannot be bothered. Michael says when that happens, 'it's just weird'. I press him on his choice of the word 'weird'. 'Weirdness' turns out to mean that such behaviour traduces his deep sense of fairness: 'Because like it's – how can people do that to other people – when they've been told to do something and they're getting other people to do it? That's not on really. Because they're getting paid to do that job.' Thus Michael will be very accommodative, providing that reciprocity rules, but without give-and-take towards him, and without fair-play in terms of job descriptions, 'that's not on really' – no one has the right to expect something of him 'just because they don't like doing it'.

It seems reasonable to suggest that Michael has thought through this ethic of inter-personal reciprocity, in relation to his work-mates, precisely because work is of such dominant importance for him. Therefore human relations must not be allowed to jeopardise his occupational performance or advancement. What his notion of fairness does is to accommodate the legitimate expectations of others on the building site by dovetailing them with what he sees as his due and which will allow him to move smoothly through his apprenticeship. Outside work his personal relationships are handled much more roughly and are forcefully subordinated. Having voluntarily put himself on the fast-track to gain his formal qualifications, he thinks competitively that it will be good to outdo his mates and to be on better money than they are. If by doubling-up his college modules he will be less free for nights out with his mates, then so be it; if they are around when he is not committed, then time spent with them will be welcome. Since these are relations which, in any case, he envisages leaving behind, given his project for working overseas, they can be dealt with on a *laissez-faire* basis. What these mates must not be allowed to do is to impede his ambitions, and already we have seen him deriding their expectations that he will not stick to his three nights of college per week. In short, the finesse of his ethic of reciprocity is reserved for accommodating those inter-personal relations that matter to him and thus have to be dovetailed with his ultimate concern.

At the opposite extreme is Farat, who has only just reversed her priorities from 'family' to 'work' and is still elaborating how to give both their due – that is how to achieve an effective but fair dovetailing. The self-knowledge she has acquired, by learning from her own avowed 'mistakes', finds her at the point where she has to justify 'working and combining the two, rather than just giving it up'. She can no longer accept her occupational subordination in a job which is lacking in intrinsic satisfaction, challenge or status as justified, merely because it enables her to make better financial provisions for the advancement of her sons. Farat now seeks her own advancement, but she is acutely aware about the difficulties of dovetailing her concerns. She cares for her children far too much to adopt a pragmatic approach. Therefore, achieving the career she wants cannot be done, in her words, 'by slotting them in, but by working out what's best for them'. Only Farat can work this out. With a baby to consider, she cannot resort to Michael's ethic of reciprocity, because young children cannot be partners to reciprocal accords. Her dilemma is that she has come to a point where 'I want a career – but then I don't want the little one to suffer because of my needs.'

In the past, when her priorities were 'family first', she had simply renounced her needs for theirs. In the following comment, which is both retrospective and prospective, Farat is struggling to articulate an ethic of fairness based upon respective needs. 'I'm a qualified youth worker, so that's something I was going into. But then, as soon as I had my second child, I thought, "well it's not fair, because I'm leaving him in the day, it's not fair on him for me to sort of leave him in the evening as well". So that's something I had to give up. So I'm thinking ahead now. When he's a bit older I can perhaps go into that [teaching] – but I'm thinking as well, if I go for a better job I've got to be committed to it.' Here, Farat is deliberating about how to balance fairness to herself, her children and to her future employer and pupils. What helps here is that this is not only the self-knowledge she has acquired: she also has her first-hand knowledge of children's needs, because of the fifteen-year gap between her two sons. She feels confident that her elder son was not harmed by her return to work, when he was two, and that at fifteen he is rapidly becoming independent.

Thus Farat is now able to articulate her own 'ethic of accommodation', in which 'fairness' is defined in terms of the relative needs of those in question. She sees no need for the radical subordination of her own aspirations in relation to her second child, as she did with her first. Certainly, for the next year of her baby's high-dependency, she anticipates remaining in secretarial work and stretching time in order to complete the foundation level of her course. However, when he enters nursery school, Farat sees no 'unfairness' in her undertaking a degree. Living out this particular 'ethic of accommodation', will take up a significant portion of her life-course, and is proportionately damaging to her future life-chances. Nevertheless, when Farat is thirty-eight, she feels that she will be able to dovetail her concerns, such that legitimate family demands no longer preclude the realisation of her ultimate concern for a career.

If societal expectations about gender roles caused Farat so much frustration and delay, they performed precisely the opposite role for Paul. He declares that his concerns are 'all related' and that work and the family dovetail smoothly. When he became self-employed, at the age of thirty-one, 'I could do that because I didn't have any children and my wife was working.' Fair enough for that time, but when the children came along a few years later, how did he then maintain his smooth dovetailing? Paul volunteers that he 'certainly cares a lot about them', but that he had sacrificed his part in their growing-up to launching his firm. 'When I was running my own business I probably didn't spend enough time with the children, in as much as I was out before they got up and I'd be home after they'd gone to bed. I didn't spend much time with them.' How though, when working around the clock to establish his business, to the point of making himself seriously ill, did Paul justify this subordination of his family? His 'ethic of accommodation' was completely dependent upon a division of domestic labour, which justified him prioritising work if he behaved fairly as a good breadwinner. To Paul, fairness consisted 'in providing for the family essentially. Making sure you can do that.'

If some have negative reactions to Paul's 'patriarchal' ethic, his notion of 'fairness as providence' was not unthinking traditionalism, but a genuine 'ethic of accommodation' which proved costly for him to live out. When Paul was forty-four, his children still under ten, and the business had been running for thirteen years, he had a severe heart attack, resulting in by-pass surgery. His decision, which will be examined later, was to return as full-time project manager to a large construction company. This allowed his career to continue, without working around the clock, for Paul says he no longer takes work home. Yet when I question him about his concern for his health, in relation to what is still a strenuous job, he reveals two attitudes of great interest about his physical well-being: 'I don't think about it. No point is there – as long as I keep providing for the others.' On the one hand, there is his determination to live up to his 'ethics of being the provider'. For a quarter of a century he has 'accommodated' his family through the belief that he treats them fairly if he provides for them. Now, he is not willing to redefine the terms by which he performs his dovetailing, even though this means subordinating his health to the lowest position on his list of priorities.

On the other hand, he is revealing something which is also common to the two older 'autonomous reflexives' – the younger pair having no significant health problems. Although a loss of physical well-being can occur at any time in the life-course, if its incidence post-dates commitment to an ultimate concern, then the 'autonomous reflexive' refuses to allow it to disrupt his dovetailing of concerns. Work will go on, 'accommodative ethics' will continue to be honoured, so health is relegated to the lowest possible level of concern that is commensurate with carrying on. At fifty-seven, Eliot admits that he does sometimes worry about the sheer physicality of book handling and packing. Several years ago he feared a hip-joint failure, determinedly shed three stones, takes a homeopathic treatment and (with accommodative stoicism) packs on. Vincent's attitude is identical. After being operated upon for cancer last year, he refused convalescence in order to return to his household and was publicly celebrating Mass two weeks later. As he puts it, 'I'll carry on while ever I have the health and strength to do so.' Eliot fondly imagines that he will die while parcelling, cross that someone else will have to finish the job (less neatly).

However, to return to the theme of accommodating subordinate concerns when these involve other people, Eliot is again typical in declaring smooth dovetailing to be unproblematic: 'to balance the three [work, household and dog] – no, I don't have to spend over much time'. We have already heard him say that if, as a self-employed bookseller, had he not made a fair financial contribution to school fees and domestic expenses, this would have been a blot on the enjoyment he has derived from his work. However, his concept of 'fairness' is much broader than 'fair-shares' in monetary terms. This emerges when he becomes rather shame-faced in talking about his affection for his dog, which he follows up by a revealing comparison with his family: 'Somehow or other I expect that the dog has her own agenda, but she really would be pretty hopeless without me.' The dog has legitimate expectations by virtue of her dependency, but his (grown-up) family are expected to be independent beings who successfully manage their own concerns. He extends a respect for their autonomy, which he expects to be mutual. Eliot endorses an 'ethic of decency' in his inter-personal relations, which includes a willingness to support his sons' outdoor enthusiasms, to shop, cook and garden, and to proof-read his wife's manuscripts, but one which excludes the intimate exchanges and general 'togetherness' which are supremely important to the 'communicative reflexive'.

Thus, he talks about how this dual-career family collaborates considerately, but without undermining his working life by emotional dependency or intrusiveness: 'I think I have to say that either I have a very understanding wife or a wife whose behaviour is as akin to mine as I'm likely ever to find on earth. The idea that I should be married to someone who would have emotional responses to every aspect of my existence – that of course would be a horrible prospect for me.' Perhaps unsurprisingly, the elder son, who has now graduated, also started his own business: the 'ethic of decency' required that Eliot offered financial assistance, but as someone rightfully 'in charge of their own affairs', it was properly declined by his son. The 'ethic of decency' accommodates family to work, largely because family members appear to share it, but it is clear that it performs a regulatory role towards inter-personal relations in general by strictly demarcating legitimate expectations from what are held to be unfair ones. 'I hate letting people down more than I probably used to. I have a fairly clear idea in my own mind what other people expect of me, but if I feel that I have let them down, then I'm much more severe on myself for so doing. If I think they're entertaining far too great an expectation or invade to the extent that some do, then I'm likely to cut them or say I cannot cope with that degree of interference in what I regard as my private existence.'

Vincent had an entirely different problem about accommodation, because it was one which was set for him. Therefore he had little control over his situation and no preparation for it. In effect, Vincent was seconded by his Order to become a university chaplain, to offset the shortage of priests in a diocese that was unable to staff the proliferating new universities. A modest stipend and a large diocesan house went with his appointment. The only way to make ends meet and to maintain the property was to take in four or five postgraduate tenants. Vincent's task was how to accommodate his office with this secondary role of landlord. He has dovetailed them by elaborating another 'ethic of decency', which can be seen as both an extension to and a protection of his office.

On the one hand, he charges very fair rents, which are even more advantageous to students because he takes responsibility for providing all domestic products and staple provisions – tea, coffee, milk, bread, butter. He himself explains this pragmatically: 'it would be daft for six people to be buying loaves'. As a man with a clear distaste for sanctimoniousness, I wonder whether this decision to supply basics is not underpinned by a Christian concern that no one should go really hungry under his roof? Be that as it may, it is a task he takes seriously: 'if I've forgotten something and we've run out, then I've let myself down and I've let my tenants down'. Rather than do so, he will turn out in the dark to fetch the milk. His consideration goes further; he offers to drive the tenants to the supermarket several times a week, to save them a three-mile walk, buys each new intake any items of furniture they require, and never charges them for the weeks when they are away. He takes a gentle pride in the execution of his new role and his ex-tenants become regular visitors – another part of his extended family.

On the other hand, Vincent takes care that domestic arrangements in no way compromise his office. Shortly after his appointment, nearly nine years ago, he had the diocese construct a small self-contained bedroom and bathroom, to obviate potential embarrassments in sharing with female tenants. Moreover, the household seems to run on a series of unspoken understandings: that others enter his sitting-room only by invitation, that boyfriends or girlfriends do not stay overnight, and that entertaining members of his flock takes precedence for use of the dining room. In these ways he smoothly dovetails the domestic concerns, which he did not seek, yet cannot avoid, with his ultimate concern as a working priest.

Thus, every one of the 'autonomous reflexives' has, in quite different ways, succeeded in accommodating their different inter-personal concerns. Two factors distinguish their achievement of smooth dovetailing from that accomplished by 'communicative reflexives'. Firstly, their accommodation does not and cannot rely upon established custom and practice. 'Contextual discontinuity' spells a break with the traditions of their upbringing, and the thrust of their ultimate concerns usually precludes the adoption of the conventions prevalent in their new *milieu*. Consequently, it has been seen that all our 'autonomous reflexives' elaborate a much more abstract 'ethic of fairness' to accommodate their inter-personal commitments, precisely because these were matters of concern, rather than such an ethic being a corollary of 'autonomous reflexivity' itself.

Secondly, and of much greater import to the question of 'mediation', the 'autonomous reflexive' dovetails his subordinate concerns in such a manner that they are never permitted to obstruct or to dilute commitment to his ultimate concern. To 'communicative reflexives', 'family and friends' came first and work was subordinate; for 'autonomous reflexives' these two priorities are reversed. For 'communicative reflexives', the consequence was a systematic reduction in their occupational aspirations, as the price for protecting their ultimate concerns – and the result was to reinforce their social immobility. For autonomous thinkers, the outcome was the exact opposite. Because inter-personal concerns were effectively subordinated, though treated with fairness, they did not impede pursuit of the ultimate concern with work. It follows that if work is the prime concern of the 'autonomous reflexive' (and this is not a necessary association), then the unimpeded pursuit of work-objectives will not allow this sub-group to evade structural constraints and enablements, as was the case for the 'communicative reflexives'. Instead, those with an autonomous life of the mind will be more alert to social enablements and more vulnerable to social constraints because of their ultimate concerns and the projects to which these give rise. It now remains to be seen how these subjects cope strategically with the pressures to which they have voluntarily exposed themselves, and whether or not they can forge a satisfying and sustainable *modus vivendi* within their new contexts of social placement.

'Autonomous reflexivity' and exposure to constraints and enablements

The final proposition about 'mediation' states that agents *subjectively* deliberate upon their courses of action in relation to their *objective* circumstances. Reflexively they must seek to establish a *modus vivendi* at the nexus between their voluntarily defined priorities and the socially determined characteristics of the contexts that they now confront. The biographies of the 'autonomous reflexives' have been considerably more eventful than those of the 'communicative reflexives'. Their life histories entailed multiple adjustments of their circumstances in the light of their concerns and of their projects in relation to their changing contexts. This means that they will have been much more exposed to the powers of social constraints and enablements, because they themselves have activated them by virtue of the transformatory projects to which they became committed. Such projects are necessarily transformatory because they involve a distancing of the subject from his original context of involuntary social placement and his re-location in a new social context. Therefore, the last question to answer is how good as strategists were these subjects? How proficient were they at using enablements and circumventing constraints, to arrive at a *modus vivendi* through which their concerns could be realised and expressed – one which was both sustainable and satisfying?

The biographies of all five subjects show that their desired ways of life were quite different from those of their social origins. All but the youngest had already been through the process of establishing 'intermediatory' ways of living. By 'intermediatory' is meant a *modus vivendi* which was discontinuous with agential origins, but which had also been left behind: Farat as a qualified but non-working mother, Paul as a young company employee, Eliot as a university lecturer and Vincent as a school or hospital chaplain. The lives of 'autonomous reflexives' tend to move through a variety of *modi vivendi* as a result of learning about themselves and their society, whilst also coping with the inevitable quota of intervening contingencies.

For purposes of presentation, this is why all five respondents were biographically 'suspended' around the point when they had articulated their latest project. This allows us to conclude with an assessment of their virtuosity in coping with constraints and enablements. The evaluation is made in their own terms, using their own 'currencies' to judge whether they have forged a *modus vivendi* which is expressive of their ultimate concerns within circumstances which, as ever, were not of their making. For Michael and Farat, it is not possible to go very far because they have only just articulated their new priorities and the projects reflective of them. For Eliot and Vincent, now approaching or beyond the normal age of retirement, it could be tempting to assume that we are examining their 'final' pattern of established practices. However, Paul's life-course stands as a warning about the ability of contingency to disrupt the powers of both self and society – a reminder that if our subject-matter is human, then social 'science' can never aspire to prediction.

This reminder is appropriate when approaching the case of sixteen-year-old Michael, who has framed his project for a very different life, working overseas. At the moment he is severely financially constrained, to the extent that he cannot even begin to establish any of the practices which are expressive of who he wants to be, and thus of what he cares about most. On his low pay, he has to live at home for the next few years; much of his timetable is ruled by his reliance upon his father for lifts and he does not expect to afford his own wheels for some time; he lacks the resources for even a trial bungee jump; and he has not yet been abroad. Although the stringency of these constraints may gradually lessen, they are likely to be operative throughout his apprenticeship.

Within these constraining powers, derived from his original and involuntary social placement, Michael endeavours to act as strategically as he can. His social position has not dealt him many enablements, but mentally he plans to seize upon those available. He can fast-track his way through day-release, by taking on extra modules, and even complete his qualifications in two skilled trades in order to increase his employability overseas. As an individualist, he is already resisting peer-group pressure to conform to apprenticeship norms, both in training and in social life. However, Michael's present commitment will have to withstand two of the most powerful sources leading to the abandonment or re-definition of agential projects – the acquisition of self-knowledge and an increasing knowledge of society. Over the next few years he may discover that he cannot stick to the tight training schedule he envisages, or he may be distracted from it by his first serious girlfriend. He has yet to learn whether his trial paraglide is as exhilarating as he expects, or is simply terrifying. Even if all of that is successfully negotiated, he might still suffer a huge disappointment as he surveys the contractor's compound in somewhere like Dubai. Nevertheless, as a developed 'autonomous reflexive' and barring catastrophe, he should be as adept as the other four subjects at re-adjusting his concerns and re-designing his life-projects. What he cannot do is what nobody can do, namely act with strategic prescience in the absence of so much self-knowledge and knowledge about society.

Farat, much further along her life-course, still has the big decision before her about whether or not to undertake teacher training. Her major difference from Michael is the extensiveness of her knowledge base; in a personal sense, Farat is expert about the interplay between structure and agency. On the one hand, she is familiar with constraints and their power to frustrate projects. From the start she was constrained by the engendered nature of her Asian family's plans for her education and that of her brother – plans which bifurcated after the sixth form, the son being supported through university whilst the daughter was expected to attend a further education college. Further, her nascent projects of becoming a nurse or beauty therapist were incompatible with cultural expectations. Yet, far from being a strategist, Farat knows that she compounded her disadvantages by refusing to formulate a project, but rebelling by walking into a dead-end job. Effectively, she has been trying to extricate herself ever since, and has learned so much from this mistake that she will now intervene to prevent others from making the same error. Thus, she tells the story of her niece who abandoned her 'A'-level course half-way through. 'She'd had enough of education and she ended up working at [one of the big supermarkets]. So, I went in one day and said, "Do you want to work here for the rest of your life? Because I certainly wouldn't." She just looked at me – and then a few weeks later she's working in [a high street] bank. So I know I was a bit mean, but I made her get off her backside and think, "What am I doing here, I'm too good for this job, I need something better." '

Farat's encounters with enablements were another hard lesson about structure and agency. After qualifying as a secretary, she gained a good job with prospects at the county court, but uncompromisingly resigned upon the birth of her first son – 'and that was the most stupid thing I've ever done'. Although she quickly learnt that full-time childcare was not for her, and now warns her pregnant colleagues not to burn their bridges, she herself virtually repeated this cycle at a higher level. She took advantage of the 'elastication' proffered by her next job with the city council, who sponsored her training as a youth worker. As an agent, Farat again contracted her occupational mobility upon the arrival of her second child, when she decided she could not justify meeting the evening requirements of social work. Since she now knew that she must work, she fell back upon secretarial employment, where she conceived the project of gaining a degree and becoming a teacher.

Is she likely to succeed in entering a profession that will give her intrinsic satisfaction, as well as the social mobility that she wants? Structurally,

Farat knows that there are enablements – which she can ride. She is fully aware of the teacher shortage and equally knowledgeable that her qualification as a youth worker should guarantee her admission as a mature student. Farat also volunteers that childcare provisions have vastly improved since her first child was born and is fairly optimistic that her husband could now be induced to pull more domestic weight. What could stop her? Once again, it is her own agential powers. We have seen that she is saving in order to put her own sons through university, debt-free, and this is part of her 'accommodative ethic' of fairness towards them. She is unwilling to sacrifice this commitment, yet one wonders where she can find the time to do a degree during the day, work to keep up her earnings in the evenings, and still take a major responsibility for her household. Farat could become like the hypothetical woman at the end of chapter 4 – a victim of her own postponement. To succeed will take not only her commitment, but also enormous energy and near-perfect health. Yet failure would leave her without a *modus vivendi* which is satisfying because expressive of whom she wishes to be. Since Farat's own currency is 'intrinsic satisfaction', one way in which she might strategically ride the enablements, without reneging on her maternal commitments, is by taking out a financial loan herself. However, only the subject can weigh such incommensurables in her own scales and according to her own 'weights and measures'.

With Eliot we are dealing with a retrospective decision, taken seventeen years ago. In this case, it is possible to insert his own subjective 'weights and measures' into the sum of his constraints and enablements. He has also an established *modus vivendi*, whose sustainability and satisfactions he himself can reflect upon, in relation to the expectations which led him to quit university lecturing. In terms of enablements, Eliot had been the subject of considerable 'elastication', prior to his decision to enter antiquarian bookselling. He volunteered that he was fully cognisant of two objective enablements, and factored them in to his decision. Firstly, we have heard his nuanced declaration that being married to a successful academic did weigh with him as a guarantee that their children would not suffer. Secondly, he was also aware that his transferable skills constituted a powerful enablement: 'Bookselling was related to my career as a university lecturer, and I knew that the field I was going into was academic books. I could judge whether the books that I would be selling were worthwhile and I sell within my [disciplinary] field. I could make some sort of assessment – should I be touching that book, should I exploit its relative cheapness or its scarcity? And I would probably be in a better position to do that than nine tenths, more like ninety-five per cent, of fellow dealers in that market.'

Eliot mentions a third factor that constituted an objective enablement, namely the *fact* of his successful 'elastication' in the past. His proven intellectual ability was something upon which he reflected, as subject upon object. Hence, 'the confidence that I had that I was reasonably intelligent and probably more so than those amongst whom I would in future be working – that would see me through. I saw no reason to believe that I would be moving into a world where the big boys would stitch me up. No, I never feared that at all, and it wasn't because I thought that bookselling was just a nice exercise where nice, slightly eccentric people operated.'

Where constraints are concerned, Eliot's aims are a good illustration of the fact that it is the *precise* nature of an agential project which is responsible for activating constraining powers. With only his voluntary redundancy payment to invest, it might be thought that he was constrained by under-capitalisation – forever to remain a small enterprise. Yet this was exactly the type of business he wanted. Eliot had seen too many local bookshops fail through inability to cover the costs of their premises, so he determined to make use of the rambling family house, to work from home, and to sell by catalogue. He intended to specialise within his area of academic expertise, which implied equally specialised customers and a worldwide catchment area. This reinforced the wisdom of catalogue-selling in pre-electronic days. Since a specialist market would not generate a high volume of sales, he could operate as a one-man business, which allowed him to provide personal advice to purchasers. Had Eliot envisaged creating a second Hay-on-Wye, he would indeed have been constrained by under-capitalisation, but for good strategic reasons, he did not wish to be a second Richard Booth.

Seventeen years later, he is still trading, so what kind of *modus vivendi* has he established? Compared with his lecturing days, he declares, 'I'm a much freer spirit now and I indulge in my own field.' That is what is of supreme importance to him. He is unpensioned, but maintains that he would not know what to do with himself if not working. He earns less than if he had remained in university teaching, but states, 'I'm not impoverished. I've got enough. I don't work solely for money.' He may have lost status in some people's eyes, but he dismisses this: 'I would think their opinion simply betrayed a terrible ignorance of the awfulness that is British university life.' He still operates as a sole-trader, but reiterates, 'employees, no thank you. I'm much better doing it on my own backside.'

It appears that Eliot had good self-knowledge when planning his strategy, but what about knowledge of his working environment? Here he admits that, 'If I look back and think how the business has changed over the last twenty years – if I'd been told what was going to happen to my market, that would have frightened me no end.' Eliot cannot live without stock and sometimes he does not know where to find it, but he can live with the uncertainty and respond with adaptability: 'When you don't know where in the world the next books are coming from, then you have to go out and find them. But I never have an annual general meeting with myself and talk about our achievements over the past year and our prospects for the next.' It is an uncertain, solitary and hard-driven life, which only a tough individualist could sustain, yet Eliot talks about his 'enjoyment of the last seventeen years'. He has found it intrinsically satisfying, but is it sustainable? Barring ill-health, he believes that it will see him out and, as an 'autonomous reflexive', his individualism means that he takes responsibility only for himself; his 'ethic of fairness' would preclude him from binding the hands of the next generation by attempting contextual replication. 'If, as a bookseller, you ask me do I spend my time worrying about electronic publishing, the end of books and that sort of thing, yes I have these thoughts. And I normally come around to thinking, no, it isn't that into which I would have happily sent my sons. I wouldn't like to have committed them to following in my footsteps. If I say it will see me out, I have no objection to that at all.'

Professing one's final vows to a religious order might be thought to remove the possibility of strategic action from the individual and to attach it to the collectivity. This cannot be entirely the case, because many choose to leave and those who do stay have to work out a *modus vivendi* for themselves within their congregations. In fact, most have to do this several times over because of being moved from post to post. As Vincent puts it, 'taking a vow of obedience is sticking your neck out infinitely far'. One aspect of this was that his religious order came to attach more and more significance to community living, where inter-personal relations necessarily increased in importance. As a man with an independent mind, he had already discovered during his formation that getting-by consisted in, 'keeping your head below the trenches' because 'shut-up Vincent, was definitely the theme'. As time went on, the self-censorship involved became no easier. There were, 'occasions when I have thought something had to be said, and got myself somewhat trampled in the process'.

Did he have any degrees of freedom for strategic action to establish a *modus vivendi* which met his ultimate concern for being of 'useful service', whilst allowing him a less communitarian way of life? In fact, this was repeatedly the case, and both structure and agency played their part in making it possible. One enablement was the exceptionally high level of academic training of his Order – of which it was once said that final profession was the reward for a well-spent life – but also guaranteeing a ready supply of appointments in educational institutions. Perhaps his happiest two decades were spent in an ex-grammar school, where he shared a house with the parish priest, rather than living in the nearest community about twenty miles away. He sustained this arrangement, against some pressure, by his success in attracting boys to early Mass before the school day started and by becoming an indispensable deputy coach and travelling manager to the rugby teams.

When that chapter closed after an enforced sabbatical in the States ('which I neither wanted nor knew what to do with, since I had no desire to write a book'), Vincent attempted to replicate his previous position and independently obtained the offer of a post as a public school chaplain. Instead of being permitted to take this up, he was seconded to a diocese that was unable to staff the burgeoning new universities. Again, his training proved an enablement. He tells the story of a friend querying what he did when some specialised postgraduate asked a difficult question: 'Say I just don't know' commented Vincent, who has enough intellectual self-confidence to accept that the days of the polymath are over and is content simply to foster discussion. Then again, what some priests see as a constraining erosion of their authority, namely the rise of an educated laity, is very congenial to his non-directive style and emphasis on sharing the sacraments together: 'It was much easier to be dictatorial when the priest was the only educated person in the Parish. And I think that some people have awarded themselves an importance that I cannot rightly understand.' Conversely, he refuses to pontificate or even to deliver formal homilies, much preferring to say, 'well that text raises an interesting problem...' and to hope, as we all do in every seminar, that the group will respond.

Thus Vincent assimilated himself smoothly into university life, helping overseas' students with their English, holding regular dinners for the small 'family' of weekday Mass-goers, and living amicably with his tenants. Yet in many ways it is an unstructured and sometimes lonely life, for each year there is uncertainty about whether or not a new 'family' will again coalesce. In his own words, 'I described myself some years ago to my colleagues in the chaplaincy – the bottom line is I'm a "Massing Priest", that's the very heart and centre of my life. I'm not sure what else I'm supposed to do as a chaplain.' For eight years he has found enough 'useful service', he is a self-contained individualist who does not mind his own company, yet a ready conversationalist when company is around. From this he has developed a satisfying *modus vivendi*. Yet he also has to live knowing that he cannot cling to it. The shortage of priests means that, even at his age, a final re-deployment is possible. How long can his Order go on bailing out the diocese when both are in the same boat? His *modus vivendi* may not be sustainable; at sixty-eight he may still have to try to forge yet another. Vincent's response is that long ago he gave his willing consent to these terms: 'you vowed yourself to obedience, you volunteered for it – so carry on trucking'.

'Autonomous reflexives' attempt to be strategists in their own lives, that is to be active agents who make things happen rather than passive ones to whom things happen. However, strategic action is conducted in an open system and is always at the mercy of unforeseen and unforeseeable contingencies. One type of contingency over which we have very little control are the liabilities which are intrinsic to our embodiment. This is why Paul's story has been reserved until the end, as a reminder that no amount of dedication and commitment can truly allow anyone to say, 'I am the master of my fate.'

After successfully running his own business for thirteen years, Paul had a serious heart attack, followed by by-pass surgery. Medical advice was to 'slow down', which Paul, who was only forty-four, found 'depressing'. He was forced back to his own mental drawing-board. His first decision was to wind up his business. Paul was sitting at home, deliberating what to do next, when he was telephoned by his former employer and offered back his old job of 'project manager'. Given his personal need to work and his 'accommodative ethic' of providing for his family, he accepted the offer and rejoined the construction company. Now, twelve years later, how does he reflect upon this decision, made quickly and under physical duress?

The 'autonomous reflexive' is an individualist who takes responsibility for his own actions; if these are flawed he takes the blame, rather than casting himself as the victim of circumstances. Paul openly, but unemotionally, regrets his decision. Implicitly he admits that he presented the alternatives to himself too starkly, in his post-operative condition, which he will not blame either: 'Yes, I wish I'd carried on, probably at a slower pace. I'd prefer to be in charge of my own destiny.' Loss of independence is the nub of his regret; having to abide by the judgements of others is the rub. 'It's very difficult to come back to a hierarchy and line-managers. Sometimes you're answerable to people that are incompetent. You bite the bullet. You have to bite the bullet. It's quite difficult at times.' Paul compares this situation unfavourably with running his own business: 'You've only got yourself to blame when you're doing that, haven't you. If it doesn't work, you can only tell yourself off. You know whether it's working or not.' Paul's *modus vivendi* had collapsed with his health. How possible was it for him to reconstruct a new one, in the knowledge that it would be sub-optimal? Unsurprisingly, he did not even contemplate adopting the sick role, preferring to ignore his state of health and to repeat Vincent's theme of 'carrying on trucking'. His priorities remained unchanged and today, at fifty-six, his ultimate concern remains, 'Well, still being successful at work.' His currency has not been converted and remains the intrinsic interest he derives from employment. It is the variety and the challenge of different projects that keep him going. He avows that he would settle for lower pay and more interesting assignments rather than vice versa. He acknowledges that in terms of status, civil engineers are 'tarred with the same brush as builders' and, although he has travelled to countries where 'Engineer' is a distinguished title, he declares, 'I suppose it would bother everybody else, but it doesn't bother me. Not personally it doesn't.' Paul continues to endorse the personal identity he had forged prior to his health problems; what mattered most then still matters most now, for his values and evaluations have not changed.

Nevertheless, deprived of his own business, Paul knows that there are practical ways in which he cannot be master of his fate. In particular, because of enforced retirement, he cannot propose dying in harness, as Eliot and Vincent do. Can he nevertheless remain the captain of his soul? He is trying. He plans to retire at sixty-one or so, rather than clinging on until the last possible moment. He wants to do so whilst he is still fit enough to enjoy moving back to his wife's part of Wales. He is drily insouciant about life in retirement; there will be plenty to do, 'a bit of travelling, a bit of walking, the odd crossword'. Why am I left not fully convinced? Because for the 'communicative reflexive', retirement remains part and parcel of 'contextual continuity', but for the 'autonomous reflexive', whose ultimate priority has been work, retirement is one more episode of 'contextual discontinuity'. Yet, it is crucially different from earlier dislocations and re-locations, since the loss of one's ultimate concern means attempting to construct a new *modus vivendi* without an architectonic principle.

Conclusion

'Autonomous reflexives' mediate structural and cultural properties in a distinctive manner. Because they know what they want in society and formulate clear projects to achieve it, they are responsible for activating the causal powers of constraints and enablements. However, their own agential powers do not end there because of their unending capacity to reflect upon their society, as subject on object. Hence the activation of constraints and enablements and the circumvention of their powers also become increasingly reflexive activities to them.

It is simply untrue that we are all very knowledgeable about our society, contrary to what has been reiterated over the last few decades. 'Autonomous reflexives' begin life in a context of involuntary placement, about which they initially know as much or as little as their neighbours. However, as the authors of 'transformatory' projects, they willingly expose themselves to the acquisition of further knowledge about their society and about themselves. The 'communicative reflexive' becomes knowledgeable about her initial context, but as she collaborates in curtailing her own social horizons and as she contributes to contextual replication, so its confines also become the bounds to her knowledge. For her, *il n'y a pas de hors contexte*. The 'autonomous reflexive' usually experiences, but always courts, 'contextual discontinuity'. In the process he necessarily acquires supra-contextual knowledge, one of whose functions is to refine his original critique of his involuntary placement, just as the re-positioning he seeks also undergoes refinement.

Not only do 'autonomous reflexives' know more about society, but they also become more expert in understanding its workings. Constraints and enablements cease to be forces like the weather, but become powers towards which an active agent can take a strategic stance. If one's projected career has undergone 'elastication' or 'contraction', these are objective facts which can be scrutinised subjectively and from which lessons are derived. Through the inner conversation, 'autonomous reflexives' begin to anticipate the constraints that their refined projects are likely to encounter and the enablements that may assist them. This is not passive knowledge but strategic information, which they use. As their experience expands and deepens, what they increasingly deliberate about are strategies for riding the enablements and for circumventing the constraints, in order to achieve their aims. It is unavoidable that they only know about social powers fallibly, under their own descriptions, and that their assessments of strategic actions are subject to their own 'weights and measures'.

Therefore, to call 'autonomous reflexives' strategists no more implies that they possess great strategic virtuosity than does the fact that someone is called a military strategist. The ineluctable reason why they can never be *very* good at it is because contingency can always intervene to suspend or distort their own powers and those of the society they may think they have mastered. They may warm to the belief that they are 'the masters of their fate', but this must always remain hyperbole. Sometimes too, deliberative discretion will point to self-restraint, to tailoring their projects to what is possible under circumstances which are not of their making. Nevertheless, there is a hugely important difference between those agents who accommodate themselves to structures and these people who seek to harness structural powers to their own agential aims. It is the difference between the 'communicative reflexive' and the 'autonomous reflexive': both are active agents, but the former is an agent for stability and the latter an agent for change. 'Autonomous reflexives' attempt to promote what they care about most. More than those with any other mode of reflexivity, these are people who both know what they want and also know a good deal about how to go about getting it. They do so strategically, as agents who endorse the life-politics of the possible.

8   Meta-reflexives

'Meta-reflexivity' sounds a complicated mental activity, but it is one that every normal human being practises, at least on occasion. It entails being reflexive about our own acts of reflexivity. Much of the internal conversation consists in asking ourselves questions and answering them. Thus, in 'primary' reflexivity, we may ask ourselves what date it is today, and supply an answer. The subject who proposes that 'the date is 8 May', might, upon hearing this (as object), then have her doubts – and an internal discussion can ensue.[1] Here, what she is bending back upon is her own utterance. In this case it is a proposition which she has heard herself enunciate. Yet, on hearing it, she doubts its truth for some reason. The ensuing conversation is about the proposition and is an internal attempt to establish the correct date. However, she can also ask herself, 'why was I a day out?' – and perhaps provide the answer, 'you always get confused when there's been a Bank Holiday'. This is an exercise of meta-reflexivity; the internal conversation is not about the proposition itself but about why she herself uttered it.

The insertion of this extra loop into the interior dialogue is a recognisable occurrence to most people. Usually it takes the form of questions we put to ourselves, even if we cannot supply the answers: 'Why does he always rub me up the wrong way?', 'Why do I often type "becuase" instead of "because" ', or 'why did I believe I wouldn't need a jersey today?' 'Meta-reflexivity' can be about the trivial or the profound, just as any act of 'primary' reflexivity may be. Equally, those who engage in a great deal of 'meta-reflexive' thinking do not necessarily possess a 'profundity', which sets them apart from other people. There is nothing 'deeper' in someone asserting, 'I know I miss regular dental check-ups because I'm afraid of going to the dentist', than Angie saying, 'I like it here, so would my friend, we must come here together.' The former, if correct, demonstrates knowledge of one's self, the latter, if correct, demonstrates knowledge of another.

[1] See chapter 3, pp. 100f.

All acts of self-monitoring are acts of 'meta-reflexivity'. Often these are task-oriented, as has been seen over the last two chapters. The type of 'meta-reflexivity' examined here is different; it is 'self-oriented' – the subject is internally conversing about herself and not about her external actions. 'Meta-reflexivity' is something that some people practise a great deal more than others, and there were four subjects in this exploratory study for whom this seemed to dominate their internal conversations. As a group, they exercised a distinctive mode of reflexivity and their form of interlocution, during interview, was also markedly different.

Unlike the 'communicative reflexives', who sought to extend their 'thought and talk' pattern into the interview itself and to engage me for the completion of their thoughts, 'meta-reflexives' tended to withdraw into self-interrogation. Withdrawal could sometimes be literal, for members of this sub-group alone availed themselves of the invitation to pause and think over their responses, if they wished. More frequently, their withdrawal was verbal; they would begin to voice a response, qualify it, situate it in their personal biographies, link it to illustrative episodes, actively handle the topic out loud, and occasionally interject comments such as, 'that's interesting', or, 'I've not thought of that before.' This represented a huge contrast with the brevity, economy and readiness of responses made by 'autonomous reflexives'. It was telling that these four interviews were the longest of all, lasting up to three hours. They were also by far the most difficult to transcribe, because of their use of subordinate clauses, their false starts, reformulations, the interjection of clarifications and their general ruminative form. At times too, these were the only subjects[2] who manifested unease during interview, because of the greater degree of self-disclosure that they found themselves to be offering. In this context, it was noticeable that the two older subjects were much better versed in techniques for making those disclosures, using irony or humour to draw the emotional sting.

The four subjects ranged in age from twenty-nine to sixty-five, which raises the interesting question as to whether or not a much younger person could have developed this mode of reflexivity. Two were men and two women; three came from working-class backgrounds and one was middle class, although all were themselves members of the professional middle classes. The two men had doctorates and the two women either a higher degree or multiple forms of postgraduate training. At one time or another all had been teachers, and beyond that they had worked in the 'caring professions'. This, it transpires, is closely related to the first feature which they shared in common.

---

[2] Apart from the 'fractured reflexives' examined in the next chapter.

As with other types of reflexivity, the initial aim was to identify any objective features in the social backgrounds of these four subjects which had been propitious for the development of this distinctive type of life of the mind. For 'communicative reflexives', it was held to be their 'contextual continuity' which was propitious for the establishment of their 'thought and talk' pattern, and which also continued to sustain it over time, providing that this context indeed remained continuous. Stable 'communicative reflexivity' was the co-product of structure and agency. Structurally, an unbroken context had to be continuously available to the subject, so that she could 'think and talk' her way through key transitional points, of which the most important appeared to be school leaving, job-entry and partnering. Agentially, it depended upon the subjects' ability to define their life-projects within their original socio-cultural horizons, and their voluntary collaboration in maintaining these projects, which meant endorsing their social confines.

The equivalent objective factor for 'autonomous reflexives' was precisely the opposite, namely an early 'contextual discontinuity', which deprived them of a durable group of interlocutors and thus threw them back upon their own internal mental resources for purposes of deliberation. Again, the stability of this mode of reflexivity was co-dependent upon structure and agency. Structurally, a new context had to be socially accessible into which these subjects could move. Agentially, it had to be one that the subject could embrace because, within it, he could develop his (work) project and establish a *modus vivendi* which was both satisfying and sustainable. Sometimes this took two shots at a contextual target, as in the case of Eliot; sometimes it involved a readiness to settle for second best, as with Paul after his by-pass operation.

'Meta-reflexives' share exactly the same objective 'contextual discontinuity' with the 'autonomous reflexives'. Indeed, since the youngest subject in this sub-group was twenty-nine, there is no way of establishing from an exploratory study whether or not these people started adult life with an autonomous mode of reflexivity, and only later acquired that pre-occupation with interrogating their own motives and reactions, as is characteristic of the 'meta-reflexive'. All that can safely be said of these subjects is that, both structurally and agentially, they now stand in a very different relationship to society from that of the 'autonomous reflexive'.

On the one hand, no available context is such that they can embrace it uncritically and lastingly. Generically they are 'contextually unsettled', internally they ask themselves why, and uniformly they produce a critique of both self and society and, above all, of the relations between them. Hence, 'meta-reflexives' are not firmly rooted in any context, as is witnessed by their combined patterns of geographical (even inter-continental) mobility, job changes, career shifts, professional re-training, and the progressive diversification of their skills. 'Meta-reflexives' were themselves responsible for weaving a goodly part of this unsettled pattern.

'Meta-reflexives' are not good at permanent 'rooting' because there is always (eventually) something, if not many things, that they find wanting, undesirable or deleterious about a given context, which generically impedes the full expression of who they want to be. Because they are not entirely intra-punitive, 'meta-reflexives' are amongst society's critics, not only in relation to their own pre-occupations but also in terms of distributive injustice. This does not make them political activists, though all have had their political moments. Rather, there is a deep concern for the underdog, the oppressed, and the globally deprived. This means they care about the present 'victims', instead of engaging in revolutionary politics to give jam to everyone tomorrow.

On the other hand, as agents, 'meta-reflexives' are idealists. Sooner for some than for others, they were all drawn to an ideal, which they wished to express in and through their own lives. These are people with a vocation (or in search of one) in which they can invest themselves and which is expressive of their ideal. As idealists, they experience a constant tension between structure and culture. No existing social arrangements approximate to their ideal, nor ultimately does any institution or organisation to which they are vocationally drawn. This is what makes them social critics. Simultaneously, their ideal makes them critical of themselves as persons and critical of the lives they lead.

It is this latter, which constitutes their second shared characteristic. Because they have a holistic ideal, they want everything that they do and everyone with whom they are involved to tap into the same wellspring, sharing their ultimate concern and thus reinforcing their commitment to it. This is why the 'meta-reflexives' have difficulties with the dovetailing of their concerns, unlike those discussed in the last two chapters. They want their involvements in the three orders of natural reality to be aligned to their ideal, which is their ultimate concern. Their basic problem is that these keep slipping out of alignment. As subjects, they will go through a great deal of soul-searching about why this should be the case, and how they can change themselves and their comportment to establish the harmony which they seek. Yet, sometimes they have to conclude that no amount of self-awareness or self-improvement can suffice. In any case, factors outside the subject's control, such as an absence of physical well-being, may destroy the desired alignment.

It is at those junctures, where the possibility of realigning their concerns to their ideal seems reduced to vanishing point, that the 'meta-reflexive' is propelled to seek a new *modus vivendi*. In other words, the 'meta-reflexive' has the greatest difficulties, during his or her life-course, in completing the sequence, "concerns -> projects -> practices", to his or her own satisfaction. Their practices will change considerably and so, more reluctantly, will their projects, but not their ultimate concerns. None of the four people interviewed had abandoned the original ultimate concern which fired them. Instead, they had struggled on to find a satisfying and sustainable means of living it out, in harmony with their other ineluctable concerns. What they were seeking was holistic – a life wholly aligned – as a living expression of their ideal. Had they abandoned their ultimate concern, they would necessarily have become someone else, not in terms of losing a continuous sense of self, but in the sense of having a shifting personal identity – literally somebody who identified themselves with something different. Instead, these 'meta-reflexives' had sought to adjust their projects and to re-define their practices, precisely in order to retain their fidelity to their ideal.

Because this sub-group had greater difficulties in embracing lasting projects and transforming these into stable practices, they also had greater problems than any other group in defining a *modus vivendi* which was satisfying and sustainable over the long term. Hence their restless volatility. 'Meta-reflexives' are idealists ever seeking a better fit between who they seek to be and a social environment which permits their expression of it. This environment is something which they need, for they are equally incapable of the lone individualism characteristic of the 'autonomous reflexives', or the uncritical traditionalism of the 'communicative reflexives'. Instead, they are idealists, ever in search of a creative symbiosis between 'self' and 'society'; one which nurtures the best qualities of the 'self', but which simultaneously translates these values into an external social environment – however modest it may be. As idealists, they will pay the price for their restless quest, in terms of lateral or even downward social mobility. As we will discover, this means that the 'meta-reflexive' has a relationship to social constraints and enablements which is quite different from either of those sub-groups examined thus far. Once again, we need to make the acquaintance of someone who exemplifies this mode of reflexivity in order to gain some hermeneutic feel for this life of the mind.

Cass Ballantine: a picture of a 'meta-reflexive'

Cass is fifty-five, the mother of two grown-up sons. She is now separated but not divorced from her husband, and has spent most of her life in teaching and social work. Recently she took early retirement, and in a week will be leaving for Southern Africa to work as a volunteer on a project with street children. This is a limited commitment for a year, and Cass refuses to second either those who tell her that the experience will be 'wonderful', or how 'wonderful' she is to undertake it. Her new project sets a real problem of understanding what she is doing. To gain any insight at all, we have to try to enter into her mode of reflexivity and its relationship to her entire life-course.

Cass agrees that her internal conversation is probably 'ongoing most of the time', something that she attributes to now living alone. She is one of the few subjects who had dwelt on the question of what is going on in this inner dialogue, and almost the only one who volunteered a name for it – to her, self-talk is about self-monitoring. Her 'meta-reflexivity' becomes very clear in her responses to every mental activity on the prompt list, and she engages in all of them. Perhaps the best example of her being reflexive about her own reflexivity comes from our fairly lengthy discussion of 'mulling things over'. This is a term which she herself had introduced before I employed it, but when I do, she is clearly so at home with it that she offers an entirely 'meta-reflexive' response. When 'mulling over', 'I find that maybe I'm slipping into a mood or a pattern of thinking that I know is not healthy for me. I will cognitively almost sort of re-frame it, and I will fight against what I see as negativity. There's that, on the one hand, and I suppose alongside of that will be a sort of self-admonition – an acknowledgement of the need to stop thinking like that – or of "you should not be doing that". All the "oughts" and "should nots" come into play.' Yet a moment later, Cass re-consults her own statement and adds a rider to it about the dangers of over-policing oneself: 'I'd like to think it's a sort of self-awareness. I am aware of what I am doing, or as soon as I become aware of what I am doing, I will reflect upon it. What might happen is that I would be too self-critical and get into that "you shouldn't", "you oughtn't", rather than thinking, "Oh isn't it interesting", you know, observing that you're actually going along that path again. So that may take some time, but I usually get to that point.' This pair of responses, in which the second qualifies the first, seems to be an exemplification of her mode of reflexivity – spoken out loud. In other words, internal self-control must not be allowed to shoulder out self-knowledge – especially the knowledge that one is controlling oneself to a rigid, formulaic pattern.

Nevertheless, since we have to be actors as well as observers in our own lives, I press Cass for a concrete example of a form of self-censorship that she would consider legitimate, even on further inspection. She volunteers instances of having negative thoughts about someone or their behaviour, particularly those with whom she has no deep involvement: 'It could be anybody really and that's something I do try to cut off, because it's useless, it's got no merit in it. I think, "you haven't always thought that about this person, some of this just popped up today, but something else popped up yesterday". So why, you know, what is it in me? How's my perception being distorted? Recognising that it's more to do with me than them. And yeah, I do stop that, because I know the uncomfortable feeling, it is more to do with me – but not always.' The addition of 'not always' is important, because the 'meta-reflexive' monitors others as well as herself and is not uniformly intra-punitive. Sometimes other people are indeed at fault and responsible for provoking the responses they do.

All the same, it is easier to control oneself than other people, and within the inner conversation this is the only thing one can do. Thus Cass frequently refers to the self-controls she exercises in relation to the mental activities on the prompt list. In referring to the practice of self-control she often stresses that this is not habitual to her, but rather something that she has gradually learned to do, perhaps quite recently. This is important, because Anna, who is ten years older, emphasises this learning process even more strongly. The two young men are more pre-occupied with pattern-recognition within themselves, rather than having learned what to do about their unwanted mental tendencies. The acquisition of this self-control is summed up in Cass's response to the question about whether or not she engages in much 're-living' of episodes, events or relationships. 'I suppose the answer for me is, I probably used to. And that was usually when there was a very sort of dynamic personal situation around that was ongoing and unresolved. The very nature of it meant that one was hiked back into the past. But now – maybe for ten or twelve years – if I have gone against my will into the past, you know those times when we're hiked back, the self-monitoring will take over and say, "it's not helpful to go there". So that would be to do with painful things – painful or unhealthy emotions.'

So far, the examples cited make it sound as if Cass engages in nothing but strong doses of self-censorship, and, as she herself volunteers at this point, 'I seem to be a very controlled person.' This would be to give an erroneous overall impression. Conversely, there is also a good deal of self-acceptance, as emerges when we discuss decision-making. What Cass emphasises is the futility of unending self-flagellation over what is past: 'I'd say of the decisions that have been made – that's fine.' Equally futile is any pretence that experience adds up to infallibility where future decisions are concerned: 'So I would tend to say, well I've decided to do this, and it may not be okay, but it doesn't matter.' This is not a version of post-modernism's 'anything goes', but an internalisation of the sane advice of Francis de Sales, '*soyez doux envers soi*' – be gentle towards yourself.

Indeed, it is not the case that 'anything goes', because when we discuss 'budgeting', Cass begins to reveal her ideals and idealism. Significantly, this topic does not suggest money to her. She raises 'cost-benefit analysis', as a principle for the apportioning of time and effort, and laughingly dismisses it as something which she has learned to put aside. In its broadest sense, budgeting is, 'something that I would find myself doing more now than in the past. I think what influences that is a deeper self-awareness of why I might have done things in the past. So, now, I may decide to do something that maybe doesn't benefit me, but I choose to do it, whereas before, I might have done it just because I thought it would benefit me. So, maybe, I'm not as driven now to respond in a certain way.' She is saying that her ideals have become more influential, but shows the reluctance to appear pious by drawing attention to their grounding in her religious commitment: 'spirituality apart, only it's not apart, I think it's central . . .'

When I question Cass about the main areas of concern in her life now, this is followed by a remarkably long pause, after which she slowly says, 'I suppose it's about integrity, [pause] about personal integrity – integrity in the sense of wholeness, of things coming together. Not just to have it, but to act on it – integrity towards other people. That would be sort of the ultimate goal. Trying to eliminate the self-seeking – even in the most subtle, manipulative ways – to meeting my needs. I don't know if one ever gets round to that.' She is struggling to articulate an ideal 'quality', which would permeate all her doings and relationships. Instead of supplying a list of concerns, such as the ones which the other two sub-groups produced so readily, Cass has taken a mental step back, surveyed the problem of dovetailing, and come up with her own holistic contribution to the problem of alignment. This entails a reflexive diagnosis of where she feels she succeeds and where and how she fails: 'I suppose it's often easier for me to take integrity into situations where people don't know me – colleagues at work. I suppose it's in one's dealings with one's family, extended family, where sometimes stuff from the past can colour – not so much my actions – I'm alright if I'm acting, but it's thoughts.' Indirectly, Cass has pinpointed which one of her concerns (family relationships) has created most problems by being unstably aligned to her ultimate concern. In a moment, this will be seen to be closely related to two major changes in Cass's *modus vivendi* over the years.

When questioned directly about which of her activities are most important to her, she highlights the centrality of her vocation. 'It would always involve other people. There's an awareness that no matter what you do, it's about how you do it. That's the central tenet, but one recognises where one's strengths and gifts really are. So that would be in some vocational task, like the social work bit – without all that stuff about caring and compassion, all that rubbish that goes with it. Tough love's in that as well. It would always be around that area, yeah, I'm sure.' What is particularly interesting is that Cass recognises a general area of social service which would be expressive of both her skills and values. However, she mentions social work merely as one exemplar of it, rather than nominating it as her ultimate concern *per se*. In turn this makes a great deal of sense of her biography, which is one of considerable 'contextual unsettlement'. She can move flexibly between those vocational areas in which her 'strengths and gifts' can be put to good account. However, whilst this flexibility may explain or rationalise her *ability* to change her *modus vivendi*, it does not account for what produces this pattern of unsettlement.

What is missing is an explanation of why she should move at all, once she has found herself in a professional context which draws usefully upon her manifest social skills. To account for this, we have to examine the part played by the three factors, characteristic of this sub-group, throughout her own life-course. Until her early thirties, Cass experienced an intensification of 'contextual discontinuity'. The first major shift came with her entry to teacher training, immediately after leaving school, which placed her on a career-track that was discontinuous with her working-class background. When she married, a year after graduation, the discontinuities were compounded because her social mobility was coupled with an intense geographical mobility. She had left one social context, but did not have another stable context in which to put down roots. As Cass puts it, for the next fifteen years, 'we seemed transient'. There were seven moves around the country, prompted by her husband's employment. During this time, and between the births of her two sons, Cass taught intermittently, but necessarily on a part-time or casual supply basis. Towards the end of this period, Cass's sense of social injustice seems to have risen through her experience of 'teaching the lower streams at school'. There is also evidence that it expanded to embrace the educationally deprived more generally, for she undertook a course in 'adult literacy' before the family eventually settled in the Cotswolds. At that time, teaching posts were tight in the area and Cass did voluntary work for a year in a Probation day centre. This seems to have been very important in re-focusing her ideas about her own vocation. At a purely personal level, this experience might seem to explain her decision to re-train as a social worker, in conjunction with the shortage of teaching posts: 'my empathy level rose at that point, so it seemed like the natural thing to do'.

Yet this was not just a personal matter of Cass gradually crystallising her vocation, for it represented a radical shift in her *modus vivendi*, and one which took place against the background of increasingly misaligned concerns. Being rich in self-knowledge, and now placing great value upon integrity, she is unwilling to leave me believing that in re-training for social work she merely did 'the natural thing'. Cass volunteers that this 'was a very difficult period of my life'. She is not very explicit, but amongst these difficulties were the death of her (supportive) mother, growing marital tensions, and the problems of childcare, were she to realise her vocation in full-time work. As she analyses it herself: 'it was the "Diana thing", that when you're in emotional turmoil you actually tell yourself that you're going to turn outwards. Sometimes that's how it starts, but given the natural bent, it was already there.' Vocationally she wanted to 'turn outwards' and do so wholeheartedly; practically she sought financial independence for the freedom this would give her, but there remained the problem of adequate childcare.

Looking back, Cass says that at such points, you have to ask yourself, 'is that really what you still want to do?' If the answer is negative about maintaining an existing *modus vivendi*, then 'you have to re-evaluate'. Re-evaluation resulted in a commitment to re-training for social work, but she immediately had to abandon the course because of the problem of making after-hours provision for the care of her primary school son. Two years later, she brought about a radical change in her *modus vivendi* which re-aligned her concerns. She began the course again, solved the problem of childcare by the bold move of inviting a widowed aunt to live with her family, and could then look forward to both vocational fulfilment and financial independence.

That was Cass's second major transition, which lasted as a *modus vivendi* for over ten years. Then, this way of life became destabilised as her concerns again slipped out of alignment. Her search to re-accommodate them once more resulted in contextual unsettlement. We will postpone examining the factors surrounding Cass's growing disenchantment with social work and her abandonment of it until a later section. Immediately afterwards, she began exploring the practicalities of a potential third transition. This involved extending her skills to include a qualification in Teaching English as a Foreign Language and seeking openings for work in the third world. She had specified that she was looking for a short-term commitment, but promptly agreed to the assignment in Southern Africa.

For Cass, this experience may only result in a further increment in self-learning, or it may presage a shift to a future *modus vivendi*, thus adding to the volatility which has characterised her life-course. In order to understand what makes this pattern possible, we will later have to introduce the part played by constraints and enablements in the unsettled life of a 'meta-reflexive'.

'Meta-reflexives' across the age-range

'Meta-reflexives' share the same 'contextual discontinuity' with their original and involuntary social placements that characterised the 'autonomous reflexives'. For the latter, it was suggested that these discontinuities deprived subjects of a permanent group of 'similars and familiars' who could act as both interlocutors and commentators, thus throwing individuals back upon their own mental resources to resolve their problems and to formulate their projects. Hence, 'contextual discontinuity' made a significant contribution to the development of the autonomous mode of reflexivity. There is no reason to suppose that this same factor plays any different part in the making of a 'meta-reflexive'; that is, it fosters a self-contained life of the mind. Therefore, it is necessary to look further to discover what *in addition* serves to differentiate the internal conversation of the 'meta-reflexive' from that of the 'autonomous reflexive'.

The answer seems to lie with agential rather than structural features. Specifically, it relates to the kinds of projects which subjects pursue. In the last chapter it was found that the ultimate concern of all 'autonomous reflexives' was their 'work', or more generally their performative achievement. There was evidence that to accord top priority to developing *performative skills* also contributed to fully fledged 'autonomous reflexivity'. From young Michael, seeking to be able to 'think for himself' about wiring an electrical installation, through to much older Vincent, talking about the need to concentrate deeply when saying Mass, the importance attached to performative virtuosity accentuated the need for autonomous thinking, because no interlocutor could help these subjects to 'think and talk' their way through their tasks. Consequently, their inner conversations became profoundly 'task-oriented'; as Eliot put it, 'I'm sorry, this seems to be business yet again.' In short, the projects pursued by this sub-group encouraged independent thinking in relation to work tasks, because these entailed constant self-monitoring to ensure proficiency.

Matters are very different for our 'meta-reflexives'. All of them are fired by some particular 'vocation' (meaning that they had each become so at the point of interview). To succeed in a 'vocation' is very different from acquiring the performative skills which constitute success at work. As was noted in the last chapter, the latter entails becoming sufficiently proficient that one's performance meets external standards of assessment – be these of public building inspectors, the market, or the satisfaction of one's congregation. Conversely, a vocation requires that those who are drawn to it also progressively develop personal qualities that are expressive of it.[3] Such qualities are not amenable to assessment by objective performance indicators, as all the 'meta-reflexives' agree, given their howls of protest about the imposition of this form of quality assessment in teaching, research and social work. Indeed such qualities are very difficult for the novice to grasp, let alone acquire. What does it mean for a young academic to be 'creative', as opposed to productive? What makes a good teacher, as opposed to satisfying OFSTED? What does it take to be a successful social worker, as opposed to 'all that stuff about caring and compassion'? What constitutes living out a religious vocation, as opposed to merely keeping one's vows? These are the questions which our four 'meta-reflexives' ask themselves. The answer they give is about cultivating some 'quality' within themselves, rather than acquiring some measurable standard of performative proficiency.

Because of this, far from being task-oriented, much of their inner conversation turns upon whether or not they are becoming the kind of person called for by their vocations. Consequently, much of their internal dialogue is concerned with themselves. It is about the recognition and nourishing of qualities tending towards the ideal, and the uprooting or taming of those which are antipathetic to it. This is the crucial additional feature which shepherds them towards 'meta-reflexivity'. Since the desired 'quality', be it 'creativity', 'integrity' or 'holiness' is always evasive, in the sense that no one ever feels that they fully and adequately personify it, this is what fuels 'meta-reflexivity'. The proviso has to be, so long as the subject remains faithful to his or her vocation. Being human, there are many ways in which love can grow cold. The subject will be the first and perhaps the only one to know that this has happened, since their routinised behaviour may be impeccable. They will know it precisely because their internal conversations cease to be pre-occupied with their own relationships towards their ideals.

This potential occurrence has not affected any of our four subjects, and from them it is possible to chart the intensification of 'meta-reflexive' mental activities, from the time at which the youngest was first drawn to his vocational ideal. Before beginning to examine them, it is important to signal that possession of a 'vocation' is quite different from simply occupying a role – any role. It is obvious that not every teacher has a

---

[3] Conversely, what are commonly and objectively held to be 'vocations' can be interpreted by subjects in 'task performance' terms. For example, Vincent, in chapter 7, describes himself as 'a Massing priest', and regards his principal obligation as that of making the sacraments readily available to his congregation.

vocation to teach; for some it will have been an occupational default option. A vocational commitment entails a subjective investment of the self and a voluntary quest for self-transformation, such that one comes closer to personifying the ideal qualities which ideally express it.

Once again, we will begin with the youngest subjects and work through to the oldest, hoping to provide indicative 'snapshots' (which are entirely non-predictive) of different phases in the development of 'meta-reflexivity'. As the two older subjects repeatedly insist, self-knowledge and self-transformation, which lie at the heart of this life of the mind, involve a great deal of learning. How then does this process engage and how does it colour the inner conversation of those who have just begun the process of living out their vocations? Both Andy (aged twenty-nine) and Ivan (a few years older) are young academics, each with a recent PhD, and each in his University post for less than three years.[4] The two are powerfully drawn to an ideal of 'academe', which has more to do with the 'invisible college' than with their present places of employment, and to a notion of academic 'creativity', which resonates much better with the image of the 'lone scholar' than with the scientistic model of working with a 'research team'. Simultaneously, both are under huge time pressures to combine teaching, administration and research.

As soon as the question of holding internal conversations is broached, Andy concurs that he engages in a lot of internal dialogue and he immediately says why: 'I mean it helps because it indicates particular facets about me as a person – what's important to me.' This is an entirely 'meta-reflexive' reason; Andy wants self-knowledge and he indicates this in his reactions to every kind of mental activity on the prompt list. Many of his responses display anxiety and uncertainty, but not as unexamined emotions. They are rather attempts to gain self-understanding so as to deal better with whatever provoked them. Two examples will suffice. As far as 'reliving' episodes is concerned, Andy construes this as 'reconstructing an episode in my own mind. Particularly if something has upset me, I'll sort of want to try and understand why it's happened so that I can deal with it.' Similarly, for him, 'clarifying' matters is something 'we have to do because otherwise I think you'd just go mad – about things that I find incomprehensible and hurtful, at the same time. And I think you can cope better if you come to some sort of caring understanding. If so-and-so was rude, well perhaps other things are going on for them.' As Cass said retrospectively, much of her earlier internal conversations were prompted by anxiety, but this has diminished over the decades, 'from experience.

---

[4] It is possible that they might have jibbed at the notion of 'vocation' as applied to them, except that both are familiar with Max Weber's paper, 'Science as a Vocation'.

I don't get so anxious, I don't feel uncertain, because, I suppose, I'm more practised in problem-solving for myself.'

As far as writing is concerned, some of the things that one can only learn from experience are how one responds to time pressure, whether or not one can handle plural assignments or needs to be single-minded, when to say no, and the importance of setting one's own intellectual agenda and keeping to it. Few of us achieve anything like mastery of these issues, but here is a story from Andy about how one starts. 'I've had to withdraw from [a particular] conference, and I know they had made an effort especially to fix the date to fit in with me, so I feel awful about that, but I haven't got time to write a paper. I've written the abstract and thought I had enough time. You know, you're thinking, I don't really want to be instrumental in saying, "well, you'll get a publication out of it". Anyway, it doesn't fit in with what I'm doing at the moment. So you have to say, "look, I've got to withdraw", but going back six months, it was a great idea. It's a learning curve – a learning experience. I have a project in mind, and I know that I'm not going to get involved in any other major projects, if I want to do that. It's too easy to say, "yeah, I'll do this and I'll do that". So I'm learning, in my conversation with Andy, to ask, "actually can you do it?" – and knowing when you mustn't commit yourself.'

Those are the pressures, the principles and the pragmatics involved, but more important is how does one come to self-monitor the quality of one's writing in terms of the 'quality' which it should begin to exemplify? Andy gives plenty of examples of false starts, of self-admonition, of voluntary deletion, but also of the odd days when he feels he is 'on a roll' and keeps going. Important as this is, as self-learning, it is probably not so different from Michael recognising when he has bodged a piece of circuitry. What is different is that an electrical apprentice cannot pretend to himself that it will work when it won't. Yet the academic is ever open to self-pretence. Sometimes, as Andy says, 'I rush my work a bit too much and I'll write six thousand words, and sort of know that I'm kidding myself that it's satisfactory, but I also know it's not.' He knows when he has fallen short, but then so does every other self-monitor – who need not be a 'meta-reflexive'.

Much more interesting is when Andy then talks about getting the 'right feel' about an idea. This is something that can be thought of as developing an 'intellectual conscience'. Andy describes a familiar experience and his reaction to it: 'I was reading something by [a well-known philosopher] and thinking, "Oh this isn't right", but I don't know why it's not right.' He then tried to pad out this insight into a paper, accepted that his product was pretty confused, sensibly decided against sending it for publication, but then oscillates wildly about his original intuitive sticking point. Should he stick to it, or reluctantly bury it and go along with this thinker whom he genuinely admires? This time, Andy does the latter. Then, a few months later, he comes across his own original reservation, well spelt out by another author whom he respects: 'and I thought, "heck, I was right". You feel a bit of an idiot, but then I knew instinctively there wasn't something right about the whole thing. So now, I'm asking myself, "well why did you go along with it then?", and "what was going on in your own head?" ' Probably we have all been there and done that – at least *mea culpa*. It is hard, lonely, time-consuming and frustrating to follow one's 'intellectual conscience', especially when it goes against the tide. Yet, if Andy wants the 'quality' of creativity (as reflexively he does, because otherwise he would not question, 'what was going on in your own head?'), he will have to accept the uncertainty and also bite the final bullet. After all that, one's 'intellectual conscience' is fallible and the end product may also have to be scrapped!

Andy is reflexively pre-occupied with himself in relation to the writing process, as is necessary because he wants to write well. Ivan has the same pre-occupation, but for the opposite reason, he wants to be well in order to write. In other words, Ivan is acutely aware that many of his mental activities impede his goal of being a creative academic, and he is an equally acute critic of how other externally imposed activities also act as impediments. He avows that he engages in internal conversation nearly all of the time, especially when alone, and that his inner dialogue spans every item on the prompt list. He is undoubtedly 'meta-reflexive' and, even more than Cass, is critically aware of the negative tendency of his thoughts to spiral downwards: 'You reflect on things when you go home, if you live alone, and at work if you're alone. And something happens and you get into these pre-set patterns – depressed about something, worrying, angry, and you're voicing it in your head, "So that's going to happen and then that's going to happen." And you can tell that once you start going down that track, you can't pull the lead and stop.'

Ivan acknowledges his own proneness to depression and anxiety. He characterises this as, 'it's raining cats and dogs', where 'cats' stand for a tendency to 'catastrophise' and 'dogs' for Churchill's old black dog of depression. Ivan knows which kinds of internal conversation exacerbate this tendency and also how to use other forms of internal dialogue to combat it. Thus, 'mulling over' allows the present to be swamped by the past: 'The problem is that there can be plenty of good things, but good things tend to get ushered out, in the way I think. It's easier to dwell on bad things, well, not easier, but it happens. The good things get the colour sucked out and the bad things come in.' Conversely, 'clarifying' is a reflexively controlled activity which he employs to resist spiralling downwards. Thus, when he starts saying to himself, 'I'm depressed, or I'm angry, or I'm worrying for these reasons', he follows this up by asking himself, ' "Are these reasons appropriate? Is there evidence for that view?" It's all about trying to untangle things or turn down noise . . . But it's not something you sit down and do at once – [as in] it's Monday, there are problems in the past, so have a cup of tea and the problem is solved. It's something you do continually – it's in you, but it's something you train yourself to, not do automatically, but to recognise . . . I think a lot of people have chronic problems because they're not trying to be reflexive about them in terms of a solution. But I'm saying put the brake on it.'

Ivan fully acknowledges this need for self-controlled transformation and recognises that this is most effective when he can become absorbed in what he is writing. Given the space to write, he feels that this can become an upward spiral: 'It's like feeling comfortable with the good things – to be more productive – and then you can cope better with the bad things.' However, this upwards felicific spiralling is vitiated if his engagement in writing becomes a matter of external imposition. He gives an example of an extremely onerous task, which he was assigned in his first year as a new academic, namely writing course materials (which I will call the 'Units'), under time pressure and amounting in size to that of an average book. Generically, this would not have been an uncongenial task to him, but the combination of it being imposed, pressurised and monitored, represented a vicious circle. This initiated a downward spiral in the one area which otherwise has the reverse effect for him. To Ivan his, 'generic priority is to feel more life, if you like. One aspect of that is writing, being engaged in writing . . . I've written the "Units" and I'm much more depressed and annoyed with life because they are not as full-blooded as they could have been. There might be more of me in there, and it gives me more energy with writing if I'm doing it because I want to – because then it's creative and not routine. It [the finished product] was stilted . . . So it's not a question of writing or not writing.'

Ivan is articulating a common problem amongst 'meta-reflexives', the need to give themselves wholeheartedly to their ultimate concern, to cultivate those personal qualities that are conducive to this end and to discourage those that are inimical to it. Because they are such close monitors of themselves, rather than monitoring their task-performance like the 'autonomous reflexive', they know that 'self-work' needs to be done if they are to approximate to their ideal way of being-in-the-world. What is revealing in Ivan's case is that although 'meta-reflexives' may engage in profound self-criticism, they refuse to be completely intra-punitive. Ivan was extremely open about some of his problems, which may be more painful and debilitating than most, but Cass expressed the same self-critique when pondering upon personal integrity and its imperfections: 'as one

gets older one's far more aware that one's a shit basically'. Nevertheless, acceptance that the self continually falls short of the ideal does not
preclude an accompanying contextual-critique. On the contrary, it precipitates it, because the 'meta-reflexive' also questions whether a given
context is helping to nurture a 'better' self or is militating against it.

We have seen Cass still struggling with the same problems, but also
avowing how much she has learned as she has gone along. Thus, in turning to Anna, who is now sixty-five, the question is whether this mode of
reflexivity condemns its practitioners to life-long self-dissatisfaction, or if
it is possible to learn how to be 'gentle towards yourself' without compro-
mising one's ideals? Anna is a religious sister who now works as general
secretary to her congregation, after recently returning from Latin America
because of ill-health. She has a volatile biography, which will be examined in the next section, but for the moment, I want to focus on a comment she made in the course of the interview: 'I think, yes, I've learnt –
there's an awful lot of my having learnt coming into this!' So what does
a 'meta-reflexive' learn?

There is no doubt that Anna, who again engages in every mental activity
on the prompt list, is a 'meta-reflexive'. She explicitly repudiates the
'thought and talk' model because the 'completions' which other people
supply are theirs and not hers. They are outsiders with their own concerns
and contexts, they are not the one person on the spot who has to cope
with her own situation in terms of her own values and ideals. This Anna
illustrates by reference to one biographical episode when she had left
the congregation and was also about to leave her post as deputy head:
'I went through a very bad patch when I left the school. It was a sort
of re-living, and sometimes it doesn't help if you talk to other people,
because they were saying, "Oh you should have done this or you should
have done that", or, "If I'd been in your place I would have done such
and such." That is sometimes all very well if you're on the outside, but
they're not there, and they're not having to deal with it.'

Similarly, she is far more concerned with monitoring her own reactions
and behaviour than with any form of task-performance, which is typical
of 'autonomous-reflexives.' Anna admits that she has a 'worrying streak'
which influences her 'imagination', and that anxieties prompt some of
her mental activities, like 're-living': 'I would say on the whole, if I'm
sort of re-living in my own head, I'm reliving something that disturbed
me, something that I haven't accepted as far as I think I've accepted
it.' These responses are very recognisable and could have been spoken
by any one in this sub-group. However, Anna does highlight several activities where she believes that self-learning makes her today's reactions
different from what they would once have been. 'Imaginary conversations' used to be 'full blown' and 'ferocious': 'I think when I was young,

I concocted all those blistering comments that I would have said – but I don't do that so much now. I think it's gone out of my character or my personality as I get older. I don't have to have the last word in every conversation.' Equally, 'mulling over' can be 'unproductive dissection', so instead of allowing it to prey upon her now, 'sometimes it's much better to put things into cold storage for a while and let them surface again at a later day'. Finally, although 'decision-making' can still leave her 'grumpy' and 'snarling', 'I think I've learnt that you take your time and you make a sensible decision. I've learnt to say no, if I know it's more than I can cope with in any way, physically, or mentally or emotionally, whatever. Having made the decision, then I take it in a quiet moment and abide by it.'

However, there is an important sense, Cass's sense of 'integrity', in which a 'meta-reflexive' cannot change her spots, because that would be a betrayal of her ideal, of the person whom she seeks to be. Anna talks about continuing to defend the 'underdog', in this case a much older nun who could not stick up for herself: 'defending her at cost to myself. But you have to decide where you point and where your line of demarcation is.' Some principles are non-negotiable. Some practices are, but only at the price of using self-knowledge to augment self-control. Thus, Anna says that she has come to put her 'peace of mind at quite a high premium', which means self-consciously avoiding certain confrontations. Hence, she continues, 'if I have a blistering row with you today, it's not going to make for peace of mind on my part. You go off and we don't see each other for a few weeks and then we'll see each other and try to pretend. Very often now I don't think it's worth it. So I'd say that it's more about evaluating its value for present or future relationships.' The last sentence is a crucial one. Pragmatism can never be the resort of the 'meta-reflexive'. As people seeking to conform themselves and be conformed to their ideal, their responses are evaluative through and through. Growing knowledge of themselves and their society can enhance their coping strategies, but they can never become *very* gentle towards themselves, or their surroundings, because that would be a betrayal of their ideal. Let Anna have the last word: 'I think the day I lose my idealism, I might as well give up. I keep saying, people can change, it is possible. I keep hoping I'll change and they'll change and everything will be wonderful.'

'Meta-reflexives' and the mediation of social structure

The making of the 'meta-reflexive' entails its own distinctive relationship to their involuntary placement within the social structure. It has nothing in common with that of the 'communicative reflexive', who remains continuous with her original context and actually deploys her agential powers for its replication. It does share a starting point with the 'autonomous reflexive', namely an objective 'contextual discontinuity' which is dialectically related to the subjective formulation of initial projects – ones which carry individuals further away from their original social *milieux*. However, once an initial project has been formed, the 'autonomous reflexive' then has to locate a different social context within which to execute and express it. As was seen in the last chapter, for Farat, Eliot and Paul, this can involve a lengthy quest for the appropriate context, during which their first projects may undergo substantial revision because of growing knowledge about self and society. Nevertheless, the 'autonomous reflexive' does eventually find a new context to adopt that he finds suitable (if not optimal) for the establishment of a *modus vivendi*, reflecting his prime concern.

This is where the 'meta-reflexive' differs. The projects which they embrace, against a background of 'contextual discontinuity', are not ones that can be readily accommodated by any of the new contexts which become accessible to these subjects. Primarily, this is because of the nature of their projects, which draw upon some cultural ideal for which a contextual approximation is always lacking in social reality. Subjects will seek to embed themselves in one context after another, but, sequentially, they find them wanting. Thus, whilst the 'autonomous reflexive' can (eventually) find circumstances which permit him to concentrate upon living out his concerns and to become concentratedly task-oriented in his reflections, this is consistently denied to the 'meta-reflexive'. No structural context ever matches his or her cultural ideal. Therefore, instead of their inner conversations becoming pre-occupied with performative achievement in a stable context, as is (eventually) the case for the 'autonomous reflexive', the internal dialogue of the 'meta-reflexive' remains riveted upon the relationship between the self and the ideal. Self-monitoring is a matter of attempting to bring about sufficient self-transformation, such that the person acquires more and more of the 'qualities' which represent embodiments of their ideal. This life of the mind is pre-occupied with self-examination. The aim is that the sequence, 'self-knowledge – self-criticism – self-improvement' will gradually nurture the 'quality' desired.

Nevertheless, since 'meta-reflexives' are always condemned to inhabit some concrete social context, they travel in the hope of finding one which is more congruent with their ideal. They will try hard to content themselves with new settings, but consecutively find them wanting. Thus, whilst a large portion of their self-talk is devoted to self-criticism, another portion dwells upon contextual critique. Because life in some context is ineluctable, but also necessary to them, the 'meta-reflexive' is always scanning the social horizon for a new setting. Consequently, their biographies are much more unsettled than those of the other subjects examined over the past two chapters. Moreover, where they are found now, at the point of interview, is not a fixed resting place for any of them; their current contexts are subject to exactly the same kind of critique as their previous ones. Further moves can be anticipated, especially for the younger subjects, and one question to be answered is whether or not a 'meta-reflexive' can ever become fully reconciled to a concrete context, even with the approach of old age?

Since these are quests for a setting in which the subject hopes to realise something of their ideal *modus vivendi*, they are also related to social constraints and enablements in a distinctive manner. Instead of responding to them strategically, this group will generally be willing to pay the structural price for re-locating themselves in a different context, which they evaluate as preferable. Hence their biographies will not only be restless trajectories, they will also be chequered patterns of upward, lateral and, most significantly, downward mobility, which bear little relation to the powers of constraints and enablements. This is because 'meta-reflexives' tend systematically to discount objective 'costs' and 'benefits' in their search for a social environment suitable for the expression of their concerns.

In this way, they are not merely the critics of the social institutions that they encounter, they are also society's subversives. They can neither be bought-off by societal inducements, in the form of enablements which give the subject access to objective advantages; nor can they be repressed by constraints which impose an objective price upon engaging in given courses of action. They remain subversive as long as they hold tenaciously to their ideals. There is no guarantee that they will, for compromise is an ever-present temptation. However, for as long as they resist, then the life of the mind of the 'meta-reflexive' also represents the conscience of society.

Contextual unsettlement and biographical trajectories

It should by now be unnecessary to labour what early 'contextual discontinuity' means. For the three subjects who originated from the working class, Andy, Ivan and Cass, the crucial break was the same, namely entering higher education. None of the three could design projects that lay within their original social confines. Andy and Cass looked to a future in teaching and made a direct transition from 'A'-levels to university or college. Ivan took a more roundabout route. Leaving school at sixteen, he immediately distanced himself from what he described as a dysfunctional family, by joining the army. This lasted a year, and was followed by three more stints in various unskilled and semi-skilled occupations, before he took an Open University foundation course and then gained university entry. Anna's story is very different, but her middle-class background was packed with geographical mobility as a result of her father's occupation, and included a period living with her grandmother in order to complete her primary schooling. At school she became attracted to a very small missionary order, which she entered as a novice at the age of eighteen. More geographical disruption soon followed: Anna was sent to Ireland to become an undergraduate.

What next needs to be identified is the point at which these subjects became fired with the ideals that they still upheld at the point of interview. The two younger subjects volunteered much more data about this, because all four of them were pre-occupied with the present – with their current contexts and their immediate past history. Andy and Ivan tell very similar stories, which began with educational 'elastication' and then led to a passion for doing a particular type of academic research. Since this aspect of their biographies is so alike, Andy can supply the illustration. Both began by taking joint-honours (for which they gained first-class degrees), both then honed their interests to a specialist MA (for which they both gained distinctions), and both then crystallised their intellectual concerns into successful PhDs.

Andy's awakening began during 'A'-levels, which he took at a college of further education. He recalls with some amazement that, 'it wasn't a shock that you had to read on your own, and it was actually interesting. I suppose in a way that should have been a miracle, if you like, because my parents don't read and you don't see any books in the front room.' Before entering university, he had 'always wanted to teach', but then his intellectual horizons began to expand. Given 'the sort of background that I come from – Council estate – University wasn't what I expected. I found I was quite good at [his discipline], which I really enjoyed . . . and I sort of lost the chip on my shoulder.' His horizons not only expanded but became more focused in his final year: 'I did a course for which I wasn't registered, and enjoyed that more than anything else. Even now, I think, "God there's so much to be done" – for me it's a passion.' His MA year was spent deepening his reading in this specialist area and realising that, 'I am actually able to do this.'

The next step was to undertake a doctorate, which for most people, Andy included, not only signals an interest in an academic career, but also effectively defines one's intellectual specialism. As he puts it, 'I just took the plunge. It was very scary and when I got studying for the PhD, I thought I don't know if I'm up to this really. I really want to do this but . . . And then, secondly, by reading stuff, you realise that the path

I wanted to take wasn't necessarily fashionable, or *au fait*, and in fact it's bloody difficult.' In his doctoral thesis, he applied this particular theoretical approach in an area to which he is deeply attached, but which is not noted for its theoretical sophistication. Yet, this is his ideal, to push these ideas forward, by teaching, research and publication. He will not consider relinquishing his area of study: 'that's my passion, and I don't want to move away from that at all'. He will not countenance reneging upon his theoretical convictions: 'so now, it's a matter of convincing people of the approach I've taken'. Even given the heterogeneity of most university departments, it might be expected that Andy would have difficulties in finding an academic environment supportive for realising his ideal.

This was indeed the case, and for Andy it signalled the beginning of that chequered biographical pattern, which is characteristic of all our 'meta-reflexives'. Faster in some cases than others, they become critical of a given context and move on. In an imperfect job market, Andy took a lectureship in a Business School, but was so unhappy and discontented that a year later he moved to a similar department in a university nearer home. Matters did not improve, and within months he was making a third application to a different kind of department, and was even considering 'downward mobility' to enter school teaching. Ivan's beginnings in the same job market were also contextually unsatisfactory. He took a post at one of the former colleges, newly promoted to university status. Again, within the first couple of years, he had made several applications to move elsewhere. He admits to having been close to the point of walking out, but was deterred, 'because I haven't anything constructive in mind. I don't know – I feel I've got what I want. I don't want to work nine to five in an office with suits.' He too can be so dissatisfied that he will also voice the 'downward mobility' option: 'I'll probably end up going abroad – voluntary work in Africa or something. It's meaningful.' Quite significantly, if neither of these two young men can realise their ideals in academia, then their thoughts turn to working with the deprived; idealists are not people 'on the make'.

At fifty-five and sixty-five respectively, Cass and Anna have much longer biographies, but ones which display the same pattern. Cass's major contextual shifts have already been sketched in the 'portrait' – from teaching, to social work, to a temporary project in Southern Africa. Anna's life history is possibly the most contextually unsettled of all, although unfortunately she spoke little of her earlier years. After graduation and taking her final vows she went out to south-east Asia and became a school head at the age of twenty-six. When she returned to England about eight years later, and after a period recovering from surgery, Anna was posted to Latin America. Her short time there coincided with the rise of one of the more brutal military dictatorships, and she found herself running a small 'underground railway' to get political dissidents out, before also having to leave. These experiences appear to have precipitated a near-breakdown, during which Anna determined to leave her congregation, and did so for twenty years. After various dislocations, including a time of undoubted 'downward mobility', she assumed her old role in teaching, eventually becoming deputy head. We have already heard her refer to the painful experiences in her last school, which culminated in her resignation. Approaching retirement age, and with her sister with whom she had kept house having died, Anna was drawn to re-approach her old congregation and to request re-admission. She happily returned to (a different) Latin American country, but came back four years later because of ill health. Her desire was to return, but now, another four years on, we find her engaged in administrative work for her congregation in the north of England.

Since the biographies of 'meta-reflexives' are so eventful and because the interviews concentrated upon where subjects are now placed – their reasons for being there and their reactions to it – it is these recent contextual deliberations which will be examined. If some understanding can be gained about these subjects' relations to their current situations, then it may be possible to formulate hypotheses about the personal and social dynamics underpinning their chequered and unsettled life histories. The problem is to diagnose what it is about a 'meta-reflexive' which means that context after context fails to satisfy, and that no durable *modus vivendi* is established. However, since the two older subjects do record substantial intervals of contextual contentment, even though these did not last, this does indicate that we are not dealing with a group of unassuageable idealists for whom no social setting can ever begin to satisfy.

The idea I want to explore is that their failure to establish stable *modi vivendi* can be attributed to the difficulties which members of this subgroup experience with the smooth dovetailing of their concerns. It seems to be the case that it is when their plural concerns are extremely badly aligned that contextual shifts occur in their biographies. Yet even if that hypothesis is correct, it is first necessary to account for why the 'meta-reflexive' has such difficulty in accommodating his or her subordinate concerns. Why are they so unlike the other two sub-groups, who achieve this unproblematically? Why is it that the others can translate their cluster of concerns into lasting projects, and then establish durable practices, in a manner that seems to be denied to the 'meta-reflexive'?

Difficulties with dovetailing concerns

The 'meta-reflexive' is not fundamentally a communitarian, unlike the 'communicative reflexive', nor an individualist, unlike the 'autonomous reflexive'. Although they are people in quest of an ideal, they are also people who are seeking an environment in which to realise and express it. Since they have all broken with their original social backgrounds, then the traditional community can no longer be of service to them. As is often remarked, we stop being traditionalists as soon as we realise that there are alternatives. Equally, since 'meta-reflexives' are not lone individualists, then the possibility of focusing upon performative achievement with nothing but a subordinate, accommodating cast of actors, is not for them. They need an environment that they see as supporting them in working towards their ideals.

What they want this environment to foster is an alignment between three factors, such that all are positive and thus mutually reinforce the living-out of their ultimate concerns. Firstly, they seek to work in a so-cial setting where the gifts and talents they would ideally develop are not continually frustrated by incongruent definitions of *performative skills*. It is their difficulty in finding such settings that makes 'meta-reflexives' such forceful institutional critics. Secondly, they also seek at least a small group of colleagues or friends who are on the same 'wavelength', and whose active support serves to increase rather than to diminish their own *self-worth*. Again, they seem to have problems in either establishing or in maintaining this small, necessary and complementary network. It is significant, in this connection, that none of the four subjects is married or partnered, and that nearly all sustain much closer relationships with family members, to the point of co-habitation, than would be the case for most of their peers. Thirdly, they also seek an environment conducive to their *physical and mental well-being*. This is presumably a *desideratum* of most people, but again members of this sub-group record more interference with their projects because of an absence of well-being than any other, and some of these health problems do appear to be related to their other difficulties.

In short, the 'meta-reflexive', like everyone else, needs a satisfactory re-lationship with the three orders of natural reality. However, their approach to dovetailing is quite different from the radical subordination of lesser concerns which is practised by both 'communicative' and 'autonomous reflexives'. Instead, they work for an organic integration between their concerns, rather than to a (principled) formula for their accommoda-tion, in hierarchical order. Thus, if one concern begins to slip, their holistic approach will incline them to attend to its restoration, such that overall alignment is maintained. Ultimately their problem with organic integration is that it is hard to sustain; either the three concerns will not come into alignment with one another, or they slip out of alignment. The holistic approach is harder to make work because it is much more demanding; something positive is sought from all three orders, namely mutual reinforcement. Conversely, the other two sub-groups will accept what is basically a negative principle for the 'accommodation' of their subordinate concerns, namely non-interference with their prime concern.

This section will explore the difficulties that all our 'meta-reflexives' experience with dovetailing their concerns. It is then hoped to be able to answer the question, is it the times when their concerns slip badly out of alignment which also represent the points at which the *modus vivendi* of each of them displays volatility? Again, let us start with the youngest subject and work up to the oldest, with a second question in mind. Does the sequence of transforming their ideal concerns into practical projects which then result in stable practices, become any easier as the 'meta-reflexives' grow older?

Andy presents a very clear statement of the difficulties he has with dovetailing his concerns: 'I do prioritise but for me it's not a simple, well there's A, there's B, there's C. Sometimes A can go down one and B can come up, and it's quite hard to disentangle quite clearly and categorically that this is most important now.' Disentangling is difficult because A, B and C are all important to his holistic ideal. This he puts simply, 'I want to be happy in what I'm doing. Not in a selfish way. Obviously it involves other people. And it's an ongoing concern – I wish it wasn't an ongoing concern.' As becomes clear, it will only cease being one if he can bring his concerns in the three orders of natural reality into a mutually reinforcing relationship.

Taking his present job in a Business School was itself a compromise between his academic ideal, his desire to be closer to his tight-knit family, and his quest for friendship and keener students. Immediately after he was offered the post, Andy started thinking: 'what the hell am I doing? Is this really what you want? But you're coming back home [to live] and it's been an exhausting year... Don't worry, you can hang on in there. Your brother's here. He needs your support and you're bound to meet some interesting people. But my heart's not in it. It's not me – not what I want to do, being in a Business School.' In performative terms, the job has indeed proved a hindrance to realising his intellectual ideal. Although he has managed to be very productive and to stick to his own academic agenda, it has not proved a supportive environment. Andy cannot teach his own specialism, finds standards are low, some assignments traduce his notion of professional ethics, that the probationary teaching certificate bears no relation to what he does on his hind legs, and that he is constantly being chivvied to take a greater interest in business issues. His conclusion is, 'I'd like to be in a department where I can say, yeah, it's part of my identity' – and here he cannot.

As can be seen from his first reaction to being offered the post, the social support of family and friends were the considerations that reconciled him to this appointment. However, on every front he finds little that supports and fosters self-worth. Attached as he is to his family, he now realises that he cannot resume his old role of domestic prop: 'I do care about my family and I worry about my brother. But I'm realising that they're making mistakes, but you can't always interfere – just advise. I'm changing as well. I don't feel as dependent as I used to. But it's important, so in terms of movement I don't want to be on the other side of the globe.' Neither has the new job yielded the friendship he hoped, and again he highlights the difficulty of separating work from collegiality: 'My job's important to me, but that again is banged up with what I'm looking for out of life. What's very important is that people like me, I like people, and I have a job and a relationship that's actually meaningful to me – there's real genuineness about them. With my current job, there isn't an opportunity for having a meaningful relationship – I'm not saying with lots of people, just one, two or three.' He wants friendship and he wants a partner, but again one who would be fully aligned with his concerns – 'a fulfilling relationship. I would like to share my passion with somebody who is like minded – on my wavelength, but it's important that I don't make a mistake and find somebody for the sake of it.' Nor can Andy find compensation in his teaching, and teaching is something he enjoys, but once more there is the problem of alignment: 'I like to be with students and I'm very passionate about my subject. Some of my students are quite negative. It gets me down. I don't say that I get overly depressed, but I don't get a high – not many highs at all.' In terms of a social environment, the new post has given Andy nothing and this has even prompted him to consider doing a PGCE, recalling the enjoyment he derived from temporarily working in a primary school.

Finally, in terms of well-being, Andy suffers less than most 'meta-reflexives'. Nevertheless, he talks openly about stress, anxiety and lack of confidence, especially in relation to making conference presentations: 'it's making the effort to go that I find stressful. I still think I'm not up there yet, and I really wish I wasn't like that because it's preventing me from really going for it.' He recognises that these anxieties are seriously holding him back and hopes that, with the publication of his book, they will diminish – 'then the career would really start for me'. They seem unlikely merely to dissipate, given that everything else is out of alignment. With a core of close friends and collegial allies, he could tackle this problem – given their supportive presence at a couple of forthcoming conferences. The absence of close academic friends may well account for why, at twenty-nine, he still lives at home, where he is appreciated. Yet he also knows that *la recherche du temps perdu* of familial working-class traditionalism is something for which he has now unfitted himself; there is no going back. What he is trying to do is a holding operation: 'I think at the moment what I'm doing is trying to devise coping strategies, and I do feel a lot better. So, I'm making an effort to go in more [to the university]. I'm doing French in the evenings on campus. That's the sort of self-deliberation with one's self, "Pull yourself together – yeah, it's not easy but try and make it easier for yourself." But ultimately I know I'm not going to stay there.' Given this combination of dissatisfaction, loneliness and anxiety, his conclusion seems inescapable.

Ivan took up his first post a year later than Andy, and so is now half way through his second academic year. They are thus very similar in terms of qualifications and experience, but even more so in relation to their *desiderata* and disappointments. Ivan too provides a very clear statement about the holistic nature of his concerns and the components that he wishes to be organically integrated with one another. His generic priority is, 'to feel more sense of living, which is a sense of being happy and productive'. This, in turn, involves the alignment of the three types of concerns pertaining to the three different orders of natural reality. Firstly, it means being able to get on with research and writing, without being diverted by the intrusion of calls to exercise different skills: 'to be more engaged in writing, rather than doing things by imposition, as in, got to do the Research Appraisal Exercise, got to do the teaching, and got to do the social thing with these people'. Secondly, Ivan's generic ideal also requires supportive friendship, which would dovetail well only if it were in the form of like-minded collegiality: 'more contact with the nicer people, not only people that have got problems, but the non-superficial, easy-going and sensitive people'. Finally, as Ivan says, his overall sense of well-being 'would tend to unfold between the two'; it is not something separate, but is closely and organically intertwined with them.

Ivan is acutely and reflexively aware of his need for this alignment and also about the futility of imagining that it would automatically come about were he merely to exchange one professional activity for another: 'So, yeah, I'm thinking of how I can improve. I don't mean practically, but how to improve the quality of life. I think more generally about how can I improve my social life and how can I feel more comfortable with the job I've got – overcoming problems, rather than sitting around thinking, well if I leave activity X, it's not going to be Y, and I'll have more time for activity Z . . . I don't think about it in those terms. I think more about how can I feel more comfortable in how I am, and that may be more productive for writing.' So let us briefly unpack these three components, to discover what is awry with each and how this precludes their dovetailing in the holistic manner sought.

Ivan was relieved to take up his appointment in one of the newly upgraded universities, because the job market was particularly quiet that year and his alternative might well have been a post in further education, leaving him with no time for research. Immediately, he experienced frustrations with every element of his newly created lectureship – teaching, administration and research. In his view, which doubtless would be contested, 'my post was created with no thought for my research development, because it was a matter of employing me to mop up some teaching and mainly deal with big administrative jobs, to take the pressure off them'. He finds that the teaching can be 'disheartening', because although the part-time students 'can be really great', the full-time taught postgraduates generally have 'no sense of wanting to engage'. Ivan blames this upon a subsidised programme, intended for the re-skilling of redundant manual workers, having been appropriated by those who simply want to go on enjoying an undergraduate lifestyle. Therefore, he claims, 'what we do is morally wrong', because instead of those who could benefit from it, the course has been hijacked by 'mainly white, upper working-class, lower middle-class, second-hand car dealer type kids, with their mobile phones and cars. And they're not interested in it, got no passion for doing it.'

His administrative responsibilities were heavy; he felt pressurised over writing the 'Units' and at sea when given sole responsibility for other departmental tasks, 'with no mentoring or training' and no guidance. To him, these two sides of the job were squeezing out his real interest, research. 'I feel rusty because I haven't been able to do any decent writing since I got the job . . . I just felt suffocated in the last year and a half.' A major factor, which intensified this, was an absence of colleagues upholding the same research culture that he had absorbed during his postgraduate days: 'there is a bad culture here. That's what I probably feel uncomfortable with. It's not bad as a former poly, but the culture is anti-intellectual.' Most of his colleagues are 'too laddy': relaxation consists in drinking lots of beer and discussing football.

Where then is he to turn for friendship on his own wavelength? He knows the impossibility of reverting to his traditional class pattern, but not how to go forward out of his relative isolation: 'if you went for . . . say, school friends and family, then you've got a group and you've got the support there, but at the same time it's probably stifling . . . The opposite of that is being cut off . . . So it's a problem – also a problem of fear I think.'

How do you engage in risk-taking behaviour, i.e. meeting new people?' In terms of reversion, he has tried and re-tried tapping his family as a resource, but his mother is not in a stable relationship and one of her partners was aggressively abusive about Ivan taking four years over a PhD. Time in that environment was only survived by developing a 'siege mentality', and by Ivan reflexively telling himself not to conform to the status of 'victim' which can license any form of retaliation. Conversely, these experiences seem to have given him a genuine empathy with victims, several of whom he has generously befriended, only to find that damaged people cannot reciprocate, are unreliable in their shifting demands, and unpredictable in their rejections. Since his close friends are geographically scattered, Ivan asks himself how he can find or form an environment which enables him to do 'all the normal things', like having a house, wife and kids, given that he is 'cut off' from the conventional path belonging to his original social context.

Without support at 'work' or 'home' he knows that his general well-being deteriorates, that the depression and anxiety to which he is prone then seriously intensify. He has sought and gained help from a clinical psychologist, but bad experiences like family rejection and aggression prompt deep unhappiness and panic attacks, thus triggering the downward spiral about which we first heard him speak. Nothing could be clearer than the holistic realignment required to reverse matters in an upward direction, but where can Ivan start? Of his three concerns, the one most readily under his control is his job. Until the market picks up he, like Andy, tries to make the best of it, taking on editing and hoping that the publication of his book will make a difference. He sums up his present post by saying, 'it's a default option at the moment'. Already he is making applications to traditional universities and is buoyed up by getting short-listed. Given his circumstances, another instalment of biographical volatility seems to lie just around the corner.

Andy and Ivan are extreme cases of 'meta-reflexives' who failed to root contextually because the mis-alignment of their concerns precluded the establishment of a satisfying and sustainable *modus vivendi*. Cass's 'portrait' revealed a biography which unreeled in slow-motion in comparison with theirs. Nevertheless, the dynamics are fundamentally the same, with the difference that Cass could temporarily bring about a sustainable degree of alignment between her concerns. Her transitions to a different *modus vivendi* coincided with her concerns slipping badly out of alignment. Earlier I undertook to return to her decision to take early retirement from social work, and now want to examine this as a serious point of slippage in the organic integration which she, like other 'meta-reflexives', seeks and needs to find.

Cass volunteered that her first seven years in social work largely fulfilled her expectations. However, her awareness of the various social philosophies, warring throughout the profession, meant that she knew her work context would not remain unchanging: 'So I suppose I always knew that there would probably be a time when I'd make a decision that this wasn't what I wanted to be doing.' She gives an acute diagnosis of the bifurcation which she soon recognised amongst colleagues; between those who devoted most of their energy to changing 'the system' from within, versus those who were more client-oriented, amongst whom she placed herself. She agrees that nearly all entrants join the profession in the hope of effecting change, but then as an idealist herself, 'you have to re-visit that as the years go by and you have to be content with the small changes'.

Yet how small can these changes become and still leave one feeling that one is usefully serving one's ideal? Over the last decade, Cass admits that 'I was actually becoming a disenchanted sort of person. I was losing my enthusiasm and it was to do with the way the job spec was changing. You know, the whole thrust of all the quality-control stuff... and the phrase "more out of less"... it was just more and more assessing. The assessment was about people who didn't need our services rather than people who did – the whole philosophy had swung so much.' Here Cass produces a lengthy critique of the 'new managerialism', which closely parallels the criticisms levelled by Ivan and Andy at the same trends within higher education. This type of institutional critique is typical of the 'meta-reflexive', and a major reason for their contextual volatility. What prompted Cass to resign was 'the business of "right, now you can close the case", when, as a professional, one knew that it might close this week, but that two months down the road it would blow open again'.

This was a major reason, but not Cass's sole reason for her resignation. Equally important was the fact that the bold yet careful family arrangements, which she had designed to be in alignment with her professional commitment, began to unravel. Most obviously, her sons were now independent and their care no longer supplied the rationale for domestic life. Next came the death of her aunt, bringing to an end this inter-personal commitment, which had made Cass's full-time working possible at first. In fact, her extended family ceased to be a factor in the equation. Like her aunt, her father had joined the household, but his deteriorating health led first to residential care, and soon after to his death. Most important of all, Cass had finally taken the decision to separate from her husband. As a practising Catholic, re-marriage was not on the agenda. Therefore, her domestic situation, which had been set up to complement her professional life, changed at exactly the time that her disenchantment with social work was peaking. She was now in an unprecedented position of freedom, but increasingly asked herself why she was there at all. Her *modus vivendi* was objectively sustainable, yet subjectively it failed to satisfy, and there was no reason to shore it up when its two basic components were so out of kilter with her ideal.

Given that Cass enjoyed good health, what she did was to design a new project for herself, one which entailed a further contextual resettlement, in the hope of bringing her concerns into a better (more organic) alignment. She undertook a further qualification in teaching English as a foreign language and then bound two of her concerns even more closely together by offering her services to a couple of religious orders for work in the developing world. The project with street children that she will be working on in Southern Africa represents an extension of her vocational commitment, and will enable her to exercise it, untrammelled (she trusts) by performance indicators and quality controls. Nevertheless, she insists that this one-year 'experiment' should not be understood in terms of pure altruism: 'I'm doing this for myself – all the things I'm going to be doing there, I could do right here.' So why not have taken that seemingly easier alternative? Because there is one more concern that she seeks to bring into alignment.

At first she says of the African project, 'well I can't lose, it'll give me a different perspective on life'. Although this is true, it is such a truism that I query exactly what she means by a 'perspective'. Cass does mean something very specific. Her husband is a local public figure and significant employer; in a rural borough, it is impossible to escape his orbit and avoid being constantly 'hiked back' into the past. Despite their apparently amicable relations, this new venture 'is as much to get away from it all as anything'. What Cass means is that before she commits herself to another *modus vivendi*, she needs to be able to engage in undistorted 'meta-reflexivity' – from her own perspective, uncoloured by past concerns which it has been impossible to put into the past tense. Hence, 'I want to get away and put it under a microscope.' Cass has gone away to initiate a new round of the internal conversation, to research a new context in the hope of designing a new life-project – with integrity and in line with her holistic principle.

At the age of fifty-five, there is no reason why she should not succeed; Anna made an equally dramatic revision when she was two years older. Their two sets of circumstances were very similar and precipitated the same quest for a new *modus vivendi*. For Anna too, her previous alignment between 'work' and 'home' had slipped completely. She had only moved to the south-west to take up her deputy headship, and had made a home there with her retired sister. When her job ended and her sister died, this represented a transition point. In less than a year, she had conceived the project of re-entering her old religious order, having been out of it for twenty years. Like all the other members of this sub-group, Anna has a holistic ideal about a satisfying way of life: 'I think there's got to be a certain wholeheartedness in what I'm doing.' Above all, it was this organic integration that she sought to re-establish. In her own words, 'my relationship with God is very important to me now. I think it's an extension, if you like, of my relationship with other people. I'm very conscious that you can't live in community with other people and not get on with them . . . and there are concerns about the wider – the terrible situation of people in other parts of the world. It's all obviously linked with my choice of way of life.'

These are the elements that Anna sought to align by re-entering her order, but their organic integration seems to have remained problematic. To begin with, she was again sent out to Latin America, to a country which she loves: 'that's I think where my heart has been and always will be, sort of working – and it's always something I've been able to do and very happy to do. I can work among the poor and uneducated and not feel deprived in any sense or superior in any sense.' The work was satisfying and Anna is full of initiative, perhaps too full of it for this to dovetail with her inter-personal concerns. As she volunteered, 'I mean one of the reasons I said I wanted to re-enter was I felt I wanted a community. And you come back and it's not so easy to form communities.' At least to an outsider, petty jealousies appear to have played a part in moving her from community to community in that Latin country: such as those deriving from her desire to get a school building operational in the slums of the economic capital, or from her organising the funding and construction of a hostel in the countryside. Doubtless other factors were also in play, but when Anna was moved to the high Andes, she had to work out her own ministry, and, just as she was beginning to do so, she became ill, which dictated her return to England.

Having accepted that her health would probably preclude returning to Latin America, Anna's problem was to re-design a *modus vivendi* within her religious order in this country – one which successfully aligned her concerns. Clearly there are difficulties, and she admits to 'worrying about how to get them all to dovetail together'. Most obviously these involve 'work' and 'community', and both elements are accompanied by the on-going contextual critique which is one of the hallmarks of the 'meta-reflexive'.

In terms of work, she was promptly made secretary general and immediately confronted tensions between this task and 'community'. On the one hand, the job gave her access to much confidential personal information, leaving her unable to confirm, deny or participate in speculative discussions with 'ordinary' sisters about what was going on. On the other hand, she was not treated as a member of Council, yet expected to prepare documentation about deliberations in which she had not participated. This left her as neither fish nor fowl, and matters deteriorated when the Council decided to set up community together elsewhere: 'The situation job-wise has become worse because they've all moved out to another house, and in a sense this place is almost dead now. I feel I'm sitting there saying, "right I'll be your archivist", but as secretary general, you know, I'm not really operating.' The work had become routinely clerical, and once again Anna was casting around for a new project to supply fulfilment. Thus, at the age of sixty-four, she enrolled on a part-time MA, which potentially could lead to a new and highly specialised professional qualification. As Anna says, 'it can become very repetitive, typing up lists of sisters and things of that nature. You need something – just some stimulation. I find that in the course.' What she is trying to do is to advance her own personal well-being, but in a manner which will also protect her relations with the community. 'I really did believe that if I went and did something a little bit more testing mentally, then I'd have more to give. Otherwise, I genuinely felt that if I sat in an office five days a week, I'd be certifiable and everyone else too. It would affect other people as well.'

Community was one of the things that Anna sought when she re-entered, and it is still crucially important to her now: 'the relationship with God and the community, in one sense must come first. Otherwise I'm not fulfilled as a person, and then I find I'm miserable and unhappy and scratchy.' Yet, 'making community' with a diverse group of people, with different educational levels, experiences, backgrounds and ages is not easy and tends to be a major pre-occupation in female congregations. Anna describes some of her ploys: 'I sometimes sit down and watch "*Coronation Street*", and play really dumb about it. Because there are two or three in the community who watch it regularly, and it gives a point of contact with them.' She honestly admits that she had expected to encounter much greater attitudinal transformations: 'I didn't realise. I find in fact that for all the changes that have been introduced, after all that they say and do, there's still an awful lot of the old routine. For example, this morning Sister X in the community, who's seventy-five now, said, "Well I know this is the kind of community we are, but I would prefer it if we were all living in the house and working in the house." She doesn't like the idea of people going off and doing different things . . . Yes, the rigid timetable maybe has gone, but there's an awful lot of unchanged thinking and unchanged ways of behaving.'

From this, it seems that the difficulties which 'meta-reflexives' have with dovetailing never do disappear. Alongside it, three other features also persist. Firstly, their contextual critique is life-long, for no context ever fully exemplifies their ideals. In Anna's words, 'I thought things were going to be different. . . So I am an idealist in some ways. I always expect something to be better than it ever turns out to be.' Yet she is determined to remain with her congregation and thoughts of doing otherwise are 'fleeting things'. Secondly, there is also a life-long re-configuration of practical projects, in the (enduring) hope of producing a better alignment. Thus Anna is determined to finish her MA, and, although she finds the weekly journey to London tiring, it gives her an intellectual stimulus which is lacking in the community and also the chance to stay with members of her family, who are also important to her. The trouble is that the MA will end this year. She wants to make use of it, but would need to study to doctoral level in order to practise professionally. So much turns upon whether she can find the health and strength to face this. It would give her very useful employment, regardless of age; professional autonomy, rather than her ambiguous secretarial role; and a window on wider needs, all of which could represent a new *modus vivendi*, but one still within her congregation.

Thirdly, and precisely because both their contextual critiques and their difficulties with dovetailing are life-long, so is the pre-occupation of the 'meta-reflexives' with acquiring more self-knowledge. Although they remain social critics, they still have to develop coping strategies for living within institutional contexts. Moreover, they are not claiming that all of their difficulties are the fault of 'the system'; with greater self-awareness and self-learning they all believe that it is possible to cope better, more constructively and more creatively. With the aim of doing so, members of this sub-group have consulted (variously) clinical psychologists, therapists, counsellors or spiritual directors, something which was not encountered among either 'communicative' or 'autonomous' reflexives. To be pre-occupied with their own subjectivity is one of the distinguishing features of 'meta-reflexives'. This is very understandable; the 'meta-reflexive' looks to and fro between self and society, is equally critical of both – and of their imperfect fit. Goodness of fit can only be produced by a self-change that complements circumstantial change, and defective circumstances call for a changed self who can cope more readily with them. In this sense, they are practical dialecticians, people who practise the dialectics of objectivity and subjectivity, which is why there is no lasting set of established practices for them – no final *modus vivendi*.

'Meta-reflexivity' in relation to constraints and enablements

Generically, courses of action are defined and produced by reflexive agents. They subjectively deliberate upon their objective circumstances when determining what projects they will pursue. The deliberations of 'communicative reflexives' were markedly 'traditional' because their pattern of 'thought and talk' opened up their subjectivity to the guidance of their surrounding community – to the influences of 'contextual continuity'. The deliberations of 'autonomous reflexives' were distinctively 'strategic' because these individuals, with their clear hierarchies of concerns, simply interrogated their circumstances and came to their own conclusions about how best to realise their aims. The deliberations of 'meta-reflexives' are different again. Personally they *judge* courses of action in relation to their ideals, rather than canvassing the views of 'similars and familiars'; normatively they *evaluate* right action, rather than strategically assessing the politics of the possible.

Subjectively, the 'meta-reflexives' are the strongest of 'strong evaluators', in relation to their objective circumstances. Their normative orientation to the situations that they confront means 'meta-reflexives' have a unique relationship to constraints and enablements. They neither evade them nor seek to circumvent them, but exhibit outward *immunity* towards them. They will try to advance their projects in the face of constraints by resisting their powers, and will pursue them with indifference to whether or not enablements are on their side. Of course, they are not objectively immune to the causal powers that they activate, which impose their opportunity costs and exact their toll when they are resisted. Yet, subjectively, this group displays a willingness to pay the price, thus subverting the causal powers of society in the attempt to realise their ideals.

'Meta-reflexives' are *subversive* because the courses of action that they set for themselves are immune to directional guidance from the social structure. The latter cannot determine action, it can only condition it by attaching penalties and bonuses to acting in one way or in another. If the 'meta-reflexives' will absorb the costs and shrug off the incentives, then they 'buy' freedom of action, but at a considerable cost to themselves. Whether they can summon up the price of subversion and continue to pay it throughout their life-courses is a matter of fallible human judgement. There must always be a temptation to capitulate and to compromise their ideals because resistance takes its toll, day by day and year by year. Hence, as with all other modes of reflexivity, there are no guarantees that the younger subjects will persist. Both Andy and Ivan might land plum jobs, gain academic recognition, and gradually subside into becoming career strategists. 'Meta-reflexivity' is just as mutable as any other life of the mind.

However, as long as these subjects remain subversives, it is important to recognise that their resistance is not that of some other-worldly idealists who are oblivious to the powers which they have activated and the costs entailed in subverting them. Nothing could be less true of this group, which should not be surprising since its members all have more social science expertise than was found in either of the other sub-groups – each member has at least a joint-honours degree in one of the social sciences. As respondents they freely use the language of constraints and enablements for examining their own dilemmas. Thus Andy reflects that there are *some* constraints which he could not resist. If the posts he wants are not available, then he could have protected his ideal by remaining jobless, but he could have done nothing to advance it whilst living on the dole or in casual employment. That would be the other-worldly response; his this-worldly reaction is to have taken a post in a Business School, where he hopes to push on with his research trajectory. As he says, 'structurally the jobs aren't there at the moment, that's a constraint, an extreme constraint for me emotionally'. Similarly, Ivan, who has little that is positive to say for his new university, admits, 'I've done okay so far, given the constraints.' He goes further and furnishes his own analysis of why he finds himself where he does: 'I'm too good for the further education/higher education borderline places, and not good enough for the better places, obsessed with the forthcoming RAE.' It will be recalled that Cass too reflected upon the trends pervading social work and recognised from the beginning that it would not always be the environment for her.

In other words, 'meta-reflexives' cannot be fully immune. They need to work somewhere and thus take one of the jobs available to them. This is true even of Anna. Although at eighteen she seemingly turned her back on the occupational distribution by joining her religious order, she was still restricted to the postings which her congregation had available. What is different about the 'meta-reflexives' is their subjective awareness that they are searching for structural approximations to their cultural ideals. Simultaneously, they are also aware that the approximation is not good enough and that they would be guilty of self-deception if they tried to convince themselves otherwise. Here is Andy reflecting on his impulsiveness in accepting his first appointment, as he stands at the station to catch his train home: 'I knew for some reason I'd got the job, and I can remember putting my briefcase to one side and thinking, "what have you done?" in my mind . . . but sometimes I kid myself in this conversation. I'm wanting to say, "Andy, if you go for this job you do realise it's going to be a nightmare." And it's there in the background so, in that sense, although I'm kidding myself, I'm actually quite aware of it and try and ignore it.' Here, Andy articulates the classic argument against the possibility of genuine self-deception, namely that he does know what he is 'kidding himself' about and should not be doing it.

Moreover, once having done it, he also knows that he cannot follow through and live up to the job expectations. Here he is comparing his own reaction with that of one of his colleagues, when both came under pressure to attend a business conference. 'He's saying we ought to go to the [particular] conference, and I'm thinking, "Oh God, I don't really want to go." So he's being strategic in a way that emotionally I can't be – it's not me. It doesn't bother him, but emotionally it bothers me, whereas for my colleague, it's not a problem. If that's how he gets his Chair, fine, it's not that important to me.' Yet, if Andy now refuses to become a strategist in working this part of the system, he has only one alternative, which is to get out of it. This is precisely what he did and is trying to do again. The 'meta-reflexive' makes his or her judgement, condemns the context in question, subjects it to critique, and then moves on. It is at this point that the 'meta-reflexives' willingly pay the objective price, rather than conform, collaborate or compromise. This is evident in the willingness of all these subjects to resign their posts, to re-locate in other areas or countries, and to re-train.

Is this pure expressive action? If the 'meta-reflexives' can be over-impulsive in taking up a position, are they also being over-emotional in dropping one, by deeming its imperfections to be normatively intolerable? This would again make them into other-worldly idealists who never count the costs. In fact, the converse is the case. These are people who are acutely aware of the objective price that their resistance incurs for them. This becomes very clear when I question them about the remuneration and status associated with their preferred ways of life. Even if Andy and Ivan could have a post in the department of their choice, it would make no great difference to their earnings or their public esteem. Ivan, in his mid-thirties, thinks the salary is derisory: 'It's a joke, spending all that time in higher education and get a crap salary. I want to get a mortgage. By myself, what can I get? A maximum of sixty thousand – you're talking about a terrace house in a working-class area.' Although he thinks that the public does look up to university lecturers, nevertheless, if he achieved what he wants to do in his writing, then after all those exertions, 'who would notice?' Andy also admits to being hard-pressed on his starting salary: 'moneywise I'm in debt and I'm getting into more debt. But I'm thinking that in a few years' time, I'm going to be okay. Alright, I'll be in my late thirties. But again, that's well worth the price.' These are hardly the reflections of other-worldly people. Andy's last comment, about the price being worth paying, is a remark from someone who is also fully aware of the objective cost.

So too are Cass and Anna. Thinking back on her years in social work, Cass reflects that the low pay level threatened the very financial independence she sought, because she always had to think of her husband or father as fall-backs. She is also very aware 'that even now with my colleagues, it's a struggle and it's a source of grievance'. She also comments on the low status of the profession and how 'my neighbours think I just go and sit around people's houses and have cups of tea all day and be nice'. This she could laugh off, but not those situations where she was put-down by other professionals, when seeking to defend a client: 'You go to a professional meeting, particularly with medical people and you're quite keen. I can remember a couple of occasions when I wanted to smack him across the face. But I suppose I had a degree of fulfilment in what my job meant to me, so how others saw it didn't actually matter too much.' This is spoken by someone who is also well aware that her fulfilment, at that time, was bought at a price.

This is clearest of all with Anna, who objectively bore the heaviest costs when re-entering her order. 'When I decided to come back to the congregation it was in a sense – I suppose there was every sense really – of calculating. There was the money, the commitment, but it was the commitment I think and what it involved, because it was quite a bit. I had my own car and could get into it and go where I wanted, when I wanted. You sacrifice a certain freedom. I've lost my dog. I gave up smoking. All of which were stipulated. Is the price worth paying? Yes, the price is worth paying.' Moreover, this is not a once-and-for-all payment, but a daily one. Anna admits, 'sometimes I find the financial limitations irritating. Sometimes I think if I have lamb stew once more, I will throw it at somebody. You can't choose what you're going to cook; you can't choose what you're going to eat... On the odd days I might see an Aston Martin or something of that nature. I can say to myself now, "you had a lovely sports car and you chose to give it up"'. In short, Anna does not stop objectively registering the price she is paying.

Throughout, we find the same refrain. The 'meta-reflexives' are fully cognisant of the costs of their actions and do not seek to minimise the objective price paid, including obligatory lamb stew. Yet, in different words, they all re-iterate that the price is worth paying to exercise their vocations. What this means is that subjectively they are employing their own currencies and that according to their own 'weights and measures', the balance is positive. So what kind of currency do they employ which can outweigh these knowing sacrifices? As I have maintained throughout, our currencies are coined by our ultimate concerns, they are non-convertible and their gold standard is the value that their ultimate concern enshrines. This means that in worldly terms they seem to get by on very little and all of it intangible, but subjectively this is what they care about most.

Andy gains his greatest satisfaction from being read and from the knowledge that a few individuals appreciate his work and engage with his arguments. 'I think this is great. I'm being taken seriously by people, and, yeah, I really enjoy it. It's funny, if someone will say, "I read your article on [X]", and I'll say, "well, it wasn't that good, I mean compared to other people's work". But if somebody says, "no, but I like it", that's good and you get a dialogue going.' Subjectively this is what keeps him going. It offsets the better remuneration he would have gained from entering the legal profession and the greater conviviality he would have derived from joining the teaching profession. Temporarily, it helps to counterbalance the alienation he experiences in the Business School.

Ivan too gets by on short commons; a light diet of a little appreciation and encouragement for the kind of research he wants to continue doing. He tells the story of a recent application for a job, which could have been depressing since he was long-listed out of several hundred applicants, yet did not quite get onto the short-list: 'but the head of department thought I had some good research ideas. So that helps you keep going, saying to yourself, "well, I've done okay, so far" '. For Ivan and Andy this type of appreciation reinforces their determination to stick with the research agendas they are pursuing by signalling that the ideas in which they have invested themselves have recognised worth. Also it encourages them to keep trying to leave their present contexts. For both of these young academics, a great deal hangs on the reception of their first books which will be published in a few months. Good reviews and citations are the most tangible forms their currencies take, and are as close as these currencies come to being negotiable – by improving their access to the posts they seek. If their books do not receive any recognition at all, and these young academics are not expecting their first books to set the world on fire, then it becomes questionable whether or not they will continue as they are doing at present.

What is distinctive about 'meta-reflexives' is that they constantly evaluate their situations in the light of their concerns and *not* vice versa. When situations are deemed too disparate from their ideals, then they quit, which is what makes for the biographical volatility of the 'meta-reflexive'. Conversely, ideals are *not* modified to produce a second-best fit with circumstances. Instead, they are re-cast into different projects with the hope of their realisation. This is the source of their immunity to constraints and enablements, namely that they are willing to pay the price and to move on, rather than to compromise their concerns. It is what entitles them to be the critics of society's institutions (and what prevents them being dismissed as 'whingers'), because not only do they hold up different societal values but also pay the costs involved in so doing.

'Meta-reflexives' are subversive because they are unmoved by the penalties and bonuses through which constraints and enablements discourage some courses of action and foster others – instead they pass judgement and move on. This is the most clearly marked by the *indifference* shown by the 'meta-reflexive' to the general social evaluation of upwards, downwards and lateral mobility. The two younger members give intimations of it: the two older ones gave evidence of it.

When his current job feels particularly alienating, Andy is tempted by the prospect of downward mobility, of undertaking teacher training and joining the kind of primary school which would be expressive of his values. For the time being, he mentally resists this inclination, saying to himself, 'alright, things haven't worked out yet, but don't be stupid, don't go and do this just because you're unhappy. Don't go and do a PGCE, come on, sort yourself out.' So far, he is hanging on, but not too many people actually wrestle with the *attractions* of downward mobility.

Yet, Ivan is similar and reflects that he would refuse promotion at his new university because this would decrease his prospects of getting out of it. 'I'm a perfectionist. If I was still in a new university and was offered a readership, I wouldn't take it . . . someone was headhunted from here to be reader in an old university, but I think that's the exception that proves the rule. So I'd actually be ambitious enough not to take the readership here, if I was offered it eventually.' That is on a good day – one on which Ivan manages to sound like a strategist. On a bad day, he has been close to walking out and to thinking that voluntary work in Africa would be preferable – which no strategist would ever do. Many people will say such things when disgruntled, but the 'meta-reflexive' will actually do them, as Cass did – not out of disgruntlement but as her normative pronouncement upon the state of social work. Cass had first moved laterally, for which she had trained and re-trained, and recently she re-trained again – for downward mobility.

Anna has no doubts that in re-entering her order, she too embraced downward mobility, after a life-time of moving in all three directions. She reflects that religious sisters today, no longer wearing habits, have definitely moved down the social scale, particularly in developing countries where they would rank lower than the local school head. She talks very revealingly about how her own repeated shifts in social status can be acceptable – to a 'meta-reflexive': 'very often I say to myself, it doesn't matter. I've been there, done that, I don't need to prove myself now. I mean definitely, yes, I don't have the clout that I had in many respects – and that doesn't matter either . . . It seems I've spent my life being number two in this job. Maybe, if I'd stayed, by this time I'd have been somebody. But I'd have been a very unhappy somebody – so that doesn't matter . . . Because this has been very much a free choice – you know, I chose to live with these stupid women.'

Conclusion

It is proper that Anna should have the last word, because at sixty-five she has sustained and is still sustaining a life of 'meta-reflexivity' and continuing to pay the price for resisting constraints and enablements. Yet, in conclusion, there are several points to draw out of her summary comment. Firstly, Anna is being self-consolatory as she reflects upon her chequered life-course. Its very volatility allows her to say, 'I've been there, done that' and thus to interpret her trajectory of 'contextual unsettlement' as a rich life. I do not doubt the authenticity of her assertion, but nevertheless wonder whether all our 'meta-reflexives' could reflect on the consequences of their actions in this positive manner. There are many alternatives, including embitterment, disillusionment and capitulation. After all, Ivan and Andy had undergone considerable 'elastication' before they conceived of their vocations, both are ambitious for their realisation, and they also want the 'usual' things – houses, cars, families. Although they both voluntarily contemplate downward mobility, how would they respond to it if it became a reality? At the moment, both are engaged in 'contextual re-location', as a 'game' that they hope to win, in objective terms; each lateral job-change and every new job application is meant to bring them closer to their ideal. If it does not, will they cede their title to being contextual critics and merely become embittered individuals, who, unlike the 'communicative reflexives', cannot find contentment in the 'usual' things?

Conversely, if they succeed objectively, might they gradually succumb subjectively, their ideals atrophying with their success? Success might signal a gradual drift towards task-orientation, in which their ideals become reduced to what is institutionally acceptable. Twenty years on, we could be looking at two heads of departments who are busily implementing the quality controls of the day. Anna could envisage that situation and reflect that she would have been a 'very unhappy somebody', had it occurred. Yet she says this precisely because she did *not* do it, but seems set to remain a 'meta-reflexive' to the end. The problem is that had she done it, her mode of reflexivity itself might well have been transmuted in the process. As an idealist she may then have become an instrumentalist, and as a subversive she could have become a strategist, whose resistance gave way to the art of the possible. In that case, the restless search for self-knowledge would have been displaced by self-monitoring for performative achievement, and the internal conversation would increasingly have assumed the form of 'autonomous reflexivity'. Whether that would have spelt greater happiness or unhappiness is impossible to determine; 'autonomous reflexives' seemed to have their share of both.

By sustaining her own subversion, Anna had also maintained her capacity for 'free choice', that is for self-determination uninfluenced by the powers of constraints and enablements. Yet if we look back to her last phrase, this was a choice to 'live with these stupid women'. She herself has commented upon their limitations, she has admitted her frustrations, and her self-knowledge has led her to conceive of and begin to execute a new project. The moral seems to be that there is no durable re-positioning, there is no final elaboration of stable practices, and there is no end to the biographical volatility of the 'meta-reflexives' – who persevere to the end with this life of the mind. In that case they will always forego a sustainable *modus vivendi* because neither the self, nor society, nor relations between them can ever be evaluated as satisfying, let alone as satisfactory – that is, worthy of being sustained.

Postscript

Six months after interviewing him, I received a letter from Andy, who is one of the subjects whom I knew before undertaking this research. With his permission, extracts from his letter are reproduced below.

25 February 2002

Dear Maggie

Having read your chapter, I think it's best to say at the outset that I have decided to quit the academy, possibly *pro tem*, but I am not worried about it. The amount of inner dialogue over the past month has surpassed previous stressful dialogues about my career. Anyway, I have applied to do a PGCE primary teaching and Graduate Teacher Programme (which would provide a salary-based route, in contrast to PGCE). I thought that being a project co-ordinator would improve things here [in the Business School], but they haven't; and, coupled with the loneliness of research, I have decided that the academy isn't making me happy. Regrettably I can give one thousand and one reasons why to change career and only one reason for staying – namely the kudos of being published!

The main barrier to making this decision has centred on the sheer amount of work I have undertaken to get where I am today... However, I don't want to be one of those embittered people in ten years' time, even if, as you say, as Head of Department or Reader in [my discipline].

I am indeed adjusting projects in order to remain faithful to my ideal – in this case "making a difference" to people's lives through teaching (now "relegated" to primary). Well, six years ago I would never have contemplated downward mobility! Like Cass, I always wanted to teach (vocation)... did well at University, loved the subject, didn't foresee the loneliness of writing up PhD and, fallibly, forgot that lecturing in top-class universities ever enjoins at least three days per week of what I now want to call "solitary confinement"! Having spoken with colleagues, they readily admit to frustration and loneliness, yet state that they develop coping strategies. I was advised to get a partner to help me cope! For me, my vocation should not involve the development of coping strategies . . . I may find in my career change that this may enjoin it, but am prepared to take the risk . . .

I am well aware of the OFSTED regime in schools but know (fallibly) that I will cope, because I will be caring for children and doing the best for them in full recognition of target mania. For me, having spent so much time in primary schools, I find that whilst children are not ever easy to teach, at least they are not cynical and make judgements about you *qua* you rather than some course-provider-cum-executor who gives them the goods for which they have paid £1000. This would apply equally in any other department or university.

For me, changing to primary teaching isn't a compromise as such; going along with the management stuff would be, as would the structural inability to teach in a way that I want to (i.e. care for students and get to know them). Here [at my present University] I know that a job would be mine in [the Department I prefer] if I wanted it. But I *now know* that I would encounter the same problems – loneliness and pettiness (among academics). Conversely, I can ignore such people (to an extent, though not completely) if I teach at primary level, since one can work with the kids rather than politick in the staff room!

Yes, in an ideal world most of academics would not be insecure, not inclined to be jealous when one gets published, not inclined to network in order to publish instead of network because they like people for genuine reasons, not be petty (this applies to the not-so-bright from my experience!) . . . So, I need an environment that provides for stable mental well-being. . . . Having been to universities like X (where I was messed around by so-called like-minded colleagues) and worked in other universities (Y and Z) I now know, regrettably, that this environment, at present, will not provide a stable mental setting . . .

Clearly (from the book!), you won't be overly surprised by my decision.

Take care
Andy

9   Fractured reflexives

Reflexivity, exercised through the internal conversation, has been examined as the process that mediates the effects of structure upon agency. However, such mediation depends upon agents exerting their personal powers to formulate projects and to monitor both self and society in the pursuit of their designs. The last three chapters have examined people who are capable of doing that. This chapter turns to those who are not. Human powers are like all others: they are generative mechanisms which may be activated, or whose exercise may be suspended – by the intervention of other such mechanisms or by contingency.

Some of those who will be examined here are people whose powers of reflexivity have been suspended. In other words, they previously possessed the power to hold an internal conversation about self and society, which allowed them some control over their relationship. However, subsequent contingencies had rendered these personal powers inoperative. The particular mode of reflexivity that they had developed no longer enabled them to deal subjectively with the objective environment they confronted. These have been called 'displaced persons'. By rough analogy, they are like someone who, having learned French then finds himself in an exclusively German culture and is unable to participate, until or unless he begins to master the new language. Alternatively, since all human powers only exist *in potentia*, events may also intervene which inhibit the realisation of the potential for conducting inner conversations. Those who do not develop a mode of reflexivity, to the point where it could be exercised to converse internally about the relations between self and society, are called 'impeded persons'. Again, by very rough analogy, these are like someone who has begun to study French but finds her knowledge inadequate for catching the gist of a conversation or making any contribution to it.

Together, the 'impeded' and the 'displaced' are 'fractured' reflexives. What has been suspended or inhibited is their capacity to hold an internal conversation about themselves in relation to their circumstances, which has any efficacy. It is not that these people are incapable of inner dialogue, for we shall see that they do indeed engage in internal conversations. It is rather that their self-talk provides them with no instrumental guidance about what to do in practice. The reason for this is that their inner conversations are predominantly expressive. They are too exclusively affective to be practically effective. However, there is no reason to assume that this is a permanent condition. That was why the term 'fractured' was adopted, because 'fractures' can often be mended. That was also the reason for employing those rough linguistic analogies, because most people can learn new languages or increase their level of proficiency in a given language. In other words, these subjects are 'fractured reflexives' now, at the point of interview, when 'impediment' or 'displacement' profoundly undermines their subjective orientation towards both self and society. To be 'impeded' or 'displaced' also undermines the objective abilities of these subjects to monitor their circumstances with any degree of mastery. Nevertheless, there is nothing *in principle* that condemns them in perpetuity to this condition.

This does leave one major issue outstanding. Throughout Part I it was maintained that an entirely non-reflexive subject would be incapable of life in society and, conversely, that a society of non-reflexive people was impossible, on the transcendental argument. However, are there human beings who are even less capable of exercising reflexivity than these 'impeded' and 'displaced' subjects, that is people who barely hold internal conversations? If such near non-reflexives exist, who nonetheless cannot avoid being social subjects, then what is the fate of such an individual in society? At the end of the chapter, we will examine the case of one young man, whose life of the mind is so bare that it only allows of rudimentary reflexivity, and seek to answer this question in relation to him.

In the past three chapters, it has been maintained that the exercise of their reflexivity had practical implications for the kind of agents that our subjects were in society. In general, that is regardless of which of the three modes of reflexivity they practised, the internal conversation allowed all subjects to monitor the self, their society, and relations between them. Certainly, this did not permit them to make what they wished of these three elements, and their properties and powers, purely by acts of will. Nevertheless, their internal conversations enabled them to be 'active agents', that is people who exerted (some) control over their own lives. They are people who can help certain things to happen, especially ones that matter to them a great deal, rather than people to whom things merely happen. The latter defines a 'passive agent'. 'Passive agents' are people whose subjectivity makes no difference to the play of objective circumstances upon them. Their mental activities (whose existence is not denied) perform no mediatory role for them; they permit of no intentional relationship between self and society. In short, they make no difference. The main argument, developed in this chapter, is that 'fractured reflexives' are 'passive agents'.

In discussing the three different modes of reflexivity, the common denominator was that practitioners of all three were agents who could take a *'stance'* towards society. Taking a 'stance' means that agents direct their own powers towards social powers in a systematic manner, which facilitates the achievement of their ultimate concerns. Thus 'communicative reflexives' systematically *evaded* constraints and enablements, 'autonomous reflexives' acted *strategically* toward them, and 'meta-reflexives' behaved *subversively* by absorbing the structural costs of their actions. Thus the adoption of these three 'stances' made for three groups of 'active' agents. To call all of them 'active', by virtue of having a 'stance' towards society, is not to endorse any of the following as implications.

Firstly, there is no assumption that any 'stance' entails extensive (let alone full) understanding of the structural or cultural properties and powers involved in their social lives. Agents monitor themselves within *situations* and initiate courses of action in the light of their concerns, including modifying their projects according to the circumstances that they confront. However, there is no presumption that they can diagnose what social properties (or, usually, combination of social properties) have shaped any situation in that particular way. This is an unnecessary assumption and it would be erroneous. We can, by analogy, take very different 'stances' towards rain, depending upon our aims, without having the least idea why it is raining.

Secondly, there is no implication that the 'stance' adopted entails a *correct* reading of the situation. People can be as fallible about their circumstances as about anything else: misunderstanding the need for evasion, misdirecting their strategic actions, and miscalculating the price that will be exacted. Certainly, they can and probably will learn more by bumping up against the real consequences of their actions (because any 'stance' is corrigible), but to have learned something about one's society is far from having learned all. An 'active agent' does not have to be right every time, any more than an active motorist has to be someone who never makes mistakes; in both cases, they may pay heavily for their errors.

Finally, there is no implication that the 'active agent' is left objectively 'better off' by virtue of having adopted his or her 'stance' towards society. Often this is not the case, as has been seen for all the 'communicative' and 'meta-reflexives', and also for individual 'autonomous reflexives'. Yet, there is no reason why it should be so. What the subject is subjectively seeking to attain is something that he or she values highly and is expressive of whom he or she wishes to be. This is an end in itself, not a means to something beyond it. The achievement of these 'ends' defies their representation as objective losses or gains (except by those who still coin the counterfeit single currency of 'utiles', in which to conduct a bogus 'felicific calculus'[1]).

The only assumption which is made about the 'active agent' is that, in relation to his or her subjectively defined projects, the adoption of a 'stance' towards society, as developed through the internal conversation, also accords them a certain degree of control in and over their own lives. It is indeed the case that it is only because they have employed their personal powers to define projects in society that social constraints and enablements can impinge upon them. Yet the power of human reflexivity does not stop there. In addition, the three different 'stances' inform subjects about what to do in the light of the social powers that they can unleash upon themselves: respectively, take evasive action, take strategic action, or take subversive action. Obviously, such courses of action are conceptualised under the agents' own descriptions, rather than in the theoretical terms just employed.

There are no guarantees that any such form of action will be successful, yet without such a 'stance' there is no chance of success, beyond that which is associated with random action. It is to the latter position that the 'passive agent' is condemned. Because they are 'passive' this does not mean that they cease to act, which is impossible for a human being living in society. Yet, their 'fractured reflexivity' precludes the monitoring of either self or society, and hence the emergence of a monitored relationship between them. In consequence, the 'fractured reflexive' has forfeited control over his or her own life. This is not a voluntary occurrence for, as will be explored in this chapter, the process of 'fracturing' is itself involuntary. Both 'impediment' and 'displacement' can be attributed to things which happen to agents, to matters beyond their control, and to which they would not willingly have lent their assent. The consequent inability to hold an instrumental internal conversation protracts 'passivity', by continuing to deprive the agent of any interior control and exposing him or her to the vicissitudes of the external environment.

For the purposes of argument, if the three modes of reflexivity did absorb the entire population, as practitioners of one or another, then society would be made up exclusively of purposive people. At any given time, all of its members would be pursuing clearly defined projects, designed to attain (something) of what they most care about, establishing practices, which helped to realise their concerns, and elaborating these

---

[1] See Margaret S. Archer and Jonathan Tritter (eds.), *Rational Choice Theory: Resisting Colonization*, Routledge, London, 2000.

into *modi vivendi*, which they found satisfying and sustainable. In short, there would be few members showing chronic distress or disorientation – far fewer than we see and know to be the case.

Furthermore, because all three types of reflexives are purposeful, many of their actions are about realising the subjects' concerns in reality. Therefore, all practising reflexives must have some proficiency in means–ends analysis. To talk about them engaging in self-monitoring and societal-monitoring, means that, in their different ways, they deliberate about themselves in relation to their environments. Though their knowledge, like all our knowledge, is fallible, that does not deprive it of practical utility. Moreover, in all three chapters, there was evidence of subjects claiming to have learned from experience, including the experience of their own mistakes. In short, they are the opposite of being disoriented. They know where they are trying to go, because this is defined by their ultimate concern, and they know a great deal about how to get there, even if this knowledge has been painfully acquired through repeated self-correction. This is not the case for 'fractured reflexives' who may be disoriented about their concerns, or about how best to act to realise their priorities, or usually both. I am thus using 'disorientation' to signify the opposite of 'purposefulness'; it refers to individuals who lack an orientation towards society and towards themselves – and therefore towards the relationship between them.

In every respect this means that 'fractured reflexives' differ from those practising one of the three modes of reflexivity which have been examined. These differences can most readily be identified if we consider where the 'fractured reflexive' stands in relation to the process of mediation between structure and agency, and its three stages which capture the interplay between objectivity and subjectivity.

(i) Structural and cultural properties *objectively* shape the situations which agents confront involuntarily, and possess generative powers of constraint and enablement in relation to

(ii) agents' own configurations of concerns, as *subjectively* defined in relation to the three orders of natural reality – nature, practice, and the social.

(iii) Courses of action are produced through the reflexive deliberations of agents who *subjectively* determine their practical projects in relation to their *objective* circumstances.

By working backwards through these stages, three propositions can be advanced which differentiate 'fractured reflexives' from practitioners of any of the modes of reflexivity which have already been discussed.

Stage (iii) necessarily implies agents who can internally deliberate about what should be done in order to realise (something) of what they care about most, under circumstances which were not of their own choosing. In short, it entails somebody who can adopt a reflexive 'stance' towards herself in relation to her society. To do so involves engaging in the internal conversation *to that end*. Through internal dialogue, the subject specifies to herself the goals she desires to achieve and delineates the means for achieving at least something of them. Such internal conversations are necessarily conducted under the subject's own descriptions and the courses of action that are defined are always fallible in terms of their intended outcomes. Nevertheless, the intentionality of internal discourse is instrumental; it is about determining the course of practical action to adopt in order to achieve those ends that are defined by one's concerns. To designate the general *orientation* of the inner conversation as 'instrumental' is to endorse none of the assumptions about 'rational choice'; purposeful actors need neither be maximising nor satisficing.

What distinguishes the 'fractured reflexive' is that his or her internal conversation has no instrumental orientation at all. Their inner dialogue does not work as a guide to action. It supplies the subject with no orientation towards the question, 'what is to be done'. Instead of leading to purposeful courses of action, the self-talk of the 'fractured reflexive' is primarily expressive. Its effect is to intensify affect. It leads the subject to feel an ever more poignant emotional distress about her condition. I have argued elsewhere that our emotions are commentaries upon our concerns.[2] Although this is indeed the case here, what transpires is that the 'fractured' subject merely dwells with increasing misery and frustration upon the impossibility of realising any of his or her concerns. Their internal conversations simply do not work for them – by enabling subjects to propose courses of action to themselves. Instead, their inner dialogues go round in inconclusive circles, which increase the subjects' disorientation. These people may hark back nostalgically to what once was, which merely intensifies the subject's sense of loss; or they grasp in desperation at unrealistic projects, without the requisite self-knowledge or societal-knowledge to translate these into feasible courses of action – which then augments both their distress and disorientation.

Why does this occur? Here, I believe that it is crucial to resist reduction to psychological explanations, that is to accounts which are cast exclusively in terms of individual pathology. Certainly, two of our subjects (one 'impeded' and the other 'displaced') suffered from anxiety and depression, but the other three did not. Moreover, for one of those who did, her biography indicates that her affective disorder was the product of the

---

[2] See Margaret S. Archer, *Being Human: The Problem of Agency*, Cambridge University Press, 2000, ch. 6.

situation in which she found herself rather than its cause. 'Fractured reflexivity' is a broader phenomenon, whose origins cannot be identified reductively. Instead, what takes place at stage (ii) seems more germane to the aetiology of the 'fracture'. Stage (ii) refers to subjects subjectively defining their configurations of concerns. It is these configurations which are purposefully pursued by agents at stage (iii). Significantly, the 'fractured reflexives' had the greatest difficulty, at the point of interview, in articulating such a constellation for themselves.

A subject's precise constellation of concerns is what gives him or her strict personal identity.[3] All 'fractured reflexives' had problems in defining such a relatively durable configuration. Even during the course of interview, every subject displayed uncertainty, often to the point of volunteering different lists of concerns. It seems indubitable that an agent who cannot complete stage (ii) is incapable of moving forward to stage (iii), because they cannot define that which they seek to accomplish in society. What they lack is the strict personal identity which both defines *who* they are and also *what* kind of social actor they would need to become, in order for this to be expressive of their identities. Two different but allied questions will be examined in relation to these subjects. What 'impeded' some from developing a strict personal identity, and what occurred which meant that some individuals were 'displaced' from the identities which they had previously acquired? As stated above, the answers to these questions cannot be given in psychological terms. Only in one case did factors at that ontological level appear to be of major importance.

At stage (i), the proposition asserts that structural and cultural properties objectively shape the situations which agents confront involuntarily. However, these can only be operative as the powers of constraints and enablements if they are able to constrain or enable projects that are subjectively elaborated by agents. Since the 'fractured reflexives' are incapable (*pro tem*) of designing such projects, it follows that they neither activate constraints and enablements, nor do they act in such a manner as to suspend the exercise of these powers. Such social powers therefore have no efficacy in relation to 'fractured reflexives'. This is because the causal effects of constraints or enablements, as expressions of structural or cultural emergent properties, is dependent upon the exercise of personal emergent powers, as maintained in chapter 4.

Nevertheless, 'fractured reflexives' have no alternative but to live (with difficulty) in society. Since they do so, structural and cultural properties are still objectively shaping the situations they confront involuntarily.

---

[3] Ibid., ch. 7.

These situations are influential, even though the nature of their influence cannot be construed as constraining or enabling action. What then is the nature of their influence? Their social environments have effects in exactly the same way as do their natural environments. These are sites where things happen to people. Socially, these are places where subjects may be rendered homeless, where they may lose their jobs, or suffer discrimination. Yet, *qua* happenings, these are no different from the vicissitudes experienced in the natural environment, where people may have accidents, their houses may be flooded, or they may prove to be infertile. In both types of cases, it is a passive agent to whom these things happen. Since in each type of case we are talking about animate human beings, it is always possible to adduce some generic human interest in matters being otherwise; no one wants to lose their home, either by being thrown out or by it being flooded. However, these two kinds of events remain as 'happenings', unless it is possible to identify an agential project designed, however ineffectually, to prevent their occurrence. Having such a project carries no assurance that it will succeed. Someone may quit smoking, eat a healthy diet and take regular exercise, with the explicit aim of staving off heart disease, yet may still succumb to it because of circumstances beyond their control – such as a genetic pre-disposition (if such there be).

Whilst an agential project has no guarantee of being successful, it remains entirely different from an 'innate' human preference for one state of affairs rather than another, but where nothing is done to try to make one outcome more likely than the other. Merely to harbour a preference (or many) still yields a passive subject to whom things happen; to maintain otherwise would be to endorse the efficacy of pure will over matter. Without the insertion of mentally designed projects and practical, purposeful action, the subject remains passive. This is the case for the 'fractured reflexive'; they are passive agents because all happenings are beyond their control. It need not always remain the case, but will do so while ever their passivity precludes the formation and pursuit of projects.

In sum, the following three characteristics will be examined for members who have been grouped together as 'fractured reflexives':
(1) An inner conversation which generates only affective responses, and thus does not work as a guide to purposeful (i.e. instrumental) action.
(2) An absence of strict personal identity, which precludes the prioritisation and accommodation of concerns and thus blocks the formation of projects (hence precluding the sequence, 'concerns' → 'projects' → 'practices').
(3) A resignation to agential passivity.

Attention will be devoted to explicating these shared characteristics. It will then be shown how the 'fracturing' of reflexivity deprives these subjects of control over their own lives, in a manner which sets them apart from those who can hold any of the three types of internal conversation which have been examined.

'Impeded' reflexivity and agential passivity

An 'impeded' reflexive is someone who displays a particular bent towards one mode of inner conversation. Nevertheless, he or she cannot exercise it purposefully and therefore cannot develop any 'stance' towards society. There are two subjects who appear to suffer from such 'impediments', one whose interior dialogue gives evidence of tending towards 'communicative reflexivity', and the other whose tendency is towards 'autonomous reflexivity'. Both will be examined in this section and the format adopted will be similar for each of them. First, their internal conversations will be scrutinised to identify *why* they generate affective responses and *how* they fail to guide instrumental action. Secondly, evidence will be adduced to support the claim that these subjects do indeed have a bent towards a particular mode of reflexivity. Thirdly, an attempt will be made to answer the question, 'what went wrong?' and arrested the full development of the life of the mind to which they are inclined. Particular attention will be paid to those features and factors which appeared propitious to the emergence of that mode of reflexivity amongst the subjects who have been discussed in previous chapters. Finally, flesh will be put on the bones of what is meant by holding both of these subjects to be 'passive agents', who lack control over their own lives.

The only features, apart from their 'impeded' reflexivity, which these two people share in common is that both were encountered as tenants now living in a 'Foyer'.[4] This sheltered block of flats and bed-sits is situated in the same market town as the hairdressing salon, which was discussed in chapter 6 and which will be re-visited in the next section. Lara is eighteen, from a working-class background, and hopes to enrol in a college of further education for a qualification in performing arts. Lawrence is thirty-one, middle-class in social origins, wants to become a film-maker, and is enrolled on a preparatory course to this end. Although both had volunteered to be interviewed, neither finds the process easy, despite their openness, and the reasons for this seem to reflect the problems that they have with reflexivity itself and its inconclusiveness for them.

[4] A national network of 'sheltered accommodation' for young people at risk, whilst they undertake some form of education or training, and where they may remain until they are in steady employment.

Lara: an 'impeded communicative reflexive'

Lara speaks in a small voice and her most frequent comment is 'I don't know' – reiterated fifteen times during the interview. This becomes the most obvious sign that the internal conversation is not really working for her, although she admits to engaging in it 'quite often'. She does so, 'more when I'm on my own than when I'm not alone'. In other words, Lara is attempting to engage in 'autonomous reflexivity'. However, from the evidence that she supplies, I will be suggesting that this is neither her original nor her preferred mode of self-talk. It is one towards which she has been driven, over the last two or three years, because of the drastic dissolution of her previous 'contextual continuity'. The clearest indicator of this breakdown is the fact that Lara became homeless and, as far as her family relations are concerned, these are 'still going through a patch of ups and downs'.

Before discussing either her past or her future, we explored her self-talk, where it emerged that she engages in only six of the activities on the prompt list. Her responses to these six divide into two equal groups. One of these groupings consists of reflexive acts which prompt negative emotions in her – an affect which intensifies as she proceeds with them. We begin by discussing 'planning', and although her reply mentions 'worrying', this alone is not distinctive, because other subjects have often mentioned it. Lara says, 'I do plan a lot. I worry about my future as well, so I want to get everything right.' Because she does not continue, I ask what kinds of things go through her head when contemplating the future. Unlike most subjects who then make a positive statement about what they would like to achieve, even if this is laughingly qualified as dreaming, Lara reflects in negative terms about not wanting to spoil things. It is as if she and her life were separate entities, and that her own influence could only damage her potential for having a good life: 'I want to have a good life and everything and I don't want to ruin that.'

Lara does not relish looking backwards and volunteers that she tries to evade 're-living', because 'I didn't have a good life when I was young and I tend to sort of worry about that. I used to live in [a small nearby town] and, like now that I've moved out, I don't want to go and live back there. It would scare me to live back there because of the stuff that went on – I can't really look at the past and face it. It just scares me.' The emotions which are stirred by re-visiting these experiences (about which Lara remains reticent) also have the effect of inhibiting this mental activity.

The difficulty is that attempts to censor the lives of our minds are often ineffectual. This is the case with 'mulling over'. In the following short exchange, Lara admits to attempting self-censorship, but also that she cannot prevent negative emotions being unleashed:

L 'I tend to leave it really. Sometimes then it kind of like all gets to me, and then I get all upset over it. Because it's more than one problem – sort of like loads and loads. I tend to leave it.'
M 'What happens when you try to leave it at that point?'
L 'It gets worse – then I do start panicking.'

There are two elements to note. On the one hand, 'mulling things over' greatly intensifies the negative affect Lara experiences. On the other hand, 'dwelling upon' these matters is not doing any practical work for her; it does not help her towards analysis, evaluation, or the self-learning, to which other subjects have referred. Hence her response is to 'leave it'. Otherwise, all that can ensue are further negative emotions, culminating in panic.

The other group of three activities in which she engages does not provoke the same emotionality, but neither are these activities of any assistance to her in exerting more control over her own life. Where 'imagination' is concerned, Lara says that she practised 'what if' thoughts when younger, 'but now I'm more a bit of a daydreamer'. She agrees that her daydreaming blots out real issues, and effectively serves as escapism. 'Budgeting' money, time and effort are of little help to instrumental action, and Lara simply states that it is 'something that I can't do very well'. Finally, 'deciding' is not a process which enables her to come to conclusions, but one which 'goes round in circles'. Once these have begun, she does not know how to break out of them. In short, these mental activities are not helping her to become more purposeful by envisaging the future, marshalling her resources, or determining what to do.

Indeed, if the two groups of responses are put together, the former seems only to exacerbate her distress, whilst the latter merely intensifies her disorientation. Her attempts at 'autonomous reflexivity' are simply not working, as epitomised by the oft-repeated coda – 'I don't know.' If so little self-knowledge is forthcoming, is this indeed an inner conversation in which Lara can examine her own internal utterances and then respond to them as subject to object? Alternatively, could this be the first part of the 'thought and talk' pattern of the 'communicative reflexive', which gets nowhere because of the absent other whose contributions would complete the sequence?

Evidence for Lara being an 'impeded communicative reflexive' begins to emerge when we discussed 'clarifying', because she maintains that she does not try to sort matters out in her own head. So, if a relationship or a situation is in a muddle, I ask her what she does. She gives a more revealing and more animated reply than to any of the foregoing: 'I try and work things out, but I tend to work out other people's problems more than I can do for myself.' Does she mean working out these problems for others in her own mind or in conversation with them? Lara says, 'by talking to them and helping them out more than what I can do to help myself out'. Here, Lara is volunteering that she is a willing conversational partner, with whom others can share their thoughts, and also that she is more effective in this role than in her autonomous thinking. Therefore I ask her directly whether talking or thinking is more useful in relation to her own pre-occupations. She answers unhesitatingly, 'the talking. Then you know someone's there for you really.'

This interpretation is reinforced when Lara thinks back over our discussion and contrasts it with the exchanges she has with friends, which are clearly much more familiar to her: 'your friends don't normally ask you that kind of question. You don't have conversations where you have to deep think and think about you and how you think. That was quite strange.' If Lara needs to know that 'someone's "there" for her', completing and continuing her thoughts, and if she finds lone thinking both distressing and unhelpful because inconclusive, then why does she not practise 'communicative reflexivity'?

The answer is sadly simple, and starts to surface when she talks about her relationships within the block of flats: 'It's like here at the minute everyone seems to call me mother hen. Because they all come to me about their problems – and I seem to talk them through. I've always wanted to be there for other people, but sometimes I do need it.' She needs it, but she does not get it; the Foyer's population is transient and relations with her family are partly severed. 'Well there's like not really much support in here, at the minute. I don't know why. I get support from my friends that live near here, and my mum, she sort of helps me out a bit as well. But apart from that, I don't really have anyone else.' Lara is lonely. She lacks the density and continuity which contextual embeddedness furnishes for conducting the 'thought and talk' mode of reflexivity. At rock bottom, Lara is an 'impeded communicative reflexive' because she lacks those 'similars and familiars' who would complement her thought processes. Her 'impediment' is that she has no one of this nature with whom to talk. As she reiterates, 'I don't really know anyone.' Hence, circumstances have propelled her towards an alien mode of 'autonomous reflexivity'. This induces agential passivity, because Lara cannot properly engage in lone deliberation, and therefore her internal conversation remains unhappily partial and unproductively inconclusive.

Further support for this understanding comes from the supreme importance that she attaches to inter-personal relations, as was typical of the 'communicative reflexives'. This colours her everyday behaviour and the way in which she interacts with her few friends: 'I do like helping other people out. I like making people happy and seeing them happy. When I'm with my friends, I'm always trying to make them laugh, you know. I try to be a bit of a clown – keep them amused.' By assuming the clowning role, she has discovered how to exorcise misery on a daily basis. Perhaps spurred on by the success of this performance, she has formalised it into acting as an amateur DJ. This she now sees as her future career. The motivation is identical; in this role she lifts herself and lifts others, in a Durkheimian 'collective effervescence' which dispels loneliness: 'I think that's what I like about being a DJ, because everyone's out having a good time on the dance floor. That's something that I do like – you know, going out and being someone's DJ. I'm having a good time and I find everyone else is having a good time by seeing that. So I wouldn't mind like giving that sort of pleasure.' This has much more in common with the celebration of conviviality, central to 'communicative reflexives', than with the single-minded 'task-orientation', common to 'autonomous reflexives'.

If Lara is indeed a 'fractured communicative reflexive', then what went wrong to prevent the smooth development of this life of the mind? Lara herself volunteers a series of biographical episodes, which represent a complete breakdown in 'contextual continuity' and which she believes caused her to become a different kind of person. These divide into three phases and span the same number of years. At the start of the first phase, before Lara left school at fifteen and a half, she envisaged going into factory work, like many of her friends and like her mother. She was then caught in a cross-fire between her friends' expectations and her mother's aspirations – the same kind of inter-personal 'cross-fire' which will later be found to bear responsibility for Trish's 'displacement'. As Lara puts it, 'ages ago, I was on about going into a full time job. I went through a bit of a mad patch when I was really bad for money. I was talking to my mum and she told me, "at the end of the day, if you're going to get a factory job, you'll be stuck then – dead end job. And you're young, you can still go to college and get your education." And I was just saying, "my friends seem to be able to go out and go on the town, and I can't always afford to go out". And my mum said, "at the end of the day, you've got that to come."' Lara is caught between the instant (financial) gratification she seeks, by following her friends into the factory, and the deferred gratification her mother preaches, based upon her own experiences of this 'dead end job'. Faced with the choice, Lara admits that 'I always took my mum's advice, even though we've had our ups and downs.'

Whether or not her mother behaved tactically to enforce her point of view, she did move the family to the nearby market town. This signalled phase two, which represented a profound 'contextual dislocation' for Lara, by severing most of her friendship network. The result was anomie and dissonance. After the move, 'my mum tried getting me into other schools, but I couldn't get into any and I was sort of like at home for a whole year waiting to get into college. And that really got an effect on me – like socially. Because I was always like loud – not loud, but, you know, just sort of not this quiet person. And then when I went to college and that, I was really paranoid and scared of other people. I think that had a big effect on me.' Deprived of her network and left in suspended animation for a year, Lara became timidly subdued and could not form new friendships at college. It seems plausible that the 'fracturing' of her reflexivity starts here, with her deprivation of dialogical partners whose experiences were anchored in the same continuous context.

Finally, Lara sought to engineer a truce in the cross-fire; propitiating her mother by attending college (briefly) and retaining her residual friends by taking an evening job to fund her clubbing. In this final phase, we find Lara's agential activity backfiring badly, leaving her homeless, and further denuding her of inter-personal continuity: 'I went to college for a bit and then I came home and my mum ended up kicking me out because of all the arguments we had. Because I began college and was then going straight to work, as soon as I got in. I kept doing that and every day she'd like moan, because her life wasn't going great. We ended up having this one big argument and I ended up leaving home. It was hard to be independent by myself – sort of not being able to cope with it.' This is Lara at seventeen: without a single qualification or reference for a job, lacking in the tough individualism associated with 'autonomous reflexivity', and now unfitted 'as this quiet person' for making new friendships in the sheltered accommodation because she finds her fellow tenants 'angry and aggressive with themselves'.

It is suggested that at this point, Lara becomes a 'passive agent'. She was identified by social services, housed and enrolled upon a GNVQ course in performing arts run by a voluntary organisation to attract young people back into education (this entitling her to housing benefit). What was conducive towards 'passivity' was that she had now become thoroughly confused about her concerns. When we first discuss her 'priorities', it is as if the 'old' Lara peeps through and volunteers a list of what is important to her, which is indistinguishable from those concerns regularly identified by the 'communicative reflexives': 'Family are important. My mum's important. And my career's important. Some of my friends are important.' Later in the interview, when we talk about what matters to her most, she gives a very different answer: 'well the thing that matters to me most is getting my career. Making the right decision and just making the most of life basically.' Because of this discrepancy, I ask her directly if she means that her career is now top of her list of concerns. The ambiguity of her response seems to be indicative of the fluidity of her concerns, and that the 'old' and the 'new' Lara have neither been able to consolidate a hierarchy nor, consequently, to achieve dovetailing. She answers, 'sort of like. In between that, it's just like, relationships – being happy with my family and everything else and my friends. And then, yeah, my career.' It is thus far from clear where her career does stand, which confirms the impression that Lara has lost strict personal identity because she does not have a definitive configuration of concerns.

There are two indications which suggest that she has become a passive agent. On the one hand, her case officer and advisers seem to have picked up on her interest in entertainment and to have built upon it, encouraging her to write scripts, lyrics and to perform. She seems to be wide-open to their suggestions and has gained a place at college, thirty miles away, to undertake a higher GNVQ in performing arts. This 'new' Lara, who has now enjoyed the 'buzz' of being on stage and has received disco equipment from the Prince's Trust, talks about her career ideal in the following way: 'Oh, it's like really major. It's kind of like big and everything. Kind of DJ-ing, say right up to the age of twenty-five or twenty-nine, and then moving abroad and then running my own club – like a big club.' She has been encouraged to develop this interest, to endorse it as a career, and to sign up for the next stage of training. Yet is she doing more than passively going with the tide of these new influences that have come with her re-housing?

On the other hand, there are plenty of signs that she is simply adrift and being tossed about between these influences and her 'old' inclinations. Immediately after voicing her career ideal, she adds, 'but sometimes I just don't know where I'm going. If I do something in life, I find you've got to go through obstacles to get there, and it's really hard to get your way around sometimes. That's how I find it. Sometimes it is hard and I just give up. But sometimes I think to myself, "Oh no, don't – go for it."' These obstacles turn out to be matters such as applying to and being interviewed for college, finding out how to get there, and moving thirty miles away. Since all but the last have already been surmounted, with plenty of guidance, I begin to wonder whether she is inwardly reluctant about this re-direction of her life from outside.

We go on to talk about what she is really looking forward to doing on her college course, starting next summer. Her response is equivocal, showing none of the commitment to honing her *performative skills*, which is characteristic of the 'autonomous reflexive'. Simultaneously, she reveals a hankering to use her abilities to generate the convivial company, which typifies contentment to the 'communicative reflexive'. 'I want to learn to play the guitar, and I want to do a bit of vocal work as well, which I've done, but I don't really like my voice. But I wouldn't mind being in a band for a couple of hours one evening, just for something to do, some people to be with. But, no. I don't like my voice anyway. I'm just really scared of everything.' That sad last sentence says that Lara is drifting frightenedly with the tide of external advice. She cannot work reflexively to define her own goals and think instrumentally for herself, whilst her 'impeded' tendency craves for 'people to be with' who will remove the burden of lone thinking by enabling her to engage in 'thought' and 'talk' – and leave her feeling less scared.

Lawrence: an 'impeded autonomous reflexive'

In some ways, Lawrence is the obverse of Lara; he has very clear ideas about what he wants to do and film-making has been his goal for as long as he can remember. He engages in internal conversation 'a fair bit' and does so when he is alone. The difference is that 'autonomous reflexivity' does seem to be his bent. Although Lawrence lives in the same housing project as Lara, his reasons for doing so, at the age of thirty-one, are about being in close proximity to college. Since childhood, he has lived with an increasingly debilitating anxiety condition, which rendered him housebound for six years. He now feels sufficiently recovered to try to make an independent life for himself. In other ways, Lawrence and Lara share a common problem, namely that their current exercises of reflexivity are not working for them, tending to exacerbate emotional distress without increasing their ability to control their own lives.

Like Lara, Lawrence only engages in a minority of the mental activities on the prompt list, but unlike her, he is more analytical about why he shuns those that he does not practise. The two themes, or two variations on 'passivity', which run throughout his interior dialogue, emerge prominently when we discuss 'rehearsing' and 'planning' – activities in which he does *not* engage. Where 'rehearsing' is concerned, Lawrence says, 'I think about doing it, but I don't – how can I explain it? I don't know that it would do any good, in my mind. I can't see that it would do any good to rehearse things. In situations – I suffer from anxiety problems and am very nervous anyway. I can't see rehearsing things is going to make me any less nervous. So, I don't usually.' I comment that some people 'practise' in order to feel more prepared, and thus less scared about some forthcoming encounter, but Lawrence is convinced that anxiety defeats such attempts to reduce it. 'I have it in my mind that it's not going to make any difference anyway, so I don't do it. Maybe if I tried to do it, it would help. I guess I see it more as a magical thing, that you can't really get to do anything about easing your anxiety a bit. It's [practising] not really defeating the main problem, so there's no point in doing it really.'

Because he sees his affectivity as subject only to 'magical' regulation, he correspondingly accentuates the futility of attempting to exert practical control over it. This is the first intimation of his passivity. However, this acceptance of impotence towards his own condition, which is understandable from someone who has struggled with it for most of his life, also spills over into the same passivity towards his circumstances. Thus, in relation to 'planning', he articulates the second *leitmotif* of his subjectivity, namely that neither does it secure any degree of control over matters which lie outside himself. Whilst he will make everyday lists of what he needs to do at college, planning cannot serve to extend his mastery over future eventualities beyond that. Hence his practice is one of 'just taking each day as it comes'.

Turning to those activities in which Lawrence does engage, these divide into the same two categories as were documented for Lara: those which generate negative affect and those which fail to guide instrumental action. Both 'mulling over' and 're-living' exemplify the former. Lawrence agrees that he dwells on problems, situations or relationships 'a great deal. Especially when I suffer from anxiety really badly. I get something in my mind and it just won't go away, you know – like a video repeating all the time. So I guess it's still there, but it doesn't hang around as much as it used to.' Thus, dwelling on such matters does not serve to clarify them, but merely re-invokes negative emotions which Lawrence feels unable to control. He refers to them like animate entities, which inflict themselves upon him of their own volition and only depart at their own pleasure. This is even more accentuated where 're-living' is concerned, with the additional thrust that not only can he not control the negative feelings that it elicits, but that they control him. 'I used to re-live things all the time in my past – what happened to me as a kid and so forth. It's gone a fair bit now. But it's probably still running my life more than me running my life. I still don't do things because of what happened to me in the past.' These emotions are both distressing and also immobilising. This Lawrence himself employs to explain why he finds 'decision-making' near impossible: 'It's probably harder to make decisions with things that I'm very anxious about. Making decisions depends on how I feel when I wake up in the morning. Some days I don't feel like going out and doing things.' Engaging in these mental activities is either distressing or paralysing; in both cases, Lawrence is at their mercy.

In the second category are mental activities that are not distressing in themselves, but prove depressing because they do not lead on to instrumental action. They are frustrating reminders of the internal impediments which prevent him from harnessing his inner conversation to productive outcomes. In many ways, Lawrence welcomes being imaginative because this is what he can bring to film-making, yet it only serves to remind him that he is not in fact making films – and comes to constitute another barrier to doing so. Thus, he says of 'imagining': 'I wish I could switch it off because it's there all the time. I want to learn to film, so I'm always imagining that we're in wonderful worlds – I'm very very creative and artistic and that's always there. You can't switch it off. It does get depressing because you can't – you always feel like you need to be creating something. And your imagination wants you to create something that you haven't got the enthusiasm or energy to do. And, yeah, through the anxiety, I imagine, not so much now, but still especially if I have to do something new, I'm imagining all the different possible things that could go wrong.' Coming up against his own absence of 'enthusiasm or energy', his imagination is without issue. Instead of being able to turn it outwards creatively, it is turned inwards, resulting only in escapism. Thus he talks about having 'an obsession with science fiction', about his fascination with alien worlds and creatures, and of how he becomes absorbed when watching science fiction on television. Lawrence is perceptive about the consequences of his problems and offers the following analysis of what happens and why he watches such programmes. After seeing 'those TV series, I did dream a fair bit afterwards that I was like the third member of the team. It's quite good. But, yes, it's probably easier to deal with to go into those worlds than to deal with everyday life sometimes.' In this way, an instrumental orientation towards film-making gives way to inertia.

Reinforcing this is the use that Lawrence makes of 'imaginary conversations'. The example he volunteers is significant: 'sometimes I pretend that I am on a talk show or something – talking about a film you've made or ideas for a film, things like that. Or I'll pretend that I'm in one of my ideas on TV. It's quite fun really sometimes – more so when I'm on my own. Just to go and develop something like that.' Thus, positive affect attends both his escapism and his imaginary dialogues. Yet, importantly, both of these mental activities are substitutes for practical action, rather than ones that mentally guide and orient him towards it. His self-confessed escapism is what he does as a displacement activity, instead of sketching out an idea for a film. His imagined contribution to a talk show is one in which he mentions talking about a film *he has made*. Together, his escapism and his imaginary conversations represent the 'before' and 'after'; what is missing in the middle is the practical endeavour of actually trying to make a film, or at least working towards it. Lawrence's active imagination is of no assistance in orienting him to action, even those actions which he is keenest to execute. In short, his inner conversation does no practical work for him; it does not help him to define or to determine how to proceed instrumentally. Because it does not do any work, he then falls back upon 'taking things as they come' (repeated several times), which epitomises his passive 'stance' towards his social environment.

Nevertheless, Lawrence shows a clear bent towards 'autonomous re-flexivity', which is being impeded by his anxiety problems. On the one hand, 'thought and talk' could not be his preferred mode because it is precisely the area of inter-personal relations which have been most dif-ficult for him, since childhood. 'I've always been trying to keep in the background. Not through my choice really, but more that I couldn't do anything else. I wanted to be at the forefront of things – be the life and soul of the party. But I couldn't do it.' Indeed, one of the active uses he makes of the internal conversation is to talk himself into, and talk himself through, the stress of sociability – be it encouraging himself to chat to other residents, to go down to the office, or to volunteer for this interview. As he puts it succinctly, 'talking to people is very demanding, easier now than it used to be – but I did used to have to talk myself into talking to people'.

On the other hand, Lawrence is clearly 'task oriented': 'I can't actually remember a time that I haven't wanted to make films. As a kid I wanted to go into visual effects and special effects in films, I think from watching *Star Wars*, and then it gradually grew into wanting to make my own films and direct my own films.' This concern remained constant and has spanned the period of his psychological problems. What it discloses about Lawrence's proclivity towards 'autonomous reflexivity' is the significance he attaches to autonomy itself. To him, internal autonomy is closely allied to external anonymity. He would like to work his imagination into a film and then, in complete anonymity, to observe its impact on an audience. His projection of this event also represents a huge contrast with Lara's desire to be under the spotlight as a DJ, seeing and being seen, amidst the happiness she has generated. 'More than anything I'd like the idea of if I made a big film that a lot of people liked, more the general public than the critics. I'd just like to sit in the audience and feel their reactions. It would be good that – just to sit there and feed off their reactions to what the film was about – and then just walk out. And they wouldn't know that the director of the film was actually there watching it with them.' He emphasises that he wants to be the autonomous producer of these effects, who retains his anonymity. 'I like the idea of being in the background. That would make me feel quite good really, when they laughed at the right point and cried at the right point and things like that.' Lawrence is insightful and volunteers his reasons for this (benign) manipulative dream: 'maybe this is because I felt so out of control for such a long time. So with the audience, the feeling that I'm controlling these people would be quite a powerful thing.' As a dream, it implies 'autonomous reflexivity'; a desire to hone his *performative skills* to produce this effect, of which he would be maestro and not participant (unlike the 'communicative reflexive'), and for which he would be responsible, without questioning his responsibilities (unlike the 'meta-reflexive').

Since the factor which impeded the development of Lawrence's reflexivity was his clinical condition, which in his own view goes back to events taking place when he was only five, it is impossible to provide a narrative account of 'what went wrong', which would parallel that given for Lara. Both the necessary expertise and the requisite data are lacking for examining the interplay of psychological and social factors over his past life. All that can legitimately be undertaken is an examination of where this past leaves Lawrence in the present. He considers that he is now recovering and that having left home, where he had been effectively housebound, he could begin to prepare for the career he has always wanted, by enrolling on a foundation course in art and design.

What impedes him at the moment is his inability to establish a strict personal identity, by determining his hierarchy of concerns and dovetailing them together. Without such a configuration, it is impossible for the subject to move through the sequence 'concerns –> projects –> practices', since each stage requires conclusive (though revisable) internal deliberations. Lawrence's 'fractured reflexivity' manifests itself in his inability to use the inner conversation to design purposeful courses of action. In his case it quickly emerges that 'prioritising' is his main difficulty and that this necessarily precludes the formulation of a coherent and comprehensive life-project. This is evident in his response when we discuss whether or not he spends time 'prioritising' his activities: 'Not a great deal. Maybe if I have college work to do – things like that. And that comes first, so I've got to get that done. But I don't know really. No – I just take things as they come really, more than anything. I don't really put one thing ahead of another. I don't know.' There are four points to note here. Firstly, Lawrence's concentration upon the proximate and the short term – his college assignments. Secondly, his passive attitude of 'just taking things as they come', rather than attempting any mastery of his future or his environment. Thirdly, his repetition of 'I don't know', which was encountered so often with Lara, and is a direct avowal of his lack of self-knowledge. Finally, his assertion that, 'I don't really put one thing ahead of the other' goes to the root of how and why his internal conversation is not working for him – because he neither privileges his ultimate concern nor accommodates others to it.

The latter point is amplified when we go on to talk about the things that matter to him most now. Whilst he readily furnishes a list, he makes it clear that these cannot be ordered because they are all only means to one end, that of feeling 'normal'. In other words, only if he can overcome the impediment constituted by his anxiety condition could he properly address these concerns in their own right. Thus he says of what is important now: 'Finishing my course in art and design – another year on that. And then going on to do another course after that. Try and defeat this anxiety problem that I have. That's something I'm dealing with reasonably well at the moment. Relationships – I find I'm very nervous in those situations, and that's something I need to deal with – all tied in with the anxiety problems and things in my past. Basically, it's just trying to build myself up to a point where I feel like a member of the human race, which I haven't felt like for a long time. It's probably my main – I'm doing all these different things, college, going to the Foyer, making friends and so forth – it's that, building up to be more normal.' Thus, Lawrence sees his mental and physical *well-being* as being absolutely central. This has become his sole concern, usurping the place of others and precluding him from generating an ordered configuration of concerns. Unless he can become a functioning human being, he rightly recognises that he cannot give priority to, or begin to prioritise other concerns – which would give him strict identity as a person. What leaves Lawrence in thrall to his lack of *well-being* is that it not only impedes his 'autonomous reflexivity', but it also leaves him reflexively unable to do anything to improve his mental condition itself. He has no idea of how to tackle it, having tried self-help books and forcing himself to socialise, he concludes, 'I can't really do anything about it.'

The consequence is that Lawrence has become a passive agent in relation to his own future. This is epitomised by his reaction to my question about looking further ahead, beyond his foundation course, and how he envisages getting into film-making. 'I guess get onto a film course and then go from there. I don't know really. I've always felt that I'd like to go and make some short films on my own, to show people what I can do. But I haven't made anything, I haven't had the confidence, I don't think. I don't know why. I don't know. The tutors at the college, they've talked about having to move on to a different area because there's no courses at the college to do with film. Other than that, I don't know, I don't know. I haven't really looked into it a great deal. Just really finish college and go from there.' Up to this point, near the end of the interview, Lawrence has been articulate and often insightful. Confronted with the future, his 'fractured' reflexivity leaves him powerless to cope. Hence his reiterations of 'I don't know' and of just 'going from there'. The former admits to a lack of self-knowledge and the latter to a lack of societal knowledge – both of which are necessary to formulating a project. In their absence, then 'going from there' indicates a passive agent to whom things will happen, rather than an active one who can participate in making his own future life.

After a moment, Lawrence continues speaking in rather a sad tone. What he says shows that he himself is also aware of the connection between his psychological impediment, his inability to use the internal conversation to shape his future, and his consequent (childlike) passivity. 'I think because I still have the anxiety and I don't have a great deal of confidence, it [the future] still seems more of a dream than anything else. I still feel like I've got to remain that little child – can't go out into the big wide world and do things, film directing, because I'm still that little child. I'm still dependent on people and things like that. So it's something I'd like to do and I think I'm building more confidence to do it, but it's still very frightening. I think I've just got to take it one step at a time really.'

Displaced reflexives and unrealistic agents

No mode of reflexivity is regarded as immutable. This is because they are not fixed psychological traits or faculties. The reflexive life of the mind pertains to a different ontological level. This statement is warranted because of the associations found between social factors, like 'contextual continuity', and different modes of reflexivity. Each mode is an emergent property that is dependent upon the relationship between the individual and his or her social context. Consequently, the mode may change because of some independent alteration in either the subject or their context, which then transforms relations between them. Suggestions have been made, at various points in the text, that particular subjects or their circumstances could alter in ways which would precipitate a transformation in the agent's type of internal conversation. However, any such suggestion was purely speculative since all interviews were conducted at a single point in time.

Nevertheless, this exploratory group of subjects did yield two cases of agents who appeared to be undergoing the process of transition. Since there were no follow-up interviews, this exploratory study has no longitudinal dimension. Therefore, it is not possible to trace through what is involved in making the transition from one mode of reflexivity to another. Nor is it possible for the data to support the assertion that such a transition can be made completely or successfully. What the two cases do indicate is that the transformational process is neither easy nor immediate. Yet, it is still necessary to remain agnostic about the eventual outcome.

The two women in question, Trish aged eighteen and Gwen aged fifty-eight, are both working class in origin and both provide sufficient evidence to judge that they had been proficient 'communicative reflexives' up to about two or three years preceding the interview. (This prior proficiency is what distinguishes them from the 'impeded' subjects.) Beyond that, the circumstances which led to their 'displacement' are divergent. In the case of the younger woman, the changes taking place in her mode of reflexivity seem attributable to the *qualitative breakdown* in her 'contextual continuity', such that it lost its consensual and cohesive properties. In the case of the older woman, her 'contextual continuity' remained unbroken, but an acute illness radically disrupted the smooth dovetailing of her concerns that she had previously achieved. Taken together they illustrate how changes in either of the elements constitutive of 'communicative reflexivity', as a relational property, can initiate a transformation of the internal conversation. For Trish, this began with a change in her context, and for Gwen, with a change in herself.

What will be documented for both is how precisely they became displaced from their previous mode of 'communicative reflexivity' and how the identities which they had earlier established, using that particular mode of deliberation, were simultaneously undermined. Secondly, attention will then shift to their attempts to grapple with 'autonomous reflexivity' as an unsought and unfamiliar method of conducting their mental activities. Both experienced great difficulties and ones that are very similar to those of 'impeded' reflexives. Firstly, their novel and lonely internal dialogues yielded the same negative affect as was experienced by our two 'impeded' subjects. This is hardly surprising. On the one hand, negative experiences had occasioned Gwen's and Trish's 'displacement', so it is unsurprising that they would be inclined to dwell upon them. On the other hand, both are tyro practitioners of 'autonomous reflexivity' and are therefore very like the 'impeded' subjects who are also 'learners', rather than proficients. This new life of the mind is pre-occupied with emotionality, and 'displaced' subjects too have major problems in getting this unfamiliar mode of internal conversation to do real work for them. Specifically, they are unaccustomed to employing lone deliberation to determine those instrumental courses of action that would make them effective and purposeful people.

Instead (and perhaps *pro tem*), both Gwen and Trish become 'unrealistic' agents. By this it is meant that they have subjective difficulties in designing realistic projects in the light of their objective circumstances. To be realistic only signifies that the projects entertained give due regard to their practical feasibility *in* the circumstances; it has no connotations of 'rational choice', for a realistic project may well be a sub-optimal project. Presumably, because of their forty-year age difference, Trish is found looking forward, but is unable to design realistic courses of action that will carry her forward. Conversely, Gwen looks backward nostalgically; but any notion of restoring a *status quo ante* is necessarily unrealistic.

Gwen: a 'displaced communicative reflexive'

Gwen is a very ready interlocutor, with a facility for finding words and a willingness to share both her past and her present. Her openness makes it possible to grasp the import of her recent displacement for her own subjectivity and her established way of life. In her own eyes, these events constituted an upheaval in half a century's contentment with her *modus vivendi*. Gwen, the daughter of a bus driver, continues to describe herself as working class, and looks with gratitude on the warmth of her own family life, growing up on Merseyside. Her background does seem to be one of outstanding 'contextual continuity'; she married her first boyfriend in her teens, mum remained her 'best friend', and she dwells affectionately upon life in the two-up and two-down in which their sons were born. Over the years, Gwen and her husband generated another close family unit, with both of them working hard to supply the best material environment for their two boys. For this couple, house and home are interchangeable terms, and their joint focal point. As the children reached their teens, Gwen gradually extended her secretarial hours, her husband worked around the clock, and they eventually purchased their 'dream house' in the Cotswolds.

All appeared to be going smoothly and contentedly for this family. As the boys approached 'A'- levels at the local comprehensive, Gwen recognised their increased independence and began working full time as secretary in a nearby independent school. Her intelligence and organisational abilities were acknowledged, she was given significant responsibilities, and the new post of 'Registrar' was created for her. Therefore Gwen, who had never been a careerist, was nevertheless poised for her work to assume more importance after the boys left home. As her maternal role receded, so her occupational involvement would advance to take up the slack. This could reduce the work-pressure on her husband, thus giving them more time together for their leisure activities, which were still significantly home-centred. Then Gwen suffered an unexpected but acute heart condition – life-threatening for a few days and entailing several months off work.

When her period of sickness benefit expired, she was sent a note of dismissal. Gwen, now largely recovered, instigated legal proceedings against the school, but she settled out of court for a derisory cash sum in compensation. This derailed her neat plans. Personally she became penniless, but more importantly had nothing to do; the home to which she had devoted her creative skills began to feel like a place of house-arrest. Gwen developed a depressive illness, which was unresponsive to treatment, her husband took early retirement, and this is where we find her three years later, at the point of interview.

Gwen herself sees what I am calling her 'displacement' in 'before' and 'after' terms. Retrospectively, Gwen is clear that her life was governed by her willing acceptance of working-class, female role expectations. 'In my generation your first priority is your home and family, and if you wanted a job, that's your decision. You could go and have a job on the understanding that this part is sacrosanct – it means that you've got to work and run twice as fast.' Although she is analytically aware of the change in female roles and tolerant of her daughter-in-law's rejection of traditionalism, she herself had wholeheartedly endorsed the traditional role. 'I felt it was very important being a mum. I worked hard at it and I didn't feel as though I was missing out. I did once they got to school – and I had to go and do something else because the day was long. But, yes, they were my priority, and Brian [her husband]. They've all been very constant. I've never had any major hassles. So, it's a nice, safe area.' This theme of security and predictability colours her retrospection. If this *modus vivendi* left her with little breathing space for other activities, and Gwen loves singing in a choral group, 'well at least you had the satisfaction of being on track. Still in control.'

This calmly controlled *modus vivendi*, which may have entailed ironing shirts at one in the morning, is something she sees in stark contrast to her present position as a 'damaged' person. 'I've got a major problem now. I think I'm suffering from depression, following my heart op. and my finishing work. And together, they've spoilt me, damaged me.' They have demolished someone who felt in control of her own life, with everything in its place and a place for everything, even if it was a tight fit. Moreover, 'together' (which shows Gwen realises the significance of their conjuncture) these events have precipitated her into a situation with which she cannot deal, and towards a new form of lone thinking, which does not help: 'I love boxes. Fitting things into boxes, and I can't fit this in anywhere, because what has happened seems very unfair. And I can't deal with that – I have to make things right. So there's unfinished business. You know, I'd like to go and run over somebody, write a letter, face them or something. And it's not resolved – it's not tidy. I like things tidy. So I do think a lot about that. I spend a lot of time thinking about what's going to happen.'

Not only does Gwen have this problem, but also plenty of time to dwell upon it, now she is no longer working. She is being propelled to engage in 'autonomous reflexivity', which is both novel and alien. 'It's a new thing. Because being a very practical person, I do something. That's who I am – somebody who does things, not somebody who sits and thinks about it. So it's a complete change. And it's been very difficult making your brain *not* solve practical problems, but actually having time to wonder – just wondering, What if, and what if, and why.' Although Gwen herself describes these autonomous thoughts as attempts at 'problem-solving', she is self-consciously uncomfortable with this mode, to the point of resistance, and it does not recommend itself by solving her problems. 'I listen to the radio a lot. I tend to switch on the iron and switch the radio on and things like that. It's when I stop that I start thinking. Sometimes I don't want to and that's when it starts. And I almost fight against it – and give myself things to do to stop me thinking, because thinking's not particularly joyful.' In the last phrase, we get the first hint that her recent excursion into autonomous thought is mainly expressive.

Gwen provides plenty of evidence that this is indeed a foreign mode of reflexivity to her and that, until recently, she lived her life as a 'communicative reflexive'. As we move down the prompt list, her responses to two mental activities reveal her familiar reliance upon interlocutors, and the life of the mind with which she is most at home. When we discuss 'clarifying' matters, she volunteers how the four nuclear family members share a common interest in current events and have frequent discussions: 'So we always talked. And I sometimes play devil's advocate. And by doing that, it clears my head as to what I really think.' She also mentions one of her few women friends, with whom she had just had a lengthy telephone discussion about a news item on the eligibility of servicemen's partners for widows' pensions: 'I like those sort of discussions, and they do clear your head. Sometimes they get your thoughts clearer.' This is redolent of the 'thought and talk' pattern, and Gwen reinforces this when she says, 'also I find explaining how things work to other people helps me as well. So it's all sort of thinking and talking that clarifies what's going on.'

Yet this 'thought and talk' pattern is no longer so easy or all-sufficient as it used to be. Close as she and her husband remain, Brian cannot really enter into her depression, a 'failure' which she seeks to minimise by generalising about male reactions: 'Poor old Brian's locked up there [in the house] with me, and he can't understand it. A lot of men are like that – got a nice house, nice family, nice garden, so everything's fine.' Yet it goes much deeper, because now, whilst she is saying one thing to him, she is also (traitorously) thinking the opposite. She cannot prevent this autonomous running commentary, but neither can she sustain communicative consensus: 'You're sitting there having a cup of coffee, and the sun's shining and there's a squirrel on the lawn, and Brian says, "Isn't this lovely?", and I say, "Yeah" – I think it ought to be. It's all sort of you know, disloyalty, because you want to say, "Actually it's all shit. It's horrible – nothing." And you feel disloyal that there's this man there who's doing everything to try and make me happy, but it's not working.'

Similarly, when we discuss 'imaginary conversations', Gwen reveals the importance of her 'contextual continuity' and the central role she still assigns to her mother, even though she is now dead. Thus, Gwen still projects her 'communicative reflexivity' into imagined dialogues with her mum, to whom she still takes her troubles, although she is careful to make clear that this is entirely imaginary: 'She's very reassuring – she reassures. Well, I don't hear her talking to me. But I ask the questions and I know the answers would be very reassuring. It's a comfort.' Yet Gwen cannot stretch out her old 'communicative reflexivity' in this manner, to cover her current problems, because these are ones for which she has no adequate interlocutor. Consequently, her 'imaginary conversations' are extended in an attempt to deal autonomously with her disruption, by generating an internal, dialogical closure: 'On the other hand, I do have conversations with Mr X [head of the school], because when I finished work, he ran away and wouldn't talk to me. So I have conversations with him that would make everything alright. It would bring it to a conclusion.' Note that her frustration is directed towards his unwillingness to talk, rather than to her dismissal itself, and that instead of generating closure, Gwen is really rehearsing the grievances for which she is denied the outlet of voicing – and so her sense of outrage increases.

This is the case with her uses of 'autonomous reflexivity' in general: they intensify negative emotionality, rather than producing solutions or resolutions. 'Planning', especially for the long term exercises her greatly: 'That's the sort of thinking I'm at, at the moment – what's happening in the future. I'm efficient, so that I don't have to think about the day-to-day things. But not working means it's a whole different ballgame. I worry about the future for myself, because it seems a very, very big black canvas to me.' Things become blacker rather than becoming clearer. Gwen knows she has to fill the void left by her job, but cannot discern any concern that could replace it. Hence her distress increases without her disorientation diminishing: 'So it's big thinking at the moment. How am I going to keep going like this for the next thirty years? I need a project. It's thinking along those sorts of lines – I need a passion. Yeah, trying to think about how to fill my time in a positive way.'

Similarly, 'mulling over' either exacerbates her grievances or leads her to dwell upon the failure of her depression to respond to treatment: 'It's there all the time [depression], something that makes you think a lot. You know, little everyday things, you can sort those out. But this won't go away, and that's why it gets you down – so keep taking the tablets! Not that they're helping.' Unsurprisingly, 're-living' again serves only to intensify negative affect and to signal the desire for expressive action, this time augmenting anger rather than accentuating bleakness. She 're-lives' those recent events 'over and over. Wake up thinking about it – cruel things. Why couldn't other people see what was happening at work, or perhaps they did see but they didn't care. Isn't it terrible that they didn't care for me? I would have done something – I would have spoken up. So it chips away. I'd like to get Mr X in a room and beat him up [chortle]. But it would be a waste of energy.' Gwen acknowledges that this is unproductive, but she cannot help it, any more than she can prevent her 'imagination' from picturing the loss of her husband. What this brings home to her is the realisation that she would be unable to cope. Thus, this last use of autonomous thinking only underlines her dependency and inadequacy (as with Lawrence), which is the antithesis of the internal conversation assisting her towards greater purposefulness. 'It's a big question, what would happen if Brian died. I ask that a lot. Yes, because I lean on him tremendously. He's got me through. I don't think I could cope – no that's the problem.'

This is Gwen's paradox. She has been 'displaced' from 'communicative reflexivity', because it simply did not work for her recent problems; those to whom she is closest could not enter into them, since their shared context did not cover this tract of her life. Thus, she has had to introduce herself to autonomous thinking, but that does not work either; it intensifies her anguish, without suggesting any instrumental course of action. Since all that 'autonomous reflexivity' yields is yet more negative affect, it is understandable that Gwen 'fights against it', tries to block it out with the radio, and generally concludes that, 'it's nice not to have to think about things'. Yet, since Gwen now devotes so much time to lone thinking, what is preventing her from moving forward into 'autonomous reflexivity' and becoming adept at making it work purposefully for her?

The answer is contained in her own previous cries, 'I need a project', 'I need a passion', or rather what lies beneath them. With the loss of her job, Gwen also lost her strict identity. Her previous dovetailing had accommodated her subordinate concern, employment, to her ultimate concern – the family. Nevertheless, the role of work was expected to grow as family demands diminished; now there is just a hole instead, and depression has rushed into the vacuum. When I ask her what matters most in life now, she still answers, 'Brian and the children. They're the most important. They've never let me down.' Gwen has given thought to the possibility of extending her role in the family, particularly with regard to the son who is doing less well, but has sensibly decided against such intrusion: 'What if we raised some money on the house and paid off David's bills, would that help? What if we moved a bit closer and I could look after Adam [grandson] and Karen [daughter-in-law] could go out to work – I do worry – I give time to it. And then I have to say, "Hang on, it's not up to you. Step back. Leave them alone."' She knows she cannot buy indispensability; she recognises that her need gives her no right to trespass.

Yet her only other concern is an ineffable one, 'finding peace of mind', whose absence is undermining the contentment she would otherwise derive from her ultimate concern. 'Now my other personal priority is finding peace of mind. Which I feel I ought to have, because I've got such a nice family. It's a bugger, because it doesn't work like that! You can have all the nice things around you and still feel grotty.' Her previous configuration of concerns has collapsed, and in its collapse it is endangering what she most cares about. Thus Gwen correctly diagnoses that she needs a 'passion'. This is partly to plug the gap left by her satisfying job, partly to protect her ultimate concern from insidious discontent, and finally to give *self-worth* in society and an outlet for her *performative skills* – which cannot be confined to ever redecorating the house. It is precisely because she is without such a 'project' (her own term) that 'autonomous reflexivity' cannot work for her. It cannot guide her purposefully because there is nothing for it to be instrumental about. Internal deliberations require an objective; they can then help us diagnose, delineate and dovetail our concerns, or to evaluate, promote and demote our concerns. Yet, if our concerns are expressive of who we are and what we want to be, then our internal conversation cannot act independently of us and invent a concern for us. We can talk ourselves into being more concerned about something, but this requires a minimal concern upon which to build.

Therefore, 'autonomous reflexivity' cannot carry Gwen forward instrumentally. Instead, since it only increases her distress and disorientation, all she can conceive of nostalgically is the unrealistic project of 'going backwards' – what she calls 'getting back on an even keel'. Much of this is understandable, for no one would want to live with depression, but the lack of realism comes in wanting to turn back the clock: 'It's just wanting not to have panic attacks. Not going into [the market town] and hoping that you don't meet anyone you know. And breaking out in cold sweats. If I'm in the lounge and Brian drops something in the kitchen, I break out in a cold sweat. I want all that to go away. I just want to be like I used to be. Just jogging along really.' What is ultimately unrealistic is Gwen's entertaining the project of cherishing a void: 'So you know, finding something – like I said a passion or a project, it's because it would fill my mind. So what I really want is not to. What I really want is not to feel it necessary to have a passion.'

Gwen appears to be stuck, and her reflexivity is not helping her. She cannot realistically move back into 'communicative reflexivity' and her old *modus vivendi*. The 'thought and talk' pattern is of no avail because it is predicated upon anchorage in common experiences, but no one in the family can share her two pre-occupations – with dismissal and depression. There is no re-establishing of the old *modus vivendi*; her ex-employer destroyed part of it, yet the family concern would inevitably have shrunk, as part of the life-cycle. She cannot yet move forward through 'autonomous reflexivity', because lone inner conversation increases her distress, without diminishing her disorientation. Gwen knows that to make a future, she needs a project, but she cannot embrace one: 'I think I need things to do, but anything that comes along so far, I don't want to do.' This renders Gwen, like Lawrence, a passive agent. As she retreats more and more into the house, then she is in danger of ceding all control over her own life and being treated literally as a patient, not an agent – as the bearer of a mental illness. Regretfully, the conclusion has to be that 'displacement' from one life of the mind does not necessarily spell its 'replacement' by another – at least, not in the short term.

Trish: a 'displaced communicative reflexive'

Trish, who is eighteen, in good health, and nearing the end of her apprenticeship is a subject who could potentially put a more positive gloss on the outcomes of 'displacement'. She was one of the three girls who left school together to become apprentices in the same hairdressing salon. Like Mel and Kim she stresses their importance to one another, thus accentuating the significance of 'contextual continuity' at key transition points, such as from 'school' to 'work'. 'I like the girls I work with and I couldn't imagine not working with them. We do get on quite well. Yeah, we do have goes at one another – but it's like sisters do.' Any one of the three young women could have said the same, just as some of her responses are indicative of the same 'communicative reflexivity'. For example, here is Trish talking about deciding: 'I'm not very good at that. No [laugh], I really have to ask people's opinions. Oh I don't know what to do. I'm so indecisive.' Equally, she displays many of the patterns of behaviour common to this group, such as a voluntary curtailment of her ambitions. Thus, at fifteen and already 'going steady', she renounced an ambition to enter dress-designing and fell back on hairdressing. She had wanted to do this since she was seven and she could train locally, rather than going to London and attempting to enter a fashion-house. As she now puts it, 'I'm happy doing what I'm doing now. It [designing] was just a little phase I went through. Like lads saying, "Oh, I'm going to be a footballer."'

In all of these ways and more, Trish conforms closely to the profile of a 'communicative reflexive'. More strictly, she seems to have done so up to the age of sixteen and, like Gwen, still retains many traces of her original mode of 'thought and talk'. Trish's history over the last three years constitutes a warning against construing 'contextual continuity' as an objective set of properties whose *qualitative* dimension is of no importance. For the particular 'communicative reflexives' examined (in chapter 6), their 'contextual continuity' also denoted inter-personal harmony and attitudinal consensus. Clearly, these latter are not necessary accompaniments of families whose objective attributes are geographical immobility, intense interaction and socio-economic stasis. Trish gives the opportunity to explore the consequences for 'communicative reflexivity' when these two clusters of features are not mutually reinforcing. Indeed, it is suggested that it was because Trish was caught in the inter-personal cross-fire, between her significant others, that she was displaced from her 'communicative reflexivity', over a three-year period.

Essentially, during this time, Trish was confronted with a series of *choices within her context*, which precipitated her towards the lone deliberation of 'autonomous reflexivity'. As a life of the mind, 'communicative reflexivity' provides completion, confirmation and continuity, anchored as it is in common points of (experiential) reference and communal orientations towards the involuntary context of social placement. However, it is relatively weak in its ability to arbitrate upon inter-personal disputes, because it does not foster those 'ethics of fairness', which enable 'autonomous reflexives' to accommodate the disparate demands of other people. 'Communicative reflexivity' 'appeals' to inter-generational traditionalism and personal loyalty, but these become blunt instruments when different sets of 'similars and familiars' make use of them simultaneously, since they neither eliminate the need for choice nor regulate how to choose sides.

To find oneself in this inter-personal situation is simply termed 'cross-fire'. In Trish's case, the 'crossfire' was extremely important because it impinged directly upon her (listed) concerns themselves – family, boyfriend, career and friendship – and did so almost simultaneously. These are not independent episodes, but I will try to disentangle three of the threads in order to show how each propelled Trish towards having to make a choice – whose consequence was to precipitate her towards 'autonomous reflexivity', in order to do so. The single story into which these threads were interwoven unfolded over a short period of approximately two years.

Firstly there were ugly, divisive rows within the family over Trish's school leaving, with her father, a warehouseman, and her older sister on one side, and Trish and her mother on the other: 'my mum was there to support me. My dad wasn't, because my older sister, she went to sixth form and she's gone off to university. And it was like, "leaving school at sixteen, doing this dead end job, blah, blah". My dad just wants me to be a lawyer or a police officer – someone with high status like my sister. And it's just not me – I'm not like my sister. We had this big bust up with my dad over that. I get, "Oh, why aren't you like your sister?" I just think eff-off. I am who I am.' As Trish said, 'we' had this 'bust up'; with her mother's support she held her own and left school. This was probably not such a difficult choice to make because her friends were doing the same thing, and siding with one parent rather than the other was likely to have been encouraged by their own mutual animosity – culminating in divorce a year later.

In addition, Trish's boyfriend, to whom she was already engaged, sup-ported her leaving school. This is a second thread in the crossfire. The pair had been together 'for years', her mum liked him, and they were plan-ning their wedding for later that same year. As Trish puts it, 'I wanted it and planned so much that we rushed into it and it didn't work out.' The pair had a violent (though temporary) break-up, 'did some stuff that we shouldn't have done', and the pattern of alliance changed. Predictably, Trish had gone to live with her mother, after the parental divorce, but now her previously supportive mum became hostile to her boyfriend. When Trish and he got back together again ('on and off'), her mother's attitude hardened over the next eighteen months, because of car accidents and his drinking bouts. This culminated in Trish being 'kicked out' of home. She was now alienated from both parents, with only her friends from school and work to sustain the remnants of her 'contextual continuity'.

Apparently her friends had never taken to her boyfriend, and now they sided with her mother. Just before the point of interview, they had effec-tively presented Trish with an ultimatum: 'My friends say like it's either us or him sort of thing. And then I've got to sit down and work out which one I want more. But unless I have to, I don't really do that. They're really good friends and they've always been there for me, and I don't want to hurt them or lose them. But I really like him – we've been together for years.' This is the final strand, in which Trish is again being forced to make a choice. Abandon her friends, and she scuppers the last remaining element of her 'contextual continuity' – her supportive reference group of contemporaries. Opt for her boyfriend, and she is left with one unstable relationship, with a 'rocky past', and an 'on and off' pattern.

This is where we find her at the time of interview; confronted with a choice, very reluctant to make it, and ill equipped to do so because 'communicative reflexivity' cannot avail her. If she attempts 'thought and talk' with her friends, they neither complete nor confirm her thoughts, but re-present their ultimatum. If she tries this pattern of deliberation with her boyfriend, then far from stabilising their relationship, it prompts recriminations: 'We had a really rocky past and we used to like dwell on that – well, "you've done this and you've done that". And that was years ago and it was pointless – we just used to argue about it. So we got like a fresh start and forgot about it – we don't go back to the past. So just live for now sort of thing.' On neither front can Trish talk through her thoughts to achieve some resolution, so increasingly she is thrown back on her own mental devices to try to resolve matters through the exercise of 'autonomous reflexivity'.

Simultaneously, Trish's strict personal identity seems threatened by this 'cross-fire', because her growing uncertainty about what is most important to her also mirrors these inter-personal tensions. Early on, she presents a picture of her ideal future, which is typical of the 'communicative reflexives' in its domesticity and self-acknowledged modesty: 'I imagine myself in a nice house, my own place, a car, Labrador, kids – that sort of thing. I don't let my imagination run wild. That's about it.' Later, when I ask her what is most important in her life at the moment, she presents a very different list and gives the reasons for this: 'My job – that's about it at the moment. The main things, of course, are like my friends and family and my boyfriend. But I've been having disagreements with all of them at the moment. So, you know, just mainly my job – it's been important, but it hasn't always been the most important.' Here we see a lack of strict ordering, and therefore of dovetailing, and also a promotion of the importance of her job. Is this new concern with her job a result of her equally new autonomous deliberations, or does it merely represent the one stable point in her current turmoil, as she suggests? The latter seems to be the case, because Trish states her unwillingness to engage in prioritising her concerns: 'I'd rather just go with life and not have to put anything before anything else, unless I have to. Unless I'm put in situations, then I don't really do it.' There are two important statements here: that prioritisation represents a forced choice, dictated by circumstances, rather than being autonomously controlled by Trish, and that her preference is to evade the process and 'just go with life', which evokes her previous references to 'just living for the present' – and agential passivity.

Both statements indicate that Trish is not able to assume control over her own life, which would only be possible if she could move through the sequence, 'concerns → projects → practices'. She cannot do this because she refuses at the first fence; her previous identity having been eroded in the 'cross-fire', she does not ask herself who she is or what she wants to be, but goes along with what is circumstantially available to her. Therefore what work is her recent foray into 'autonomous reflexivity' doing for her? It is important, in trying to answer this question, that when reflecting over the prompt list, Trish *does* agree that she attempts these mental activities autonomously: 'The stuff you've been asking me is like stuff I like to think about on my own. Like planning for the future and my job and what I want to do and everything. But, it's not stuff I talk about. It's stuff I think about.' So what actually takes place in her lone internal conversations and how do they relate to the governance of her life?

There are three points to highlight here. Trish regards her lone internal conversations as being *expressive and ineffectual*, though obviously she makes these points under her own descriptions. Firstly, her own general characterisation of her internal dialogue is both expressive and, like Gwen, is largely retrospective. These conversations take place 'when I'm on my own, yeah, just sort of thinking – running things through my head. Mainly, usually, when I feel sorry for myself. "I wish I'd done this", "How could I have changed that?" Just sort of sit there, going over and over in my head. Working out if it could have been different. How to have avoided the situation. It just sounds stupid really.' It is deemed 'stupid', I suspect, because Trish derives no 'lessons' from her past actions, despite the cognitive and analytical thrust of this thinking. Therefore, when it comes to the present, lone thinking is just an occasion for negative affect: 'Well, I've had a bit of a downer at the moment. I've had a car accident and I got kicked out of my mum's, and my boyfriend – we've been having problems because he drinks a bit. I'm walking home on my own at night or I sit in the back garden, and I dwell on it and feel sorry for myself.' Trish freely admits that this self-pity is because she cannot think of a solution, which would be a way forward: 'I'm just like "where do I go from here?" and nothing's going right. I'm not depressed or anything. It's just when I'm on my own, especially at night time – it's like, "Oh no."'

Trish feels very ambivalent about planning as a means of seizing the initiative, rather than just living with this emotive 'Oh no'. On the one hand, 'I try not to plan because of the past and everything. I've planned stuff in my head and it hasn't gone according to plan. Just got let down.' Here she is reflecting upon her plans as a sixteen year old: 'a couple of years ago I was engaged and I think because I wanted it and planned so much that we rushed into it too quickly'. On the other hand, Trish does warm to the idea of assuming control through planning: 'I'm still like that now. I will have a mortgage in a couple of years and I plan like where I'll be. I just sort of plan everything I want for the future.' Is this realistic planning or is it daydreaming? From Trish's description of her financial budgeting, it appears to be more of the latter: 'I sit and work out my finances and I think, "Oh, I'll just take a bit out of my savings account and I'll put it back next month when I get paid" – and I don't. It's just terrible. I tell myself to do it, but as soon as the money's in my hand, you can kiss that goodbye.'

As Trish goes on to explain her finances, it is manifest that the notion of taking out (or being granted) a mortgage is completely unrealistic. 'I still only get about eighty pounds a week working here [the salon]. I've just moved into my flat and I just can't afford it. Not with – I've just got a car. Car insurance, and going out, and saving! So I just had to take on a second job, because I got myself into so much debt. I took out a credit card to like help finance me, and then, being eighteen and stupid, I didn't pay it off.' She is actually in financial difficulties, and these have further repercussions.

The second job she has taken on is bar-work, starting in the early evening. Immediately, this created problems because Trish was expected to travel to the sister salon in the Spa town for two days a week, meaning that she was back late for the bar. An argument ensued with her salon employer in which he confronted her over which of the two jobs mattered more. Her retort was that 'they're both as important as one another'. This may be the case in strictly financial terms, but on the other hand, she has less than a year of her apprenticeship to complete, and, as she says herself, 'I've done so many years' training and I've almost come to the end of it now. It's what I want to do and there's no point in chucking it away.'

How realistic is she being about seeing through those last crucial months of her apprenticeship? Trish recognises that, 'I'm walking on very thin ice. And I don't want to lose it because I enjoy working here. I like the people I work with and hairdressing's what I want to do.' Her job and some of the friends with whom she works are the only elements remaining from her previous context. Yet Trish is rather insouciant about running her two jobs in double-harness and skating over thin ice: 'I've fitted it in so the hours I work here don't clash with the hours I work there [the bar]. And I enjoy both jobs – I think they're both great. And I can handle like working the extra hours.' Yet can she?

Earlier, when we were discussing budgeting time, Trish appeared to have self-knowledge that made her claim, about being able to handle it, seem questionable. What she had then said was: 'I'm terrible with timekeeping. I panic – it's like, "I'm going to be late", "Oh it doesn't matter", "I'll just manage to have enough time."' She did not, as I learned later when visiting the salon as a client. Working all day and into the night, she was often late for the salon next morning and, after several such occurrences, Trish was given a formal warning. Not only did she fail to heed her self-knowledge, but also her societal-knowledge, for Trish had been very acute about clients and their expectations in this 'image trade'. Being so short of time, she began to cut corners; personal hygiene slipped and she collected another formal warning. Just a few months short of completing her apprenticeship, Trish was dismissed from the salon.

'Living for the present' is indicative of agential passivity. This is because the future has to be made, and the present is largely where it is forged. Either the agent takes her place at the forge, to hammer out something of her design, or she cedes her role as artificer to happenstance. The latter was the case for Trish. Trying, quite unrealistically, to hold down two jobs, in order to secure her future in hairdressing whilst hanging on to her boyfriend, she was attempting to evade the 'choice' with which she had been confronted. In turn, this meant that the choice was made for her, rather than by her; she lost her apprenticeship, lost the remaining friends from her contextual network and was left with unskilled bar work and an uncertain relationship. This is a case where objective costs of 'rejecting' structural benefits are accrued uncomprehendingly by the subject – and structural 'penalties' are accumulated in the same manner. She had sacrificed obtaining a skilled qualification this summer, but also, were she to seek to retrieve the situation at a later date, then Trish would have to pay the penalty of starting her apprenticeship all over again. (Sadly, there is no happy ending. Six months later, Kim and Mel told me that her 'rocky relationship' had ended, meaning that she had paid the social costs of sacrificing her apprenticeship without any inter-personal compensation.) Just as there was no going back for Gwen, so there now seem to be huge obstacles preventing Trish from going forward. In short, the failure to master a new mode of reflexivity creates passive agents who surrender control over their own lives, but cannot suspend the play of circumstances upon them.

Near non-reflexivity: the case of Jason

The personal accompaniments of 'fractured' reflexivity have been found to be distress and disorientation. The social denotations are those of agential passivity. A passive agent, to whom things happen, may also be one who is simultaneously collecting structural 'penalties' which would come into play were he or she later to become active, to formulate projects and to monitor them instrumentally. Such penalties would then have to be paid in terms of steeper opportunity costs for accomplishing a given course of action. For example, Trish would have to do another three years' training to become a qualified hairdresser, or Gwen would find it much harder to obtain another position as school secretary, now that she is approaching sixty and has a record of litigation. These costs would only be extracted from a 'fractured' reflexive who then developed or recovered the ability to formulate and monitor projects – by deliberating upon themselves in relation to their social circumstances. Those who remain 'fractured' and 'passive' pay no such toll, but continue in their distressed and disoriented state.

It might therefore be thought that as subjects approach near non-reflexivity, these two features would be accentuated. This is not so. The reason for this is clear, if we compare the 'fractured' reflexives, already examined, with a hypothetical case of non-reflexivity. Disorientation and distress were chronically reinforcing for both the 'impeded' and the 'displaced' subjects examined. They cannot project a way out, which intensifies distress about their suspended animation and, in turn, intensifies their paralysis. Yet someone with no reflexivity at all would also have no inner conversation. Without it, they would lack the self-knowledge that augmented 'regret', 'frustration', 'dismay' or 'nostalgia' in our four subjects, because as people who knew nothing about themselves, they could not experience such emotions. Without reflexivity, neither could they give a considered response about the relationship between self and circumstances. Thus, they could not be said to be disoriented, but only to be lacking in any orientation whatsoever towards society.

In seventeen-year-old Jason, we encounter a subject who is not non-reflexive, but who has the most restricted internal conversation of all those interviewed. He engages fully in only one mental activity on the prompt list, and in a second to a limited extent. On the one hand, even such a spare and bare life of the mind does distinguish Jason categorically from the (hypothetical) non-reflexive, because he can identify concerns as his own and can begin to articulate a project which would represent the realisation of one of them. On the other hand, he shows neither the distress nor the disorientation which characterised the 'impeded' and the 'displaced' subjects. Yet, in objective terms, Jason has experienced the worst life of any of the interviewees, so his lack of affect about it begs for explanation. Equally, he displays none of their disorientation, none of their paralysing uncertainty about what to do. Yet, he has no better idea than they do about purposive action, which also calls for explanation. In these two respects he is closer to our (hypothetical) non-reflexive.

The suggestion is that we can account for these differences by reference to the bareness of the life of his mind. Jason is unlike the 'impeded' subjects whose reflexivity was sufficiently developed for them to show a bent towards a particular mode of inner conversation. There is no evidence that he has any such inclination, given such a paucity of avowed mental activities. Conversely, Jason differs from 'displaced' subjects, who at one time possessed full mastery over a mode of reflexivity. Instead, his subjectivity appears to have been arrested before it had reached that stage of development.

In order to gain some purchase upon Jason's subjectivity and some understanding of how a near non-reflexive lives in society, let us begin by painting his background and analysing the underdeveloped inner conversation that he conducts today. I met Jason at the Foyer; his dress was neatly uninformative, unlike the 'statements' of many seventeen year olds. His responses were ready and unfaltering, bereft of those uncertain 'don't knows', unlike Lara and Lawrence, and drily factual, unlike the anguish of Gwen or insouciance of Trish. Gradually, Jason un-reeled the following appalling story.

He is the son of a train driver, of parents who split up during his childhood and presented him with three full siblings, one half-brother (on his mother's side) and six step-brothers and sisters (on his father's side). Jason was suspended from school at the age of thirteen and 'just never went back'. Instead, he took to the streets, something whose implications he says, 'to be honest, I never really thought about'. He lived rough for a couple of years, got into drink, drugs and juvenile crime, and was then presented with the option of living in a children's home. As he puts it, 'my mum didn't really care. If she did, then she would have let me live with her, but, no. When I was fifteen and just before I was about to go into a children's home, she turned round and goes, "You can live here if you want." And I'm like "No", because I didn't see the point. Because if I'd have moved in there, within a week she'd have kicked me out again – and then I wouldn't have been able to go to the children's home, because someone else would have took my place.'

When the home 'did not work out', he returned to the streets, to underage labouring, and he then tried turning to his father. When still fifteen, 'I moved in with my dad for about four or five months. Then I was working, earning two hundred and ten pounds a week, cash. I was really chuffed, and then my dad kicked me out – and then I was back on the streets again.' That signalled the end of his relationship with his father. Jason then moved from the West coast to the market town with his mother, but now sees little of this part of his family, because his brother is in the Army and he avoids his sister who is 'doing drugs'. Jason sums up his life until the age of sixteen: 'No one ever thought of me. So I thought, well I'll make my decision of what I want to do to make my future look better.' This involved moving into the Foyer, where he has lived for over a year, whilst gaining a GNVQ certificate in computing, preparing for one at a higher level, as well as for a certificate in general administration – with a view to office work.

Jason immediately understands the notion of the inner conversation, but his use of it is distinctively different from that of any other interviewee. When he says, 'I don't really do it when I'm alone', this dissociates him from 'autonomous reflexivity' without it pointing towards the 'communicative' pattern of 'thought and talk'. His following statement is understandable, given his background of rejections: 'I tend to do it more when I'm around people. Well, like people talking to me and I just think more about what they're saying and just try to see if they're lying or telling the truth, I suppose. Because I've got a problem with trust. That's about the only thing I ever think about – whether I can trust them or not.' Small wonder about that, but what is surprising is bareness of his inner life, which he confirms as we work down the prompt list. Only two mental activities elicit positive responses from him, and one of these is qualified: Jason engages in 'a lot' of 'rehearsing' and in restricted 'planning'. Both responses repay attention.

I ask him to give me some idea of what he 'rehearses' mentally. His reply is: 'Just what I'm going to say. Something like, if my girlfriend's coming round, I plan out what I'm going to say before she comes round.' Conversely, 'if I go to a job interview, I don't plan it out. I never plan anything out about what I'm going to say for a job interview, because I like just to take it as it comes.' Probably this will strike most readers as a strange reversal; to 'rehearse' for informal encounters and not to 'practise' for formal ones. Yet, there is logic to it.

Firstly, Jason's 'rehearsal' for exchanges with his girlfriend are closely related to the matter of trust – he is testing her out. 'I've always been wary of everyone and just sussing them out before I make a judgement. Even with my girlfriend now, I've been with her, what four months. I mean it's not that long, but I still don't trust her, not fully. I love her, but I don't trust her.' This statement allows that his girlfriend could eventually turn out to be trustworthy, so Jason will give her time and set her tests until he can be sure into which category she falls. This is a lot of hermeneutic rope for him to pay out, because he sets tight limits to human understanding. Jason divides the world into 'Them', meaning 'people who are higher, that just don't care' (including the well-off, officials, social workers and his parents), and 'Us', who include his fellow tenants, his girlfriend, his full brother, sister and half-brother – as the 'main people who mean something to me'. The latter is his small 'hermeneutic in-group', with whom mutual understanding is possible, and towards whose needs he shows considerable sensitivity. Beyond, lies a vast uncaring residuum, the majority of society's members, who do not understand but readily dismiss 'Us'. 'If I went out and asked people what they thought of people like us, they'd say we're all drug users and alcoholics and stuff like that.' There is no reaching across this chasm of non-understanding. Since one of 'Them' would be conducting the job interview, there is no point in preparing, because the question of mutual understanding does not arise. Either the job will be offered if Jason fits their bill, or it will not if he does not, but nothing he could do would change the outcome.

In Jason's 'objectified' outlook, either a complementary state of affairs exists, or it does not. This also explains the partial nature of the second mental activity in which he engages, namely 'planning'. 'I don't think that I really plan a lot. I mean I plan things like my career, and that's probably about it, I suppose. I don't plan how my life's going to go or anything like that.' By career planning, Jason means that he can change his objective characteristics (becoming an applicant with qualifications in computing), and he can consult the posts which are objectively available, but he cannot be more of an active agent than that, as will be seen.

This is the extent of his inner conversation, but there is a further point about our discussion of it that is of significance. In general, Jason simply says 'No', that he does not engage in activities like 'reliving', or 'holding imaginary conversations'. However, where activities like 'deciding' and 'prioritising' are concerned, he gives a reason why he does not go through a deliberative process, namely, he accepts his occurrent desires or reactions unquestioningly. Thus, in terms of working out his priorities, Jason asserts, 'I don't really think about it. Because I just know if it's important to me. My girlfriend and my career. That's it.' Thus, again unlike the 'fractured reflexives', Jason is quite clear about his concerns. It is significant that his scanty reflexive activities, 'rehearsing' and (partial) 'planning', are devoted to the two things about which he most cares – for these are matters which he does not wish to blot out.

We come to discussing the reasons, as he understands them, for the bareness of his inner conversation, when talking about the two or three years he spent on the streets, using drugs and drink. 'It was just the fact that it was so much easier. So much easier to forget your problems. If I was high on drugs, or if I was drunk, it was so much easier. And now, the last six–seven months, when I come off the alcohol – I'd come off the drugs before that – but it was sort of so much harder. Because I had to think of it. I had to think about what's going on. I had to decide, and it was just a lot harder – and a lot of the time, at that point, I just wished I'd carried on drinking. I mean, now I don't. But it's so much easier just to drink and be drunk all the time and not worry about it. I think I've always done that – and it's never done me any good.' Understandably, Jason finds it painful to dwell upon himself in relation to his circumstances, so at one time he retreated into oblivion to avoid doing so, and now he still evades it. However, this does not mean that he is incapable of reflexivity, for the above statement is a fully self-reflexive one, nor that he is unable to engage in self-monitoring, because this is precisely what he must have done to kick both habits. Nevertheless, he continues to practise evasion as far as possible, and fails to cultivate his reflexive potential, which thus remains undeveloped. This is what accounts for his lack of self-pity and the absence of the affect that overwhelms the 'fractured reflexives'. Jason avoids mental activities like 're-living', 'mulling over', and 'clarifying' which would re-animate painful experiences; as he puts it, 'I don't see the point of letting my past get me down.'

Yet, how can he evade other activities, like 'deciding', 'budgeting' and robust 'planning', if he wants his future to be different from his past, as he does? Rather than developing these reflexive skills, all of which would involve his deliberating upon himself as subject to object, Jason treats himself as an object with occurrent desires, the source of intuitions which require no inspection or evaluation, and therefore no internal conversation. Hence his earlier statement about his priorities, 'I just know if it's important to me', hence his repeated motto, 'I never do anything I don't like', and hence his decision about his future career, 'working in computers, because I like working with computers'. In this way, his life of the mind is that of a passive recorder, which simply registers his intuitions and inclinations, without engaging in internal dialogue about them – about their appropriateness, feasibility or likely consequences. He thus lives as Humean man, a slave to his passions, without using internal reasoning as their 'ingenious servant', to compare and contrast the merits of concrete projects for the realisation of his desires.

In other words, Jason does not reflect upon himself as an agent, whose own actions have imports for himself as subject. He is an object who registers his own inclinations, executes them, and lives with their consequences. As a subject he is therefore entirely passive, one who does not mentally intervene to monitor his own actions, but simply accepts their repercussions. This is illustrated when he talks about quitting his recent job because of its low pay. After a year in the Foyer, its manager placed him with a firm of solicitors who handle the charity's local affairs. Jason wishes to continue living in his flat, but 'the rent's extortionate. It's like a hundred and seven pounds[5] a week, and I was only on a hundred and forty pound a week. And I can't afford to do that, which is the reason why I quit my job, because there wasn't enough money to pay my rent and my food.' Once unemployed, and no longer technically in training, Jason became liable for rent and he now owes over a thousand pounds in arrears. I ask him what he is going to do, which implies an active response, but instead he gives a passive account of the procedures that ensue and the consequences these entail. 'They give you a letter telling how much you owe and you've got a week, and then they send you another one. If you don't pay it, then you'll get an eviction notice. But if you ain't got the money you can't pay it. Then we end up how I was before we moved in – homeless.' This sequence is presented as a set of mechanical occurrences, which will happen to Jason, but which he, as subject, is powerless to control. His inability to monitor himself in relation to his circumstances means that he passively allows this scenario to unroll. Reflexively, he had not reviewed the alternative courses of action he could have taken.

In sum, his undeveloped subjectivity also underwrites an undeveloped subject – one who cannot exert himself as an active agent. Jason does not relate to himself as subject to object, and because he cannot see himself as a subject who has powers to regulate what happens to him as object, then he is at the mercy of his occurrent desires and their reception by circumstances. The sad result of his non-reflexive behaviour is that his passivity may well nullify his previous exertions to get off the streets, by returning him there.

His passivity is intensified, because not only does Jason see himself as an object, unamenable to self-regulation, but he also views society as another object, and therefore one to which he cannot be hermeneutically related in any way. Therefore, nothing can be negotiated (because negotiation implies inter-subjectivity) and events just happen. Jason sees himself as one object and the world as another; the two are either congruent or incongruent. This is exemplified as we continue to discuss the possibilities of finding new employment. Firstly, Jason acts as a passive recorder, and simply responds that the type of work he seeks does exist. 'I've worked in an office before when I did my work experience. I weren't getting paid. That was exactly what I wanted to do. It was advertising on the Internet for [a national chain of stationers]. So it is there. It's just finding it.' What he does not reflect upon is that this unpaid work would not solve his rent problem, nor has he ascertained what the rate of pay would be, nor what qualifications would be required.

---

[5] This includes a service charge. Here I am quoting the figures he gave, not vouching for them.

Secondly, he underlines his object-to-object outlook, namely that if he has the skills and the market requires them, this coincidence will result in employment. 'It's not that hard to find another job. [The market town's] supposed to have a high employment rate. At the moment, I'm just applying at agencies and then they will try and find me a job that they think fits my description. And then I'll go and they will tell me about it, and I'll go for the interview and if it sounds good, I'll take it if they offer it. If they don't offer it to me, or I don't want it – then I'll just say no I don't want it.' The process is presented as entirely mechanical; if there is goodness of fit between his objective skills and the objective job requirements, then employment will follow, and if there is not it will not. Jason does not reflect upon the influence of self-presentation or the need to give a positive account of himself, especially since he will approach employers without references, track record, or many qualifications.

Finally, when I attempt to steer the conversation in this direction, Jason stresses that he does not view a job offer as open to any such inter-personal negotiation. It is merely a question of 'take it or leave it' on both sides – as our following exchanges show:

M   So do you reckon that only having one IT certificate is going to be a barrier?
J   Yeah, along with my criminal convictions. They would be the two. Probably companies won't employ me because of . . .
M   What are you going to do then if . . .
J   Just keep trying.
M   Just keep trying?
J   Yeah, definitely. It's their loss, not mine.
M   But you do need a job . . .
J   Yeah, but if they ain't going to employ me because of the way they see me, then that's their problem, not mine. I ain't going to put myself down because of it. Because what's the point?
M   So would you try to cover up?
J   No. I never cover up nothing. I never do and I never will.
M   That sounds rather like 'take it or leave it'.
J   If they don't want me for who I am, it's not my problem.

It is Jason's problem, because failing to get a job will entail even more serious problems for him, yet he does not think there is anything he could do to make a favourable outcome more likely. Because he does not relate to himself as subject to object, he regards himself simply as the bearer of objective characteristics (a few qualifications and a police record). Internally, he does not interrogate himself about how to advance his case, for example by stressing that he does have a real ability for computing, as he is largely self-taught. Because he does not regard himself as a subject, neither can he allow that others are active subjects and that 'the way they see me' could be changed – by his giving them cause to think. Without subjects there can be no hermeneutic interchange, merely a market exchange of commodities. The latter is how Jason sees matters.

From Jason's conception of social relations as object relationships, there is no room for, or point to, purposeful or instrumental action. Thus the basic reason why Jason does not display the same sense of disorientation as the 'fractured reflexives', is that he does not think about orientation at all. Since his own stance towards society *endorses* his passivity as ineluctable, he does not flail around in uncertainty about what to do. Instrumental action is irrelevant in his *mechanical* view of the manner in which self and society are related.

The conclusion seems to be that the further away we move from any practised mode of reflexivity – through the 'fractured reflexives' and towards near non-reflexivity – then the closer we come to the passive agent, to the individual who can exert minimal control in his own life and over his own life course. Terrible things have happened to Jason in the past; given his passivity, the fear is that he will again be the victim of circumstances. Of course, there is always the possibility that contingency may intervene with felicific consequences. Yet, for a passive agent, such a welcome outcome would in no measure be the result of the reflexive usage of his personal powers. So, the best of luck, Jason.

Conclusion: personal powers and social powers

The argument presented over the last nine chapters has been an attempt to specify *how* 'the causal power of social forms is mediated through social agency'.[1] It was acknowledged that the word 'through' was unacceptably vague and that its specification as a process of conditioning was unduly unilateral. It accentuated the social shaping of our circumstances to the neglect of how agents received them. Instead, the full mediatory mechanism has been held to depend upon human reflexivity; namely, our power to deliberate internally upon what to do in situations that were not of our making.

This sounds dry and technical and so it is, until one sets out to explore the personal capacity to reflect upon ourselves and our concerns in relation to our social circumstances. The internal conversation, through which such inner deliberations take place, is relatively unknown territory. As exploration proceeded, the awareness of being a stranger in strange lands intensified. Internal conversations proved to be radically heterogeneous, despite the intuitive conviction of subjects that all others conducted their reflexive deliberations in the same way as they did themselves. On the contrary, internal conversations were found to be so different as to warrant distinguishing three different modes of reflexivity – 'communicative reflexivity', 'autonomous reflexivity' and 'meta-reflexivity'.

The co-existence of these three modes of reflexivity within late modernity (not precluding the future discovery of others) has much wider implications. It is far richer in its consequences than merely furnishing an answer to the technical question about the process mediating between structure and agency. These implications derive from the summary conclusion that practitioners of each of the three different modes of reflexivity adopt generically different 'stances' towards society and its constraints and enablements: the *evasive*, the *strategic* and the *subversive*. Each 'stance' goes above and beyond the manner in which a given subject responds to

---

[1] Roy Bhaskar, *The Possibility of Naturalism*, Harvester Wheatsheaf, Hemel Hempstead, 1989, p. 26.

any given constraint or enablement, and represents an overall pattern of response to the totality of structural powers.

'Stances' are basic orientations of subjects to society. In other words, the 'stance' is ventured as a generative mechanism, at the personal level, with the tendential capacity to regulate relations between the person and her society. In short, they *constitute* the micro–macro link.

The ability to take a 'stance' towards society is itself a personal accomplishment. What it produces is the 'active agent'. Not everyone achieves a 'stance' because the development of personal reflexivity may be impeded; neither is the achievement of a 'stance' a once-and-for-all matter because a mode of reflexivity can be damaged to the point of becoming inoperative as a personal power. The important question about the possibility of recuperation or mutation is one that cannot be answered without longitudinal study.

However, in the short term, at least, any type of 'fractured reflexivity' deprived the subject of an active personal 'stance'. Such people became incapable of deliberating purposefully as subject to object about their social contexts. It was not that they ceased to engage in internal conversation, but its increased preoccupation with affective distress intensified their inability to act with purpose. As their subjectivity lost its purposefulness, signalled by their subjective incapacity to conceive of the sequence 'concerns → projects → practices', so the subject withdrew from exercising directional guidance over her own life.

The root cause was that such subjects had lost their strict numerical identity as persons, defined by their unique configuration of concerns, thus depriving the deliberative process of its necessary traction. The key consequence was that subjects, experiencing something akin to paralysis of their personal powers, became 'passive agents'. Passive agents are the opposite of those taking a social 'stance'; they are people to whom things happen rather than people who exercise some governance over their lives by making things happen. Conversely, all practitioners of a given mode of reflexivity were 'active agents' and the *modus vivendi* that each had established in society was to a significant extent their own doing – the effect of exercising their personal powers.

'Stances' towards society: origins, orientations and outcomes

In the Introduction I called this book a 'tale of two powers'. This is the case whether one focuses upon the *origins* of the three different modes of reflexivity, the *orientations* of 'communicative', 'autonomous' or 'meta-reflexive' agents in terms of their distinctive 'stances' towards society, or the *outcomes* of their 'stances' for social transformation and human eman-cipation. Therefore, the task is the same under each of these headings, namely to describe that interplay between societal and personal prop-erties and powers which accounts for these differences. The key factors involved can be condensed into the concepts of 'context', contributed by the socio-cultural structure, and 'concerns', contributed by active agents. For any given subject, context and concern are internally or necessarily re-lated. Together they generate the particular mode of reflexivity to emerge and become a subject's own personal property – capable of exercising both internal and external causal powers.

Origins

The origins of the three different modes of reflexivity are found at the nexus between contexts and concerns. What complicates matters is that neither factor is static. On the one hand, the agential contribution is made by subjects who are reaching maturity, but are still in the process of identifying and prioritising their concerns. (That is by youngsters who are undertaking their preliminary circuit around the square depicted in figure 3.4.) In other words, they have not yet achieved strict numerical personal identity. The projects that they forge in their initial social con-text, which was not of their making or choosing, may be experimental (and thus corrigible). Nevertheless, some find sufficient personal satis-faction there to prolong the experiment into a life-project, thus endorsing their original and involuntary social positioning. Others do not, and this appears to be closely related to the absence of 'contextual continuity' itself. For, on the other hand, whilst many agents are completing the maturational process, their involuntary contexts of social placement may *simultaneously* be shifting and changing at the micro-level, in ways which represent discontinuities for the subject.

In order to summarise the development of the three different modes of reflexivity in terms of the interplay between context and concern, the old bagatelle board provides an analogy that can readily be pictured. Even better is the slot-machine version of bagatelle, which used to be found upon every self-respecting pier. The machine worked vertically; a ball would be released at the bottom right-hand corner and be flipped upwards by the player. The angle at which it hit the rounded top determined its initial downward trajectory, in the course of which it encountered various cups distributed at different levels down the face of the machine. If a ball fell squarely into a cup at any stage, then, once it had settled, an aperture opened and the ball disappeared. Alternatively, a ball could ricochet off the edge of a cup, change direction, but be trapped by another cup lower down. More rarely, a ball would career its way (un-trapped) to the bottom – in which case it was released again for another circuit. Like all analogies, this has many defects, the obvious one being that it is mechanical. However if the cups stand for contexts and the balls for agents with concerns, these provide the props for a sociological parable.

Each subject is involuntarily launched; he or she has no say about the natal social context that they will inhabit. Now let us say that the first ball is flipped squarely into an upper cup, it rocks around within it but insufficiently to roll over its lip and continue its course. Instead, it slowly ceases to move, the aperture opens and the ball becomes trapped by its context for that game (remember that potentially there are many games, because in figure 3.4 we can tour the circuit throughout life).

In this parable, that round of the game stands for the 'communicative reflexive'. The first cup in which they find themselves is their initial context of involuntary social placement. The cup is stable, which represents 'contextual continuity', and although the young agent may roll around exploring the potentials offered by this restricted environment, she does identify something or some things which she deems worthy of investing in as her 'concern(s)'. As she does so, she slows down and settles, for the agent is no longer casting about trying to discover something sufficiently worth caring about. Instead, she is now concentrating upon defining a project, expressive of her concerns *within* this context. Meanwhile, the context has remained stable and continuous; it has not shifted, it is the agent who has rattled around exploring it. And, in the course of her exploratory forays, she has become more and more familiar with the stable features of her context. When the agent comes to rest, it is because she has defined a life-project within her contextual confines. Its pursuit signifies that she has voluntarily endorsed her context and also that the context has embraced her. Hence the story ends *pro tem* with departure through the aperture.

Note several other features of this story. It has not been necessary to give our ball special features like 'bias', which affect its journey, because the interplay between context and concern is not secretly orchestrated by psychological characteristics of the agent. This is not a story that can be reduced to one about the ball, whose internal characteristics determine both its trajectory and also the context in which it comes to rest. Conversely, neither has it been necessary to give the cup particular features, such as a flanged lip which would prevent the ball from teetering over its brink – thus making the outcome more to do with the cup than the ball. There were no indications from the study that the 'social class' assigned involuntarily by the context, or the education afforded by it, played a deterministic role in detaining the subject and retaining agents within their initial context. Equally, there was evidence that subjects had looked beyond their context before determining that their concerns lay within it, and that their siblings had done the same, but had concluded otherwise. Obviously, the one thing a mechanical analogy cannot capture is the essentially 'communicative' nature of this developing life of the mind. It cannot picture how 'similars and familiars', who share a common contextual reference point with the subject, can thus enter into her concerns to the point where they can complete and confirm her internal dialogue, which then becomes yet more firmly anchored in and to its context.

The second ball to be flipped also falls into a cup, but this cup is loosely attached, promptly tilts and decants the ball into a lower cup, out of which it bounces because of its acquired momentum. It careers on, ricocheting from side to side, but eventually comes to rest in one of the lower cups, through whose aperture it then disappears. By analogy, this is the making of the 'autonomous reflexive'. Such agents, like all others, are born into an involuntary context. However, unlike that of their counterparts above, this initial context itself lacks stability. Before the subject has become familiar with it, and vice versa, she is deposited in a new context. Frequent geographical moves on the part of the family were the main feature that objectively distinguished the 'autonomous' from the 'communicative' reflexives. There were also intimations that, for the 'communicative reflexives', the context had to be smooth as well as stable, such that their concerns could unfold into established practices, without environmental friction. Conversely, geographical mobility and changes of school, made rolling stones (to change metaphors) of the nascent 'autonomous reflexives'. They gathered no enduring network of early friends whose lasting companionship was anchored in a common context and whose interchanges were densely localised. Instead, they were thrown back upon their own resources to deliberate upon the *variety* of contexts that they had involuntarily encountered. As rolling stones, it is unsurprising that when as they began to define their concerns, these should be performative in kind. Performative skills are primarily personal and generically transportable. Moreover, to concentrate upon honing the competence of one's performance involves constant self-monitoring, which thus reinforces the 'autonomous' mode of internal conversation.

Although to have an ultimate concern that is focused upon a performative skill does indicate a preoccupation with the practical order, nevertheless it also requires a social context for its expression. It is the quest for such a social environment that the image of 'ricocheting' was intended to capture. Subjects inspect (and may try out) various new contexts in the hope that each in turn will prove to be the environment in which their concerns could be successfully commuted into a project, whose realisation would result in the establishment of a satisfying and sustainable *modus vivendi*. Like the ball, zigzagging on its way, these subjects may take a quantity of hard knocks. Through them, their concerns themselves may become clarified or modified and their contextual desiderata may become clearer or less demanding. Sooner for some than for others, the subject settles for a combination of concerns and context that are sufficiently complementary for her to conclude that a particular slot does permit the expression of who she wants to be. Since she knows the answer to this, having no difficulty in ordering her concerns, she accepts to go through that door.

At the start, the third ball follows the same course as the preceding one. Again, there is no early 'contextual continuity' to detain it and bind it to a stable social environment. It too is a rolling stone, thrown back upon its own autonomous resources before it has reached maturity. What is unclear is quite how much of the journey the 'autonomous' and the 'meta-reflexive' share. What is different about the third ball is that somewhere *en route* it has acquired a (non-rounded) shape, which gives a distinct bias to the trajectory then taken. Thus whilst it may indeed fall into cup after cup, a roll past each aperture demonstrates that it would not be able to pass through, and in any case its velocity carries it on over the lip. Eventually, this ball bypasses all the cups, neither staying nor being stayed, drops to the base and is immediately back in play.

What the 'meta-reflexive' acquires fairly early on in life is a driving ultimate concern. In accounting for this, the data collected allow one to go no further than insisting upon the relative autonomy of the structural and the cultural domains. The personal powers of these subjects have seized upon a cultural ideal and their guiding project is to come to embody and express that concern as closely as possible. Thus, they know what they would become and recognise how far they fall short. Simultaneously, they are acute monitors of any context because an acceptable context is one that should nurture their ultimate concern, facilitate its expression and promote its diffusion. Unlike the 'autonomous reflexive', who will countenance mutual adjustments between his contexts and his concerns, the 'meta-reflexive' deliberates upon the dilution which such accommodation would entail – and rejects the compact. Their internal conversations are replete with self-critique and societal critique; their outer comportment is *Wertrational* in form. Since no context is ultimately deemed commensurate with their ultimate concerns, at most they will be sojourners in a social environment until the discrepancy between their social identity and their personal identity is judged to be too great – at which point these subjects move on. As there is no fixed resting place (no slot which fits their ideal), the 'meta-reflexives' have the most volatile biographies of all subjects. For them there is no final *modus vivendi* – no established set of practices which can be deemed both satisfying and worthy of being sustained.

The making of the three different modes of reflexivity has been explained as emerging from three distinctive types of interplay between structural properties, constituted by the social context in which young subjects find themselves involuntarily, and personal properties, represented by the nascent concerns of these young people. The resulting forms of subjectivity are irreducible to the context alone; otherwise all who share the same type of initial and involuntary context would develop the same mode of reflexivity. This was not the case, particularly if social class background is regarded as a summary index of involuntary positioning. Equally, the three modes of reflexivity are irreducible to personal concerns alone; otherwise 'contextual discontinuity' would contribute nothing to their making – yet it did strongly appear to have this effect.

In other words, neither structural determinism (the dominance of context), nor agential voluntarism (the dominance of concerns), can be sustained. Instead, the emergence of given modes of reflexivity result from a dialectical interplay in which one particular aspect of context, namely continuity or discontinuity, 'proposes', but the nature of personal concerns then 'disposes'. Thus, during the first moment, 'contextual continuity' proposes a 'communicative' life of the mind to those who have experienced it and 'contextual discontinuity' an 'autonomous' form of subjectivity to those who have undergone it.

In the second moment, as maturity approaches, some subjects can develop concerns that are complementary to their continuous contexts and become 'communicative reflexives'. These remain socially immobile and actively contribute to the replication of their social placement, which thus ceases to be largely involuntary. Others cannot – because their developing concerns are incompatible with any of the discontinuous contexts that they encounter early in life. This fosters autonomous deliberations and serves to monitor the quest for a suitable social context for the realisation of their concerns. 'Autonomous reflexivity' therefore makes a crucial contribution to the dynamics of social mobility. Still others cannot achieve this accommodation with society, from first to last. For the latter, the force of their cultural concern, and their need to personify it as well as to pursue it, drives them towards 'meta-reflexivity'. Correspondingly, their life-long contextual unsettlement generates a sequence of moves, embracing upward, lateral and downward mobility. This patterning is inexplicable within existing theories of social mobility, because inadequate recognition is accorded to agential powers as the choreographers of our movements through the social world.

In the third moment, if no 'fracturing' has occurred, the three modes of reflexivity are consolidated and become the means through which subjects determine the concrete projects which they seek to advance in a suitable context – if and when one can be located. Emergence of a given mode of reflexivity, as reconstructed above from our subjects' biographies, is thus advanced as the missing link in accounting for patterns of social mobility. Generically, explanations of this patterning have been over-mechanical and have underplayed the active role of agents as their own social artificers.

Orientations

Each mode of reflexivity is a distinctive way of deliberating about oneself in relation to one's society. It is the modality through which the active agent continues to align her personal concerns with her social context. However, the method of alignment varies directly with the mode of reflexivity being exercised. In the course of their innumerable internal conversations, every active agent had effectively reached conclusions about two matters, under their own descriptions. On the one hand, they had reflexively prioritised their concerns and crystallised these into determinate projects. On the other hand, they had arrived at some orientation towards their encounters with constraints and enablements. It is the combination of these two deliberative outcomes, which represents acquiring a 'stance' towards society. However, these 'stances' were so different that the three distinct modes of reflexivity effectively conjoined subjectivity to objectivity in three completely different ways. In other words, the internal conversation, as the fundamental process mediating between structure and agency, also canalised the personal–societal relationship in different directions, according to its mode – thus articulating the precise form of the micro–macro link.

'Communicative reflexives', firmly identifying their 'ultimate concern' with inter-personal relations (family and friendship), adopted a 'stance' of systematic *evasion* in relation to constraints and enablements. This has to be recognised as a positive achievement of active agents, despite the fact that its effect was social reproduction. Indeed it makes such reproduction (or often replication) a human achievement requiring the exertion of personal powers. Without such deliberative decisions as to forego overtime, self-employment, or to give up small businesses for the sake of the family, and without self-monitoring in order to devote time and effort to conviviality, togetherness and quality of life, their accomplishment of sustainable and satisfying practices would be a puzzle.

Those whom it should trouble are any who portray this group as passive 'losers', victims of social forces which defy their penetration, or as quasi-automatic self-victimisers, bound to a chain of reproduction through their semi-conscious dispositions. Whilst it is the case that the 'communicative reflexive' does not court constraints by promoting ambitious projects, the full import of *evasion* cannot be grasped without stressing that it is also the case that they actively shun objective enablements to social advancement. It is this combination which warrants the claim that the subjects in chapter 6 had developed and displayed a distinctive 'stance' towards their social context – as an expression of their personal powers.

Since the ultimate concerns of 'autonomous reflexives' centred upon performative achievement, it is congruent (though not a matter of necessity) that they looked towards work activities for their expression. However, since their concern is with intrinsic satisfaction, rather than ambition, they seek an occupational context which meets this desideratum, whilst imposing the minimum of undesired requirements. In the course of their quest they become increasingly knowledgeable about themselves in relation to society (learning from their mistakes) and of society in relation to themselves (learning about its constraints and enablements). Through the (often lengthy) process of seeking to transform their own circumstances in order to realise their concerns and adjusting their projects in the light of their new circumstances, the 'autonomous reflexive' adopts a *strategic* 'stance' *vis à vis* constraints and enablements. The reflexive powers of deliberating upon what has been learned and then using this knowledge to anticipate the feasibility of potential courses of action allows this group to identify a satisfying and sustainable *modus vivendi*. This active and transformative achievement entails knowledgeably capitalising upon relevant enablements and an equally knowledgeable circumvention of anticipated constraints. Since both are known fallibly, the strategic outcome may indeed be a way of life that is sub-optimal in objective terms. Nevertheless, it represents the life-politics of the possible to the subjects in chapter 7. Their resulting *modi vivendi* are very different because these agents have actively attempted to climb society's 'ladders' and to circumvent its 'snakes'.

The 'meta-reflexives' are distinctive because their commitment to an ultimate concern partakes of dedication to a vocational ideal. Their search is for a social context that both fosters its expression and also nurtures its growth. Again and again, institutional contexts are found wanting on both counts, are judged to be such, and are left behind. This produces volatile biographies because no organisational setting is ever deemed to be sufficiently commensurate with the cultural ideal. The 'stance' adopted by 'meta-reflexives' is deemed to be *subversive* because the courses of action followed by the subjects in chapter 8 resisted directional guidance from the constraints and enablements they objectively encountered. Objectively, they were not immune to the loss of 'bonuses', forfeited by refusing enablements, nor from the 'penalties' collected by resisting constraints. Subjectively, however, the 'meta-reflexives' were willing to pay the price of their contextual critique. Sometimes the bill was presented in terms of resignation of posts, re-training, and re-location – as the prices of lateral mobility. Even more significantly, these subjects would willingly embrace downward mobility and its objective losses in order to pursue their vocations in what they subjectively defined to be a preferential context. The systematic rejection of society's 'sticks and carrots' left them free to engage in societal critique because their *subversive* 'stance' meant that they personally absorbed the costs of actively promoting alternative values.

It follows, therefore, that each of the three modes of reflexivity expresses a particular orientation towards personal–societal relations. What I want to draw out here are the *internal implications* for subjects themselves, which are embedded in their adoption of these different 'stances' towards society. Once again, these can be understood in terms of the interplay between contexts and concerns.

Fundamentally, each 'stance' towards society represents a subjective judgement by the agent about the importance that she attaches to her objective social context and its place in her own life. For some this is much greater than others. Quite simply, certain concerns are more heavily reliant upon a social context for their realisation, while other concerns are less socially dependent. Another way of putting this is that according to their concerns, subjects determine how much of themselves they will invest in the social order. All invest something because every concern in some way entails a social context for its expression, realisation and development – if not all three. However, there is a huge difference between whether or not a concern is intrinsically social in kind (and thus highly context-dependent), rather than being extrinsically social (and thus less contextually reliant). This is the difference between internal or necessary relations, in the first case, and external or contingent relationships, in the second.

Of course, this series of statements contravenes every version of societal determinism – and, in social theory, this is becoming the 'new superpower',[2] which drives out the creative actor. They will provoke outrage from protagonists of the 'social action perspective' because, let it be crystal clear, the assertion is indeed that as active agents one of our personal

---

[2] Colin Campbell, *The Myth of Social Action,* Cambridge University Press, 1996, p. 28.

powers is precisely to determine how much importance we attach to 'the social' within our own lives. The three modes of reflexivity and their related 'stances' towards society represent very different answers to this question.

'Communicative reflexives' are fundamentally 'investors in people'. Since their ultimate concerns are 'family and friends', these agents vest themselves fully in the social order. Logically, their concerns cannot even be articulated without entailing pre-suppositions about society – about the family unit and about the spatial distribution of friendship networks. Necessarily, the expression and realisation of their concerns entails a deep embeddedness in a localised social context. The very practice of their mode of reflexivity depends upon a secure contextual anchorage, such that through sharing common reference points and through their communality of experiences, 'similars and familiars' can be interlocutors, capable of completing and complementing a subject's own internal deliberations. In short, the personal flourishing of 'communicative reflexives' is utterly dependent upon their receiving good returns upon their self-investment in society – in terms of their own currency of contentment.

'Autonomous reflexives' invest themselves in performative concerns. Because these are transferable skills, subjects whose personal identities are vested in their expression put the practical order first and foremost. To them, it is a subsidiary matter *which* context provides the social framework compatible with the realisation of their ultimate concerns. This is the case even though it is undeniable that performative concerns cannot be realised in a social vacuum. Hence, far from being embedded in a given context, much less in one of those encountered through their original and involuntary social placements, these are active agents who are actively seeking a context which will prove compatible with that which they care about most. Instead of becoming engaged to a context early in life or married to one later on, the 'autonomous reflexive' sits light to society and accepts that his over-riding concern may spell contextual changes. Even those who appear to 'take root', because of a lasting compatibility between their lasting concerns and some amenable context, are not embedded in that social environment. Instead they are fundamentally 'loners'. They can accept that certain legitimate demands and expectations will emanate from their social surroundings, but meeting them is effectively a social contract, in which the subject reserves his right to a private life – that crucial area of self-defined activity which, being individualistic, repudiates communal incursions from the context. 'Autonomous reflexives' are accommodative individuals; 'investment in people' is never their ultimate concern and, in so far as it figures as a subordinate one, then it will be served in due order, which means maintaining its subordination.

The 'meta-reflexive' is even more reserved about forging tight links between her ultimate concern and any context whatsoever. Those who share this life of the mind have basically invested themselves in a cultural ideal, to which no structural context is ever anything more than a temporary approximation. Each context is a base, which initially seems to allow for the expression and development of that ideal, but always then falls unacceptably short of it. Since 'meta-reflexives' can rarely be eremitic, though the most important part of themselves may be vested in activities such as lone writing or solitary prayer, their ideal of a holistically integrated life precludes them from instrumentally endorsing 'social contracts' and condemns them to life-long frustration as social utopians. Of course, some will object that if their ideals are 'cultural' then they are necessarily social. This would be to misunderstand that these subjects have raided the cultural system and found there something that has become their 'banner with a strange device' and that their own 'excelsior' is independent from its socio-cultural popularity or practice.[3] Effectively, they have invested themselves in the transcendental order, which means a quest for truth or goodness, one that transcends the best that any social context ever represents.

In summarising the implications of these three 'stances' towards society – the evasive, strategic and subversive – for those who hold them, what has been stressed is the fact that our personal powers are crucial in mediating the importance of society to us. It is we who deliberatively determine how much of ourselves will be invested in the social order. Although there is no dispute that we are all ineluctably social beings, nevertheless, contra the huge and growing swathe of imperialistic thought in sociology, it is persons who reflexively determine to what extent they will become 'Society's Being'. Moreover, in exercising this personal power, practitioners of the three different modes of reflexivity come up with three different answers. The 'communicative reflexive' is 'collectivistic' towards the social (concerns and context are inseparable); the 'autonomous reflexive' is 'accommodative' towards the social (context is a means towards the realisation of a concern); and the 'meta-reflexive' is 'transcendental' towards the social (context is always inadequate to concerns).

These represent general orientations towards society on the part of three groups of active agents. However, the particular 'stances' that they adopt do mean that the *internal* causal consequences of exerting their personal powers are quite distinct from one another. This should not be surprising because to take up a 'stance' is not akin to holding an

---

[3] For the distinction between the 'Cultural System' and the 'Socio-Cultural' levels, see Margaret S. Archer, *Culture and Agency*, Cambridge University Press, 1988.

abstract point of view, but is rather a commitment to a distinctive course of practical action in society. It is a commitment which subjects make to themselves, within the internal conversation, and although it can only be made under their own descriptions, it is an acceptance of a particular way of being-in-the-world.

Thus, generically, the *evasive* 'stance' of the 'communicative reflexive' towards socio-cultural constraints and enablements is a commitment to use their personal powers in practical actions – in a manner that will entail 'self-renunciation'. Subjects, of course, do not put matters to themselves in this way. Yet, every time an enablement is reflexively evaded, subjects do renounce self-interest for the benefit of the 'contextural' community. Subjectively this is not altruism, because the subject's concerns are invested in the collectivity, but objectively they do forfeit the opportunity of becoming 'better off'. It is this renunciation that is involved when a young hairdresser foregoes working on cruise ships or when middle-aged men reject self-employment, overtime or promotion to spend time with their families. Similarly, the evasion of constraints by the determination to 'live within one's means' is also a renunciation of greater pleasures than those represented by annual holidays and modest home improvements. These subjects are fully aware that there is more to be had – hence their regular purchasing of lottery tickets. Again, the renunciation of ambition is not self-sacrifice for those whose concerns are vested in their proximate context, for they know that their own contentment depends upon the stability of that micro-world. Ironically, these are the last people who can afford to win the lottery jackpot.

Each 'stance' towards society embroils those who take it in a specialised form of self-monitoring. The *strategic* orientation of the 'autonomous reflexives' means that the internal effects of their personal powers commit them to a life of vigilant self-discipline. If constraints are to be circumvented, agents have to show ingenuity in carving out niches for their practical activities that are least vulnerable to socio-cultural penalisation. One common strategy is self-employment or the lone exercise of skills. This entails the self-discipline of taking sole responsibility for the guidance of the undertaking, self-restraint in not following trends which would attract high opportunity costs, and long hours of hard work, with the subject acting as his own task-master. Taking advantage of enablements is largely a matter of marshalling one's resources and deploying them to the best strategic effect. Usually, it involves accepting every 'elastication' afforded by educational opportunities, the self-discipline to extend qualifications and skills, often informally and outside mainstream channels, and then capitalising upon these self-improvements to advance the *modus vivendi* desired. Strategic mastery of the politics of the possible takes single-mindedness, a determination not to be deflected by others, and a disciplined acceptance of loneliness – for there are few to give support and none to blame.

When the 'stance' of the 'meta-reflexives' is characterised as *subversive*, this tends to accentuate their external face as contextual critics. The inner effect is a constant striving for self-transformation. If coming to embody the ideal 'quality' enshrined in their ultimate concern is their goal, then constant self-improvement is their means. It is for this that they monitor themselves and the contexts in which they try to live out their commitments. Indeed, their willingness to pay the price of subversion, through absorbing the costs of their own lateral or downward mobility, is their attempt to locate an environment that will better nurture their self-transformation. In this way, they are the antithesis of the agents of rational choice theory. They are not acting as instrumental rationalists seeking to become 'better off'; their action is *Wertrational*, discounting both means and costs with the sole aim of becoming 'better'. The effect is to produce their volatile biographies, but ones whose constant theme is an internal interrogation to ascertain whether or not the transformation sought is progressing or receding. There is no resting-place, no durable *modus vivendi* because internally these subjects ever deem their self-transformation to have fallen short of their ideal.

Adopting any 'stance' towards society *always* has internal causal effects upon those upholding it. This is necessarily the case because a 'stance' is an attempt by the subject to regulate the personal–societal relationship. Part of that regulation, and inevitably the larger part, consists in self-monitoring in relation to society – because the personal powers of the agent are more effective in generating self-change than societal change. In their lifetimes, which is the human measure of time, active agents can fallibly engineer an alignment between concerns and context, predominantly by monitoring themselves in relation to their social environment. Only in this way can they achieve significant governance over their own (short) lives.

In adopting any of the three 'stances', the respective agents assume the task of self-monitoring. Significantly, the forms taken – self-renunciation, self-discipline and self-transformation – are all personally onerous, as different means of assuring some alignment between self and society. The internal causal efficacy of their 'stances' works precisely because reasons are causes; they are reasons to which the agent gives her assent after surveying the social context in the light of her personal concerns. However, since what is found good and then practised by these active agents entails shouldering various forms of self-denial, then the 'bargain hunter' is the least appropriate way of modelling how the agent comports herself within the social context.

Finally, although agents themselves focus most upon bringing about and trying to sustain a micro–macro alignment which gives them some measure of control over their own lives, this does not mean that their activities are relatively self-contained micro-level phenomena, deprived of macroscopic social import. On the contrary, their 'stances' also have *external* causal efficacy. Their effects upon society will be less obvious to the agents, more cumulative in their consequences, but no less important for that.

Outcomes

Societal morphogenesis and morphostasis are most obviously associated with the effects of corporate agency: social movements, organised and articulate interest groups, and pressure groups of all kinds. Very few agents participate in the activities of promotive interest groups without the explicit *intent* of defending or transforming the *status quo*. Of course, such intentions do not themselves determine the outcome and the result is rarely what anyone seeks. Nevertheless, the effects are significant and noticeable. These have not been examined in the present book, because of its pre-occupation with the relationship between personal powers and social powers. Their importance is mentioned now as a caution against giving the individualist too much comfort from what follows. Despite the fact that the practices of individual agents are not intentionally geared towards producing societal effects, nonetheless these are the external outcomes of the exercise of their personal powers. In general, they are small in scale and undramatic, but their microscopic nature does not deprive them of cumulative significance.

To appreciate the consequences for social stability and change of the actions undertaken by the three types of reflexives, it is helpful to make use of the distinction between 'social integration' (the orderly or conflictual relations between members of society) and 'system integration' (the orderly or conflictural relations between parts of society).[4] Here the influences exerted by 'communicative reflexives' and 'autonomous reflexives' are precise opposites. Because the ultimate concerns of 'communicative reflexives' are vested in inter-personal relations (family and friendship), their main effect is to strengthen 'social integration'. Because the

---

[4] David Lockwood, 'Social Integration and System Integration', in G. K. Zollschan and W. Hirsch (eds.), *Explorations in Social Change*, Boston, Houghton Mifflin, 1964.

ultimate concerns of 'autonomous reflexives' are vested in the institutional order that provides the contextual outlet for their performative skills, their main effect is to augment goal-achievement in different part of the social system.

This sounds reminiscent of Parsonian functionalism, with the 'communicative reflexives' promoting 'systems-maintenance' and the 'autonomous reflexives' advancing 'goal achievement'. However, whilst in functionalism these two effects were held to be necessary for and complementary in any functioning social system, no such harmony is assured here. Fundamentally the 'communicative reflexives' foster morphostasis, whilst the 'autonomous reflexives' encourage morphogenesis, thus pulling society in two different directions. Since the cumulative effect of the 'meta-reflexives' represents a critique of both tendencies, there is no sense in which society is underpinned and held together by shared values.

The 'communicative reflexives' have been called 'investors in people', and indeed every exertion of their personal powers reinforces 'social integration', under their own descriptions. The consequences for 'system integration' are secondary and derivative from that, but unintentionally, the nature of the extant role-array and, more distantly, the institutional configuration of society, also derive positive reinforcement as the effect of this group exercising its personal powers.

The social integration promoted by 'communicative reflexivity' is flexible and adaptive. The dense life-world of inter-personal interaction maintained by these subjects is indeed localised and sustained by the frequency of face-to-face contact, but it is neither neighbourhood based nor traditionalistic.[5] (The endurance of such dense 'contextual continuity' in the face of globalisation raises important issues needing further exploration.) Networks of family and friends are adaptive for their members: resilient to growing trends, such as divorce, re-partnering and amalgamated families, open to novelty in cuisine, tourism and technology, and experimental in life-styles and consumption patterns. Yet, the other face of adaptation is selective assimilation, for the network functions as a collectivity, inserted between the individual and society. Collectively it sieves systemic novelties for personal endorsement. By inter-personally regulating the absorption of *novelty*, the informal collective reduces internal *variety* amongst its members. The mechanism through which intra-group integration is achieved is 'communicative reflexivity' itself. By mutually holding their inner deliberations open to inter-personal commentary and

---

[5] Unlike M. Young and P. Willmott's discovery that Bethnal Green in the late 1950s survived as a village in the centre of London, where traditional working-class practices continued to flourish as a means of cushioning families against the enduring rigours of capitalism. *Family and Kinship in East London*, Penguin, Harmondsworth, 1962.

completion, personal powers are offered up for collective approbation, filtration and censure. These effects, which serve to heighten social integration, are only possible because such agents have invested so much of themselves in their context, which is the focal point of their concerns.

Because this is so, we have also seen how the *evasive* 'stance' towards constraints and enablements then serves to preserve the contextual *status quo*. The consequence of 'living within one's means' is to protect the context from intrusive difference. Individuals deliberately protect the quality of life within the privatised unit of family and friends by self-monitoring themselves to resist over-involvement in work, and ultimately turn their backs upon social mobility. But the unintended consequences of these protective practices are morphostatic for the social system.

Work is secondary and subordinated to social interaction; the orientation towards it is one of financial instrumentalism, rather than deep personal involvement. The roles that they assume occupationally are not only conventional to their context, but also their personification is governed by the maintenance of conviviality in the work setting. Task-performance takes second place to social integration, even within employment. When coupled with the strong inter-generational tendency to replicate roles between father and son and mother and daughter, institutional continuity is reinforced by this supply of new recruits. These are pre-socialised to the 'old ways', yet able to 'think and talk' one another through adaptation to the new technological society, whilst their lack of ambition secures their stable occupancy of positions. In short, social integration works to underwrite systemic stability and thus 'communicative reflexives' make a significant contribution to morphostasis at both levels.

The macroscopic consequences of 'autonomous reflexivity' are almost the direct opposite. The subjects' prime concern is vested in their relationship to the 'parts' of society, rather than the 'people'. As products of early 'contextual discontinuity', who embrace some form of performative achievement as their ultimate concern, their *strategic* 'stance' eventually succeeds in locating a new context for them, which enables them to do that which they care about most. This part of the social system absorbs their energies, whose consequences are morphogenetic for the system itself.

In living out their prime concern, often within the context of their work, these agents are consistently engaged in the self-monitoring of their task-performance. In that and other ways, the social system is the beneficiary of their exertions. These are people who dwell deeply upon their performative skills, subjects who will devote countless unpaid hours to cogitating about their work, to deliberating over the problems it presents, and to devising innovative means for overcoming difficulties. Indeed, they would probably disown the distinction between paid and unpaid work. As such they voluntarily contribute huge amounts of 'surplus value' to the institutional sector in which they are engaged – thus augmenting its 'productivity' and development.

Similarly, their role-incumbency has the same morphogenetic thrust, for they personify their roles individualistically. The preference of 'autonomous reflexives' for self-employment, sole trader status, or working as lone practitioners, reveals their individualism – in stark contrast to the collectivist orientation of the 'communicative reflexives'. They neither need nor welcome supervision because they are their own task-masters and shun the conviviality of group-working as a distraction. These are neither team players nor traditionalists. Cumulatively they contribute to role stretching, by introducing new styles of execution and idiosyncratic forms of efficiency. Their active role-making introduces novelty and variety into successful performances and is thus also morphogenetic in its consequences.

In accommodating their concerns to a social context, where they devote themselves single mindedly to that about which they care most, 'autonomous reflexives' foster institutional growth and development because of their hard work and innovative contributions. Hence their effects were morphogenetic. Less obviously, they have the same effect for social relations. If personal relationships feature amongst their concerns, they do so as subordinate ones, which are given their due without allowing them to usurp or encroach upon the ultimate concern. Subjects handle this by adopting their own accommodative 'ethics of fairness', all of which are quasi-contractual in character. These subjects have discharged their obligations towards other people when their legitimate expectations are met. The effect upon significant others, especially partners and children, is to encourage them to develop their own independent activities, because 'autonomous reflexives' repulse any overtures to bind them to a shared microcosm of intensive togetherness. What these others will do depends upon what they themselves are, or come to be, but the effect of life with an 'autonomous reflexive' is to throw them back upon their own resources, rather than fostering their social integration. 'Ethics of accommodation' can be generous in their terms and demanding upon the subject who promulgates them, but this is nevertheless their effect upon others.

However, what also has to be considered are 'autonomous reflexives' whose configurations of concerns may attach no importance to interpersonal relations. In that case, their (unavoidable) social congress would not be ethically regulated, but only legally policed. Consequently, interactions with others would be subject to commodification, with human value being reduced to exchange value. The exploratory group contained no subjects of this kind, but there is nothing intrinsic to 'autonomous reflexivity' that precludes them. Thus, the overall effect of this mode of reflexivity may be expected to be even more negative towards social integration.

Hence, if the external consequences of these first two modes of reflexivity are juxtaposed, they are diametrically opposed. 'Communicative reflexives' foster social integration at the expense of systemic development and morphogenesis. 'Autonomous reflexives' intensify the latter at the cost of reducing social integration. In the absence of knowledge about the proportional distribution of these modes of reflexivity in the population, it is impossible to say anything about the magnitude of these two effects in relation to one another. However, *a priori* there is no reason whatsoever to conclude that a functional balance results between system-maintenance and task-performance in society (assuming there is any way of measuring this). On the contrary, the factor that supposedly represented this 'hidden hand' in functionalism, namely the central value system, is precisely what is absent here. Not only are shared values lacking, but also the two sets of unintended consequences just discussed are underpinned respectively by those two most hostile of values – 'collectivism' and 'individualism'. From between them, the highest compromise possible, as Donati has emphasised,[6] is some variation on the 'lib/lab' theme.

It is here that the social significance of 'meta-reflexivity' is found, for its practitioners view such 'third ways' as poverty-stricken. What they refuse is any notion of trading-off social integration against systemic development, in a compromise between justice and efficiency. Hence their *bête noire*, the third way's executive instrument, the performance indicator. To them, this yields the worst of both worlds – dehumanising participants and robbing tasks of their intrinsic worth. It is the enemy of goodness and truth, of compassion and creativity and of public service and private well-being alike. What they counterpose is an orthogonal ideal, in which social integration and systemic development are reciprocally related rather than mutually compromised. This can take a variety of practical forms, but common themes are subsidiarity, co-operative organisation, voluntary association, community service, inter-generational solidarity, social inclusiveness and other constituents of a robust civil society and civil economy.

It is an environment characterised by reciprocity between the social and the systemic which they seek in their own lives and fail to find – without being deterred from the search. That is their contribution. Their subversion consists in resisting any concordat with the structural *status*

---

[6] Pierpaolo Donati, *Teoria Relazionale Della Società*, Franco Angeli, Milan, 1996, ch. 8.

quo because of their relentless contextual critique. In consequence, they become birds without nests and foxes without holes, finding no resting-place. The sacrifices they make are devalued by the rhetorical portrayal of their life practices as 'anticipating the good society'. Such would also be a deceptive rhetorical flourish because it is precisely their inability to establish satisfying and sustainable social practices that precludes their own flourishing – in society as they now find it. Indeed, part of the price paid is the absence of any guaranteed systemic recompense – any sense of precipitating the macroscopic transformations desired.

Meta-reflexives are such because they pursue cultural ideals that cannot be accommodated by the current social structure and the array of contexts it defines. Instead, fidelity to their vocations counterposes lasting cultural idealism to present structural reality. The cost of accentuating the contradiction between them is paid throughout the individual life course of each meta-reflexive. Yet, their subversion does have one crucial systemic consequence. In dedicating himself or herself to upholding a cultural ideal, each meta-reflexive animates one element of the Cultural System. Meta-reflexives give contemporary social salience to their ideals, without which those ideals would sleep on, in the Universal Library of Humankind, unmarked amongst the shelves of humanity's forgotten dreams and slumbering utopias.

By personifying their ideals of truth and goodness, the meta-reflexives awaken them and re-present them to society. In so doing, they re-stock the pool of societal values, by displaying alternatives to the aridity of third-way thinking – and its repressive consensus. Ultimately, what the meta-reflexive does is to show that the *Wertrationalität* is alive and active in the third millennium, and, as in all previous ages, this constitutes its leaven.

Index

active agents *see* agents: active
actors
    and agents, 118–19, 122, *124*, 126,
      127–9
    and persons, 118, 119, 120–1, 122, 123,
      124, *124*, 127–8
Agassi, Joseph, 47, 48
agency and structure *see* structure and
    agency
agential passivity *see* fractured reflexivity:
    as agential passivity; passive agents
agential reflexivity *see* personal reflexivity
agents
    active, 299, 300–2, 343
      see also autonomous reflexivity;
        communicative reflexivity;
        meta-reflexivity
    and actors, 118–19, 122, *124*, 126,
      127–9
    and agential projects, 5–8, 132–4, 135,
      141–8
    corporate, 118n, *124*, 127, 133, 133n,
      135, 137, 146, 356
    as cultural constructs, 10, 12–13, 14, 40,
      99
    as inseparable from social context, 10,
      11–12, 13, 14
    morphogenesis of, 115–16, *124*,
      124–9
    passive, 25, 164, 299–300
      see also fractured reflexivity: as agential
        passivity
    and personal reflexivity, 9–14, 25–52
    and persons, 119, 121, 122–3, 124, *124*,
      126–7, 128–9
    primary, 118, 119, 124, *124*, 126, 127,
      133, 133n, 135, 137
    stratified concept of, 118–21
    as 'strong evaluators', 32–3, 141–2,
      143
Alston, William, 48, 49, 50
American pragmatism, 56, 78, 93, 153

analytical dualism, 71
    and 'internal conversation', 113–15
    and morphogenesis of persons, 115–16,
      124–9
    and morphogenesis of structure, 3
    and morphogenetic (M/M) approach,
      2n, 3, 71–2
anthropomorphism, 85
Antigone, 45, 46
Antigone's dilemma, 41–2
Archer, Margaret S., 3, 353n
autonomous reflexivity, 210–54
    and contextual discontinuity, 93,
      211–12, 218–19, 221, 228–35, 252,
      257, 265, 346–7
    and dovetailing of concerns, 213,
      219–20, 235–44
    and 'ethics of fairness', 213, 219, 236–7,
      238–40, 241, 242–3, 359
    as individualism, 213–14, 220
    and mediation of structure and agency,
      212, 227–8, 244–54, 257
    and *modus vivendi*, 213, 219–20,
      235–44
    origins of, 346–7, 348
    as self-assurance, 211, 215, 224
    as self-discipline, 216–17, 225, 226,
      227, 354
    and social malintegration, 359–60
    and social mobility, 212, 227–8, 348
    societal outcomes of, 356–7, 358–60
    and structural conditioning, 212,
      214, 243, 244–54, 300, 350, 353,
      354–5
    and system morphogenesis, 357, 358–9,
      360
    and 'ultimate concerns', 213, 217–18,
      226, 235–6, 243, 266n, 346, 350,
      357
    see also communicative reflexivity;
      fractured reflexivity; meta-reflexivity
Ayer, Alfred J., 48